Archer Fullingim
A Country Editor's View of Life

ARCHER FULLINGIM
A Country Editor's View of Life

*Being a 25-Year Chronicle of Writings by Texas' Most
Outspoken Liberal Newspaper Editor, with Irreverent
Reflections on LBJ, Nixon & Sundry Political
Matters, Commenting on Vietnam, Ecology,
Youth & Journalism, with Excursions
into the National Conscience,
Reminiscences of the Depression
Era & Tributes to Poke
Salad, Country Pleasures
& Other Matters.*

EDITED WITH AN INTRODUCTION BY
ROY HAMRIC

Heidelberg Publishers / Austin, Texas
1975

Photography credits
Blair Pittman: frontispiece, 265, 420
Archer Fullingim: 111, 157, 196, 286
Roy Hamric: 431

Published by Heidelberg Publishers, Inc.
3707 Kerbey Lane
Austin, Texas 78731

FIRST EDITION

Library of Congress Cataloging in Publication Data
Fullingim, Archer
Archer Fullingim: a country editor's view of life.

1. Texas—Politics and government—Collected works. 2. United States—Politics and
government—1945—Collected works. 3. Big Thicket National Park, Tex.—Collected works.
4. Fullingim, Archer.
F386.F84   320.9'764'06   75-29497
ISBN 0-913206-07-5

*This book is dedicated to country journalists
who work on in the great tradition
in a time when lightning
no longer excites the world*

CONTENTS

INTRODUCTION

Archer Fullingim is a 73-year-old, small town country editor. His story begins with the land. All stories start there, but in Fullingim's life there are two lands.

The first is the West Texas land of his youth. An arid, sweeping earth of browns and blues and curves which take miles to unfold, it gave grudging sanctuary to the families who tried to scratch sustenance from its surface in the early 1900s. The second is the land of his old age, the forested heart of East Texas where narrow bands of black asphalt stretch out between walls of green pine and hardwood trees. Birds spiral in the stillness above the tightly drawn tree limbs and on the forest floor fallen branches rot near seeps of brackish water and mud-banked creeks. This land is called the Big Thicket.

To Archer Fullingim, the retired editor and publisher of *The Kountze News*, the two lands are more alike than not. In West Texas, he first felt the wind in his heart; and in the Thicket woods, he now walks, listening to bird calls and communing, he says, with a "Holy Ghost feeling." Before he retired from writing and printing his small, 2,000-circulation weekly, Fullingim experienced 50 years of the trials and pleasures of country journalism. He is one of the last of an era, for the day of the lone, devil-take-the-hindmost editor is almost gone. Most young journalists today want to practice "New Journalism," but Fullingim would understand that.

In his weekly front page column, "The Printer Fires Both Barrels," Fullingim unleashed a blistering, tan-the-hide, anvil pounding, thundering prose that stung most of the major politicians of the past 25 years. When he wasn't zeroing in on his favorite targets, he wove delicate reminiscences of the Depression days in West Texas.

The six-foot-five, 240-pound "Printer" was called cantankerous, eccentric, fiery tempered, tempestuous, peppery, prejudiced, iconoclastic, fickle and a self-made son of a bitch. He was

1

also called courageous, honest, loyal, ahead of his time, human-
istic, poetic and a protector of the little man.

This book is the story of Fullingim's 25-year career at *The
Kountze News*. It is a portrait of two lands, two eras and the best
part of a unique man's life. Fullingim's paper was a journal of the
past and present. He remembers his family at the turn of the
century. They were poor, but they believed they were rich.
Memories are of one-room schools, brush arbor revival meetings, serial novels, family traumas and quaint neighbors and
friends, in a time when people were more important than
television. In the pages of the *Kountze News*, the life of a small
village in the woods unfolds and Fullingim's vision grows as he
chronicles three decades. His contemporary political comments
and essays are written in a direct, salty style rare in today's
journalism. To find parallels, you must go to the giants of
another era: to William Allen White and Brann, the iconoclast,
or to P. D. East of Petal, Mississippi and Hodding Carter of
Greenville, Mississippi. Most of the pieces in this collection were
composed directly on a Linotype. Much of the writing is literally
thinking in public, on the printed page. Yet the prose is alive
with involvement, whether about simple pleasures or mourning
the death of cherished leaders.

As the country moved through a tumultuous 25-year period
with three Democratic and three Republican administrations,
Fullingim viewed the emergence of civil rights, brutal racism,
black power, political assassinations, the Vietnam War, student
protests, ecology and political corruption from the state to federal level. Apart from the tides of current fashion, with memory
and rage fueling his prose, he observed, decried and challenged
until a thread of verities converged to form a simple philosophy
of brotherhood and good for the greatest number. The story,
like Archer Fullingim, is one of a kind.

The first son of Alfred and Mahala Fullingim, Archer Jesse
Fullingim was born May 31, 1902 near Catlett Creek within sight
of the rocky white hills that ring Decatur, Texas.

The family put in crops of cotton in Wise County until the
small, 300-acre farm dried out in 1916. Fourteen-year-old
Archer helped pack their belongings on a train and they mi-

grated to the wheat lands of Lynn County, in far West Texas. Within a year they moved again, this time in a horse drawn wagon, and trekked 150 miles northeast to Paducah where they settled near Salt Creek.

When he turned sixteen, his parents decided Archer should return to Wise County and attend classes at Decatur Baptist College, an imposing, red brick, four-story Gothic building on the town's highest hill. At the first junior college in the nation the lanky and gangling youth was exposed to a once-in-a-lifetime teacher, Miss Bernice Neel, who guided him to serious poetry and literature and encouraged him in his writing. After graduating at eighteen, Fullingim taught for two years in a one-room school, saved his money, and decided he should complete his education. He enrolled at the University of Oklahoma, majored in English and minored in journalism.

His journalism teacher was a fireball addict of the "Front Page" school of reporting where the "scoop" was everything. But Fullingim was not thinking along those lines. Secretly, he was plotting that very next year to start an opposition paper against the great Harry Koch of *The Quanah Chief-Tribune.*

"Of course, I never got anywhere with that," he recalled, "but for the next twenty years, during most of which I worked on newspapers from Florida to California, I dreamed of starting my own weekly at Muleshoe, Texas, because I liked the name."

Graduating in 1924, Fullingim's life took on a Jack London mystique as he dashed across the country in an odyssey of newspaper reporter, migrant farm laborer, merchant seaman and, somewhat improbably, the enraptured camp follower of several leading concert pianists and opera singers of the era. His first newspaper job was at *The Wichita* (Kansas) *Eagle* and his first story exposed the gory details of a job he had earlier in the Kansas wheat fields where he was beaten by the owners when they suspected him of being a member of the Industrial Workers of the World. After a year learning the craft of daily journalism, he hopped a freight train east, following the southern tour of Ignace Paderewski, a Polish composer and pianist. Ending up in Florida, where the Italian-American opera star Amelita Galli-Curci was scheduled to perform, out of work and fed up with the road, Fullingim stalked into the impersonal city room of *The*

Miami Herald and asked to see the city editor.

A dour, gruff man, the editor solemnly looked the raw-boned youth over. Standing before his desk, Fullingim said he loved opera and great music and told him he should be hired as the paper's music critic.

"I know you don't have a music critic and nobody around here could do the job, because it takes a special talent and they don't know anything about real music," Fullingim exclaimed.

Setting his trap, the editor inquired, "Well, son what do you know about music?"

Taken aback, Fullingim gathered his wits and replied cockily. "I know that Amelita Galli-Curci is going to sing here this week and that when she sings in her pure soprano voice it sounds like smoke rising from a white rose!"

The editor, in a bow to bravado, said, "You've got the job."

But he was soon restless again and he signed on a merchant ship commissioned to carry sugar from Cienfuegos, Cuba, to Japan and back to British Columbia. Leaving the ship in Canada, he hitchhiked to Washington, picked apples, then wandered down to California to pick cotton and potatoes. In 1929, he found another reporting job on *The Shafter* (California) *Progress*, a weekly in the foothills of the Sierra Madres. The experience convinced him that weeklies were his field. Nearing 30, he returned to West Texas where he worked the summer picking cotton in Cottle County. Recognizing that stoop labor got him no closer to his own weekly, he ventured to Galveston and found work on the now defunct *Tribune* before he and a friend decided to sign on a merchant ship bound for Europe. Before the ship left the Houston channel, however, they were involved in a fight with other crew members and were forced to jump ship. After briefly roaming the state, Fullingim was hired at *The Panhandle Herald*. Later he moved to *The Pampa Daily News* where he stayed 13 years, eventually becoming city editor. Although 42 at the outbreak of World War II, he enlisted as a seaman, but was later commissioned a second lieutenant and served on several South Pacific islands.

After the war, he finally fulfilled his dream by purchasing the smallest weekly in Texas, *The Normangee Star*. "I loved it," he said. "I might have stayed there the rest of my life, but one night a friend and I were arrested for being drunk at a carnival.

"Actually, he probably was drunk, but we weren't talking to anybody or disturbing the peace, so I refused to pay the fine. We had a little justice of the peace trial in the barber shop and I was acquitted, but I didn't want to stay there anymore."

Within a few days, Fullingim learned that a small town 450 miles southeast had been without a weekly newspaper for three months. Scanning the classified ads in *The Dallas Morning News*, he found a print shop for sale in Paris, Texas, for $845. Buying the entire shop, he piled the equipment in a truck and the flat expanses of West Texas he knew so well passed behind him as he drove through the verdant curtains of East Texas to a fecund, tropical hardwood forest called the Big Thicket. Fullingim was nearly fifty years old, but he was entering a world none of his travels could have prepared him for.

Touching three counties, the Big Thicket begins 40 miles north of Beaumont. It lies between the Trinity River on the west and the Neches River on the east. Winding, clear streams, dark hardwoods and pines and rolling hills mark the Thicket's northern half, while its southern half is made of tangled palmetto stands, moss-draped hardwoods and sluggish bayous. The earliest American settlers cautiously pushed into the forest about 1800. Early on, the country was dominated by lumber barons and oil kings, and by the end of the 19th century the region had put down the roots of the strange, populist-racist tradition that has characterized East Texas most of this century.

The heyday of the timber and oil era stretched from 1865 to the 1920s. Railroad tracks, ox cart trails and lumber camps were hacked out of the Thicket's green, inner sanctums. Almost overnight, mud-street settlements of 20,000 drifters and laborers sprang up. Saloons and brothels prospered and in Batson, an oil boom town, the jail became a large oak tree in the center of town. Wrapped around the trunk was a "mystic chain" which was attached to an offender's neck. The legendary bear hunter, Ben Lilly, prowled the Thicket during the 1890s and brown bear and panthers continued to roam the wood's impenetrable recesses until mid-century. The last bear killed in the thicket, however, died ignominiously in 1955 when it dreamily sauntered out of the woods onto a Woodville street where it was struck by a goggle-eyed motorist.

All of the bear and probably most of the panthers have now disappeared. But the flora of the Big Thicket holds fast. Its unique mixture of trees and plants, which make it a priceless island of biological diversity, was recognized in 1975 when Congress created an 84,500 acre Big Thicket National Preserve. Within a 30-mile radius you may find 30 species of orchids, four of the world's five insectivorous plants, a lime-green beech forest, cool, leafy baygalls, rare ferns and desert cactus. In one spot, by turning in four directions, one can see landscapes that resemble the Appalachians, the Florida everglades, the Southwest desert and a Carolina pine barren.

The wisdom of the woods is still a lingering tradition. Even after heavy timbering, the Thicket forms a barrier that shelters local residents from most forms of 20th century civilization. Suburbanization is just a six-syllable word and natives take pride in the orneriness implicit in the local compliment, "He's a hard man to starve." There is a heritage of quick-to-fight and quick-to-help and even young people talk of "fitting" the country. An evening's pleasure might consist of waiting for a red wolf to skitter across a clearing at dusk, or being heart-stilled by the groan of a hunting horn in the woods. Most folk believe a man ought to be able to make it with just about any job, a gun, a garden and some fishhooks and people are slow to let go of old ways. Collard greens, opossum, raccoon and armadillo meat can be bought at small-town groceries and services have a way of blending together for convenience. One sign on the highway advertizes "Johnson's Pit Bar-B-Que and Beauty Shop." And the trunks of trees frequently talk at dirt road crossings through hand-lettered signs that announce "Pies—½ mile," or "Lord Jesus Comes." Back in the shade are rickety, white board churches with names like "Jesus Thicket Name Pentacostal Church," and mysterious place names like "Devil's Pocket" mark the countryside. The spoken tongue is sprinkled with pioneer words. For many, a funeral is still a "burying," a religious conversion a "perfessin'," a quarrel a "cuss fight," and should a man's eyes fill with tears he may complain of them "souring."

Because most Big Thicket residents work with their hands, a

single lifetime may involve work as a cowboy, oil field roustabout, sawmill laborer, truck driver, farmer and store clerk.

The Big Thicket is like a favorite grandfather's treasured attic, a storehouse for natural and human history. The people who live there endure the summer heat and pesky mosquitoes because the arcadian rhythm and backwater ways somehow seem a little closer to the continuum weave we call human experience.

When Fullingim drove into Kountze (pronounced Kōōntz) it was a scruffy little town of about 1,500 people, the seat of Hardin County, named after a pioneer family of Methodist preachers, one of whose sons was the gunfighter John Wesley Hardin. With one of the highest illiteracy rates in the state, the county performed an eerie twist of conscience when it overwhelmingly supported John Kennedy against Richard Nixon in 1960, only to revert in 1968, giving Nixon 60 per cent of the vote. Political feuding is one of the county's main characteristics, and old-line families still wield clout and frequently clash.

Despite strong civic pride, the life blood of the town runs thin today. Main Street is clothed in fading colors and the town's mainstay is still the nearby sawmills, with their steady stream of tractor-trailers heavily ladened with freshly cut logs. Stores form a respectable block or two before the ever-present pines close in. In the summer of 1950 Fullingim surveyed the town and rented a single room behind Birdwell's Department Store. On September 15, the first *Kountze News* appeared, a four-page issue of 600 copies. For the next six weeks the *News* was distributed free at the post office, and when he tallied up the books, Fullingim learned he had 600 subscribers, and realized he had found a home.

The *News'* familiar jabbing, barbed approach, however, didn't get underway until the mid-1950s. For the first few years, the paper's stories were short and breezy, carbon copies of most country weekly fare. But as Fullingim settled in he began to develop his political views.

For many years, he labeled himself a "brass collar" Democrat who supported all party candidates. But gradually, like other liberals, Fullingim came to believe that the philosophy of conservative Democrats in Texas was actually more aligned with the traditional principles of the Republican party. In his mind,

Republicans and state conservative Democrats became one, and both curried the favors of big business and supported establishment control. As a result, in his column, he frequently labeled conservative state Democrats and major state newspapers as "Republican."

With an abiding veneration for Franklin D. Roosevelt, he found it hard to accept Harry Truman, even though a Democrat. He vigorously supported Adlai Stevenson against Eisenhower in 1956 and sounded ominous warnings about Ike's running mate, Vice President Richard Nixon, calling him "a potential dictator." With unclear views on integration, he blistered the Republican administration for its tactics, calling its actions at Little Rock High School unconstitutional, and in several columns he came dangerously close to sounding like many of the people he later chastised for racism. By 1959, he knew where he stood on integration. He warned irate readers that if loving the human race made him a "nigger lover" he was proud to be one and their taunts were compliments in his mind. From the beginning, he derisively nicknamed most of the politicians he wrote about. Lyndon Johnson was simply Lyndon, John Connally became "St. John," and Senator John Tower became "Useless John." It was Governor Preston "Pious" Smith, former Texas House Speaker "Greedy" Gus Mutscher, Congressman "Timber" Charlie Wilson, and since the early 1950s, "Tricky" Dick Nixon.

When Kennedy challenged Nixon in 1960 the battle lines were clearly drawn. The "Both Barrels" column picked up the "New Frontier" banner, and entered its apex as a forum of humanist philosophy. Reveling in the Kennedy victory, a rich series of childhood memories appeared, producing at least one classic, "The Love and Wrath of Old Matt," a moving tale of death and manly pride seen through a child's eyes. Gradually, the *News* evolved into an individualistic weekly that broke many guidelines.

"I expressed controversial opinions in my front page column and most editors thought I was some kind of nut," Fullingim recalled. "I had a simple rule for writing local news: print the truth as I see it. I supported long hair, feuded with the timber companies, advocated saving the Big Thicket and eventually ran a quote by Chief Crazy Horse on my masthead: '*Man does not sell the Earth upon which he walks.*' But I never got into any real trouble until I took sides in a school board election. Then everybody wanted to whip me.

"It really wasn't worth it," Fullingim drawled, "since most school boards are alike in the main. But it was all highly enjoyable and the people gradually came to expect the *News* to take a position on everything."

Throughout its life, Fullingim's *News* was a joy to read, and its homespun approach was unmatched. For instance, readers regularly encountered ominous black headlines normally used to herald war or armistice. But to Fullingim, mundane matters might call for large, screaming type. Some favorite headlines from over the years, all set in bold type:

**Boy Has Favorite
Cake For Birthday**

**Ticks Kill Roy
McCormick Cow**

**President of School Board Begs
Members Not To Curse In Meetings**

Appearing in 60-point type in a single line across the top of an inside page:

He Knocks Toe Nail Off Getting To Bed!

That apocalyptical headline ran above a full page of correspondent "briefs" from area communities and referred to a one-inch story buried in the middle of the page. Another, with the story that followed:

**Termites Ate Up Foundation
Of House While Gilmore
Watson Was Sick In Bed**

Gilmore Watson, who lives near Fletcher, and who has been in bad health this summer, had to get up out of bed last week and replace the foundation and lower three feet of the walls of his house, because, as Watson said, "The termites had come like thieves in the night and eaten away the lower part of my house while I slept."

9

It was all in keeping with Fullingim's belief that some of the paper's best news appeared in small stories on inside pages. Typical were his personal "I Heard" and "I Saw" vignettes sprinkled throughout the paper.

A life-long bachelor with few close friends, Fullingim's heart was in the dimly lit, two-room tin building he eventually acquired across the street from the post office. The yellow, green and red sign above the door read, "The Kountze News," and inside were the tools of a bygone era in journalism. Looming in black masses several feet behind his ink-stained desk was an imposing, 75-year-old Miehle flat-bed, cylinder press which took hand-fed, single 44 X 32 inch sheets of newsprint. To its side stood a venerable Mergenthaler "Blue Streak" Linotype. Next an 18 X 12 inch Chandler & Price platen job printing press; an Omaha Folder; a Hammond Easy Kaster for reproducing pictures; a cutter-perforator; four worn Hamilton Type Cases; a Mustang Mailer for address labels; steel chases to secure type; pica poles, make-up rules, oil cans, pig lead molds, red wiping rags and buckets of black, red and yellow ink.

Looking down on the clutter from a mural which swept across the top half of two walls were eleven mustang horses with wind-tossed manes, flared nostrils and prancing feet, pursued by mounted cowboys. Five feet wide and forty-four feet long, the mural was painted in 1958 by Fullingim's brother-in-law, Tom Simms, an artist and Methodist preacher.

"I knew after I read *The Mustangs* by J. Frank Dobie that I wanted to work in the company of mustangs and the freedom they expressed," Fullingim said, explaining its origin. "I tried to get Tom to paint the mural for months and I tried to get him to read the book so he could get the feeling, but he didn't show any interest. All he wanted to do was paint Jesus.

"But he eventually did it and he captured their spirit. And, you know, he never once got Jesus and the mustangs mixed up."

Following his retirement in 1975, Fullingim reflected upon country journalism and drew up a list of "The Ten Best Weekly Newspapers in Texas."* However, after considering more than

---

*Top weeklies by name and county: *The Highlander* (Burnet); *The Tulia Herald* (Swisher); *Diboll Free Press* (Angelina); *Canadian Record* (Hemphill); *Hays County Citizen*; *Castro County News*; *Quanah Tribune-Chief* (Hardeman); *Post Dispatch* (Garza) and *Rockport Pilot* (Aransas).

500 Texas weeklies, he couldn't come up with a 10th place. Exasperated, he created his own imaginary weekly, *"The Jeff Davis Countian,"* named for a West Texas county which has no weekly paper. "Picking No. 10 sort of did something for me," he said, pleased.

"My selection didn't take into account whether the editorial stance was conservative or liberal," he said. "Actually, there are no strictly conservative or liberal weeklies in Texas. One year they will be conservative and liberal the next. They were picked on whether they printed local news, whether they consistently took note of the environment, the tax structure, the kind of law enforcement they had; and whether the editorials were hard hitting or simply for mother, home and heaven, with a lot of blue sky and flag waving.

"Four of the ten are in the Panhandle. That's probably because it's nearer the frontier spirit than any part of Texas. Now think of those 500 other weekly newspapers. How am I going to explain them? Well, most of them are alike: nice cute pictures that print well on those offset presses. Their editors believe every word of the old saying that a picture is worth a thousand words and they cram their pages with pictures of people. The editors of my nine best believe that if you print the right words, any picture has got to take a back seat to them.

"One longs for the days of Brann, and *The Iconoclast.* Hardly ever do newspapers attack the editorial policies of its neighbor, which was a frontier custom. No editors are ever shot at, none maimed, no type cases are overturned. The point is that no reader can ever leap to his feet, wave his arms, tear up the paper or clutch it to his bosom after reading the milktoast editorials of most 'weaklies.'

"Most weeklies are like pet dogs that you pat on the head and you know they are never going to bite anything but dog food. Country journalism has now taken on the characteristics of city journalism. Their main business is to make money. Their aim is to protect their status, to protect big business, big oil, to protect period, because they figure if they do, they'll make money.

"There's a great field for people who want to go into country journalism, if they make up their minds they will not only write the news, but also will lead the people, will recognize injustices in the world. Anyone who goes into country journalism solely to make money is not only a phony, but a fool. And he's a fool to go into weekly journalism if he's afraid to express an opinion.

"The Texas weekly editor must derive inspiration from himself. He can't look to the dailies in Dallas, Houston or San Antonio. They are all super rich and super establishment. The only formula for an editor to follow is simple: to tell the truth as he sees it, and not ride the fence. But most weekly newspapers hide, bury or reject enough real news each week for fear of ruffling feathers to make it a great newspaper."

Typically, Fulllingim's assessment goes straight to the point, and most observers of rural journalism would generally agree with him. Most weekly editors have abandoned the tradition of ruminative essays and shrewd, personal commentary on local, state and national affairs that once made weeklies an important and entertaining part of national life. There is much to admire in the type of journalism personified by Fullingim and other weekly editors who print good newspapers, but who go largely unnoticed outside their own communities. It is journalists like them, on the political left and right, who freely and distinctively voice the breath of democracy. Their voices may be discordant, unsettling, even devisive, on the surface, but they are the energy and inspiration which shapes our nation. And in such voices there is an unspoken passion and faith to match a dream.

In retirement, Fullingim looked forward to three things. He wanted to spend more time in the Thicket with the "Holy Ghost feeling;" he dreamed of sighting an ivory-bill woodpecker, an elusive, perhaps extinct bird; and he hoped to return to work on a novel, long uncompleted. One day in early spring, he took one of his rambling walks near Village Creek. He had been slightly ill. He carried a five-foot, hickory staff garlanded with a seven-spiraled rattan vine which circled its way to the top. Hard-carved into the staff were the words "Save Thy Thicket."

His age showing, he stopped briefly every few hundred feet to study the wind-tossed leaves, gaze at the lacy clouds and listen to bird calls.

"Let's go this way; it's something, ain't it!" Fullingim boomed, pointing to a maze of bramble and twisted vines called "tight-eye" Thicket. "I want to go right through the heart of the woods," he said, leaving the trail.

Stopping again with a slightly tilted forward stance, his white hair shining, his voice suddenly fractured the still air, sending birds scurrying.

I come from haunts of coot and hern
I make a sudden sally
And sparkle out among the fern
To bicker down the valley

I chatter, chatter as I flow
To join the brimming river
For men may come and men may go
But I go on forever

"That was by Tennyson or Keats," he exclaimed. "I've forgotten, but I must have liked that in school. You see, it was a small school where you had to memorize everything.

"Smell that yellow jasmine," he said, leaning on his staff, inhaling mightly, trying to prolong the stop.

Walking deeper into the woods over a carpet of mulchy, brown and gold leaves, he passed tree trunks lightly caked with new, lime-green moss. Tiny scarlet and yellow mushrooms shone iridescently on the sunlight-dotted floor and insects floated lazily through slanted shafts of light.

Under the darkening web of limbs, birds flitted about as the wind rolled the crowns of trees in a constant, soft moan. Just ahead a bird sang.

"Count those calls!" Archer shouted. "Listen! That's a red-eyed vireo . . . one, two, three, four. Now, I wonder what he just said?"

"Well, I think it's God's music," he answered himself. "It's all a sweet concord of sounds.

"You know," he said. "I like Merle Haggard and Jimmy Rogers and that kind of music, and Mozart and Beethoven and that kind of music, and nothing in between. That's pure-dee hillbilly and pure-dee beauty.

"Hand me that flower!" he demanded, eyeing a finger-nail sized purple bloom. "I've got to have that."

13

His large hand grasped the tiny blossom and shoved it under his nose like a pinch of raspberry snuff as he inhaled an endless draw of breath. Walking on between armored, columnar pines, he sighted three blue dots painted man-high on the trunk of a squat, muscular hundred-year-old oak.

"That tree's marked for cutting," he said, disgustedly. He pulled out a blue handkerchief, wiped his sweating brow and flipped it over his left shoulder, adding, "Those sons of bitches."

Asked how he first found the Holy Ghost feeling in the Thicket, he said:

"I never have given a good explanation of that, have I? Hmmm, well the first time was with Neil Wright, who took me into a beautiful part of the deep Thicket. We walked forever. I got so tired I couldn't go on anymore, so I told Neil, 'Go on, for God's sake, leave me alone.' I sat down against a tree. He'd been gone a long time and I sat there and pretty soon this feeling washed over me like a wind in my heart and I felt like I'd been there before.

"I was suffused with a spirit something like what Adam and Eve must have felt. It's a feeling of lightness. I don't think it's mystical. I used to find it only in the Thicket's depths, but I can find it anywhere in the woods now."

Approaching the creek the country changed. A dark tangle of muscadine and rattan vines in twisting curls snaked up the trunks of trees toward the sunlight in the overstory. Mixed hardwoods and pines were replaced by the more gentle trees and plants of the stream bank. The trail passed over a spongy flood-plain pierced by tubular cypress knees jutting out of the ooze. The creek flowed steadily. Next to the bank were delicate ribbons of green fern. Bearded Spanish moss draped the tips of limbs. Water hickory, black willow, tupelo, river birch and cottonwoods.

"It was in cottonwoods like these that I used to read those books up in Salt Creek Canyon," Archer said, pointing to a flickering green-and-silver tree. "When we were young we'd go to the canyon about 400 yards from the house. We'd climb up in a cottonwood and sit there reciting poetry and reading books. We were very poor all the time we lived there. We had beef twice a year. In the summer, we'd have vegetables, but in the winter we wouldn't have anything to eat, hardly, except beans. We didn't have enough to eat, we didn't have no clothes. But you know something? We owned that farm and we thought we were rich.

"We said, 'We live down there on that creek, Salt Creek, and we've got a hundred acres up there in cotton, we've got a hundred acres in corn and we got a hundred acres in grass. We got horses, we got cows, we ain't got no car, but who wants a car? They'll just go out of style.'

"The people down here don't realize what they have," Archer said, sadly. "If I were you, I'd get my girl friend and backpack. Don't be in a hurry! When daylight comes, get up and listen, just listen!"

"You know," he added slyly, eyeing his watch. "Birds don't sing at noon. By then they've already loved out, fed out and sung out."

Asked if he was glad to be out of newspapering, he said, "Well, I'm 73 and for the last two years I've been doin' manual labor, because I got some eye trouble and I couldn't run the Linotype, which is sittin' down work. So I had to do the standin' up work. I had to cast the pages, make up and kill out and that's hard work. I was getting tired, I ain't lying to you. I was getting tired.

"Then the newsprint company quit making the 44 X 32 single sheets I used. I had about four tons and we used two bundles per week so I saw that the last paper would be used up in February. I had a choice to go offset or sell.

"But I'm rich," Archer shouted into the air. "Yeah, I'm retired and rich. I told that to a man yesterday and he said, 'Archer, I didn't know you were rich. You must have been squirreling away your money.' I told him, 'Listen, here, I've got enough money to buy anything I want to and to go anywhere I want . . . provided I die by Thursday.'

"But I'd have kept on, if I'd gotten the paper," he added seriously. "I'd have kept on."

The clear, black-tinted water of the creek flowed gently over the muddy, orange bottom. Wind-whipped leaves floated on the water.

Asked how he believed people outside of Kountze viewed him, he said:

"Oh, I don't look upon myself as any hero or anyone that par-

15

ticularly brilliant, because, you know, I'm aware of my faults. I realize that a person like me who fires both barrels every week at something is intolerant. Because of the things I've said, I've made a lot of political enemies, but I regard myself as a person who loves humanity, the underdog and the people who are in need. I wouldn't try to take advantage of them and I think anybody who does should be run out of office."

What about his image among Kountze citizens?

"How do they see me? Oh, well, they see me in various ways. They see me as a liar, an agitator, a person who tells the truth, a fool, a hero. It depends on whether they got stung by me or not.

"One time a candidate told me he was going to beat me to death. I told him, 'All right, you devil, come ahead. But they'll carry you out first, because I'll kill you just as sure as you're breathing.' You see, here's the thing. I've always got just about as many on my side as those against me have. And if they're going to whip me, they've got to whip the whole damn bunch.

"But you know, most people aren't aware of the way I really think," he sighed. "I'm sort of a loner. And to me the most important thing has always been books. They have been my major interest all my life.

"I guess I'm most scared of being misunderstood," he said. "You see, I'm a bachelor. My sister lives next door and my brother lived in the next town. My life has always been intertwined with my brothers and sisters. At times people in Kountze, when we had a hot, local campaign, questioned my masculinity. Of course, it never bothered me any. A man who is one of my best friends now made a remark like that once that came back to me and it upset my sister but it didn't me.

"You see, I opposed him that year. I've changed friends in this town, friends and enemies, two or three times. The people who are my closest friends now were my enemies years ago and my closest friends then are now my enemies."

A dampness and stillness entered the evening air as the sun fell below the tree tops. Turning to begin the walk back, Archer said, "I love America. The people who criticize me sometimes don't, but the country isn't suffering. The basic American character, the American feeling, is all right. American youth, which is the gauge of our life, hasn't suffered a bit. It's only the corrupt politicians that have suffered."

Asked what he was most proud of, he paused. "Well, before John Kennedy became president, I was sort of a racist. Publicly at least, I don't know that I approved of integration and I was so mad at Eisenhower all the time, I couldn't decide if Little Rock was bad. But just before Kennedy came on the scene, I saw the light, and I thank God. We had no trouble in Kountze on integration. That, and helping to save the Thicket for a national park are the best things I've done."

In the deep woods again, dark shadows sealed out the light as Archer asked, "Shouldn't we go that way?" The woods were quiet and moist and Fullingim's exhaled breath hung white in the air. "Or this way?" Ahead, fireflies blinked. An owl called. Pulling away clinging vines, he pushed forward, stepping over rotting branches, edging up a steep incline.

Continuing, he said, "You see, all my life I wanted to be a writer. I come from a long line of poor white trash farmers and I love that and working the soil. But from the time I was eleven I wanted to write. I remember the day I told my mother I wanted to be a great writer, because I got a whipping for it. I got this can of shoe polish, you see, and marked a large religious cross on the living room door. When my mother found it, she grabbed me and demanded, 'Why did you do that?' I promised myself then I was going to be a great writer. You see, I was just a kid and that's the only thing I knew to copy."

Ahead were large gaps of soft, evening light. The country flattened out abruptly and the grass thickened as the trees thinned and the light gradually grew brighter. Coming suddenly on the trail near the point where he had entered the woods, Archer noticed a stack of weathered logs, soft from rot.

"Man won't stop," he said. "He's self destructive. He'll probably destroy himself and the earth all at the same time. He's naturally a destroyer. I wonder why that is?

"I sometimes ask myself, why do we have the trees, the streams, the rivers? Why do people weep, cry, beg and sorrow? I don't know why, but I know we can be overcome with this earth and with the people on it and it has something to do with beauty and spirit."

Returning quietly to the car, he edged his large frame into the passenger seat, rolled down his window, and suddenly sang:

Oh, you can't grow 'taters
in the sandy land
You can't grow 'taters
in the sandy land

He turned, smiling.

A NOTE TO THE READER

When I agreed to edit a 25-year record of *The Kountze News*, I had the support of Archer Fullingim, who gave me complete freedom in choice of selection. At one point, when I searched for counsel, Fullingim replied, do what you think is right, but, if I were you, I'd take bits and pieces and get only the important points of the stories. This is what I've tried to do. The selection does not pretend to be an historical record in the chronological sense of covering all of the major events of the period. Nor does it pretend to be a verbatim copy of his columns and news stories. In the editing process, I first tried to present a portrait of a man, because more than anything, *The Kountze News* was Archer Fullingim; secondly, I tried to weave the rhythm of a rural community into the account. In addition, I concentrated on topics of national interest; stories dealing with state politics were used only when the issues discussed were broad or when they included valuable insights into Fullingim's character. I have not used any stories which deal with politics in Kountze or Hardin County. A very light hand was used in editing stories for time elements, correction of syntax or repetition. Many columns and almost all of the reminiscences are essentially intact.

AMERICAN ELM

PART ONE
1950–1955

YEARS | 1950-1955

SUBSCRIBE TO THE NEWS NOW   *September 14*

Hello folks, The Kountze News is just one day old. It's small, but give it time and it will grow, especially if you subscribe to it quickly ($2 a year)—Archer Fullingim, editor.

FREE COPIES AVAILABLE

The first few issues of The Kountze News will be distributed free to all residents of this community. Of course, being a new newspaper, The News started out without any subscription list, and it is happy to give away the first few issues in order that prospective readers may see what kind of paper it is going to be.

But don't wait until we quit giving away the paper to subscribe. Bring your $2 to The News now so you won't miss a single issue. If you can't get around to visiting The News plant, then mail us your subscription.

THE PAPER IS NAMED

One of the first persons the new editor met in Kountze, after he decided to publish a newspaper here, was Pat Roden, who owns about half of Kountze, and the fact that The News plant is now located in one of Pat's buildings on Theater Street is not un-expected. I learned from Pat that five or six years ago when the town was without a paper he made plans to publish a tabloid size paper and went so far as to buy some equipment, but his printer went back on him.

I asked him what he was going to call the paper, and he said The Kountze News, and I said, that's exactly what I'm going to call this newspaper. One thing, Pat is not charging oil boom prices for rent space. He's pretty reasonable despite the fact that he and I have been arguing for five days over a job press that he owns. Pat lives at Loeb but makes Kountze and Sour Lake every day. But that's not unusual. The J. V. Overstreets live at Honey Island. D. C. Enloe lives at Hillister, but he wants to move here. Mr. Smith, the big wheel at the lumber yard and mill, lives at Woodville. The editor lives at Village Creek, and if he ever moves it will be to the Carriker Hotel, close to those hush puppies, turnip greens, chicken and rice, roast beef, chicken and dumplings and mashed squash. What food!

BRIGHT LIGHTS   *September 22*

The possibility of putting up a street light system in Kountze is the object of a survey being made by Gulf State Utilities Company.

The Lions Club engineered the deal. On September 12 at the regular meeting of the Lions Club, Mr. Brannon of Gulf States was guest speaker, and he discussed the proposal from all angles. He said that Gulf States would agree to make a survey, showing costs, where the lights would be erected, how many of them there would be and how bright they would be. The Lions think Kountze needs bright lights and so do motorists and pedestrians on Main Street which has a constant stream of traffic passing day and night.

HUNTING WEATHER

I heard that Mr. Lilly, the night it was so cold you had to use two quilts, heard a noise that woke him in the middle of the night. He said it was his gun jumping up and down, wanting to go hunting.

KOUNTZE A DEAD TOWN? *October 5*

A local woman, a native who is both young and attractive, was in The News print shop the other day, complaining that Kountze is a dead town. I was astonished because Kountze is the liveliest town I ever lived in. Take the place I lived in three years before I came here. It was not a dead town, but it was small. It had about 600 people. Kountze, with a population of 2,000, a courthouse with district court going on, crowded streets, cafes and people buying things in stores every day of the week, is a big town to me. Where I came from people came to town only on Saturday. It had three cafes, and when the watermelon and the tomato farmers splurged on Saturday afternoons they bought a bowl of chili, winter or summer.

Although the town was as dry as a gopher hole, the inhabitants voted 99 per cent dry at prohibition elections and drank 99 per cent wet the rest of the time. You could see more people higher than a kite any day than you will see here, where there are beer joints and liquor stores galore, in a week. Movies were always three years old, not like the Gay Theater, where you can see pictures like "Cheaper By the Dozen."

That little old town where I lived certainly wasn't dead. It was just small. It had a woman postmistress and a good one, too, but a town that has a man postmaster is kinda metropolitan to me, and Kountze has one of the most likable, courteous and accommodating postmasters in Mr. Crow that I've ever met. That post office is one of the liveliest places in Kountze, and it ain't going to stay third class very long.

You could put everything in all the stores in my former home town in H&H or in Williford's. We had one telephone operator there, and we got six here on duty all the time. We had to haul ice 60 miles, and in Kountze we have one of the finest ice plants in Texas. We didn't have a doctor there and we ain't got none here, but we got a $450,000 hospital on paper and the bonds have been sold.

We didn't have a single tourist court in town and look at the Gay Courts here. We had a railroad there and the whistling streamliners passed through twice a day going to Dallas or Houston, at 90 miles an hour.

25

We didn't have a lumber yard there, and just look at them here. Two sawmills and the Smith-Fagin lumber yard and the Carriker Lumber Company. (That other one doesn't count because it won't advertise in The News.) All the restrooms in the business district were Chic Sales specials, the two-hole variety. The school didn't have a band, and look at our 35-piece outfit.

These are just a few of the reasons why Kountze is the bright lights to me. I feel like a country boy come to town. Kountze sure ain't dead to me. It's the biggest town I ever lived in. I got to watch my p's and q's and keep my nose clean and take care here.

SUBSCRIBE . . . WE'LL TRUST YOU

If a lot of people don't subscribe to The News the merchants and businessmen won't advertise, and the editor can't pay his bills. Besides, there's a newsprint shortage.

So there will be only two more free issues to Kountze residents. Then no more. We really haven't bore down on the subscription angle yet, although we have about a hundred subscribers to date. But we need 400 in Kountze in the next two weeks.

We've got to have that much circulation here to satisfy out advertisers, who alone keep our paper going. A newspaper can't exist without local advertisers. And please trade with them.

So please bring, or send in, or mail your $2 to The News this week and next week. We don't have the time or the inclination (or possibly the brains) to put on a high-powered circulation drive. We know that you like The News. We know that eventually you are going to subscribe, so why not do it this week or next?

This circulation business will turn into a first class crisis if you don't subscribe. We promise to give you the news. We promise to print all the news you phone in or mail in or send in. So please make it a point to subscribe to the only paper in the world that gives a hang about Kountze, and the mail routes, and Honey Island and Saratoga and Village Mills and the people in those places.

If you don't have the two bucks, come in and we'll put your name on the list and you can pay later. We'll trust you.

YEAR 1951

THE PRINTER GLOATS   *January 11*

There was news at the courthouse and in city hall, and there were visitors in the homes of many Kountze News readers and local people made some interesting trips, but this week personals in The Kountze News are few and far between, and for a big reason.

For the big news in this newspaper office is a wonderful and marvelous new machine on which the editor almost mortgaged his soul in order to buy. He ain't got a dime in his pocket, and he's eating on credit at the Carriker Hotel and Blair's Cafe, but he's happy because he has a new Blue Streak Model 31 Linotype. It doesn't make any difference to him that this week he has no type metal to put in the pot and consequently can't operate the machine.

All last week he stood at the beck and call of the Linotype erector, Shorty Byus of Houston, who got $5 an hour for installing the machine for Mergenthaler Linotype Co., Brooklyn. That was why The News was a day late last week. That is why he decided to fill up the paper with ads this week.

The new machine cost $9,000 and the editor hocked everything in sight to make the down payment, and must pay $113 a month for five years to Mergenthaler, and quite a sum for the next 15 months to the Silsbee State Bank, but the Linotype is here, and ready to go as soon as we get 300 pounds of metal (at 30¢ per pound).

We're so proud of this machine that we want everybody to see it. After all, it's the first new Linotype ever in Kountze. It's the most expensive machine of its size and weight in Hardin County. It has 30,000 parts, most of them moving, and we know how to fix 10 if they get out of order. But we are not worrying about any of these things. I am not even worried about the fact that I can barely operate it. I just sit and look at it and gloat.

But I want you readers to see it, so on Saturday and Sunday there will be a big Open House at The News for all readers and

27

you can see it in operation. Don't come until then because it will take me until then to get to the point I can operate it with people watching me.

THIS WAS MAMMY   *March 8*

The following story about Mrs. Mahala Fullingim who died at Galveston, February 24, and was buried at Decatur, February 25, possibly isn't newsworthy enough to be published in this newspaper, since she wasn't known here and nobody in Kountze ever saw her. But it is published because in paying tribute to her, one pays tribute to all mothers.

Even in death, it seemed, Mammy and the good Lord cooperated for the convenience of her seven children. She died on a Saturday, making it convenient for all her children to drive great distances to attend her funeral on Sunday. It was a flower-lovely funeral with two beautiful wreaths from Kountze, donated by business people and others.

Of course Mammy did not plan to die on Saturday. She had been in a coma for a week and had not been able to recognize anyone for two weeks. She had not been able to take any food or water for ten days. Her veins had collapsed and she could not be given glucose.

Her children never told her she had cancer of the stomach, but as I look back now I think she must have known it, finally. She never talked with her children of dying, though she bought lasting gifts for them to remember her by. For the editor, she bought a tie clasp with a Masonic emblem. But she talked of death with two of her daughters-in-law. She told them she could not bear to see her children weep for her.

She was not afraid of Death, but she was afraid of the pain she had feared would accompany Death.

Mammy lived most of her 79 years for her God and her children. She had read the Bible and prayed every day of her life that her children could remember. She had been a Christian for 60 years. None of her children ever heard Mammy pray aloud more than a few times, yet each is positive that she prayed every hour of the day all her life for strength and wisdom.

Innumerable were the sacrifices she made for her children. I think that at the funeral all of us kept remembering those sacrifices. I kept recalling the time when we were living out in Cottle County and Ford and I were batching in a house in Paducah and going to high school, and Mammy used to walk two miles through the mesquites to a dirt road, carrying a big box of eggs, butter, milk, bread and beans. At the road, she would use her apron to flag down a passerby and persuade him to leave the box for us at a grocery store in Paducah, eight miles away. And then she would walk the weary miles back home and cook for her other children.

Estelle, the oldest, remembered how Mammy used to run breathless to the creek and look in the swimming holes to see if her sons, who should have been home hours before, had drowned.

We all remembered how Mammy had loved beautiful clothes. She had always been the best dressed woman in church, even when she had only one dress. She was born with the instinctive knack of knowing how to pick clothes and how to wear them. But Mammy was not vain. She just wanted to look nice all the time.

Even at her funeral her children kept looking around the relative-filled, richly furnished family room on the second floor of the funeral home. Finally, it came to each of us that the person who was missing was Mammy. She had always been present when all of the children were together.

The children had their regrets. Regrets that they had not done this, had not said that. But Mammy probably had her regrets, too. Everyone has.

Of one thing all were confident. Mammy is in one of those mansions prepared for her by Him.

DOGWOOD & HONEYSUCKLE THIEVES   March 29

I saw all these people stopping their cars on the highway and filling them with dogwood branches. One man chopped down a whole tree. Said he was going to put up the flowering tree on his front porch. None of those people were from Kountze or Silsbee or Woodville, mind you. The cars they drove, or most of them, bore Beaumont license plates. Suppose Kountze people went to Beaumont and started stealing out of homes and stores down there? They would wind up in jail, and that's exactly where the Beaumont vandals ought to wind up.

If the Beaumont papers loved this part of the country as much as they pretend, they'd blow their top about this dogwood stealing, but of course those two sheets in Beaumont will probably continue to devote column after column each day to cussin' Harry Truman, the government, griping about taxes, predicting that the country is going to the dogs and accusing everybody who disagrees with them of being a Communist. Apparently they don't want to see any dogwood vandalizing. It's not only the dogwoods. It's ruining redbud trees, holly trees and wild honeysuckle. Maybe somebody ought to take a shot at those Beaumont and Houston dogwood thieves who are stripping Hardin County highways of their natural beauty.

AN EXPERT AT WORK

I saw that man, H. C. Wauson, drive up in front of The News again last Thursday. He had on a $100 suit, a hand-painted necktie, a fine white shirt that was as stiff as a board, his fingernails were manicured and polished and his $20 shoes were shined. He didn't have on no hat. His hair looked better than a $40 hat. The last time he came into this print shop, he took one look at our press, from the door, mind you, and said, "You'd better tighten that big nut under there. You've been hearing a grinding kind of noise, haven't you?" We had. Then he saw something else and fixed that. He got under the press in all those fine clothes, and an hour later when he came out he had a speck of grease on one fingernail. It was from Mr. Wauson, representative of Mergenthaler Linotype Co., that this printer bought our new Model 31 Blue Streak Linotype, which N. A. Cravens of the bank and this Printer own. Well, Thursday Mr. Wauson seemed to look even cleaner and his suit more expensive. He looked at the Linotype and found that a little old bushing had been having some trouble. So this fellow, who probably makes more than the $500 a month he could earn in a big print shop, goes up to Simpson's Auto Parts and makes a bushing out of a piece of copper tubing, and the Linotype began working perfectly.

Then he sat down to the keyboard and did things with this machine the Printer didn't know could be done. By that time, this Printer had gotten greasy and dirty just from watching, and Mr. Wauson had a speck of grease on his little finger. Moral: A person is really an expert when he can work without getting whatever he is working with all over him. That goes for cooks as well as mechanics.

HOG ATTACKS SLEEPING BABY   *August 30*

Mrs. Tate, wife of Dr. John Tate of the Kountze Clinic, thought it was a nightmare she had Saturday night, but Sunday morning her husband told her it was an actual occurrence he had told her about when he came back to bed.

About the middle of the night, he treated a 4-month-old baby that had been attacked by a hog out in the woods. The baby's parents, a Houston couple, were camped out in the piney woods and the baby was in a bassinet. The parents were awakened by the baby's screams. Then they saw a hog dragging the bassinet and biting at the child. Dr. Tate treated the baby's lacerated arm. The scared parents went back to Houston.

WRITE-UP FOR A READER   *September 13*

Aunt Martha Frazier, colored, has been here since the last day of December, 1901, "dancin around on these boards," as she puts it. Way back yonder, she wet-nursed two children of Amos Rich. She said she served the Olives and learned to read from them. She has worked for the A. L. Bevils since 1915, and she took care of Martha Bevil, now Mrs. Terrel Buchanan "as soon

31

as the doctor got through with her."

She gave birth to 15 children of her own and raised 11. One of her daughters, Martha Renfro, is teaching in Houston. A son, Randolph, carries the mail in Chicago and another son, Ogden, is braking for the Missouri-Pacific at Kingsville. Aunt Mattie says she raised all her children to work. She was one of the first subscribers to The News. She says she'd like to have one write up in the paper before she dies. She is 76 years old and still gets around lively. The News is proud to have her as a reader.

THE COLLARD GREEN DEBATE   *November 1*

The mess of collard greens pictured in the new masthead of The Kountze News has drawn nothing but ridicule, indignation and resentment from local citizens. They think that the hardy collard green, a favorite mainstay in the diet of many Hardin County residents, has been maligned, insulted and falsely represented.

The caustic comment of Judge H. A. Coe of the 88th District Court was typical of scores of persons. He wrote me that the drawing "shows a total disregard of the fine quality and noble structure of the lordly collard green. It is probably a city-slicker artist's idea, but it is not how a stalk of collard greens looks in its most familiar state.

"In keeping with the real affection we all have for the collard green, let us not be content with this phony misrepresentation. Let's have a picture of the real McCoy!"

County Attorney R. A. "Booger Red" Richardson saw a Red plot. "One of the indestructible institutions of Hardin County has been libeled," he wrote. "I refer to that democratic vegetable, the collard green. Perhaps McCarthy or Kefauver should investigate for subversive influences. Mr. Editor, who drew those collard greens for you? It could be a matter for the grand jury."

Walter Simmons, H&H butcher, said the collard greens in the masthead looked like "orange trees."

County Auditor Don Allums not only was indignant over the drawing but he berated the editor for omitting Bremmer bulls,

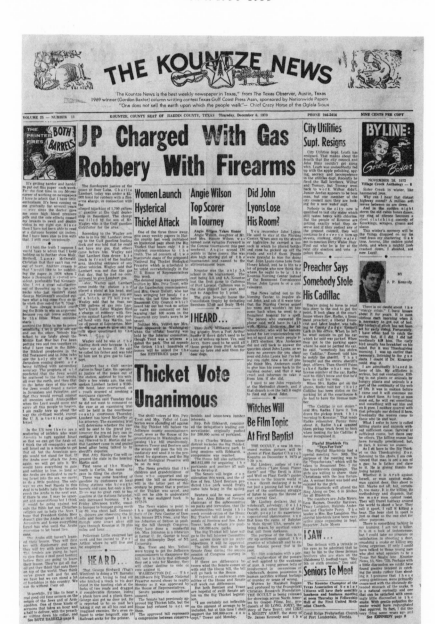

A front page of the Kountze News.

piney wood rooters and armadillos. He said that the drawing of the collard greens was an insult to the intelligence of anybody who ever saw a collard green in its most tangy and succulent state.

Joy Roberts said the collards in the picture "looked more like mustard."

John Blair said the collards were about "as realistic as Goat McDonald's bee course in Arkansas."

Judge A. L. Bevil said The News would need a lawyer but that he would not touch the case with an asbestos pole.

J. O. Fountain said the Methodist church long ago abandoned the practice of turning members out of the church, but that when a Methodist held the collard green up to ridicule in such drawings, he ought to be de-churched.

R. F. Crews said, "That picture of them collards makes my leg wound ache worse."

It looks as if the editor is out of $18. But he has an alibi. He wrote the artist for the East Texas Engraving Company at Tyler, which made the drawing, that if he didn't know what a collard green looked like he'd swipe one out of the patch near the phone office and send it to him. But he went right ahead and drawed them orange trees—or mustard greens or whatever they are. And what's more, if "Kefauver" Coe or Joe "McCarthy" Richardson want to get to the bottom of this undermining of the collard green, they can take that Tyler artist out in the Big Thicket and tie him to Red Lindsey's log. I ain't gonna take the rap for him.

COLLARDS, ARMADILLOS & BREMMERS   *November 15*

The News will have a new masthead in a few weeks which this harried and heckled printer hopes will satisfy Judge H. A. Coe, Walter Simmons, and others, including Lillie Mae Cruse, the colored cook at the Blair Cafe. The East Texas Engraving Company at Tyler has agreed to make a new nameplate at no extra cost, and furthermore, it will contain a drawing of collard greens that ought to look like collard greens, if the artist can draw the collards like the ones we sent him.

Last week, as soon as we got the engraving company's letter, Blair and the Printer got into the former's pickup and went down and made a deal with Mark Samuel, an aged colored man who has a big patch of fine collards. The Printer agreed to give Mark, who can't read, a subscription to The News for two of his plants which we pulled up by the roots. Then we went out to the Hart Florists and pulled up two fine collard specimens in Carter Hart's patch, and got a flower box from Mrs. Hart and shipped all the collards by bus to Tyler. One of the plants was five feet tall, root and all.

The new masthead should also please those, including Don Allums, who wanted an armadillo and a Bremmer bull in the scene, but we regret to say there will not be room for a piney woods rooter.

ONLY DUST REMAINS   *December 6*

I saw the corner stone of the old Methodist church opened Sunday. The elements had invaded the crypt in the 63 years since the documents and relics were placed behind the stone and nothing but dust remained. The Methodists were disappointed but not surprised. Services will be held in the new church for the first time Sunday.

YEAR 1952

WOLVES TRAPPED   *January 24*

Oney Phelps of the Thicket community trapped three timber wolves last week and another this week in Sheriff A. D. "Red" Lindsey's pasture northwest of Honey Island. Three were males and one was a female. Mr. Phelps brought the second one in live

Wednesday of last week. According to the sheriff, the wolves killed and ate more than $1,000 worth of his calf crop in 1951. Mr. Phelps is a professional trapper and is employed jointly by the county and local cattlemen to trap wolves. Hardin County is paying a bounty of $25 per wolf scalp to anyone who brings one in.

DIDN'T SEE NOBODY BUT YOU   *April 10*

I saw an old buddy coming into the printing shop last Saturday morning while I was running the big job press. This old boy had a sheet of paper in his hand. I never had learned this old boy's name but he was one of the first persons I'd got familiar with in Kountze. He used to comment on what was in The News and tell me big lies about the weather and I used to tell him big lies about fishing. I'd see him always at White's service station and I thought he was somebody helping out. Well, Saturday, I said, "What you got there in your hand?" He said, "It's a statement from the mayor." I said, "Why in the heck didn't the mayor bring it down here himself? Here, I've been in Kountze nearly two years and I've never seen Arthur Holt, let alone met him. As far as I know he's a hermit. And another thing, he don't take the paper, and as far as I know he never reads it. I've been down to his place a dozen times and didn't see nobody but you."

Then the fantastic idea began to dawn on me, but the old buddy beat me to it. "I'm Arthur Holt," he said, and he laughed so loud he drowned out Gordon Baxter on the radio. Well, what would you have done? In trying to cover up my confusion, I knocked a piece of skin off my thumb trying to shut off the job press. Also, I felt like a simpleton, especially that part about him not reading the paper. I had known he practically wore White's paper out reading it. Anyway, he subscribed Saturday, so Mrs. Holt could read it, too.

IT WAS TOO MUCH   *July 17*

I heard Gordon Baxter last Thursday describe in detail how
one hot day he jumped into a cool Louisiana bayou with all his
clothes on. It was about 3 o'clock in the afternoon and the temperature was 105 in the print shop and I was wringing wet with
sweat. Baxter kept telling how fine the water had been and he
finally said, "Everybody ought to jump in the creek at least once
a year with all his clothes on." It was too much for me. I closed up
the shop and drove to my house on Village Creek, ambled down
to the creek and jumped in, clothes and all, and didn't come out
till sundown. Best thing I've done this year.

NUDE WILD MAN   *August 14*

A gun totin' "wild" man of the woods is still the object of a
search in the Honey Island area. Last Sunday Sheriff "Red"
Lindsey headed a 10-man posse that searched unsuccessfully for
the deeply tanned, barefooted man who was first seen on August
2 by Uncle Will Kelly who lives on Sheriff Lindsey's farm.

The mysterious man was next seen last Saturday in the same
area by Dan Sutton.

Mr. Kelly was riding a horse from the farm seven miles west of
Honey Island when the naked man appeared by the side of the
road. Mr. Kelly watched the man turn around and walk through
the woods for half a mile before he was lost from sight. He noti-
fied the sheriff who, with Mr. Kelly, followed the barefoot tracks
until they lost them in the woods. The tracks were plainest where
the man had crossed an oil-dampened pipeline right-of-way.

Last Saturday, Mr. Sutton was walking from his home four
miles northwest of Honey Island and was joined by the naked
man on the road. The man walked with Mr. Sutton about 100
yards before he turned aside and went into the woods. When Mr.
Sutton told him he was going to call the sheriff, the man replied,
"I've been out here three years and the law will have to shoot it
out with me."

Mr. Sutton said the man had a heavy beard and a hairy body,

and he said the man had a gun in each hand, and that one of the firearms was a pearl-handled pistol. Mr. Kelly thought the man was about 35 years old, and Mr. Sutton thought he was about 50.

There was speculation as to whether some person was playing a trick. However, reports of a naked "wild" man in the east Texas woods have been heard from time to time during the last two or three years.

The sheriff said that the next time the man appears, he'll have bloodhounds to take to the spot. The sheriff does not doubt for one minute the accounts given him by Mr. Kelly and Mr. Sutton. He said the barefoot tracks were plain in each case. Although the first thing an insane person usually does is shed his clothing, the man modestly attempted to hide his nakedness when first sighted by Mr. Kelly, indicating that the man may not be insane, even though a "nut," or a fugitive from the law.

In the meantime, everybody in the Honey Island area is wary at night, and especially when in the woods.

ADLAI & THE DEMOCRATS *September 11*

I saw a DED (Disgruntled Eisenhower Democrat: Not to be confused with regular old line Republicans like Mr. Earl Robertson and Glover Prince) from Beaumont one day last week down at Blair's eating table, and in the course of a violent, gravy-slinging argument, the DED said, "You ain't a-votin' for Adlai Stevenson. You're a-votin' agin' Hoover and a depression and armadiller-chasin'."

At the time I thought that was reason enough to vote for the Democratic party, but later I got to thinking and decided what the DED said ain't necessarily so. I'm voting against every Republican president since 1860. I am not even thinking of the last 50 years. I'm voting against Appomattox, against Grant, against Sherman, against carpetbaggers, against the 1860's, the '70's, the '80's, the '90's and against the misery that the Republicans heaped on the South for 50 years. I'm voting for what my Confederate grandfather told my father and what my father told me. Voting against the Depression? Shoot no! I'm still voting against Reconstruction! What the Republicans did to the South between 1865 and 1932 makes the last 20 years of Roosevelt and Truman seem like hog-heaven. Sure the Republicans want a change: They want to change a lot of Southern Democrats into paupers again. The only thing that ain't changed is the Republican party, and it's still the GOP (Grand Old Plague) that, unlike the thieving Democrats who can change a dime into a dollar, can change a dollar into a dime.

So as for me, they can take the Republican party which has never changed and hasn't changed now, even with Ike the head of it, and stick it on the end of a screwdriver and rev it up to 1800 rpm's and ram it and cram it and jam it right where it has been for the last 20 years. Out of power!

THE PRESS PICTURES ADLAI   *September 18*

For months The News has been curious as to how Adlai Stevenson really looks. The nation's photographers, evidently aware that both the newspaper and news magazine press of the country is solidly behind the Republican party, seemingly try to please their schizophrenic editors by shooting Adlai from angles designed to distort his features into drooling idiocy. Thus, the daily newspapers and magazines that circulate in this area have outdone one another in publishing only gruesome pictures of the honest and intelligent Illinois governor.

For instance, The Houston Post runs only idiot shots of the man who took corruption out of Illinois politics. The Post's favorite picture of Adlai is one showing the governor drinking from a water fountain, his lips pursed out like a howling maniac. The biggest picture The Beaumont Enterprise has published to date of the man who in all probability will be the next president of the United States was one showing the bottom of Adlai's shoe which badly needed half-soling. The Enterprise also is a sucker for any picture of Adlai that makes him look like a chain gang menial. The Beaumont Journal refuses to publish his picture at all, apparently going on the theory that the worst picture of Adlai is too good to be published.

The Dallas Morning News, however, leans to shots which give Adlai a satanic look. In the Dallas News, Adlai always looks like Old Scratch.

The Houston Press, which sees everything as material for a Dragnet script, just loves shots of Adlai that make him look like the WANTED mugs you see hanging in the post office. Only the numbers below his chin are missing. The Fort Worth Star-Telegram goes in a big way for playboy pictures of the man who writes his own speeches. Old Amon Carter wants to show Adlai, who didn't toady to Truman, the Legionnaires or Shivers, as an amiable but diabolically clever comedian. The Star-Telegram publishes pictures of him with a forefinger to his temple, his eyes shut and his jaw teeth showing. A favorite picture of all anti-Adlai publications, including Time magazine, is one that shows Stevenson drinking a malt through a straw. His cheeks are sucked in and his eyes are pooped out and he looks like a bald-headed Harpo Marx.

It's strictly against the daily press's camera code for the shutter boys to take pictures of Adlai unless: he has his mouth open, his eyes shut, his jaw whonkered, his tongue out, or his back turned. If none of these occurs, the cameramen apparently are instructed to sweat it out for the idiot angle.

The Kountze News, despairing of ever seeing a reasonable picture of him (we'll take Adlai gladly), and not being able to subscribe to The Atlanta Constitution, the only other newspaper this printer knows about that is supporting Stevenson, wrote campaign headquarters at Springfield, Ill., and received a picture of the candidate. Of course, Adlai is not as handsome as Shivers, but then who wants to be? Even in his campaign picture, Adlai is as homely as, say, D. C. Enloe, Otis Smith or Truman Williford, but they say that Abe Lincoln was the homeliest man who ever came to Springfield—until Adlai came along.

HAWK MIGRATION   *October 2*

The big "chicken hawk" mystery has been solved. And it turned out that the 40,000 hawks which enveloped the Kountze area last week were not chicken hawks at all, according to Frank Watson of Houston, an amateur ornithologist who made a special trip to Kountze last Saturday to investigate the spectacular hawk migration.

Mr. Watson, who gave the impression of being a quiet, kind, studious man, viewed a gulley full of the dead hawks which had been shot by local marksmen. The hawk was the broad-winged hawk. It is a migratory bird and is protected by the State of Texas. In fact, all hawks are protected by the State of Texas except the goshawk, cooper's hawk, sharp-shinned hawk, duck hawk and vultures, so it was against the law to kill those hawks.

But the hawks were simply chicken hawks to local residents, and in justice to the local hunters who banged away at them, it should be said that the hunters thought the hawks could have wiped out the chicken and quail population.

Mr. Watson seemed to understand the actions of the local sharpshooters when this printer informed him that the hawks picked clean the bones of Charles "Chili" Daniel's horse and ran all of H. O. Peeble's chickens under the house.

"Warty" Lewis, H&H butcher, solemnly reported that while he was toting boxes of frozen fryers from the truck to the H&H market, about 40 of the hawks swooped down and tried to take a box away from him. Whereupon, he claimed, he slew 20 of them and sold them for chickens.

Mr. Watson said broad-winged hawks feed largely upon insects, especially large destructive caterpillars and grasshoppers, both of which are injurious to agriculture and forestry, and upon frogs and snakes. They prefer toads to any other food.

The hawk's nest in Canada and northern states and in the fall migrate to Mexico, Central America and northern South America. The hawks decided to light here for the first time in 25 years because some natural phenomenon or unfavorable weather steered them off their migration route. About 1926 a similar migration of hawks hit the Kountze area, and the slaughter then, as last week, was terrific.

THE WILD MAN REAPPEARS

The Honey Island wild man story just won't die. The naked man was seen a third time recently, this time standing near a creek on the Sour Lake Road. Sheriff A. D. "Red" Lindsey did not reveal the name of the couple who saw the man. The two did not care for the publicity.

The couple said they were riding in their car along the highway and saw the nude man standing by a water hole. They said he dropped his hands and turned and walked into the woods as soon as he saw he was observed.

The sheriff's theory now is that persons who have seen the man saw a naked man, all right, but that the man is not "wild," but drunk. He believes that he might be a character who is in the habit of working in the woods with his axe, without any clothes on, while he takes frequent nips from a jug. At a stage of his inebriation, the man forgets where he left his clothes and starts wandering around in search of them.

Another theory is that the man might be one who, saturated with comic book criminology, is deliberately perpertrating a hoax and enjoying it.

However, the sheriff leans to the other theory. He has known one or two men who worked in the woods naked, while they nipped the bottle, but the sheriff does not suspect any definite person.

HOW DO YOU LIKE ARMADILLO?   *October 9*

Last Thursday night old Allan ripped his britches when he said on the radio he was going to vote for Ike, but that he was still a "Texas Democrat," a label Allan himself invented, and which really means "Shivercrat." That word, in years to come, may be clothed with the same contempt that is now pinned on the old epithet, "Hoovercrat." Let both Allan and Price Daniel consider that no Democrat in Texas has ever repudiated the national party without earning the contempt of fellow Texans, without dying as pitiable political outcasts, and we predict ignominious careers for those two political renegades who have deserted the party of James Stephen Hogg, John Reagan and Woodrow Wilson and don't let anybody tell you it is not the same party! It is!

When Allan votes for Ike in November he's also going to vote for that malicious smear specialist Richard Nixon. When I heard Nixon on TV he gave me a fearful feeling that I was watching something sinister and merciless. In a few days it came to me that Nixon is the kind of person who would put you in jail if he didn't like your face or name. He hates hard and maliciously. Suppose Ike should be elected and then suppose he died. One out of every six presidents have died in office.

Suppose he should die like Harding died. A few months after he got in office. Then this Nixon, who is only one heartbeat away from the presidency, would take over. He and McCarthy. Between the two, they could start a reign of terror. Anyway, one thing Mr. Nixon will not explain is where he got the $20,000 to build that house. In my books he's a crook!

But the worst thing, I'm afraid, is that if the Republicans get in I would never make enough money to make the payments on my Linotype. I'd have to go back to Buglar cigarettes and going without underwear. And I'd be saying down at Blair's cafe:

"Please, pass me some more of that armadillo. I think I like it fried better than boiled; not so much grease in it."

YEAR 1953

TOWN WITH A SENSE OF HUMOR   *February 12*

Silsbee, the town to the east that has always been a suburb of Kountze, held a slogan contest recently, and what do you think was the winning slogan? None other than "Crossroads of Industry," and may we point out without being accused of harboring sour grapes, that endless towns in the nation are "crossroads of industry." For instance, some far larger towns, like Detroit and Pittsburgh and even Chicago, if Silsbee will permit the comparison. But if Silsbee likes the new slogan, they're the ones who have to live with it.

However, Silsbee's slogan got us to thinking about a possible Kountze slogan. Some descriptive phrase that would apply to Kountze. We dismissed all the wornout and hackneyed slogans as being not good enough for Kountze. The one we kept thinking of was "The Town With A Sense Of Humor." We like that and will use it in our masthead until some one thinks up one better.

The way we see it, a town with a sense of humor has people who are optimistic, cheerful, philosophic, and also ambitious. Whoever saw a person who saw the bright side of life who wasn't on his way to the top? Most Kountze people always have a smile, a joke or a friendly way of saying things. Even the preachers over here like to play for a laugh, and kick it around for a grin. Then, too, people that see the bright side, the humorous side, always get things done.

THE REPUBLICANS' PROMISE   *March 26*

Since the campaign last fall the Republicans are doing the exact opposite of what they said they would do. They say things that don't sound at all like the things they said then. They want you to forget all the slogans they shouted. In fact, they are now saying the same things about the budget, taxes, the war and the Reds that the Democrats said.

It has now come to the point that criticism of the Republicans, including Governor Allan Shivers, is a naughty deed, an unwholesome act. To disagree with the state or the national administration is dangerous. An act that possibly should be investigated by Joe McCarthy.

Do tell! Well, remember last fall when Ike and his crusaders stumped the country and won the election on the issue of the Korean War as a partisan political issue? Didn't he promise to "do something" fast? It's becoming increasingly evident that Ike is not going to rule the Republican party. As the Democrats predicted, Ike can't get along with McCarthy, but who can? Only the Democrats are now backing Ike to the hilt. The reason: he's carrying out the Democratic platform. The Republicans are rejecting his nominations and his program right and left. Ike, now that he's facing the facts of life, sounds like a Democrat.

As the Republican promises made in the campaign begin to face things as they are, the shining honesty and moral courage of Adlai Stevenson takes on a new luster. He tried to talk horse sense to the American people. He told the truth about taxes, the budget, and the Korean War, but the Republicans said he was Harry Truman's boy. As time goes by, it will become crystal clear that he was as far from Truman's influence as Ike was. Ike is really a Democrat at heart, and everything he has done since he entered the White House shows it. But Ike did not have the moral courage to run on the Democratic ticket and Adlai Stevenson did.

Ike and the Republicans made many promises about what they were going to do, but they are winding up doing exactly what Adlai Stevenson said he would do.

YEAR 1954

VIOLETS   *February 12*

I saw just about the prettiest violets in the county out at the home of Mr. and Mrs. Carter Hart. They flanked the walk from the front gate to the house in the old-fashioned way. There were a thousand in bloom the day I saw them. What flower is sadder or sweeter than the violet?

CIRCULATION NOW 1,000

The paid circulation of The Kountze News reached 1,000 last

week for the first time. That means that The News will print that number and more every week. That's pretty good when you consider that The News had to give papers away the first six weeks of its life in September and October of 1950.

This printer figures that now just about everybody in the Kountze and Honey Island area is reading the paper.

As soon as we get everybody in the Village Mills and Saratoga area taking the paper, we are not going to take any more subscriptions.

They could just keep on coming in, but I'll be durned if I'm going to stand up there and feed that press for more than 3 hours at a time.

KEEP COWS OUT OF KOUNTZE   *February 18*

The city of Kountze has hired Morgan Key to keep illegal livestock out of the city with instructions to do just that and no ifs, ands, or buts about it. Mr. Key, who works at the Kountze Ice Company, promised he would do it. He said he took the job "for business and not for friendship," and will make an all-out effort to enforce the livestock ordinance.

If he does, that means he will pick up all untagged dogs, all female dogs whether tagged or not, and all cattle, horses, mules and hogs. Mr. Key is empowered to impound all animals he finds loose within the city limits.

The city council is determined to rid the city of stray animals this time. Mayor Holt said that the decision to enforce the livestock ordinance has been in the making for weeks. Last week's city council move was coincidental with the "organization" of the KKK (Keep Kows out of Kountze).

BIG THICKET SIZE EGGS   *March 18*

A large white hen, 7½ months old, which belongs to the John Lewis family here, is quite outstanding in the poultry world. For some time she has been laying eggs with a double yolk but recently she surpassed that. One day last week she laid a large brown egg that weighed three-fourths pound. It measured 4½ inches long and 7½ inches round. When it was broken it contained a yolk and white plus another egg complete with shell. Quite a hen. Perhaps she belongs on the nameplate alongside the Bremmer bull.

CRANK TELEPHONES REPLACED

The old crank telephone is now a thing of the past in Kountze and this Printer misses it. It was a pleasure to ring off the old crank phone. You could put a lot in a ring-off.

One time I got so mad at the friend on the other end of the line that I rang-off for a full minute. Ah, I miss that ring-off! You simply can't cuss a machine, but boy how I could cuss those operators. But have you tried cussin' the dial phone? No kick at all in it. It just sits there as inhuman as the machine it is. Every time I look at that dial I feel like hunting up the old operators and making love to them. And I was the one person in town who just couldn't wait until we got the dial system.

Alas and alack no longer can I lie to the operator: "I've mislaid or lost my directory, please ring Amos Laird for me." Now I gotta look it up and remember four digits. Half the time I don't know my own number. The other day I got five wrong numbers before I dialed the right one. Why, oh why, did we want to get rid of those crank phones?

THE REPUBLICANS' TV ACT   *May 13*

Have you become aware of the technique the Republicans have worked out in their appearances before TV cameras? You will remember that at the beginning they hired the big New York advertising firm of Barton, Barton, Durstine and Osborne to put on their slick political shows? But this didn't set too well with the grassroots, so gradually the homey, utterly simple, utterly "sincere" approach evolved. It is a wedding of soap opera with the most advanced accomplishments of science. The best thinking of the Republicans has gone into it.

Now the speaker is both actor and conversationalist. He knows all the tricks of the suspended syllable or word, used to imply that the speaker, who is supposed to be ad-libbing, is groping for the right word. He just has to come up with it because what he is saying is so utterly true. They use homey variations of this trick, such as interrupting themselves to light a pipe in the middle of a sentence, or to fold their arms or to walk across the room or look out of a window, all of which, of course, is part of the script and carefully studied. They couldn't be more ingratiating if they had been peddling Alka-Seltzer or Tums. Nixon is the real expert at this, but Ike is learning fast. But the Republicans have to look and sound plausible for they have to sell us a bill of goods, including the war in Indo-China.

It's something new in Washington. Whether you like it or not, Roosevelt made no bones about reading his speeches in the best speaking voice of his generation, and Truman cussed like a muledriver and called a spade a spade. Their scripts did not say "knot fist here," "cross room here," "light pipe here." But it's going to take good salesmen to sell us on that mess in Washington.

QUAIL EGG RESCUE   *August 12*

Recently, Frank Cryer of Saratoga was coming home from work and stopped to put out a fire beside the road. As he got near the fire an old mother quail came out near him. Mr. Cryer thought she might have some young ones nearby and found the nest just as it caught fire.

It had 12 eggs in it. Mr. Cryer put them in an ice cream container, brought them home and put them under a hen. The next morning, Mrs. Cryer went to get the eggs and all but one had hatched, but when she picked it up it came open and out hopped a little bird.

Mrs. Cryer keeps them in a box and each day she carries them to a sand pile in the back yard. Just as fast as the chicks get out they run and get in the sand and throw dust over themselves, as if they were grown. Mrs. Cryer sits in the yard and waits for them to get through. When they get tired, they all come back to her and sit down. Mrs. Cryer feeds the birds seed and chick starter, and they follow her all over the house just like baby chicks.

YEAR 1955

THICKET'S LAST "LEGAL" BEAR KILL   *January 20*

Richard Noack of Saratoga claims to be the last man to have legally shot bear in the Big Thicket. But the 79-year-old hunter says he wasn't "aiming to kill the bear," and he admits the incident scared the daylights out of him.

The shooting occurred about 30 years ago, just before it became illegal to kill bears. Mr. Noack was hunting wild hogs, which he says were plentiful at that time, when he saw what looked like a big black hog in the dense undergrowth. He leaned back and fired and a huge black bear reared up and almost fell on him.

"I wasn't scared at all at the moment," he said. "I tied a rope to the animal and dragged him out of the underbrush. But when I got down to look at the thing I was shaking so I had to lean on my horse to keep from falling."

Bear hunting was pretty profitable in those days. Folks around Saratoga flocked to the Noack home when they heard about the kill. They bought the meat for a dollar a pound. When they had bought all they wanted, Mr. Noack sold the remainder to Fuller's Cafe in Beaumont. He got $50 for the skin. The bear weighed 460 pounds, and the sale of the meat and skin gave the seasoned hunter the best day's return on a hunt he ever had.

COWS KILLED IN KOUNTZE

May 3

There were two dead cows in the road Sunday morning on south Pine Street within the city limits and B. A. Mitchell's car was badly banged up. One of the two young Bremmer cows was killed and the other was injured so badly the Sheriff's Department was called to destroy it.

Mr. Mitchell said that he was passing a car headed in his direction, and that he could not see what was behind the car because of its bright lights. When he passed the car, the two cows were in front of his car, and there was no time to turn or put on the brakes.

SWIMMING HOLE ALLIGATOR

June 9

Boys hunting a swimming hole this summer better steer clear of the pond about 200 yards behind the home of George Daniel, a mile east of town on the old Silsbee road. The other day, Mr. Daniel's son killed a 7 foot, 5 inch alligator in that old swimming hole. And he thinks the gator's mate may still be in the pond and mad because his mate is gone.

Last summer boys went swimming in the pond quite often. The pond is about 30 feet wide and 100 yards long and is about five feet deep at the deepest point. Daniel's son was down at the pond late Sunday afternoon and saw the big alligator floating with its head sticking out of the water. He went back to the house and got a .22 caliber rifle and hit it in the head first shot. The alligator shuddered and thrashed around throwing water before it died and sank to the bottom. He then got a hook and pole and fished out the dead alligator and skinned it the next day. Alligator hides now bring about $4 a foot.

THE PRINTER MEETS SHIVERS

September 30

For 10 years I have been driving through Woodville, enroute

to various places, but in all that time I have never stopped. One night last week I went to Woodville and stopped. The occasion was the visit of the Grand Master of the Masonic Grand Lodge of Texas, State Senator George Moffet of Chillicothe. My main impressions of the meeting were: First, I saw Allan Shivers in the flesh for the first time, and, second, I'm glad I live in Kountze instead of Woodville, for Woodville appears to be loaded with VIP's (Very Important Persons).

What is a VIP? He is a person who gives the impression that he is an important man and that he knows what's best for you, and that if you don't think like he does or do what he says, you don't amount to much. But if you think like he does and bend the knee to him, he'll see to it that you get along okay. Much of the time, the VIPs of this world, including Woodville, go around with immense dignity, bestowing a handshake and a patronizing smile here and there. They like to wear blue serge suits, collars and ties.

In line with the present national tendency to distrust quips and puns and any kind of humor, the VIP scorns a sense of humor. The national brand of VIP distrusts higher education and they distrust so called "eggheads." Most of the time they are too dignified to joke. For instance, when I got to Woodville I told one fellow that John and I thought we might as well deliver a load of liquor as long as we were coming up anyway. I thought the fellow was going to throw us in jail before I could convince him I was joking. You must not even insinuate that anybody in Woodville would take a drink, though the bread man who comes up there every day from Beaumont was arrested for selling it one day last week.

But the reason I'm glad I live in Kountze is because there are no stuffed shirts or VIPs here. Nary one. No Big Shots. Or can you think of one? There may be one or two who would like to be VIPs, but we all know too much on them. Come to think of it, there are few VIPs in Hardin County. There may be one or two in Sour Lake, but there are none in Saratoga. You'd think that Oscar Prewitt of Silsbee ought to be a Stuffed Shirt, but I've seen old Oscar put a nickel in a juke box, and a VIP wouldn't be caught dead doing that.

The nearest thing to a VIP in Silsbee should be N. A. Cravens but he chews gum at times, and if them VIPs at Woodville chew gum they do it behind the barn. Another thing about a VIP, he's already got it made. They're sitting back and enjoying it and hoping you never make as much as they have. Now you take John Crosby here in Kountze, or Z. Blair, or Thomas Sydney Hooks. They got it made, too. But they're the last people on earth one would call a Stuffed Shirt. VIPs just don't wear khakis.

Another reason I'm glad I live in Kountze instead of Woodville is that I'd probably be run out of Woodville. The VIPs there wouldn't tolerate anybody who differed with them. Probably nobody would advertise. Take here, businessmen in Kountze read the paper. They don't care what's in it, just so it's read. Because businessmen in Kountze are not stuffed-shirts, they believe anybody has a right to his own opinion and beliefs.

Then there was Shivers. He made a good speech because it was the first time I ever heard him when he wasn't spouting his off-key brand of stuffed-shirt politics. He said there's an old saying that a person who drinks out of Turkey Creek will always come back to Tyler County. He said he's often wondered what happened to all the old swimming holes he used to swim in when he was a boy. You could tell the man really loves Tyler County. And if Allan Shivers loves Tyler County, he loves Texas. But there are other people who also love Texas—people who disagree with him.

After the shindig was over, Cecil Overstreet grabbed me by the arm and started dragging me toward the governor. I said, "Cecil turn me loose, I'll go quietly." Cecil introduced me by yelling that I was "one of your worst critics." The governor and John Ben Shepperd, the attorney general, have one thing in common besides the veterans land scandals. Each knows how to give you a piercing eyeballing, a full whammy. They must have practiced it a lot, or else they just have big eyeballs, but the governor's eyes got as big as buffalo nickels when he looked at me. John Ben's did the same thing up at College Station last February.

The governor said, "Oh yeah, you're the editor at Kountze. You used to send me the paper but you quit." Then somebody else came up and the governor shook his hand. I turned away and he yelled, "Put me back on your list." So I did not have a chance to tell him that his name is still on the list and the paper is mailed to him every week, and that his subscription, paid for by Houston Thompson of Silsbee, will not expire until next January.

I never had much grounds to form a personal opinion of Allan Shivers and now that I've seen him I still don't have anything to go on, but my political opinion has not changed.

FLOWERING DOGWOOD

PART TWO
1956–1965

YEAR 1956

DANIEL IS NOT THE MAN   *January 5*

Every day even the Republican daily papers get fuller of the incompetency of the state government and this is as good a time as any to single out one Price Daniel and say that if you are going to elect him governor of Texas in 1956 you will have more of what you've got now. Because he's the dear, dear friend of the boys who have been running Texas into the mud and slime for the past 10 years.

One can see now those who got into high office by slinging mud are now reaping a harvest of mud. Let's go back nearly 10 years to the Jester-Rainey campaign for governor. Remember how the great financiers who now rule Texas libeled Dr. Rainey as being a man who wanted Negroes to attend the University of Texas and who protected a cell of sexual perverts? Utterly filthy lies, but they beat Rainey. Then came on the Allan Shivers machine and it elected its hero by calling working people in Port Arthur Communists and by promising that there would never be desegregation in Texas schools.

Because the ruling machine has lost control of the state government, it is important that Texas this year turn out the ins from top to bottom.

Texas needs a governor who is not supported by the same daily press, the same lobbyists and the same Big Money which have kept Shepperd, Shivers, Lock, Ben Ramsey and all the other incompetent tools of their masters in office.

Anybody this group supports should be rejected by the voters of Texas. Otherwise, the same old clique will continue to rule Texas—and loot it. There will be other scandals, even though the top officials may be honest. Any man who is elected governor by this group will not be able to shake loose from the group now in control—corrupt Big Money.

REPUBLICAN PARTY BAD FOR SOUTH   *March 8*

The Republican party is not good for Texas and the South. It never has been good for us. It was born in 1856 and its parents were Hatred for, and Envy of, the Southern way of life. Texas and the South have nothing to gain by voting for the Republican party. We always lose when we do. When the Republicans get in they get the South with its back to a wall and a shotgun at its head —the exact position we are in now. The Republican party has never given the South a break. Not even the Ike administration.

The Republican party is not good for the country. For instance the Republican party is now not only giving away timber and dam sites and national resources, but is also giving away the Indian lands of this nation and moving the Indians to the slums of big cities.

Don't think that if you vote for Ike you will be voting for the man. You will be voting for the Republican party, the natural enemy of the South. That party and not Ike is running the country, just like it ran the country under Grant and Harding. Ike has never run the country one minute since he took office; the party has. We pay right through the nose when the Republicans get in, and it does not matter who is president.

This writer is glad that Ike is going to run because his give-away administration must be the issue in the campaign. Seeing Ike on TV, one became aware that he has lost a lot of weight and has aged considerably since 1952. He looked like Roosevelt before FDR went to Yalta. In other words, he looked to this writer like a man with one foot in the grave.

Ike said that if he is reelected he "must eliminate many of the less important social and ceremonial activities." That list could cover a lot of ground. It could mean that Ike would be only a part-time president, as he has been since his heart attack. We have never had a president who was merely the chairman of the board of directors. We have never had a president who eliminated "social and ceremonial activities." And this writer for one does not want one. The "social" activities do not worry us, but the "ceremonial" part might include just about everything. We need a president who won't eliminate any of the duties the Constitution says he must perform. We want a president who has the inclination and the passion to eliminate nothing—even if it means giving up golf.

WE THOUGHT WE WERE RICH   *March 29*

Mrs. Herrington, the pleasant Mrs. Herrington, the dignified but pleasant woman who serves your plate at Boyd's Cafe, said the other day that as a girl she and her brothers and sisters regarded it as a treat when they got light bread, instead of the biscuits they got twice a day, and that now her children whoop and holler when she makes biscuits.

That observation of the great change in American eating habits in one generation brought back memories of life on that cotton farm where I grew up. There were seven children in our family and we had biscuits twice a day and cornbread once. Maybe once in a while we had mush and sweet milk for supper. We would eat nearly a half gallon of syrup for breakfast and biscuit after biscuit. It was Mary Jane syrup. Karo syrup was for Sunday morning. Then for supper there would be what we called "thickening gravy" and biscuits. We did not think that diet was unusual because all our neighbors had syrup and biscuits for breakfast and gravy for supper. At noon, in the winter time we had red beans or blackeyed peas and anything we canned during the previous summer. In summer, we had fresh vegetables if there was not a long drought on.

Every once in a while, somebody in the community would butcher a "beef" and would come by selling "beef steak." My pappy would buy 50 cents worth. That would happen five or six times a year. The rest of the time we ate fried pork. At hog killing time, and for weeks afterward, we'd have sausage, liver and the choice bits of pork. I can still hear Pappy sucking the marrow out of the pork bones.

Sometimes in the summer we'd can 100 jars of tomatoes, half-gallon, jars, too. All winter long we'd have breaded tomatoes (biscuits and sugar added). Then we'd have dried peaches that we'd dry on the chicken house. Many's the time I've run 200 yards at top speed from the cotton patch to take in the peaches at signs of an approaching rain or shower. Next day we'd put them out to dry again.

Late in the summer we'd all go down to the blackeyed pea patch and pick the peas, cramming them in long cotton sacks. If there were watermelon vines in the pea patch, and there usually were, we'd have a watermelon fight. When we'd get all the peas picked and in the barn, we'd take them outside in a sack and beat them with a board and then "wind" them out, holding shells and peas in a dish pan high above our heads, letting the peas fall on the wagon sheet and the wind take away the hulls.

Pappy would make hominy and sauerkraut by the keg. In the early summer, we'd go down to the plum thicket in the canyon near the house and pick a wash tub full of plums and my poor Mammy would stand over a hot wood stove all day boiling that juice down to jelly.

During the cotton hoeing season, my poor Mammy could be seen coming across the fields with a bucket and then we would have a snack. It would be about 4 o'clock. The snack would consist of cornbread, onions and thick sliced bacon. In the fall, Mammy would appear in the wagon at noon with a covered dishpan full of baked sweet potatoes, cornbread, beans, onions, and fried peach pies. No matter what I have eaten or will eat before I die, I will say that nothing has ever tasted as good as those fried peach pies she made. I can just see that dark brown dried fruit and feel that squashy pie with the juice running out as I ate it, sitting on the cotton pile in the wagon.

But the big thing then was that Mammy and Pappy never had to persuade their seven children to eat. Then parents just wondered if their children's appetites were not too big. Children in that community in which we lived would have regarded present children as lunatics for not bolting everything in sight immediately. We would have marveled at the children of today who won't eat greens, cabbage, steak or syrup.

Then there were the sweets. Bananas once a year. Apples and oranges only at Christmas. On Saturday night, Pappy would come home about dark. But we were waiting for him and as soon as we heard the wagon cross the bridge we'd come running to open the gate. We knew he had a sack of stick candy that cost a nickel. In the half dark, some of the children would grab buckets of syrup and the sack of flour, and the boys would unhitch the horses and lead them in a trot to the barn, take the harness off and feed the horses. Then we'd hurry back to the house. There, Pappy'd pass out the stick candy. Sometimes, he'd bring home a bucket of honey and we'd eat that then and there.

In the summer time sometimes he'd bring back 75 pounds of ice and that night when we milked the cows we wouldn't save one treat for the calves. Usually two freezers of ice cream would fill us up, especially if Mammy had made a cake. On election night in July all the neighbors would throw in and have an ice cream supper at our house.

By present day standards we were poor. One Sunday shirt, one pair of overalls, no summer underwear; one pair of shoes until they wore out; going barefooted until one was 6 feet tall; hair cuts on Sunday morning by Pappy; one suit of clothes until they were outgrown; never a picture show; we went to snap parties and singings. We'd ride horseback 20 miles to go to a party.

But somehow we thought we were rich. We thought we were somebody. Our horses and mules were fat. Our cows looked slick. We had Rhode Island Red chickens. The wheels did not come off our wagon because we soaked them in water during droughts and we kept the wagon and windmill greased. If there was anything my Pappy hated it was a creaking windmill. We thought we had all the comforts of life and all the luxuries. Why, we were so well-to-do we felt sorry for the town kids. By present day standards we had nothing, but we thought we had everything.

A LETTER FROM LYNDON   *May 31*

The only man in the governor's race who is a real Democrat is Judge Ralph Yarborough. He's the only man in the race who will unite Texas, who will throw Bascom Giles' pals in the pen, who will clean out the awful crookedness that exists in every state department at Austin. He's the only man who will really raise old-age pensions. You know W. Lee O'Daniel won't. He will do exactly as he did before—exactly nothing.

Yarborough is on the right side of everything, the decent, honorable, honest, upright side. And the delegates to the state convention at Dallas knew it. Those thousands of delegates in the State Fair auditorium in Dallas chanted, "We Want Yarborough" until he finally appeared on the stage. Yarborough said he considered the ovation as one for Democratic ideals. He reminded the delegates how they as Democrats had been reviled in Texas and promised, "We'll march together in July and have a great Democratic victory in November."

There is a new-found pride in being a Democrat in Texas and that pride is in Ralph Yarborough who has stuck with the party through 12 years of blasphemy by the Shivercrats whose sun has set; 12 years of manufacturing lies and scandals. Democrats are beginning to hold up their heads and are not ashamed of supporting the only Democrat in the race—Yarborough. Shivers and Daniel have tried to make us believe that we were only Communists, left-wingers, pinks, but now we know better.

You say who is Lyndon Johnson for? Is he for Yarborough or Price Daniel? You know what Senator Johnson, Texas' favorite son for president and leader of the Texas delegation to Chicago, stands for. That's all you've heard and read about in recent weeks. He wants to see the Democratic party in Texas united instead of divided. You know from Senator Johnson that Allan Shivers and Republican Attorney General Herbert Brownell held a secret conclave at Woodville. You know what Lyndon thinks about party loyalty in a candidate, else he never would have finally whipped Shivers in a pitched battle.

But what does Johnson actually say? Okay, we quote from a letter from Johnson to this Printer:

"Dear Arch:. . . I know how you have stayed with me. I remember the News was the first paper to come out for me for Favorite Son. I can tell you I am proud to have a Democrat like you on my side.

"You may rest assured that I am not going to inject myself into the governor's race. I made it a rule long ago not to try to participate in anybody else's campaign. I have always managed to keep busy with my own business. Also I may assure you further, that I am not going to 'snoot' anybody who is running for office in Texas. I know who my friends are, of course, and I am proud to count you as one of the best. (Signed) Lyndon B. Johnson."

In another letter received later by this Printer, Senator Johnson wrote: " . . . *I will take no part in the gubernatorial campaign. Don't believe anybody who tells you differently—and that goes for newspaper writers who want to see the Democratic party in Texas divided instead of united.*"

Did you see that the public relations firm which dreamed up the infamous Port Arthur story in 1954 collected $175,000 for springing it on the Texas electorate 10 days before the election? You will remember the Port Arthur story was on TV. The firm which devised it sent a camera crew to Port Arthur, and the camera started grinding at dawn one morning when the streets were deserted. They hired a colored boy to parade as a picket and put a Yarborough placard on his back. Then they showed Port Arthur as a deserted town, inhabited by a few Negro Communists, all of whom allegedly supported Yarborough.

AN ELVIS PRESLEY FAN   *June 7*

This Printer finally found a honky tonk that has a juke box with all the records of Elvis Presley on it—18. We ain't going to tell you where it is because we don't like crowds and we want to keep it quiet. The owner is also an Elvis Presley fan and is just my age: 54. Kind of silly to be an Elvis Presley fan at the age of 54, ain't it? Winston Overstreet says it's stupid to be a Presley fan at any age.

A GOOD TURN   *July 12*

I saw this old lady, slightly stooped, come into Bishop's Cafe. She had walked all the way from Hardin County Hospital where she said her husband was ill with cancer. She ate a bite and then she wanted to buy a bottle of snuff. It was after closing time for most stores, but Mrs. Bishop lit out after that bottle of snuff in her car, the old woman with her. She found the snuff at Crosby's Super Market. Then Mrs. Bishop took the old lady back to the hospital. Mrs. Bishop came back with that shining look on her face that every person has when he does a good turn.

THE DONKEY-MULE QUESTION   *July 19*

Ralph Yarborough, who will be the next governor of Texas, came out of that press conference at Houston last week the best man in that bear pit, but he didn't get too much help from the Printer, who was scared wordless the first 10 minutes of the 30 minute interview. When the Printer forced himself to get in there and ask questions, he stuttered, stammered, bit his tongue, rocked back and forth like he was rocking a baby and otherwise appeared as nervous as a bootlegger in church.

Those three Houston reporters were really laying for Yarborough and this Printer. First thing off John Moore of the Post asked this Printer about the suit I was wearing. John said it was the first time anybody ever saw me with a suit on and how come. I said, like anybody in Kountze would, that it was my funeral suit, meaning that it was the only one I had and I wore it only to funerals, but those reporters took it wrong. Whose funeral you attending tonight, John came back with. I had to think fast and I came up with, this is my resurrection suit tonight. The resurrection of the Democratic party.

Those three reporters got real mean with Yarborough before we got in a single question and we were beginning to think that we would not get to ask any when we raised our voice and drowned the others out. But the Printer did get in one question that brought out Yarborough's best smile and revealed a side of his personality that the audience had not seen—that he is kind, humble, friendly and wise.

You will remember that the Printer asked his readers to submit questions for Yarborough. We got about 20 and the last one was from Mrs. J. E. Waddell at Village Mills.

Mrs. Waddell's question had to do with the recent county stock law election. She asked a question that has been asked many times since the election. She pointed out that last year, Hardin County voted horses, mules, jacks and jennies off the highways, and that on June 30 this year this justice precinct voted hogs, goats, sheep and donkeys off the highways. What is the difference, Mrs. Waddell wanted the Printer to ask Judge Yarborough, between a donkey and a mule.

Now most everybody knows the difference between a jack and a jennie and a mule. A mule is a hybrid and cannot reproduce themselves, but jacks and jennies can. But where does the donkey come in? It can't be the same as a jack and a jennet. There must be some difference because the statutes say that both must be voted on in stock law elections.

At first, we decided to ignore Mrs. Waddell's tantalizing question but there was a gnawing doubt. The more we thought about it, the more we wished Mrs. Waddell hadn't asked the question. We called up about a dozen people in Kountze and asked them if they knew the difference between a donkey and a jackass, since both reproduce their own kind. None of them knew the exact difference. How could we expect Yarborough to know if nobody in Kountze knew? But the more we thought about Mamie Waddell's puzzler the more we decided we had to ask Yarborough the question.

Now you know as well as I do that this Printer thinks Yarborough is not only the smartest but the wisest man in the governor's race. So we reluctantly decided that he just had to know the answer to that question or he wasn't fit to be governor of Texas. It made no difference if all the others did not know. Yarborough had to know. And furthermore, we had made up our mind that if Yarborough did not know, that was all she wrote in our books for him. Yarborough was born and raised on a farm in Henderson County and he has had a brilliant law career, and sometime on the farm or in his law practice he ought to have run across the difference between a jackass and a donkey.

Just before the program, Jim Palmer, a University of Houston journalism professor who is producer of the program, asked the four newsmen who were to interview Yarborough if they had any unusual questions. This Printer spoke up and posed his donkey question. Palmer paled and looked down his nose. John Moore of the Post, Baxter of the Chronicle and Taylor of the Press, all seemed embarrassed. Palmer was afraid of the question; he was afraid Yarborough couldn't answer it and that it would make him look ridiculous. But my head was set. I said if Yarborough couldn't answer that question, I would cut bait. I think that Palmer said if he could answer it, Yarborough would get his vote.

Well, the program went on and those newsmen ganged up on Yarborough. They asked cruel questions designed to hurt him, questions not designed to bring out any facts. The previous week they had been sweet with Price Daniel but they were not with Ralph, but he showed up their cruelty and he answered their questions. Suppose somebody came to you and said, "Why did you turn your back on the Negro?" What would you say? That's what Moore asked Yarborough. Moore was evidently trying to cost Yarborough the Negro vote which he has mainly because all the other candidates have attacked the Negro. Yarborough simply said he had not turned his back on anybody, that he sought the votes of all Texans, black or white, working man or otherwise.

Along there somewhere, we asked Yarborough the question. Then his friendly human side shone through his smile. He said, "That is the toughest question I've been asked." Then he went on to explain that the donkey is one of several species and is smaller than a mule but larger than a jack or jennet. He said it is a quadruped that reproduced itself. And he wound up by saying, "You know what the Biblical name for a donkey is?"

Well, up to that time the six or eight technicians in the room, who were moving and adjusting this and that, had showed no reaction at all to the program but at Yarborough's answer they all laughed. Then we knew it was a good question. After the program Palmer said that the question made the program and he said he'd have to have me back on, but I said positively no. Nothing doing. The only reason I consented to be on the program was to help Yarborough and according to the few scattered Shivercrats in Kountze I did not help him, but I did my best.

GRAB, GREED, PILLAGE AND PRIVILEGE   *August 23*

The last four years have proved that the Democratic party is always best for Texas, the South and the nation, and that the Republican party always brings us disunity, dissension and grief. Once again we have learned that when the Republicans get in, the South suffers humiliation and grief. So I believe every word Governor Frank Clement said in his keynote speech before the Democratic convention. He put the blame for the Republican privilege and pillage, the grab, greed and giveaway right where it belongs: on President Eisenhower. He was the first Democrat who had the language and the courage to call upon Americans to "rise up as one man and smite down those money changers who have invaded and violated the people's temple of justice." The Republicans who have always shouted "smear" when anybody inferred that Ike is less than a saint had nothing to say after Clement smote them with the truth. The Republicans were struck dumb by Clement's fearful, lashing tongue. He sounded like the wrath of God to millions of Americans and his picture of Ike and Nixon opened the eyes of the American people for the first time in four years. He took the halo off Ike's head. He exposed the myth of Ike's popularity in one speech and he painted Nixon as he really is—a man without political principle and conviction whose main weapon is slander.

Clement was the Democratic party come to life at that convention. Everything else was anticlimax, even the nomination of Adlai Stevenson as Democratic candidate for president. The important thing is the Democratic party and its never-changing principles, and Stevenson is a Democrat in the great tradition. There'll be no grab, greed, giveaway, pillage and privilege when he is elected president, for the people of America are not going to put a part-time president and an unfeeling demagogue of Nixon's caliber back in the White House.

One hopes that Price Daniel was listening when Governor Clement was telling the turncoats either to support the nominee of the Democratic party or get out of it. But Daniel, who brazenly supported Nixon, McCarthy and Ike in the grab, greed and giveaway is right here in Texas now trying to pass himself off as a Democrat, when all the time he is the Republican who broke with the majority of Democrats in the senate by not supporting the $20 tax cut for each dependent, and he was one of nine Democrats who voted against the housing bill. In 1955, he ranked 44th out of 49 Democratic senators in supporting Democratic legislation.

ADLAI, KEFAUVER HAVE IT   *September 20*

If you've absolutely made up your pin-head mind to vote the Republican ticket in the presidential election on November 6, don't read any further. It will just make you unhappy. But if you haven't made up your mind, then read on.

Last time a lot of you voted for Ike. You swore up and down you were voting for "the man" and not the Republican party. But now you know that the way it turned out you were voting for the party and not for Ike, and that the Republican party is the party of grab, greed and giveaway, whether it's Texas or Washington.

In the two Democratic nominees, Adlai Stevenson and Estes Kefauver, we have vigourous, healthy men who know what's best for America, not just what's best for the corporations in America. Can you feature Ike or Nixon either one having the guts to state their convictions as do Stevenson and Kefauver?

Back in 1952, one had to admit that Ike had it when he made his speeches, even if you were for Adlai, and you had to admit that the Republicans and Ike were making Adlai the goat for Truman's mistakes, but this time Adlai and Estes have it. Everything Adlai says hits the mark and nothing Ike says seems to have any steel in it, but how can it when everyone knows that he's become a part-time president who has turned the office over to a general staff. Adlai and Estes are on the offensive this year and the Republicans are going to have so much to answer for by the time they get started that Nixon and Ike won't have time to call us Democrats traitors. The Republicans are on the defensive and they are going to stay there.

You can't fool the people forever, and they know that it's just not right to vote for Ike and his hatchet man Nixon this time. They compare Ike to Adlai and Estes to Tricky Dicky and they can see that for the good of the country they'd better take Adlai and Estes. They won't want to trust the Republican party for another four years with Ike on a part-time schedule, Dulles lousing things up from Bagdad to Bombay to Berlin and General Motors building up the capitalist dollar and whittling yours down.

Adlai and Estes have a real program for the people—the Democratic party program which is always for the people. Ike has proved again that the Republicans are good only for capitalists, not for anybody else. Ike's prosperity? Don't make me laugh. Ike and the Republicans are spending more on defense in 1956 than the Democrats ever spent. Billions and billions. And that defense spending is the only thing that's keeping the country from going under. Ike's defense is costing more than Truman's war.

ELVIS AND THE MASTER THRILL   *September 27*

There is an indignant clamor in the land, mostly among the addicts of sterile, innocuous and utterly boring popular music that Elvis Presley should be put away for keeps. They say a lot, but mostly they say he's a disgrace to the human race. The truth is that Presley's physical contortions are not half as suggestive as some that were held to be so cute in bygone years. The Pelvis has never pulled off anything as seductive as Mae West's walk, or Gilda Grey's shimmy, or any run-of-the-mill hulas of the last 50 years. Watching the shimmy during World War 1 was like listening to a dirty story. Elvis' gyrations have never approached anything as suggestive as the can-can, which is now common fare. Many of the dances you see on TV are vulgar, if you want to get vulgar. The only difference is that Elvis is a man. Women have been doing far more suggestive contortions for years, but here comes Elvis and he just can't sing unless he sings all over, and then the Perry Como purists set up a howl that he's too sexy. As if Hollywood (and now TV) has given us anything but sex all these years! Elvis is just the climax of the shimmy, the hula, the strip-tease and the leg shows we've been applauding for four decades.

I have an open mind toward Elvis because I used to listen to him when he was an out-and-out hillbilly on the Louisiana Hay-ride on Saturday night from Shreveport. I liked him and I like him now. And I understand perfectly that he could not sing the way he does if he did not combine the shimmy with the hula. At least he sings, and that's more than Mae West did. If you put Elvis in a straight jacket he couldn't sing a note, indicating that he sings first and gyrates second, and that he never gives a thought to his contortions and no true Presley fan does either. If Elvis couldn't shiver and shake when he sings, the song wouldn't mean a thing, and certainly the words in Elvis' songs aren't sug-gestive. Elvis always reminds me of Lil Abner of the comic strip. A poor boy trying to get along doing what comes natural. Elvis is amazed when critics accuse him of being indecent. He's horri-fied when people insinuate that he's not decent on the inside. He knows he is.

Besides all that, you know what Elvis said when his hysterical fans out in Los Angeles wanted to run him for president? He said, "We already got a good man in the race, Adlai Stevenson. He's the mostest."

With half the nation's teen-agers prostrate before Presley and the other half in love with a dead movie star, James Dean, what's youth coming to anyway? They're doing pretty good. I think Dean and Presley have a lot in common when you get down to it. The thing about Dean was that he wanted above all to be decent on the inside and he also wanted that decency to be a master thrill, and that's the way our boy Elvis seems to be.

YEAR 1957

Here are my New Year's resolutions:

1. To go to church once a Sunday. (That means I'll have to quit putting things off to do on Sunday.)

2. To speak to everybody and smile when I speak. (That means I'll have to overcome by absentmindedness.)

3. To go on a diet and lose 30 pounds. (That means I'll have to start cooking my own food.)

4. To spruce up my appearance. (That means I'll have to get my shirts and pants ironed; and I hate ironed clothes.)

5. To argue politics with nobody. (That means I'll have to avoid old John Blair like the plague.)

6. To try to make friends instead of enemies. (That means I'll have to quit expressing my opinion.)

Any other faults you want me to correct, just let me know and I'll put them in a resolution. Oh yes, I'm going to quit grouching and growling when I answer the telephone.

Just in case it has crossed your mind that this newspaper's opinion is influenced by antiprohibition advertising dollars, let's get something straight now. If the prohibitionists were to fill up this paper every week from now on out, we'd still be militantly opposed to the hypocritical farce of prohibition. The fact that antiprohibitionists have chosen to use this newspaper to carry their message, has nothing to do with our opinion. We have turned down too many ads for anyone to claim seriously that liquor advertising or any other advertising has the slightest influence on this newspaper.

If we had thought more of the advertising dollar than we do of our convictions, we would have supported Shivers all these years and been about $1,000 richer. I refer to the constitutional amendments which were published by Shivercrat papers and not given to anti-Shivercrat papers. We never made a dime out of supporting Ralph Yarborough and Adlai Stevenson because they ran no ads in weekly newspapers, but we did make some money out of Price Daniel and Ike ads, who we opposed. Back in 1954, we turned down at least $100 worth of Shivers ads because we felt they did not stick to facts.

As for the antiprohibition ads published in this newspaper this week and last, I think I could have done better. Those ads quote statistics and figures and they are accurate because they were obtained from the state comptroller's office. But the reason I'm against prohibition is not mentioned in those ads. I'm against it because it makes a town hypocritical; prohibition corrupts both old and young. People, especially youth, who don't drink at all, suddenly think it is smart to drink bootleg whiskey. I'd rather have a dozen liquor stores than one bootlegger, and if this precinct goes dry we are going to have bootleggers. Prohibition causes people to drink more instead of less. The very minute liquor is prohibited a lot of people suddenly want it.

A NEW DAY DAWNING   *April 11*

Price Daniel was still the uncharitable little man when he put in his two cents worth the day after Yarborough was elected senator. This was Price's pip-squeak, "It is my hope that Mr. Yarborough will find it possible to respect and represent all Texans. The majority which voted for the other candidates as well as the minority which voted for him." Now wasn't that a catty remark for a governor of Texas to make. Even Shivers wouldn't have stooped so low. It was just as little as Daniel actually is. But let's analyze that typical Daniel doubletalk. It is worse than doubletalk. It's a downright Republican whopper.

In the first place nobody will deny that Yarborough got the majority of the Democratic votes on April 2. He got more votes than Dies, Bracewell, Hart and White put together. Thad Hutcheson got 218,000 Republican votes and the Republican party should be the real minority party in Texas. The majority of Democrats voted for Yarborough. The majority of Republicans voted for Thad. So Daniel chooses to ignore the real fact that the senate race was a two-party race. The truth is that both parties are the same to Daniel and have been since 1952. If there had been the runoff that Daniel conspired to get and failed, those 218,000 Hutcheson votes would have gone to Dies.

That's been the trouble in Texas all these years. The Republican votes have always gone to Shivers and Daniel. The Republicans therefore have been running this state for years. Shivers and Daniel were not elected by Democrats, as Yarborough was, but by Republicans, yet Daniel has the gall to say now that the Democrats are the minority party. Actually every person who voted for Thad Hutcheson ought to be barred from voting in a Democratic primary.

Daniel says he hopes Yarborough will represent the minority Republican party, too. How brazen can he get? Listen, Daniel, I got news for you. Yarborough is a Democrat and he will represent the Democratic voters of Texas and the Democratic party in the senate, not the Republican party, as you did. Yarborough will represent all the people and he will do a better job than Daniel did.

Daniel represented about 16 people from Texas all the time he was in the senate and they were mostly people who voted for Thad Hutcheson Saturday. Daniel now seems awfully worried that Yarborough is not going to represent those 200,000 Republicans which landed Daniel in the governor's mansion and which kept Shivers and his corrupt administration in power for seven long, scandal-ridden years.

The one big thing that election showed was that Texas has 218,000 Republicans and that they are the ones who have been keeping Shivers and Daniel in office. You know who carried the boxes in Houston that voted overwhelmingly for Shivers and Daniel? Hutcheson carried them.

Then that little man down in Austin has the gall to ask Yarborough to represent the Republicans in the senate. There's a new day dawning in Texas, Pricey. And you better get used to it.

SOME THINGS I LIKE   *April 25*

Some of the things I like about Kountze . . . The hitchin' post back of the Methodist church and the fireplace . . . Rocky Richardson's open-all-night filling station and Boyd's Cafe which also stays open all night. A hick town is one that is closed up tight at 10 . . . the foliage-filled brick planters in Williford's Store and the hardware department where you can buy anything . . . Birdwell's Dime Store . . . the kids who go out and pick berries and mayhaws in season and peddle them . . . the small gardens in the Quarters in which collard greens grow the year around . . . the early morning whistles of the sawmills . . . the chimes of the Methodist church . . . the squirrels at Richardson Supply . . . the very sight of Shorty Langston because he's always so cheerful and friendly . . . Mrs. A. L. Downing's roses, bluebonnets and other flowers and her well-concealed, charitable disposition . . . the coffee in Bishop's Cafe and the way they cook steaks . . . the early-morning coffee-drinking atmosphere in Martha's Cafe . . . the roses at the school . . . the personality of Mrs. John Knierim . . . the devotion of Slim Englin and Rito Rodriguez and all the other firemen to the Kountze Volunteer Fire Department . . . Tom Easley's prevailing, bluff good humor.

THE REPUBLICAN PLATFORM   *June 2*

The following story is dedicated to those few misguided souls who, come Tricky Dicky Nixon or John Foster Dulles, are still determined to vote for the Republican candidate for president November 6.

It seems Adlai Stevenson was traveling by car in a lonely stretch of prairie in Iowa when his car broke down. Despite a hole in his shoe, he limped toward a distant farm house where upon arrival he knocked at the front door and announced that he was Adlai Stevenson and was a candidate for president of the United States, that his car was broke down and would the lady take him to the next town. She turned a scornful look on him saying, "I'm a Republican. I wouldn't help you at all. But my husband and three sons are out at the barn." Adlai trudged to the barn where he found the father and three sons scooping up manure and pitching it on a big pile. Adlai stated his predicament and renewed his plea, addressing the father who retorted, "Not me bud, I hate Democrats." Adlai turned to the oldest son who said, "I hate 'em worse'n he does." Adlai then turned to the second son who declared, "I'm such a right wing Republican I think Nixon is a Communist." Adlai turned to the third son who came out with, "Don't look at me. I even think Joe McCarthy is a Communist spy."

Adlai turned and started walking away when the youngest son said, "Wait a minute, Adlai, if you will stand there in that pile of manure and give me a campaign speech I'll take you to town." Adlai saw that it was the only way out so he waded into the pile of manure without even rolling up his pants. He struck an oratorical pose and began in his most courteous, cultured tones, "My honored, respected Republican friends, I have delivered speeches in Madison Square Garden, in Cadillac Square at Detroit, in the Sugar Bowl at New Orleans, in the Cotton Bowl at Dallas, but this is the first time I have ever made a speech standing on the Republican platform . . ."

MIXING THE RACES   *July 4*

Here is the gist of President Eisenhower's civil rights bill: It would give his attorney general, Herbert Brownell the power to set up a separate bureau in the Department of Justice to investigate violations of so-called civil rights in the South. The bill provides that if a federal judge finds any Southerner in contempt, his guilt would be decided by the judge, without benefit of a jury. For instance, over at Houston the school board is defying integration attempts. And that is going on all over the South. Under the law, any member of the school board could be jailed by the judge, without trial by jury. That's how the bill would work.

If the bill passes, the Department of Justice can intervene in behalf of individuals in instances of actual or threatened violations of civil rights, such as attending an integrated school, and without consent of the victim. Senator Bill Knowland is making political hay with the civil rights bill. He pushed Tricky Dicky Nixon aside. Knowland now thinks that if he can share the credit with Ike for the bill he might be the Republican presidential candidate in 1960.

Nothing like this civil rights bill ever happened under Roosevelt and Truman. In 1947, a proposed Fair Employment Practice Commission came before the senate and failed. In 1950, a new effort to enact FEPC failed. The bill never got before the senate. But Ike and Knowland got their bill before the senate. It is the most dangerous threat to the social order in the South since Reconstruction when the Yankees and ex-slaves held the South in ruthless reign of terror.

How did we let ourselves get maneuvered into the fix we are in now? In 1952, and again in 1956, Ike-likers went to the polls and set up this throwback to Reconstruction. We should have known what was coming, and we would have if we had listened to the voices coming from Confederate graves. For the Republican party has always persecuted the South one way or another, once it gets in power. But we paid no attention to history. We forgot about Grant, Garfield, McKinley, Taft, Harding and Coolidge. We even forgot about Hoover and his record of calculated persecution of the South. We made a big thing about a little war in Korea. We said it was simply awful. But that Korean War is just a patch to what the Ike-likers are going to do to the South before they are finally kicked out of office. Oh, how some of the women got on a high horse about that Korean War, not knowing that the Ike-likers were even then plotting to mix white and Negro blood in the South.

We sniffed in scorn in 1952 when we talked about mink coats and deep freezes and red herrings, and we gleefully yelped the lie that the Democratic party is the war party and was soft on Communism. But we had forgotten, or never did know that the No. 1 aim of the Republican party since Abraham Lincoln has been dedicated to destroying the Southern way of life. Well, we got only ourselves to thank for helping Ike and Knowland and Nixon along with it.

We got it coming to us. We deserve everything we've got—and we've got more vindictive rulings and legislation in the last five years, all against the best interests of the South, than were recorded between 1865 and 1952. We in Texas are responsible for what we are getting. We went to the polls and gave Ike the state twice, Senator Lyndon Johnson and Senator Ralph Yarborough are utter fools if they don't vote for Ike's and Knowland's and Nixon's civil rights bill. The people of Texas deserve that bill. They got it coming to them.

So let's hear no griping about it. Then next time, in 1960, you can again cuss Truman and Roosevelt and Adlai Stevenson and go out and vote for Knowland and Nixon and another civil rights bill and another Supreme Court ruling and another Reconstruction and enforce integration and mixing of the races.

LITTLE ROCK INTEGRATION TACTICS   *October 3*

Before you start believing what the Beaumont Enterprise editors and the Ike-worshipping Houston Post says, let's get the facts straight about Ike forcing integration in Arkansas at the point of a bayonet. Those papers which would have called for impeachment if FDR or Truman had tried what Ike has pulled, are saying what else could Ike do but enforce the orders of the Federal judge at Little Rock to integrate Central High School. They are low-rating heroic Governor Faubus and trying to make him appear guilty of treason.

But I think that Ike himself has violated the Constitution. The law on which he based his action was passed in 1871 during Reconstruction and has never been ruled on by the Supreme Court. There is no Federal law forbidding segregation. The 1871 statute on which the President is relying declares that the executive can use troops on his own initiative whenever the "laws of the United States" cannot be enforced. What evidence is there that any "law" was violated or that the order of a lower court judge was based on any valid law? These are matters of legal dispute. The Supreme Court in 1849 and again in 1911 said that, "The state itself must determine what degree of force a crisis demands."

We not only believe that Ike has violated the Constitution and has acted like Batista, that little dictator down in Cuba, but that he should be called on the carpet by Congress and the whole tyrannical business investigated. Therefore, we call upon Senator

Lyndon Johnson and Senator Ralph Yarborough to see if Eisenhower has violated the Constitution and if he has to call for his impeachment. In asking for this investigation, the pros and cons of integration should not be considered or debated, only Ike's dictatorial order to send the army to Little Rock to club and bayonet people and push them around.

Why did Ike do it? You heard him on TV and radio, and the reasons he talked about the most were those that have to do with what foreign countries think about the South. Who cares what Pakistan and Russia and China think about us when our own soldiers are sticking bayonets in people in the South to force nine colored boys and girls to attend a white school. I'm sick and tired of hearing what foreign countries think about us. They are in a big mess themselves and what are they doing about it? I don't want Ike to give up my constitutional rights to make a good impression in Liberia.

We had Ike's word for it that he would not send troops into the South, so Faubus had a right to call out his national guard to prevent violence. Ike's newspapers and a few northern commentators ignore the tradition, based on constitutional law, that a president does not send troops into a state unless asked by the governor of that state. Ike has led the South to believe that he did not believe in "creeping central law" that might result by invading the South with Federal troops. On Ike's orders, those troops clubbed citizens and pointed bayonets at teenagers. Ike usurped the authority of the governor of Arkansas.

The Ike papers say that only "radicals and extremists" oppose integration in the South. They say that Faubus is standing alone in Little Rock and the South. The truth is that it's hard to find any white man in the South who is not for Faubus and what he has done. It's hard to find any person who does not condemn Ike for sending troops into Little Rock. The Beaumont Enterprise says Ike is "a good friend of the white people" of the South. Any man who believes that should stand on his head. Would a good friend of the South send troops into a schoolroom? Ike's orders to occupy Little Rock with black and white soldiers was a day of infamy for the whole South. The South had been led to believe Ike wouldn't send in his soldiers to enforce integration. A couple of years ago when Shivers sent the Rangers to Mansfield to stop integration there Ike did not make a move, but there was a difference. Shivers had supported Ike and Faubus hadn't. There are no radicals and extremists in the South when it comes to Ike's method of integrating. Just try to find one person who approves.

INTEGRATION AND THE SOUTH   *October 10*

What makes me maddest about the prevailing integration situation is that you and I love the colored people when we judge the colored people of the South by those in Kountze, and all the time our Republican critics up north are trying to say that we hate the colored man. That is a lie. Everything we do shows that we love the colored people. We may turn down a white man for a loan but we don't turn down the colored people we know; we may refuse to pick up a white man on the highway but we stop for the colored man hitching a ride from the "Y" to Cariker mill. We want them to have good jobs and good homes and we want them to have a good school and good teachers. When you think of individuals in the Quarters you know, in your heart you know you are proud of the colored man and that you love him.

So it seems that the Republican party has a deep sinister plot to turn the colored man against the white and vice versa. Is it possible that those who plotted the Supreme Court ruling really wanted dissension, rioting and trouble in the South? That what they actually want is to turn the love that now exists between the two races into hate. What a cruel thing to do in order to get votes! For I believe that the Supreme Court decision was Republican party politics, just as Shivers and Daniel played politics with the colored man's vote! O, how those two tried to make the white people of Texas hate the Negro! That's why they ran contemptible, low-down dirty races. So the party that Shivers and Daniel once espoused now wants the South to hate the Negro. Just because the party wants his vote.

The Negro up north does not have half the opportunities he has in the South. They deny him almost everything but the right to vote and the colored man knows it. We don't think of the colored man as a second class citizen, but just as valuable a citizen as the white man and sometimes more valuable. I truly believe that we in the South love the colored man.

The colored man would not trade living in the north for living in the South, if you gave him a bonus. He knows the difference between the love he finds in the South and the cruel hate that tortures his mind and body in the north. Else he would leave us in a minute, and if we did not love him as we do, we wouldn't give him our last dime if we had to. So let's not permit the Supreme Court and Ike to think less of the colored man. We have been helping each other to improve the other's lot for many a decade and let's regard this hate campaign as something temporary.

The people in the South are moving along their traditional path of patience, calmness, reason and forbearing, even if some of its editors are preaching insurrection. For instance the chief editorial writer of the Beaumont Enterprise made a speech the other day at a press association meeting and was quoted as saying that editors of the South are deplorably preparing the people of the South for eventual and inevitable integration, as he put it. Who said integration is inevitable and eventual? The law does not say that. I do not believe that it is certain. I think that Ike has got his belly full of sending troops into the South, and that's the only way he could ever enforce it. The Enterprise editorial writer just has not caught up with the people yet. He's way behind the times. And since when does he think he could make any headway "preparing" the people of Hardin County for integration. He's spinning his wheels. Let him make that speech in Southeast Texas and see what kind of reception he gets. The preparation the Enterprise is trying to force down our throats, written as it is by Yankee carpetbagger journalists, is falling on deaf ears. The people have taken about all that kind of talk they're going to take from that Ike-liking sheet which would sell out the South in a minute to corral that Yankee money.

I HAVE SUNK SO LOW   *October 24*

While Gordon Baxter was up here during Homecoming he

said something that stuck in my craw because it's true. He said that only once in a great while now does The Kountze News sparkle with the sense of humor that used to keep him in stitches. And when it does, Baxter averred, it seems premeditated and a calculated risk. He said the Printer has been taking life too seriously, what with the great ado he makes about the politics that dominate this column.

He said all this sadly, as if a permanent, pessimistic grouch had been achieved by The Kountze News. So ever since Baxter made those telling observations, I have been down in the mouth, fully aware that I have truly sunk so low that most of the time I am indignant instead of amused.

RUBY MARSHALL DOESN'T SERVE BEER   *November 7*

This column does not want to start an argument with Mr. Heidelberg and Ray Boyd over where the farmer's colored employees should and should not eat, but if those seven colored boys who said they could not get any good food in the Quarters, except where they served beer, really meant that then somebody ought to examine their heads. Right now, I'm thinking of the food that Ruby Lee Marshall puts out. Her barbecue is unsurpassed; white folks buy her small sweet potato pies faster than she can cook them. I've never eaten any better cornbread than hers nor any better turnip greens and collard greens and brother, she can barbecue chicken, too. I'd eat down there more often, as numerous white folks do, but when I do I get dirty looks from the colored people whose looks seem to say, "You are always preaching segregation. Why don't you practice what you preach." So I've only eaten in that cafe once, but I've bought and carried the food out. But I'll swear by Ruby Lee Marshall's cooking. And on top of all that, they don't serve beer there. I repeat that: They do not serve beer there.

NIXON IN IKE'S PLACE?   *December 19*

There has been a hue and a cry in the land, principally from political columnists, for President Eisenhower to resign. They say he is a part-time president, that his last and third illness was the third and last strike on him and that Ike is down on the canvas and can't get up. They say he is neither mentally nor physically able to handle the duties of the office; that a man with a heart attack and a stroke can't physically be president of the United States. They say what the country needs is for Tricky Dicky Nixon to take over, the same Nixon who has succeeded singlehanded in chasing the nation's top scientists out of the government's nuclear and missle works; the same Nixon who taught Joe McCarthy how to get ahead, the same Nixon who would call anybody a traitor to gain political advantage; the same Nixon who sat at Ike's elbow and hissed "sick-em!" when the President was considering sending troops to Little Rock, the same Nixon who will likely be the 1960 Republican candidate for president.

Do you remember how it was when Ike first took the oath of office? When he was in good physical condition? If you do, you will remember that things were not much different than now. The biggest difference was that he was able to spend more time on the golf course and at his Gettysburg house. As soon as he became President, after spending 40 years in the army, half of that in rank below lietenant colonel, he did what any old army man would have done. He set up a general staff in the White House with himself as a sort of chief of staff. He started running the country like the army is run. Everything had to go through regular channels.

We've had the kind of government for five years that we have now. If Ike hadn't had his heart attack, intestinal block and minor stroke, would the situation be any different now? Would the Russians have sent up the two Sputniks ahead of us? Would Ike have sent the troops to Little Rock, with the hearty encouragement of Nixon and Brownell? There can only be one answer to those questions: Certainly! The Sputnik race was lost the day Ike took the oath of office. Troops to Little Rock were guaranteed that sensational campaign day in 1952 when Ike threw his arms around a sobbing Nixon and told Tricky Dicky it was all right about that money the mean old Democrats said he took, but to be a good boy from now on. We've had this missile mess going on all the time. We've been losing friends abroad and failing to influence our enemies since the day Ike moved his golf clubs into the White House.

The people who want Ike to resign now are not afraid of the future with Ike as president. They are afraid of the past. They are forgetting you can't bring back the past and live it over. What they really want is for Ike to quit because, they think, he let the country down in the arms race with Russia. But Ike would have done that if he hadn't had so much as a bellyache or a bad cold in the last five years. What they really mean is that they wish Ike had never been elected president of the United States.

So it's the past that Walter Lippmann, the Alsop brothers and old Drew Pearson, all columnists, and Senator Wayne Morse of Oregon, and Senator Style Bridges of New Hampshire, all of whom want Ike to resign, object to. They are saying anybody, even Nixon, would be better than Ike, but I do not think so. We made our bed and now we ought to be made to lie in it. Anyway, the harm already has been done and Nixon would only make it worse. The best thing that could happen to this country would be for Ike to serve out his term to the bitter end. There's nothing any of us know now that we didn't know in 1956 when we could have elected Adlai Stevenson and didn't.

Nixon is the man who chased the scientists out of the government and carried on the war against eggheads and intellectuals, knowing full well that only they could keep us ahead of Russia in missile development. Nixon. Listen, we may have our throat cut now but let's not go ahead and dig our grave by putting Nixon in Ike's place.

YEAR 1958

Who are you going to vote for in the governor's race? You have your choice of several candidates. There's Price Daniel, Pappy Lee O'Daniel and State Senator Henry Gonzales of San Antonio. Price and Pappy are Republicans and are as much alike as three peas in a pod. So Henry Gonzales who is of Mexican ancestry which fought against dictators like Santa Anna in 1836 is my boy. But I'd have to vote for him whether I like him or not (and I happen to admire him very much) because he's the only Democrat in the race. With Gonzales in the race, the campaign may be interesting, what with Pappy accusing Price of being a nigger lover and Price accusing Henry of being a nigger lover. Price and Pappy are fundamentally so much alike that people may turn to Gonzales for a fresh breath. Right now I'm going to make this statement: Texas, the nation and the Democratic party needs a man like Gonzales in the governor's office. That man has guts, gumption and grandeur. He showed more courage and brains in the filibuster he threw in the senate during the last session of the Legislature than has been seen around Austin since James Stephen Hogg squared off against railroads. I don't agree with all Gonzales says and stands for, just as you Ike-likers can't possibly agree with all Ike has done, but I'll take him before I'd take the kind of weaseling you get from either Price or Pappy. Both of the latter have the same kind of courage that Shivers had when he played the deaf mute at a time when his pal Giles was confessing to swindling millions from the state treasury. One thing about Gonzales, you know what he really is.

So The Kountze News, the first newspaper in Texas to endorse Lyndon Johnson in 1952, 1954 and 1956 is now likely the first to come out for Henry Gonzales for governor.

That hateful term above that I used, "nigger lover", should have been in quotation marks, because it is not in my vocabulary.

It is a term that I loath and one which I never use. It was used by the FDR haters, the Yarborough haters and will be used by the Gonzales haters. The term is the essence of sinful hate and any politician who uses it is as low as a snake in a wagon rut. The term infers that it is despicable and contemptible to love the Negro; but its only effect on me is to make me hold in contempt the person who uses the term.

All of us in Kountze resent it when any person infers that we do not like the colored people—and I'm talking about the colored people we know; those who live in the Quarters in Kountze. We all like them personally and collectively and I despise any person who calls me a "nigger lover" in an attempt to make me like them less. For I know they are the same in God's eyes as I. The colored people themselves don't hate that term any more than I do. My own sincere belief is that the people of Kountze love and do not hate the colored people. But Daniel and Shivers have done everything under the sun to try to make us hate the colored man. Just as all Republicans do. So let them call me a "nigger lover" for I'm proud that I don't hate the Negro, and I hope that Henry Gonzales is also proud to be called a "nigger lover" (as he will be) by the likes of Daniel and Pappy O'Daniel.

GONZALES FOR GOVERNOR   *July 10*

Oscar Overstreet said he didn't think a Mexican-American could carry Hardin County, and Saturday morning, Billy Joe Haddox, Oscar and this Printer sat at the same table and the talk got around to the governor's race again. Oscar said that he wouldn't vote for a Mexican for governor, maybe some other office but not for governor. Billy Joe emphatically agreed with him. He wouldn't vote for a Mexican either; got too many of them now in this country, he said. I left the cafe feeling sad. For during World War II, I came to admire the soldiers, sailors and Marines of Mexican ancestry because of their gallant and fearless bravery. There were more heroes of Mexican ancestry during World War II than of any other group, and that includes

Southern Anglo-Saxons. One-fourth of all the Texans who won the Congressional Medal of Honor for bravery in World War II were of Mexican ancestry, a percentage out of proportion to the Latin-American population in Texas. Not one-eighth of the population of Texas was Latin-American in World War II; four Mexicans died with Travis in the Alamo. A dozen counties and towns in Texas are named for Mexican patriots in the Texas revolution. I say this nation belongs to the people who have fought for it, died for it and bled for it and Mexican-American casualties in World War II outnumbered any other group in Texas or the United States.

Remembering all this, I was truly shocked by what Oscar and Billy Joe said, because though I have many other prejudices I have none against persons of Mexican ancestry. It never occurred to me that anyone might vote against Gonzales, who is courageous, educated and humane, simply because he is of Mexican ancestry. Mexico is one of the great nations of the earth and has a great race of people. But Gonzales is no Mexican, any more than I am English because my ancestors came from the British Isles.

Gonzales is a Texan. He was born and educated in Texas and he is a state senator and a great and good one. Furthermore he is the only loyal Democrat in the race for governor. In Texas' neighboring state, New Mexico, Dennis Chavez has been a U.S. Senator for about 25 years. He is a great and good Democrat. A Mexican? Some might call him that, but most New Mexicans might be indignant if you referred to him as anything besides an American.

If you want to live in a state that has a man in office who has a sense of humor as well as feeling for the beloved people of Texas, if you want a governor who will shatter the dreary, whining phony dignity and fake religiosity of the present incumbent, if you want a governor that will attract world-wide attention and help Texas in Washington as well as the entire 49 states, then vote for Henry B. Gonzales, the one man whose very personality can make Texas cease to be the whipping boy and laughing stock of the nation. He can do this because his very name and personality are the direct antithesis of the standard Texas joke or brag. That is why I say Texas needs Gonzales as governor.

HARDIN COUNTY'S COLORFUL HISTORY   *August 28*

There are these immortal lines and it is time to quote them because they apply: "Breathes there a man with soul so dead, who never to himself has said: 'This is my own, my native land . . .' " Our native land in the final say-so is Hardin County. It belongs to us, and we love it and are proud of it. We all know and freely admit that 75 per cent of the land in Hardin County is owned by out-of-county residents and corporations, but we also know that all the land in Hardin County belongs to us. We do not admit any "foreign" ownership. So we would not trade Hardin County for any other. We like what we have in this county above and beyond what any other county has.

We love its trees, its very soil, its streams. We all love everything about it, even though it has its faults, because in our minds its virtues always outweigh its faults.

That is why we are all honoring Hardin County on September 27 when we will celebrate its 100th birthday with our Centennial celebration. That is why all of us are making the birthday party first an individual and then a collective effort.

Deep down, because we love Hardin County's very terrain, none of us wants to shirk in the county-wide endeavor to show our pride. The party is not going to be a Kountze show, a Silsbee show, a Saratoga or a Sour Lake show, but a county celebration, aimed not at glorifying any one or two communities but aimed at glorifying the brave, touching, heart-warming history of Hardin County. This celebration is something that all of us can cotton to, can warm up to, can applaud, can help create.

It seems to each of us that no county has had as colorful a history. Start back in 1858 when there were perhaps 600 persons living in the county. Then it was truly a great forest of virgin timber. Now we call it "the woods," but then it was a forest. Open country it was; the great pine trees were so high that the ground was perpetually shaded and no underbrush grew under the trees. In that way it was like a great park. The wind moved the tops of the trees like plumes with a sound that was like great orchestral music. The sky was whispering to the trees and the trees were answering.

Then came the towns. First, Old Hardin where the first courthouse was built. That was four years before the War between the States and the guns at Fort Sumter. There were a few slaves, and a few plantations, like the Arline plantation south of Old Hardin. There are still Arline Negroes here.

Later in that century came the first oil well at Saratoga, discovered by John Cotten's hogs in a "tar pit." There were the watering places at Sour Lake and Saratoga and the big hotels and society people. Then there were the oil booms at Batson and Sour Lake and Saratoga.

A railroad was built through the county in the 1880's and a town was built on it, named for the Kountze brothers of Omaha, Nebraska. The county held an election to move the courthouse to Kountze but it failed. Then they burned the courthouse down and moved it here anyway. Then two of the leading residents, Ben Hooks and Mr. Allums, sat up all one night playing the fiddle and exulting in the wonders of the Big Thicket, and wound up naming the streets of Kountze after the animals and trees of the Thicket.

Then there is our legacy of the Big Thicket bears and the hundreds of bear hunting stories. A number of books have been written about the bear hunts and enshrined in the folklore of Hardin County is the classic story of the bear hunt. Then there are the timber stories and the oil field stories, but all East Texas has oil and timber stories, one might say. But not the kind we have. No other county has the bear stories we have. Old Hardin County has had the glory, it has had the splendor, it has had the wonder, for the bear, the timber and the oil, all combined in a single personality has made something unique, and that is why we want to honor our dear county with a big birthday celebration. She deserves it.

Yes, we have a different county with people that are different. Go to Woodville and Jasper and then come to Hardin County. Our people are unique; they are mostly silent, except some newcomers. They like to wear khakis here, even if they have a million dollars and live in a fine air-conditioned house.

We love Hardin County because its sense of humor has always prevailed. We started off that way. We named our county in 1858 after the famous Hardin family that lived on the Trinity River. In those days the Hardin family included ministers, soldiers, statesmen, politicians, patriots, but now the Hardin family is remembered mostly for one man, John Wesley Hardin, the greatest and fastest gun of all times, for no desperado ever killed more men or had a quicker draw than John Wesley Hardin. You have to have a sense of humor when you think of Wes Hardin, when you think of the many things about him that could be bad if you did not have a sense of humor. So we in Kountze are proud that we are the town with a sense of humor. There is also something about the Big Thicket's mysteriousness that gives its inhabitants a true sense of humor.

LBJ, THE DEGENERATE SON

Once a man like Price Daniel turncoats on the political party that made him you can never trust him again. The reason is that his turncoat stripe is an inch wide right down the middle of his back. And it's going to stay there because he was born with it. So only the habitual Daniel supporters appeared surprised last week when Daniel turncoated not only on the Democrats of Texas to whom he had given a promise, but also on Lyndon Johnson and Sam Rayburn.

The Houston Chronicle reported somewhat gleefully that Lyndon got down on bended knees and literally begged Daniel not to betray the Democrats of Texas by rejecting two district committee members, one from San Antonio and the other from Waco. If Lyndon did get down on his knees to Daniel that leaves me stone faced and cold of heart.

For I've had enough of Lyndon Johnson, not only at state conventions but in the U.S. Senate. I've had enough of his betrayals. He did it in 1956 at the state convention and now he did it again. Democrats might as well get used to the idea that Johnson has deserted us for the Eisenhower Democrats. We might as well quit eternally hoping that Johnson will see the light and get with us, for Lyndon Johnson is committed. Let us see him henceforth as he is, The Enemy, because we would have won both in 1956 and again in 1958 if Lyndon had not turned his back on his friends.

How does it feel, Lyndon, to double cross your oldest friends, the ones who put you in office, and side in with those who voted against you in 1947? This paper used to boast that it was the first paper in the nation to boost Lyndon Johnson for president. I have just finished washing my Linotype and my press with lye soap to get rid of the stigma of that endorsement. Five years ago I would have sooner have said a word against Roosevelt or Hogg or Tom Connally or Shakespeare, or God for that matter, than against Lyndon Johnson. So I ask how can Lyndon Johnson keep from writhing when he regards the photograph of Roosevelt at whose feet Lyndon used to sit? How can he look Connally and John Garner in the eye? Answer: He can't.

Never in my life have I known the agony of spirit Johnson has caused me. The full weight of his treachery bore down upon me for the first time this week. For ever since 1956, I have been making excuses for him, have been blaming other people, have, in my heart, been justifying his treachery, have avoided placing responsibility, but I have had to face the facts this week. I have forced myself to see Lyndon for what he really is.

Like Daniel, in my eyes he has become the degenerate son of an illustrious party. It is inconceivable, it is unbelievable, it is heartbreaking, but Lyndon Johnson has proved twice in a row that he will lead loyal Democrats of Texas to slaughter.

What should the Democrats of Texas do now? Go back to the State convention next May and at a given signal storm the platform and take over and send Daniel, Shivers, Johnson and poor old Sam Rayburn packing. That's what I say. Do it by brute force because that's all Daniel understands. Our mistake at San Antonio was not doing that the minute the opening gavel sounded. Just move like a tidal wave toward that platform and take it. Kick out the rascals and lock the doors and take the Democratic party from the immoral, corrupt, traitorous turncoats. Build the Democrats of Texas into an overpowering force, and never strive for a compromise, never seek peace and harmony, never take their word or promise and never give an inch.

SKY BLUE EYES

I saw Mrs. Arden Hooks, she of the sky blue eyes, the serene look and the peach complexion, for the first time, well in some time, and realized just how much her son, Dr. Allen Hooks, looks like her.

"TRYIN' TO RUN ME OFF"   *September 25*

"Buckshot" Flowers was indicted by the recent Hardin County grand jury on a charge "to murder J. C. Ishmael or members of his family." Ishmael was no-billed on a murder complaint by the grand jury.

Mrs. "Buckshot" Flowers was shot to death in a gun battle at Honey Island several weeks ago after more than a score of holes had been shot in Ishmael's house.

At the time, witnesses claimed that the shooting between Flowers and Ishmael started after Flowers had left the Ishmael home, saying that he was going to get his gun and kill Ishmael.

Soon afterward, officers said, shots began piercing Ishmael's house.

Ishmael said that he put his wife and children on the floor in the bathroom and shot in the direction of Flowers.

The quarrel between Flowers and Ishmael started over horses and cattle. Ishmael said that Flowers was "tryin' to run me off my place."

Since the shooting, Ishmael has moved his house and family from his place.

Ishmael had asked the sheriff's department for protection several times before the final gun battle. He had his residence and barn under a floodlight at night. Flowers claimed that Ishmael had ambushed him and had tried to kill him. Flowers ran considerable cattle in the vicinity. Alleged trespassing of livestock is said to have led to the quarrel.

GRAPEFRUIT SIZE RATTLER

I saw this giant rattlesnake with 12 rattles killed by Clyde Over-street and a cousin, Carl Marion Overstreet. The snake was as big around as a grapefruit and was nearly six feet long. They ran over it in the Village Mills area.

HOG KILLIN' TIME   October 2

Did you hear the one about the man who came into town one day shortly after Williford's opened their new air-conditioned department store? Well, this old man who had come from some place up on Beech Creek came into Williford's and stayed and stayed. He stayed there for two days and Williford let him, being too polite to throw him out. Everybody tried to wait on him, but he just stood around. Finally, about the third day, he walked up to Mr. Allen and said, "You know, if it's this cold tomorrow, I'm going home and kill a hog."

LOOK AT ME BOY, I FLAT MEAN IT!   October 9

There was this 14-year-old boy sitting in the witness chair and dabbing his eyes, when Judge H. A. Coe mentioned the boys re-form school at Gatesville.

The judge kept saying that the boy had to go to school, had to get up at 6:30 every morning when his aunt and uncle called him the first time, not the second time. And furthermore, he had to study at night and make good grades, not just any old kind of grades. The boy kept saying yes, in a low voice.

"I want you to look at me while I'm talking to you," the judge said, because all the time the boy was on the witness stand he looked down.

"You are a stubborn boy . . . It looks like you're the one at fault and that you did not do right by your aunt and uncle," the judge said. And every now and then he mentioned "Gatesville," and the boy shuddered.

The boy had been paroled to his aunt and uncle after his father and mother were killed in an auto wreck. That was in February of this year. Since that time the boy's 16-year-old brother has gone back to reform school in Gatesville.

The reason for the hearing was that Saturday the boy had left the home of his aunt and uncle and went to the home of his 17-year-old sister at Loeb. The aunt reported the runaway to the Sheriff and he picked up the boy at Loeb and lodged him in the Kountze Jail from Monday until the day of the hearing.

Why did the boy run away? It was plain to see that he did not know exactly, any more than any boy knows exactly why he runs away. Yes, he loved his aunt, or, "You might call it that," the boy said. Yes, he went fishing with his uncle. The boy kept wondering why they did not understand him, even if he could not tell them what they wanted to know.

Oh, no, the boy had committed no crime, not the slightest criminal act. But he had run away and he had been on probation in the home of his aunt, who said she drew some $52.50 in social security money from his father's death. No, he had never committed a crime. Only ran away, but there he was in court being called stubborn, hard-headed, ungrateful, and it was all his fault that he was in court being threatened and read the riot act, and worst of all every other word was "Gatesville."

His aunt was befuddled and bewildered by the boy. Yes, she had done her best, and you believed her, and she said with a catch in her throat that she had come to love this boy, her nephew, who was the son of her step-brother. She was Aunt Mary and he was Jimmy. You could tell that she had come to love this boy, and it just wasn't the Social Security.

Before the hearing, the boy had said he did not want to go back to Aunt Mary's and she had said she had come to the end of her rope with him. It looked as if Jimmy, who had a well-shaped head and smoke-blue eyes, was bound for the reformatory even if he had committed no crime except running away from the home of his aunt and going to the home of his sister at Loeb.

What was wrong with Jimmy? That was a concern of the judge. Well, Jimmy said he did not like to get up at 6:30, and he had had a fight at school when a boy called him a name and he had been resentful when his uncle got on him about wrecking the lawnmower and his girl cousin's bicycle, and he did not like to study and he did not want to do his lessons. He admitted freely that his aunt had to get on him about getting his lessons and getting up.

Then it occurred to the judge that Jimmy was a normal boy and all boys seemed to dislike getting up, going to school and studying, and so the judge then talked to him like a Dutch uncle and blistered him verbally, and Aunt Mary sat over there looking like a martyr, but feeling sorry for Jimmy.

And in the end Jimmy wanted to go back to Aunt Mary's, and in the end she wanted him back, and in the end Jimmy promised everything the judge asked, and in the final end Judge Coe said he would not revoke the probation. He would not send him to Gatesville, if Jimmy would keep his promises to get up at 6:30, study his lessons and not have fights unless jumped on (and the judge said if they jump on you stand up and fight back). Well, the judge said, boy you are getting a second chance. You let me know if Jimmy does not get up at 6:30, and if he does not study his lessons. You let me know, if he does not make good this second chance. By this time, 14-year-old, hardened criminal Jimmy must have felt like he had got off light for having committed such a heinous crime and he was beginning to relish that second chance that kept him out of Gatesville.

So the judge said "Gatesville" one more time and declared, "And I flat mean it."

I wonder what would have happened if the judge had given Aunt Mary a second chance to make good with Jimmy? What would have happened if the judge had placed some of the blame on the uncle and aunt? But that is not the accepted pattern. You've got to threaten Jimmy with Gatesville over and over, even though he never committed any crime except running away, and that technically is enough to send a boy to Gatesville. You just break a parole and see.

GRAVE ROBBERS IN THE PINES

Why would anyone want to dig a 76-year-old grave and scatter the contents of the coffin? That's what Carroll Behnken wants to know. One day last week Carroll had little or nothing to do and Bobo Jordan was in the same shape and while they were riding around, Carroll said to Bobo, "Bobo, let's drive over there across Village a little way, and I want to show you a grave in the deep woods. Not 15 minutes there and back from Kountze. I ain't seen that grave in twenty years, but I know it's still there because it's bound to be and not many know about it."

But when Bobo and Carroll Behnken got to the grave it had been dug up during the dry spell this summer. Signs everywhere. To get there, they crossed Village on the Old Silsbee Road and turned right down a lane that went into a dim road that went into a trail and as Carroll said it was on a hogback ridge that was an ideal location for an estate house, having a large pond at the foot of the hogback ridge. Big old pines all around, also redbud, magnolia, oak and hickory. The old grave was about 15 steps from the lane at the foot of a giant oak that had two trunks, both blown down from about head high. The two trunks were rotting on the ground.

"This is his arm bone," said Carroll holding a green-tinted bone, "and this one here must be a toe or a foot bone, wouldn't you say?"

There was a big hole in the ground the shape of a grave and laying about were some hard yellow pine boards from the casket.

And there was broken lead all over the ground. "Man who put that lead in the coffin knew what he was a-doin. Look how he joined it together. No amateur, I mean," Carroll said.

"Betcha' there's the rest of that coffin and the skeleton under that sand that washed in there," said Carroll. "I tried to get the Sheriff to come out here and dig it up. I, for one, I'd just like to know what more's in that grave, and why somebody had to dig it up after 76 years. Why do you suppose? Now come over here and I'll show you the gravestone."

And there behind the oak with the twin trunks was the headstone laying in a depression, broken into three pieces. A headstone of fine marble, white, and of beautiful carving. The carving read: "James Saunders, born January 16, 1862, died October 4, 1882, aged 20 years, son of John and Lydia Saunders," and below that was a verse which this Printer should have copied down but didn't.

"Uncle Jake Shepard knows about this grave," Carroll said. "This is his land, that land that Stanley Coe went clean to New York to clear up. Jake can tell you a lot about this grave. You just ask him. Tell you anothern' who knows all about this grave. Uncle Charlie Roberts. If I ain't mistaken Uncle Charlie said long time ago they caught two Negroes and one white man trying to dig up them other two graves over there. See that sunk place where the tombstone is laying flat broke into three pieces. Guess they broke it. That is where the other two graves were. Uncle Charlie disrecollected what the one white man and the two Negroes they caught digging up the two graves gave for an excuse. But they put them in jail all right, just like they ought to put whoever dug this poor old boy's grave, who was born back there in '62 and died in '82."

"I mean," Bobo said.

Why would somebody who knew exactly how to dig up that grave dig it up in the dry spell? Might have been gold or buried treasure. Might have been the same reason they tried to dig up the other graves. Could have been gold, repeated Bobo Jordan. Could have, Carroll said, in that relaxed deliberative voice of his. But, continued Carroll, "First time I'd seen that grave in 20 years and like I said I wanted to show it to Bobo, and when we get over here there it is dug up with bones, lead and that plank and that grave stone broke. It sort of aggravated me, so I wish the Sheriff would make up his mind to come out here and see what's in it. Don't you want to know, Bobo? How about you, Printer?"

It's your move Sheriff.

"THE CLUTCHES OF NIXON"   *November 13*

Nelson Rockefeller, who beat Averill Harriman for the governorship of New York last week, is no more a Republican than Ike is, and he has taken the wrong step in lining up with the Republican party, just like Ike did. Everybody knows that Ike was more of a Democrat than he was a Republican, but what everybody did not know was that the Republican party would turn Ike into a confused, frustrated, irresponsible president. Just as it will turn Rockefeller into a carbon copy of Ike. When men like Ike and Rockefeller, Democrats at heart, are elected to office by the Republican party, they always wind up confused. The GOP is bigger than any man, just as the Democratic party is bigger than any man in it. That is the reason you can not vote for the man. That's why you must vote for the party. It is the party, not the man, that is responsible. In the election last week, witness how the GOP took the responsibility, in the eyes of the voters, for the mess the nation is in. When you say that you are voting for the man and not the party you are kidding yourself.

I like Nelson Rockefeller. I wish he was in the Democratic party. I wish he had lined up with the right party, but he's following Ike's footsteps. Ike would have made a great president if he had been elected by the Democratic party, but as a Republican Ike will go down in history as one of the weakest presidents the nation has had.

So Nelson Rockefeller, it's not too late to change. You are in the wrong party, boy. Get out of the clutches of Nixon before it is too late.

GOLD, RED AND YELLOW   November 20

I saw this painting two blocks long just west of Bishop's Cafe and facing the highway at the turning circle. A painting man had nothing to do with, except not cut down the masses of scarlet sweet gum which glow like flames for all to see and enjoy. It has been the prettiest sight in Kountze for days.

But all over Hardin County, the sweet gum, the maple and the tallow trees have been giving us gold and red and yellow this fall. We have had fall all right.

THE LONE STAR EYE   December 11

One of these days a native Texan (or maybe he won't be a native Texan) is going to write the book about Texas that has never been written. You will say, after you read it, "Well now, this is finally Texas." In the past, many writers have written books about Texas, or rather parts of Texas, but none has attempted to put all of Texas within the covers of one book, until this fall when Mary Lasswell tried it, and succeeded in only one chapter. The title of her book is *I'll Take Texas*. But right off I will tell you that the book about Texas, all of Texas, that is still the most satisfying is the Texas Almanac, and it is also the most inspiring and the most readable and the most truthful.

For the most part, Miss Lasswell's book is a sort of padded out *Texas Brags*, a sort of homey, cloying treatment of the "Texas Empire" type of books. One of the troubles with Lasswell's book, as it is with all books on Texas published within the last 20 years, is that after the author deals with the Big Rich at Midland and Dallas, after they have mentioned Neiman-Marcus and counted the Cadillacs, and visited the King ranch and Big Bend, and written about how quaint San Antonio is, they call it a day—and quit —and send their book to the publisher.

The author of the ideal book about Texas should know why the population of Houston is a million plus, and is made up of 100 billionaires, 1,000 multimillionaires, 10,000 millionaires and one million wage-earning hillbillies, and why that proportion is fairly representative throughout Texas. The author should start with Houston and work out in all directions, always bearing in mind the one million hillbillies in Houston alone.

Such an author should know that one out of every eight Texans is illiterate, and that the rate of Texas illiteracy is growing, due to lack of enforcement of the compulsory school attendance law. This writer of the future should know there is a Post Oak belt in Texas that covers one-fifth the area of the state and extends from the Red River south nearly to the Rio Grande and that in this Post Oak belt there is not a town with a population of more than 30,000, and that many of the hillbillies in the Houston and Dallas area were sired in this belt (Bob Wills from Limestone County). One extended visit through the Post Oak belt would convince our future author that the denizens of the post oaks are far more colorful than the Big Rich at Midland who have elephant tusks for gateposts (which I saw and which Mary points out). Now you want to know where I got all this information about the Post Oak belt? Out of the Texas Almanac which is recommended reading before you buy any other Texas Book. Miss Lasswell passed up the Post Oak belt completely. It's doubtful if she knew of its existence. Where is Kosse, Mary? The trouble with authors of books on Texas is that the lone star in their eye is so big they can't see anything that doesn't have a golden glitter.

Being a native of the Panhandle I turned first to the chapter on the high plains and Panhandle, hoping to live vicariously again in Pampa, on the Pease, the Tongue, the Wichita, the Canadian. But all Miss Lasswell saw was Lubbock and Amarillo. She would have learned more about the people of the Panhandle and the Panhandle itself if she had spent a night on Sweetwater Creek near old Mobeetie. Oh, she saw the Palo Duro canyon all right, the Big Bend and the Cap Rock at Post. But more rewarding for Miss Lasswell would have been a night at Dripping Springs, court day at Centerville, and a dozen places in Burkesville.

Obviously, the book is what is known in the East, where she has lived most of her life, as "a fast buck." She wrote up the right Texas brags, dropped the right names, mentioned the cities which have book stores. Still, Miss Lasswell simply was not equipped to write a book about Texas even though she began the pose of professional Texan in the first sentence, in the same spirit that good old Bill Daniel of Liberty poses any place he can get invited to as the No. 1 Professional Texan.

Miss Lasswell traveled over the state in order to take in everything, but she missed the whole point of the Panhandle where I was brought up. She got lost in her chapter on the Big Bend and I could not find her again through the thousands of gushy, trite, tiresome and meaningless words until a chapter near the end of the book.

And that chapter alone was excuse enough for writing and publishing the whole book on the subject of that one chapter, "The Big Thicket." And that chapter is good only because she was privileged to see the Thicket through the eyes of Lance Rosier of Saratoga. Miss Lasswell had Lance down dead to rights, as far as his Thicket genius is concerned. For Lance knows the Thicket is beautiful, romantic, inspiring, full of wonders, and to Miss Lasswell's credit she caught Lance's mood, almost, and wrote a very entertaining, though piecemeal, account of the Big Thicket.

And I'm not prejudiced in favor of the Big Thicket just because Kountze is the capitol of the Big Thicket county. No, I'm not prejudiced. After all I have lived in Hardin County only since 1949. I dearly loved the caprock country of Lynn, Wheeler and Donley Counties. I love with a nostalgia that is delicious to recall, the mesquite flats of Cottle and Motley Counties, the Pease River country and I love the Post Oak belt and the deer country around Mason. Oh, I have loved personally and intimately the many parts of Texas in which I have lived, so I am not prejudiced in favor of the Big Thicket. It takes a long time to learn to love a thing like the Thicket, but I am learning and Lance Rosier is my teacher.

Mary Lasswell's eyes were not the only ones opened by Lance Rosier. There's Dr. Bedichek, the famous author of *Adventures of a Texas Naturalist*. Dr. Bedichek swears by Lance. A lot of famous men of letters and science swear by Lance.

Miss Lasswell praised Dr. Bedichek and J. Frank Dobie to the skies in about 10 pages, and said so little. That, too, was hard to take. Dobie had devoted a lifetime to writing about Texas, in swatches and patterns, but not in one fell swoop. Why didn't Mary take a leaf from Frank Dobie and take up one patch of ground, one breed of men, one breed of horses, one breed of dogs? Dobie has done that with a genius I revel in, and so has Bedichek, and still this Lasswell woman tries to do it all in one plunge, working herself up to the lather of the professional Texan. But I guess I'm grateful for the book on account of the one chapter. So thanks, Mary, for it.

YEAR | 1959

200 SQUIRRELS, DEER, COON, MINK   *January 1*

Do you have tensions and secret frustrations? Do you hate your job? Are you subject to the blues?

If so we have two heroes for you this week. Right smack dab in the beginning of the atomic age, we have two carefree souls, Carroll Behnken and Bobo Jordan, who have gone back to Nature for at least two months.

Carroll and Bobo have been making their headquarters at Doc Selman's camp and their hunting, trapping and fishing record for the past two months is impressive. In three days they hooked 87 big bass out of Village Creek. They bagged more than 200 squirrels. Here lately, they caught four mink. Bobo and Carroll have killed 12 coon and one night they held a big coon barbecue. Although Doc is not in on the hunting, he just can't wait to go out after work in the district clerk's office to see what Bobo and Carroll have come up with. On top of all that, they got their two deer.

Isn't it fine to live in a place where two men have the gumption to go into the woods and hunt, fish and trap? Who wants to nominate Bobo and Carroll as the Men of the Year for this part of the Big Thicket?

LETTER FROM HEMINGWAY

James Starnes, a 16-year-old high school junior, is carrying around a letter which he is going to frame. Several weeks ago, his high school English teacher, Mrs. Simms, told the class that they should learn more about present-day writers, and that a good way to do that is to write letters. One night about 11 o'clock a week later, James Starnes had an impulse to write his favorite author, Ernest Hemingway. He called Mrs. Simms out of bed and wanted to know Hemingway's address. Mrs. Simms was irritated.

"James Starnes if you ever call me at 11 o'clock, and get me out of bed, I'll give you an F. Ernest Hemingway's address! The last I heard of Hemingway he was with "The Old Man and The Sea" in Cuba. Havana, I think. Good bye! And I mean good bye!"

"Wait a minute—how do you spell Havana?"

Two or three weeks later, James Starnes received a letter from Ernest Hemingway, in longhand and postmarked Sun Valley, Idaho. In the short letter, Mr. Hemingway, the author of *The Sun Also Rises*, said he was glad to hear from James and you could tell from the tone of the letter that Ernest Hemingway was impressed by James' letter.

"James can be proud," said Mrs. Simms. "Especially to get a letter all in longhand from Ernest Hemingway. If I had written him, if he had bothered to answer at all, his secretary probably would have answered it on a typewriter. But the intellectual enthusiasm and daring of youth never go unrewarded."

CUBA AND LATIN AMERICA   *January 8*

Most Americans abhor and detest the very thought of a dictator, and so the news from Cuba on New Year's Day was welcome. My only regret about Fidel Castro's successful revolution was that they did not catch Dictator Batista before he fled to the Dominican Republic where the ex-dictators of seven Latin American countries now live in exile. Now the cruel Batista will be a next-door neighbor to Juan Peron, the ex-dictator of Argentina.

It would have been nice if the Cuban rebels could have inflicted some of the heinous torture on Batista and his pals that they have been meting out for 20 years. I'm telling you that torture is too good for Batista.

It's time our whole Latin American foreign policy was changed so we will not always be in the position of upholding dictators in South America, a policy we have always had, in both Republican and Democratic administrations. If we believe in democracy, and we do, let's tell the South Americans that we believe in freedom and not dictators. Why must we be afraid to preach freedom in South America. It's a wonder that Cuba, as well as all the rest of South America, is not already Communist, considering the way we aid and abet dictators in Latin America.

ALL A'S   *March 19*

I heard this disappointed child's voice on the phone. "I am Kay Kelley and I am in Mrs. Heaton's second grade, and you had it in the paper that I made four A's and one B and I made all A's," the voice said.

HEMINGWAY'S PEN PAL   *March 26*

One of the marks of great men is the writing of letters to persons of all stations in life, and Ernest Hemingway, with William Faulkner one of the two greatest writers of this century, writes letters in the manner of a great man, to whomever it occurs to him to write.

So it was a great day for James Starnes, a local high school youth, when the great Hemingway answered James' first letter. James promptly wrote back and now, on the very day the second part of *For Whom the Bell Tolls* is a Playhouse 90 attraction, James received another letter from Hemingway, the author of *For Whom the Bell Tolls*, *The Sun Also Rises* and *The Old Man and the Sea.*

Here is the letter:

> *Ketchum, Idaho*
> *March 13, 1959*

Dear James,

Sure was glad to hear from you again. We are pulling out of here to drive to Key West to go home to Cuba and I wanted to write you before we left. Once we start leaving it is hard for me to write letters.

Hope you're doing good (that should be well) in school and everything

*goes good with you. We had a good fall and winter. Worked hard on my
book and had fine shooting, too.*

*Still eating mallard ducks, pheasant, partridges out of the deep freeze,
also venison. It hasn't been a hard winter here and the game has wintered
well. There have been 15 head of elk only a couple miles from this cabin
up Trail Creek.*

*Thanks for sending the paper. The editor sounds like the type of man I
could get along with O.K.*

*If you don't hear from me don't think I have forgotten my friend. It is
just that I will be traveling and working and I don't write letters the way I
should.*

*Best of luck to you and your folks and my regards to Mrs. Simms. I
can't help her about the lazy children because that was what I was and the
best part about school was vacation when we didn't have to wear shoes.*

Take good care of yourself.

> *Your Friend*
> *Ernest Hemingway*

My permanent address,
> *Finca Vigia*
> *San Francisco de Paula*
> *Cuba*

Hemingway wrote the letter on thin paper in blue ink. It was
sent air mail. The News hopes that Hemingway will not hold it
against James because we coerced the letter from him for publication. Letters from the great are an irresistible temptation.
Besides they should be published now.

LBJ'S "GOOD TEXAS THINKING"   *April 30*

Here comes this letter from U.S. Senator Lyndon Johnson
which he sent to all newspapers in Texas. In the letter, LBJ
writes: "Since it is impossible for me to sit down and visit with
you and get your views as often as I would like, which in turn reflect the views of the people of your community, I wonder if I
might ask a favor of you. I would like for you to send me the editorials or any personal columns in which you are especially interested and that I ought to see. We receive several hundred Texas

papers, but I frequently am not able to read all of them every week. So, if you will do me the favor of passing on to me any ideas you think are good for Texas and the Nation, I will be most appreciative. I would like to share good Texas thinking with my colleagues."

All of that is quite in order, Senator. But I have no editorials or personal columns to send you that I would guarantee would reflect the views of the people of this community. People on occasion quote statesmen and politicians of whom they approve, but they are more prone to quote opinions they don't approve.

There was old Beebee in here yesterday. It was press day and he always comes to the print shop for his paper. While here, Beebee brought up your name. He approves of you. He thinks you will be nominated for president. Beebee voted for Yarborough. He voted for Adlai Stevenson. He is a Democrat, more or less a brass collar Democrat, and that's the only kind of Democrat I understand. Beebee is elderly, and he gets a pension. There may be a lot of people like Beebee in this community which in 1956 gave Ike and Adlai a tie vote. But most of the 1956 Ike-likers and Shivercrats still hate your guts, remembering what you did to Shivers. They gloat when Proxmire gets on the Senate floor to belabor you.

Then there are a lot of brass collar Democrats who used to worship the ground you walked on, alongside FDR, but who now feel sick when they think of you, remembering how you lined up with the Republicans at the state Democratic convention in San Antonio in 1956, remembering how you played into the hands of Jake Pickle and others. Thus the people who are still Ike-likers, the people who are going to vote Republican regardless, but nevertheless have controlled Texas thinking to Texas' disadvantage, have only contempt for you and your views.

Now take me. I represent a big group of people who aren't middle-of-the-roaders, like you're supposed to be. We are brass collar Democrats who could vote for Hubert Humphrey or Governor Orville Faubus, if nominated for president on the Democratic ticket, with equal pride and passion. We are Democrats to the end and we feel sorry for the middle-of-the-roaders.

Lyndon, we want you to side in with the people of this nation in the matter of housing, education and public welfare of its citizens.

Lyndon, if you are going to side in with anybody in Texas, side in with Democrats, not Republicans like Jake Pickle and Allan Shivers. In the past, you have tried to stay in the middle of road, but you always managed to double cross the brass collar Democrats. And I suspect that is your trouble in Washington, too. You make both sides mad. Lyndon, you better take sides, and if you do take sides, I know which side it will be. It will be on our side. You're never going to get any place with your programs by making Ike look good. Come on over, man. Sooner or later you're going to have to do it. You can't forever be thinking of yourself as a liberal Democrat and then go on acting like a conservative. The conservatives and budget worshippers are the people who got us in this fix.

Lyndon, you spoke of "good Texas thinking." I wonder what you meant by that. That sounds like the kind of slogan the Republicans and Ike-likers cooked up in 1952 and 1956. What is "good Texas thinking?" Is it any better than good Arkansas thinking, good Mississippi thinking, good California thinking? Why not "good American thinking?" Who are you going to invest with the ability to manufacture good Texas thinking? The middle-of-the-roaders? The Jake Pickles? The big Republican daily press in Texas? As far as I am concerned, good Texas thinking is done by people like Governor Faubus, like Senator Humphrey, like Senator Kennedy, like Senator Lyndon Johnson (when he is not carried away with the middle of the road.)

Good Texas thinking? You'll get different versions of that. In your position, Lyndon, you'd better be concerned with good American thinking, rather than good Texas thinking, in view of the crises in Berlin and Iraq. But to boil it down, I'd say that the big thing ahead of you is to push Ike and the Republican do nothings aside and take over. Get out of the middle of the road, and get us on an even keel with Russia, budget or no budget, and side in with the people of this world who are striving for a better standard of living, the starving, the victims of dictatorships, the revolutionaries, not to forget the rank and file of the country.

THE PRINTER'S MAYHAW JELLY RECIPE　　　　　May 7

The mayhaw market in this the mayhaw capitol of the world was building its own last week, the peak week of the season in Hardin County. Last year, when mayhaws in Tyler and Hardin Counties got ripe at the same time, the bottom fell out of the market and mayhaw pickers could not give them away. This year, those who are buying mayhaws are paying about a dollar for a syrup bucket, $1.25 for a lard bucket and from $1.50 to $2 for a water bucket full.

Of course the leading mayhaw jelly maker is the Printer of The Kountze News whose recipe is as follows:

Take a big granite dishpan; do not use aluminum. Line bottom with two inches of snow and cover snow with two inches of mayhaws. Eliminate all green mayhaws before cooking. Place dishpan over high heat. Before snow is melted add two more inches of snow and two inches of mayhaws. Continue to add snow, until mayhaws are exactly one inch from top of pan. From this point until mixture foams, do not stir. If you do, the foam will not rise to the top when you make jelly. Do not stir mayhaws until you have skimmed off all the foam. Stir after all foam has been skimmed off.

Cook exactly 15 minutes on medium heat.

Next, dip out all juice with a cup and then use a potato masher to pulverize mayhaws. Then put through a wire strainer. Then strain juice through a cloth, and squeeze pulp through a new pillow case that has been boiled. Keep on squeezing until all juice is out. This is important since the squeezed out juice is comparable to the "strippings" of a milch cow. Now you are ready to begin making jelly.

Measure out four cups of juice in stewer. Add pectin, stirring constantly. Bring the mixture to a high rolling boil. Then add 5½ cups of sugar. When the mixture comes to a high rolling boil, that is a boil that can't be stirred down, boil for exactly 60 seconds and no longer. Take from the heat and skim and pour quickly into jars. If your first batch foamed to the extent that the foam would not come to the top, add ½ teaspoon of butter to the next batch, though this is not guaranteed to eliminate foam.

Above all, don't pay any attention to the purists who say that they never use any pectin. Their mayhaw jelly usually tastes like plum or any other kind of red jelly. You boil anything for 10 minutes and most of the flavor is going to go up in steam.

Oh yes, where are you going to get the snow in a place where it snowed only one time in 7 years? Well, the Printer gets his from the ice house, but one year my rich brother Ford who lives in Colorado sent a barrel of it by airplane. However, if you can't get any snow use water. All the snow does anyway is preserve the natural flavor and make the jelly so clear you can read through it.

The Printer has trained mayhaw pickers who will not try to palm green ones off on him. The snow would be used futilely if you tried to sneak in green mayhaws.

For the benefit of those people who take The News and who live in far away places like Washington or Kerrville, mayhaw trees grow in the swamps and the most common way of gathering them is by shaking the fruit off into the water and skimming it up with strainers. The water in these mayhaw swamps is usually about knee deep. Mayhaws look like miniature crab apples, red and pink and about the size of a peewee marble or maybe a little bigger.

DOBIE WRITES THE PRINTER   May 28

Dear Archer,

That bountiful supply and generous gift of mayhaw jelly was duly delivered. My wife, her nephew, Edgar Kancaid, who wrote the Pileated Woodpecker story that you published, her father, as well as I, all enjoyed and still enjoy this jelly. I have a little place out from town where I hope to do some work now that I'm getting strong enough to drive out there. I'm taking a jar of jelly with me on the next trip.

Your editorial views often make me feel like shouting, "Amen." I expect to get another book written. I don't know when and if I do, I expect to send you a copy.

Now with abiding regards and again with thanks, I remain

Sincerely yours,
J. Frank Dobie

BEDICHEK WRITES THE PRINTER

Dear Archer,

Your politics, your writing and your jelly form a trinity (3 in 1 or 1 in 3) of pleasing impressions, perfectly harmonized, as I lap up the jelly on a hot buttered biscuit, and with The News propped up before me on the breakfast table, absorb the pungent paragraphs of "Both Barrels." You conduct as nearly an ideal rural or country newspaper as I have ever seen, and I used to run one of the things myself. The News is thoroughly identified with what the editor conceives to be the good of the community. How rare is the editor who senses the good, and how much rarer the individual who can put his ideas over in print. You have solved this problem and if I live long enough (I'll be 80 next month) I shall see in the public square of Kountze, Tex., a lifesize statue of Archer Fullingim who dedicated himself to the good of Hardin County and to the blasting of the Beaumont Enterprise.

My wife joins me in thanks for the paper and the jelly and with good wishes and power to the pen (or typewriter) that often revives our hope in an honest-to-god democracy in Texas, I am

Sincerely yours,
Roy Bedichek

SINNERS, BACKSLIDERS AND PSYCHIATRISTS   June 4

I was reminded at the hearing on the injunction to restrain the Sour Lake Pentacostal Church from making too much "noise" that 50 years ago the Oak Grove Methodist Church, three miles northeast of Decatur, bore a fascinating resemblance to the present day Pentacostal church.

The big hullabaloo in the Sour Lake plea for an injunction to keep the Sour Lake Pentacostals from shouting, acting "hysterical," "passing out," and "screaming" took me back to the Oak Grove camp meetings back in the early 1900's. I saw members shout night after night at camp meetings. I remember a woman with reddish yellow hair who wore it piled up on top of her head secured by celluloid hairpins, brownish-red and curved at the top. This woman would shout nearly every night and her long hair would come down and she would lose all her hairpins in the straw, and the next morning, early before breakfast, you could see her up there under the tabernacle, she and several of her friends, hunting the hairpins in the straw near the altar. Those were all the hairpins she had and she was proud of them.

The youngest children would usually go to sleep on pallets at the edge of the tabernacle, but we would always wake up when the shouting started. First about 6 o'clock in the evening, there would be what we called "grove meetings." The men and the boys would go into the woods. The men would pray long and loud for at least an hour. Sometimes in the grove meetings, sinners would be converted.

Then everybody would come back to the tabernacle. If there were conversions at the grove meeting, the shouting would begin as it was announced, and everyone prayed for the sinners and backsliders and there was no difference in a sinner and a backslider in the Methodist church. And still isn't. The meeting would start off with a half hour of singing that would make the rafters ring. Such songs as the Pentecostals now sing, "Come Unto Me," and "The Unclouded Day." Then the preacher would begin his sermon and it nearly always would last an hour. Then he would call for mourners to kneel at the altar, and this would be the signal for Christians to fan out in the tabernacle buttonholing sinners, not to forget backsliders, while the preacher hollered, warned, cajoled, pled and begged above the singing, which might be "Oh Why Not Tonight." Usually, if the Holy Ghost was really working in the service that night, the mourners would start coming to the altar to kneel in the straw at the foot of the rostrum about the third song, all the while the preacher shouted of hell and damnation, the Unforgiveable Sin, the last chance, and, "Do you want to meet your sainted mother in heaven?"

Once the preacher and the members decided that no more sinners were coming to the altar, he would ask members to come to the altar and pray for the sinners and backsliders kneeling there.

It would have been unthinkable for a sinner to have merely held up his hand, signifying that he had been converted and that

A Sunday gathering at Oak Grove Methodist Church in 1909. Archer's father is third man from the right in the front row (with small boy); Archer, wearing a hat, is standing behind old woman wearing black dress and bonnet seated at far left of picture; Archer's mother is behind, and to the right of him, standing and holding blonde-haired child in third row.

he wanted to join the church, as is the custom now in the Methodist church. Nobody would have believed that he had been converted. You definitely had to go to the mourner's bench and stay
until you "got it." You had to weep and repent in public. I
don't remember any talking in tongues but my mother and father did. The more times you went to the mourner's bench before
you got it, the more convincing was your conversion.

I remember one man that it took five years of camp meetings
to convert. He would ride his horse up to about 30 feet from the
tabernacle and sit there during the service. He would not get off
his horse which was black with a long flowing mane and tail. He
would listen to the members pray for him year after year, but he
kept sitting on his horse. I can see his white Stetson and the black
gloves on his hands and one leg hooked around the saddle horn,
and the reflective, yearning look on his face as the preacher
warned him over and over that he was committing the Unpar-
donable Sin. When they called for mourners, the members
would make a beeline for him and plead and plead. A lot of the
younger ones thought he was smart, and they took to staying on
their horses near him. He was already a good man, but he became the hero of the sinners who figured it was smart to wear
scornful and superior looks on their faces.

One night, the preacher pointed to the boys on horseback, and
when the call came, the members started in his direction as usual,
but the man jumped off his horse to meet them halfway, weeping and stumbling to the altar. His hoarse, repentant sobs were
heartbreaking. He was converted before he fell down in the
straw, his black gloves fisted. Nearly everybody in Oak Grove
shouted that night. That fall the man became a steward.

I remember the time when two of my close relatives, two of the
wildest young men in the community, both high born and of
well-to-do parents, were riding slowly toward church, about five
miles away. They planned to arrive just when the shouting
started. They were boys who would rob a watermelon patch and
turn a neighbor's cows and calves out and leave the gates open.
They had a wild reputation. They wore gray kid gloves and gray
Stetson hats.

That day they were eating stolen watermelons and one said
he could just feel those people at Oak Grove praying for him
that very minute, and the other said, well, it was a cinch they

were going to hell if they kept on stealing watermelons and leaving gates open and letting out stock, besides taking those three drinks of whiskey, and they would probably get struck by a lightning bolt before they were 21. They got on their horses, feeling repentant and sad, talking about how sinful they were, and spurred their horses a little and kept riding faster and faster and when they crossed old Catlet Creek bridge, their horses in a dead run, even the preacher stopped to listen and shake his head, the boys spurred their horses and kept riding faster and by the time they got to the church, their horses were lathered, the boys white and ready to sob, and they flung themselves off their horses and ran to the altar, their gray kid gloves still on their hands, and their mothers shouting. One later became the postmaster at Decatur.

Of course, nothing like that goes on in any Methodist church now. There is no weeping for past sins, no shouting, no mourner's bench, no talk of backsliding, no hour long sermons, no shouted prayers, no trances, no grove meetings.

Nowadays, in the heyday of psychiatrists, you might be inclined to look back on the Oak Grove camp meetings and murmur what they needed was a psychiatrist, but it is we who go to the psychiatrists and take psychiatry to heart. You never hear of a Pentacostal going to a psychiatrist. Those people in the camp meetings knew what to do about their emotions. The people of today may be more civilized but they are not as happy.

There is nothing in 1959 that is the equivalent of loping a horse over the Catlet Creek big iron bridge and going to the long mourner's bench under the old Oak Grove tabernacle and repenting of one's sins in public.

REGRET AND REMORSE, BUT . . .   *July 23*

G. W. "Buckshot" Flowers entered a plea of guilty on a charge of assault with attempt to murder in connection with a pitched gun battle with J. C. Ishmael last year. Flowers' attorney, Houston Thompson of Silsbee, had Flowers on the witness stand before Judge Coe in 88th District Court. Houston was asking the witness the usual line of questions asked on pleas of guilty in which the defendant seeks clemency and a light sentence.

In response to questions from Mr. Thompson, Flowers expressed his regret and remorse. (After all, his wife was killed by a stray bullet in that gun battle at the Ishmael place near Honey Island.) The apparent plan of the questioning was to extract regret and repentance from the defendant, and assurances that the defendant had so changed it could not happen again.

Thompson then asked Flowers if he was sorry for the part he played. Flowers startled both his lawyer, the court and spectators by answering, "What I should have done was waited until I got him on my land and then got him."

In an aside, Houston muttered, "Now what am I going to say?"

But at the end of the trial, in which Ishmael also testified, Judge Coe gave Flowers a seven-year probated sentence. The judge assured Flowers that any more gun play from him would land him in the pen. Flowers had come straight to the courtroom from the Hardin County jail where he was being held on a charge of drawing a shotgun on his mother. Officers of the Sheriff's department said that examination of the gun indicated it had been snapped and that the shell did not go off.

After the Honey Island gunfight, Ishmael cut his house in half and moved it out of Hardin County to Jefferson County. He and his family had come to Honey Island to build a home to settle down, but shortly after he built the house and put up fences and put land under cultivation, bad blood developed between him and Flowers over land, cattle and fences. Ishmael eventually put in an electric light system around his house that lighted up two acres at night, claiming the lights were put up to ward off a surprise attack by Flowers.

The gun battle took place after Flowers came to the Ishmael home and, according to Ishmael, threatened to kill him. Ishmael got his .22 caliber rifle and shot at Flowers in the latter's pickup as he hastily drove away, one bullet going through the windshield. It was charged that Flowers then came back and shot repeatedly into Ishmael's house. Twenty-seven bullets were taken from the walls the next day. During the fight, Ishmael shot from the window of his house and members of his family laid on the floor. Mrs. Flowers, who had run from the Flower's house nearby to see about her husband, was killed by a bullet during the shooting.

⤬

UNCLE BEN'S HUNTING HORN   *September 10*

I heard this horn blowing story about the late Ben Hooks who killed the last bear in the Big Thicket. For many years, Mr. Hooks put on an annual hunt in the Thicket each fall and he would invite people from all over to attend the hunt. One time he invited a bunch from Nacogdoches to the hunt.

During the course of the hunt, somebody stole Uncle Ben's hunting horn. About five years later at camp, Uncle Ben and Carter Hart, both in charge of the hunt, were lying on their cots in a tent. Outside the visiting hunters were whooping it up with the aid of spirits and song. A number were blowing horns.

All at once Uncle Ben sat up in his bed and said to Carter Hart, "Did you hear that horn? That's the horn that was stolen from me four years ago." All horns may be made alike but each sounds different, and Uncle Ben was able to recognize his horn from among the several being blown.

⤬

WHO'LL BE NIXON'S OPPONENT?   *December 3*

The way it looks now, Tricky Dicky Nixon, the original television rigster, has the inside job for the White House. If Kennedy is nominated by the Democrats, any Republican can beat him because, sad to say, I don't think the American people will elect a Roman Catholic president of the United States. It will be 1928 all over again when Al Smith could not even carry New York. Senator Humphrey can't go either. He's a sort of Eugene V. Debs in the eyes of most of the nation. The people who voted against Adlai Stevenson in two elections will vote against him in a third. Just name me one voter who voted against Stevenson in 1952 and 1956 who would vote for Humphrey in 1960? I don't know one. Then there's Symington of Missouri, the faceless man. I have seen him time and time again on TV and sitting at this

115

Linotype right now I can't get a clear picture of his features in my mind. He is faceless. The American people will not elect a faceless man president of the United States. Yet, all these men I have mentioned would make a great president, not good but great, and better than Nixon or Nelson Rockefeller. Then who can be elected? Lyndon Johnson can be elected president if he is nominated, but can he be nominated? You can't tell me that Lyndon Johnson, a man who sat at the feet of Roosevelt, has changed that much. The words of FDR must still be ringing in his ears. He is the only Democrat that can beat Nixon or Rockefeller. For Lyndon Johnson has not repudiated the liberal cause. He has not pleased me all of the time, but Johnson did what he thought was best for the nation. He alone can beat Nixon, who has been as rigged as the $64,000 question ever since a group of Californians advertised in a want ad for a candidate to smear Helen Gahagen Douglass. Johnson is more conservative than Nixon and more liberal than Rockefeller. That may sound contradictory but Johnson is conservative in the way that Jefferson was conservative and liberal in the way that FDR was liberal. Johnson is not a TV rigged candidate as Nixon is, and he is not the offspring of the Rockefeller Foundation and an incredible group of poll takers. In a sense, Rockefeller is more of a rigged candidate than Nixon, except Rockefeller is honest about it.

There are people in Texas who want Adlai to get another stab at being president. Nobody thinks more of Stevenson than I do. I voted for him twice. I shouted from the house tops for him but I don't believe he can win because I can't find anybody who voted against him twice who would be for him in 1960. And I am for Johnson because I believe the only way the nation can be saved is to elect a Democrat, and I think Johnson has the best chance to win if he can be nominated. Please understand that if Johnson is not nominated I will support whoever is: Kennedy, Humphrey, Symington, Stevenson. I would vote for Walter Reuther, John L. Lewis or Sherman Adams before I would vote for either Nixon or Rockefeller or any Republican because I believe the salvation of the nation and the free world depends on whether we elect a Democrat. The only way to catch up with Russia is to get a Democrat back in the White House. I am full up to the neck with Little Rocks, Sputniks and Ike's foreign and domestic policies.

YEAR 1960

THE SOARING, SURGING OR SICKENING 60'S?   *January 7*

We were all scared senseless in the Frightened Fifties. Scared of even our neighbors who we indiscriminately accused of being Communists; scared most of all of the Russians; scared that the nuclear and hydrogen bombs would start falling any minute; scared to put up the money to defend ourselves lest we would miss out on a few comforts; scared of any new taxes for the same reason; scared of youth and teenagers and their activities and delinquency and at the same time setting an example before them of soft living; scared of education; scared of discipline and dedicated to living it up. Will the 1906's be the soaring sixties, the surging sixties as the New Year writers suggest, or will they be the sickening sixties when we will sicken even more and start dying on the vine? We show no prospects of shedding any of our fears. The only thing we are not afraid of is the highway, and that's because we act like gamblers and think it couldn't happen to us. As we enter the sixties, we are scared senseless of cancer, of coronary thrombosis and a hundred kinds of heart trouble and other ailments. We would panic if an old-fashioned epidemic of Seven-Year Itch would sweep Kountze, something we took in stride 40 years ago.

The most compelling news in 1960 will be the presidential election, the conventions and the general election. It's now all cut and dried for "Ruthless" Richard Nixon, whose favorite campaign trick has been to smear his opponents as traitors to get the Republican nomination for president. All Republican chairmen, east, west, north and south, are for him. He will get the nomination unless the rank and file Republicans revolt and draft Nelson Rockefeller, but that is not likely because the South-hating Republican Old Guard is in control in the Republican party, excluding the bitter-end Taft supporters who are still mad that Ike beat Taft.

This column predicts that the Democrats will finally nominate

Senator Lyndon Baines Johnson of Texas for president at the national Democratic convention in Los Angeles because he is the only Democrat who can make Tricky Dicky turn tail and run. Only Johnson among the Democratic candidates can make Nixon look, in comparison, what Nixon is: a political opportunist and mountebank.

My political belief is dedicated to the principle that it does not matter whether a candidate, be he Democrat or Republican, is liberal or conservative, but whether he is a Democrat. For the way I see it, Texas, the South and the nation benefits most under the Democratic party, and the country always goes to wreck and almost ruin when the Republicans are in power. So if the Democrats should, instead of Johnson, nominate Stevenson, Kennedy, or Symington, I would support the nominee. Johnson may not have been liberal enough for me in the last few years and he may have been too easy on Ike to suit me, but I know that he is a Democrat, and that if elected president he would yank the country back from the fatal direction it is headed. He is just what the doctor ordered when it comes to dealing with that Nixon.

NIXON NOMINATION INEVITABLE, BUT . . .   *February 4*

About all you can read in the Republican press nowadays is what a snap Richard "Switchblade" Nixon will have winning the presidency next November. It needs to be emphasized that the only people making this prediction are Republicans and Ike-likers. These prophets will privately tell you that they don't like Nixon any more than you do, and then they start finding flaws with the Democratic hopefuls. They say ever so happily that Kennedy is a Catholic, that Humphrey is a liberal, that Johnson is hated by the ADA. They leave no doubt but that they will happily vote for Nixon because, "The Democrats just don't have anybody or any issue."

The best thing to do when you hear talk that it's all over but the shouting and that Nixon is it, just ask the speaker for whom he voted in 1952 and 1956. Of course, he will say Ike and then you can consider the source. Just last week our city officials went down to the King Edward Hotel in Beaumont to a banquet and were bombarded with predictions that the Switchblader was going in and nobody could stop him. The speech was a digest of all the Republican columns that appear in the Beaumont Enterprise and Journal. The speaker said he didn't like it, but come fall he will probably whoop it up for Nixon, along with the Beaumont bankers.

We have told you before and we say it again that when the American people finally see the Switchblader standing side by side with the Democratic nominee, whoever he may be, it will be all she wrote for Nixon.

BOB WHITE   *June 23*

I saw the Rufus Hooks house after it got its new roof. Mrs. Hooks is now settling down to steady bird watching. Early on a morning when it's really quiet just after daylight you can hear the bob white calling from almost any part of town.

THE PRINTER'S IMAGINARY TESTIMONY

The scene is the hearing room of U.S. Senator Kefauver's investigation of the drug industry in Washington, D.C. The time is the present. The hearing has just started. There is a commotion at the door. Sen. K. bangs his gavel.

Sen. K.—Will the guards quell the disturbance at the door?

Guard—There's a character here from Texas. He insists he wants to testify before the committee.

Sen. K.—Who is he?

Guard—He says he's a printer from Kountze, Texas, where he claims he publishes a weekly newspaper.

Sen. K.—Will the clerk check and see if we have such a witness scheduled to testify?

Clerk, (checking the record)—We do not, but this man, accompanied by Congressman Jack Brooks of the 2nd District,

Texas, contacted me yesterday. The printer wants to testify on the price of glycerin.

Sen. K.—Is glycerin a drug? What has glycerin to do with the printing business, or rather vice versa? But I suppose we can find out. Show the printer in. The witness we have for today, the penicillin and myclin man from Upjohn, can stand aside.

(Enter the printer who takes the witness stand.)

Sen. K.—Now what's your complaint? You say you are in the printing business—

Rep. Sen.—I object to this witness testifying. There should be somebody here to vouch for him. A common ordinary citizen can't just come in here like this and take the witness chair, claiming that the price of glycerin is too high. Clerk, what did Brooks have to say?

Clerk—He said that due to the fact that this Printer cut him off his mayhaw jelly list, he'd be compelled to take the 5th amendment if called on to testify.

Rep. Sen.—I don't get it. Does he use glycerin in making this mayhaw jelly or in printing. What I'm interested in right now is why you cut Brooks off your jelly list.

Printer—The last batch I gave him he gave a jar of it to a Democrat who is a friend of a Republican who is on speaking terms with Nixon.

Rep. Sen.—It's obvious this witness is a left-winger, un-American and a Welfare Stater.

Sen. K.—The printer will state his complaint against the price of glycerin. How do you use glycerin in a print shop?

Printer—In a print shop, any print shop, you rub glycerin on the tips of your fingers so that you can handle the paper easily. Else you might always be wetting your fingers with your tongue. You can pick up the paper you feed into the presses more easily. My complaint is that the price of glycerin has gone up 25 cents in the last year at the Kountze Pharmacy where I buy my glycerin and I want to know why. It went up 25 cents the previous year. I buy this here particular type of bottle only every three months. Of course now I could buy the same glycerin from the grocery stores cheaper, but it's a tradition in printing shops that you buy glycerin from the drug store. That started before the food stores became drug stores.

Sen. K.—You say this glycerin cost you 50 cents more now than it did two years ago? Who makes the glycerin you buy?

Printer—Black Arrow.

Sen. K.—Now we're getting someplace. Wonder what the Black Arrow people would say to that?

Rep. Sen.—My wife's first cousin's first husband works for Black Arrow and I'm against further questioning of this witness until I hear from him. I think we ought to ask Senator Lyndon Johnson about this witness.

Printer—If I had my druthers, I'd druther you ask Senator Yarborough.

Rep. Sen.—I suppose Yarborough is on your jelly list. Maybe we have a Democratic conflict of interest in the Democratic party for a change. Tell me something. If you are so famous for making mayhaw jelly, what are you doing in the printing business?

Printer—For one thing to keep my readers informed about the stupid Republicans. And I mean stupid. Look at the U2 affair, the Summit and now this Japanese fiasco. What are you going to call them if not stupid?

Rep. Sen.—We'll ask the questions here. This is not a political forum. I object to this man testifying. He's obviously here to air his political views. This man appears to be the worst kind of brass collar Democrat.

Printer—You talk about taking advantage of the situation, why Nixon can't even go to church or talk with Billy Graham without insinuating that Jesus Christ would be a Republican if He were on earth.

Sen. K.—I can't account for your animosity toward Senator Johnson.

Printer—Lyndon brags too much on Ike and the Republicans. He won't get to first base at Los Angeles. The Democratic party is nothing if it's not liberal. Johnson is too much like Ike and Nixon.

Rep. Sen.—Did you ever send any mayhaw jelly to Senator Johnson?

Printer—Yes, I did, but Brooks ate it up, and that was before Lyndon sided with the Republicans on everything. I also sent a case to Senator Yarborough at Austin and as near as I could find out the Shivercrats stole it.

Rep. Sen.—This town you come from must be the hick town to end all hick towns, judging by you.

Printer—Kountze is the town with the sense of humor. That's our slogan. But it applies only part of the time. Rest of the time we're feudin' and fightin'. But we have some people in our town that'd make old Bob Hope look like a mourner at a deaf and dumb funeral. These people can do and say things that make you laugh your head off, but I'm not going to call any names—I might get sued. But I'll put their sense of humor, that is when we are all in a good humor, against anybody's.

Rep. Sen.—If this hick town you're so fond of had a sense of humor it looks like to me you wouldn't get so wrought up over this glycerin thing. That's the way of a Democrat. Always getting worked up over little things, like for instance, how much a pill should cost, how much pay a man should draw per hour, how much interest the government should pay, how much pensions old people should draw, how much insurance old people should get for medicine and hospitalization—why don't you Democrats get interested in big things for a change, like what are we going to do with Cuba, what are we going to do about rockets and missiles and Sputniks.

Printer—You ought to know, you Republicans got us into this big mess we are in now. But as usual, the Democrats are going to have to get us out. That's the way it always is: The Republicans foul up everything and get the country into a mess nothing less than a Democratic president can untangle. And it's past time for that now.

Rep. Sen.—Mr. Chairman, I move we dismiss this witness before he nominates his candidate for vice president.

Printer—My candidate for vice president is Ralph Yarborough.

Sen. K.—This hearing is adjourned, as of this moment.

THE KENNEDY-JOHNSON TICKET *July 21*

In accepting the vice presidential nomination, Senator Lyndon Johnson appeared to prove three things to Texas, the South and the nation. 1) That the people can safely and confidently elect a Roman Catholic as president of the U.S., secure in the knowledge that the church and state will remain separated. If Lyndon Johnson can run for vice president on a ticket with John F. Kennedy, a Catholic, then all Democrats can safely vote for Kennedy. Lyndon Johnson would not be his running mate if he thought for a minute that the Catholic church would try to influence Kennedy. 2) Johnson has more concern for the welfare of the United States than he has for his own personal ambitions. He wants to regain world leadership for the United States, to make this nation the No. 1, not the No. 2 power of the world. He wants the job done and he does not care who gets the credit. 3) Johnson by his action believes that the nation desperately needs the Democratic party in the White House because the Republican party has failed. Lyndon appeared to sacrifice pride and personal ambitions in order to snatch the nation from the jaws of the Soviet menace in which the goofing, golfing Republican party has placed it.

I believe Texas, the South and the nation has enough confidence in Johnson to allay its fears of Roman Catholicism. We all know one thing: If Lyndon Johnson can vote for and support a Catholic president, we all can with confidence and safety. We mention this Catholic business first, because that is the only thing that anybody can have against Kennedy. Johnson ought to know. I trust Lyndon Johnson, as I have for 12 years, even though I have disagreed with him, and only as recently as last week, but I never doubted his patriotism.

Now for the first time in years, real party unity appears possible, not only in Texas but in the entire South because Lyndon Johnson is the vice presidential nominee. Perhaps Johnson's great goal is unity, and that can be achieved only through compromise and peace-making. A lot of bitterness faded from Texas and Southern politics with the nomination of Lyndon Johnson. It took a great man to do what Johnson did, but people are beginning to see that Johnson has no false pride when he acts for the welfare of the United States.

The Democratic convention revealed that Texans have known little about Johnson, even though he has been their senator for 12 years. Many people never heard his voice until he got to Los

Angeles. Most people did not really know the senator's stand on any issue, due mainly to the Republican press, how he really thought, how he expressed himself, until the TV cameras at Los Angeles trained on him in countless interviews and appearances. We can thank CBS and NBC for introducing LBJ to the people of Texas. For the first time the real Johnson came through for the people of the nation and most were agreeably surprised, and the liberals of Texas were compelled to admit that Johnson was the most down-to-earth, the most sensible talking candidate at Los Angeles. So in Texas, both conservatives and liberals must let bygones be bygones and help put John Kennedy and Johnson in the White House, for if there ever is going to be an assistant president of the United States it is going to be Lyndon Johnson. Kennedy showed he knows the value of Johnson as a leader and a statesman by pleading with Johnson to become his vice president.

The Democratic convention pounded home the realization that this is not a conservative world. It is a world yearning for freedom and turning to revolution to get it. It is a world ringing with the shouts, ambitions and hopes of revolutionary peoples. You can call the uprising peoples of the world radicals, but they aren't much different from radicals who shouted revolt in America in 1776. There is nothing conservative about the have-nots of Asia, South America, Africa and those in the United States. Everywhere people are clamoring for political freedom and economic security. The United States sets the pace. Now these have-not nations of the world want everything that America has, and that is a tribute to American democracy.

There is nothing conservative about the ideals of Cubans or Indians, Congolese or Russians. This is a universe dominated by liberal plans and purposes. If you look at Cuba with eyes that also see the rest of the world, you see Cuba as only a repetition of what is happening in Asia and Africa. We, instead of Soviet Russia, should be helping Cuba to achieve freedom and security. We, instead of Soviet Russia, should be raising our voice against dictators.

The Democratic party caught up with itself in the platform at Los Angeles. This new platform took up where FDR left off. It is not conservative. The platform continues the revolution we began in 1776. It projects the idea that the United States must face the facts of revolution in a revolutionary world. This platform will be the bible of John Kennedy and Lyndon Johnson in their duel with Nixon.

The platform passed up the Southern states. For the first time at a Democratic convention, nobody cared. Nobody showed any fright. The convention simply passed up the South as a deep pocket of conservatism which was out of step not only with the nation but with the world. The Democratic party, which has been held back by the South since FDR, traveled on and left the South clinging to its bastions of conservatism.

If any Democrat can be elected in 1960 it is John Kennedy. The nation had the feeling that Adlai could not do it even if given a third chance, although most felt he would make the best winner. Kennedy swept the primaries. There is no reason to believe he won't keep on winning in November.

NIXON'S ACCEPTANCE SPEECH   *August 4*

The sad spectacle of Senator Barry Goldwater was the sad story of the Republican convention. At the beginning there was Goldwater before every TV camera in the place vowing up and down that Nixon had lied, and that he would fight the Republican platform and that Rockefeller wrote it for Nixon. But in the end, Goldwater knuckled under, just as Nixon did. John Kennedy was the leader at the Democratic convention, just as he will be the leader of this nation. But at Chicago, Nixon knuckled under to anybody who would give him a vote.

The handsome Oregon governor who looked like a movie star opened his speech by saying, "The White House is not for sale," insinuating that Kennedy is out to buy it. The Republicans proved for seven years that the White House was for sale. This same Oregon governor opposed Nixon in 1956 so vehemently that he wanted to dump him as a vice presidential candidate and until two months ago, he was for Rockefeller who the average American believes really has enough money to buy the White House, and judging by the way he spent money in Chicago, was anxious to get a chance to spend it.

Every speaker harped on the theme that the nation is not behind Russia in missiles and rockets, but that if it is the Democrats are to blame. The job of the Republicans in the campaign is cut out for them. It must convince the American people that Russia is not ahead of us in defense and striking power. That's going to be hard to do because the people know that the reason Russia is pushing us around at will and is winning friends in Cuba, Japan and Africa is because we are behind. The American people are uneasy. They want a change, and they are going to look at Nixon and Kennedy and determine which one will do the best job of catching up with Russia the fastest, and Nixon already has two strikes against him because he's standing on Ike's record, the very record that got us behind.

Ike himself said he has trouble restraining his "indignation" when he hears talk that we are behind and that Russia is pushing us around. But no matter what Ike or Nixon says, they can't explain away their failure in Cuba, Japan, Egypt, South America and Africa. The American people know that something is wrong, and they know that if we don't get out of the middle of the road, we are going to get knocked in the gutter for good. They know that if we do not get a leader in the White House who will hurry things up and get us off dead center, Russia is going to take advantage of her superior war power. The American people know deep down that Ike has failed and they know Nixon will fail, just as he failed in his visit to Moscow and his visit to Peru, where in both places he came off second best. If you don't believe it, get the Republicans to play that kitchen sink argument between Nixon and Khrushchev. Nixon talked back to Mr. K. all right, but what he said no man smart enough to be president of the United States would have said.

The American people watched Nixon at Chicago, sacrificing principles right and left to avoid a floor fight, to avoid an opponent. Goldwater and Rockefeller were appeased. Nixon is right when he says he's a "political animal," and we take that to mean that an animal has no principles.

Ike said at the breakfast for him that it's best to travel in the middle of the road because there is a gutter on either side; this was no doubt the product of Ike's slogan makers who have written Ike's speeches for eight years. The truth is that people who travel the middle of the road and stay there usually wind up a bloody mess all over the gutter. The middle of the road? If Ike has traveled the middle of the road that is no travel. People travel on their own side of the road these days, and Nixon better not try to be a road hog from that position when Kennedy starts walking down to Washington.

For the last seven years, for reasons I have not been able to put my finger on, I have come to distrust Richard Nixon. The sight of him on TV, the sound of his voice, the look on his face, his mannerisms have been disturbing and that has worried me. I do not want to react to anybody like that. So the high point of the Republican convention for me was Nixon's acceptance speech. It gave me an hour to study him. I was all ears. I watched his face, his eyes, his mouth, his expressions. I was determined to find out what it was about him that upset me. I was resolved to pick out good points, but I failed. During that speech, I decided that deep down Nixon personally hates people who try to block his ambition, and that is the reason he is so disliked by many people. I did not like his acceptance speech, even though it was modeled after Kennedy's. I did not like his slogan, 'victory for freedom." It implied the very thing I don't like about Nixon, a feeling that he is a potential dictator. I did not like the look on Nixon's face when he stood so long without smiling. I kept thinking of Hitler.

THE SEEDS OF DECAY   *August 18*

This column has to do with a recent Sunday school lesson. The topic of that lesson, "Seeds of National Decay," was almost to a man distasteful, almost repugnant—to members of Sunday school classes over the nation. The reason was that no one wants to believe that there are seeds of decay in American life, and if you should find yourself arguing that these seeds exist you are reproached for low-rating America, for giving aid and comfort to Communism, yet there it was in that Sunday school lesson as big as life. It came right out and said the current, basic instincts of Americans are decadent. It's safe to guess that most of the teachers that day glossed over the "seeds" and talked about

Hosea on which the lesson was based. Israel's decadence in Hosea's time was a far more comforting subject than the idols and hate we suckle.

This leads one to ask if the austere people who write the Sunday school lessons are not way ahead of Sunday school scholars in the churches of America, students who, rolling in prosperity and security, don't want to think about the causes of national decay. The subject was almost as taboo as tolerance of race and religion which must not be mentioned because they are controversial and because they bring out the hate in us. The lesson listed some of the causes of decay as indifference to human need, contempt for people, lack of respect for personality, lack of concern for other persons, the unbridled greed of some large corporations (the exact words used in the lesson), the disparity of living standards.

But the point about the lesson that concerns me is not your relation to the church or to God, but mine. There has been a saying floating around for quite a while that you get out of religion exactly what you put into it. I think that people get a lot out of the church today; I don't know how much they get out of religion, but I do know that church and religion have become two separate things. My relationship with God began at the mourner's bench at Oak Grove Methodist Church, South, when I was 14 years old. I remember that I stayed at the bench quite a while praying, while others prayed about me. At first, my praying was rather unenthusiastic and mechanical, but as I began to realize the lost state I was in, I warmed up considerably. I knew before I went to the mourner's bench what I had to do. I had watched sinners for years go to that mourner's bench. You just did not "get religion" in one trip to the mourner's bench unless you were one of those people who is so constituted you can surrender all and make a resolution to do better in a matter of minutes. I'm not that kind. Like most people, I'm stubborn. There was the matter of being forgiven for your sins, and forgiveness was not an easy thing to win while you were down on your knees praying for forgiveness. First you had to get under what everybody called "conviction" for your sins. That was the primary purpose for going to the mourner's bench, to get under conviction for if you were not under a strong conviction for your sins, how could you be truly sorry, how could you pray, how could you know you were forgiven? The conviction was a strong conscience to work on you.

This may all sound like Greek to the modern day Methodist, Baptists, et al, but it was standard operating procedure in all churches when I was growing up. I knew people at Oak Grove who would go to the mourner's bench at the revival meeting year after year without getting religion, and in between revivals they would be somber and sad all year long, very conscious that if they died before the next revivial they would assuredly go to hell, and we all knew that too, and we were very kind to them. Some would try for years to get religion, forgiveness, but they could not feel that God had forgiven them yet, or that they were ready to give up favorite sins and favorite hates. It was a sin in those days to hate somebody so much you would not speak to them, but nowadays the churches are full of people who know other people they won't speak to. I knew one man who enjoyed a hate for a neighbor so much he could not turn loose of it, and every 10 years he went to the mourner's bench before he got religion, but when he did, he got down on his knees to his neighbor and he made the great Christian that everybody always knew he would make.

So my point is, do I now have the conviction, the Christian conscience I had then. I know that I do not. Do you really have a conscience? My point is that we held that Sunday school lesson at arm's length and talked all around it, but never got our teeth into it. For it is now obvious that we Americans don't want to tackle anything that questions our security and prosperity, we want those at all costs, and our security and prosperity are our idols and at the same time our cancer and that is our national decay. I am thinking here of why we have the cancer and how it manifests itself. That being so, we sit right up in church and Sunday school and hate people of other races and religions, other creeds. The lesson that day quoted Adlai Stevenson who undoubtedly has brought out the epithets of "left-winger," "radical," and "egghead" from people who consider themselves sound Christians. Here's what was printed in the Quarterly, written by Adlai Stevenson: "In my judgment, disparity of living standards is the most important and fateful fact in the world today.

And the worst of it is that instead of getting better it is getting worse. The rich are getting richer and the poor poorer as population grows faster than production in poor areas." And of course Stevenson was referring to other countries in addition to the United States.

But at heart we despise that statement of Stevenson's because we in the United States have no real love for the poor. What we want to do is give to the United Fund and call it quits. What we want to do is give to every charity that comes along and think boy we have done our bit to qualify as humanitarians, but at the same time we are going to lobby for taxes that will shift the tax burden to the poor from the very rich, we are going to fight health insurance for old people, we are going to fight all attempts to feed the hungry of this world, clothe the naked and help the sick.

Why? Let's start answering that question by inquiring about our conscience. Is it still working as it did at the mourner's bench? But of course there is no mourner's bench nowadays to needle the conscience. There are no really self-confessed sinners in the churches. Gone are the backsliders of the oldtime Methodist church, gone are the "re-dedications" of the Baptist church except among the young who are the only ones in any of the churches who admit any sin.

Are there seeds of national decay in the United States, despite the screaming "nos" at Chicago? The seeds of national decay are within each of us, our hates, our idols, our prejudices. But we are not going to see our own faults because the fashion in church now is to see no evil, either in ourselves or in the nation. Why, we've got all these fine churches so these fine churches can be full of fine Christians. The idols we worship in our churches are Fellowship and Togetherness. The seeds of decay that are in us, the hate we harbor for anything and anybody that threatens to rob us of our soft living, the hate we have for diverting taxes to help the poor, the hate we have for taxes after we've got ours "made."

The Sunday school lesson said: "When hunger threatens one member of the human race, it eventually threatens all . . . because Greece and Rome were never deeply aware of their poor, their civilization went down. We had best not be dulled toward the human need. Neglect of the poor is but one step to blindness concerning the privilege of freedom." I'll go along with that. And I reprint it here only because I shied away from those statements; we did not even mention them. They were there but we wanted to forget they were there.

So let us say that the seeds of decay sprout and flourish where there is no conscience, and where there is no conviction and where there is no way to goad the conscience.

THE PEOPLE WILL JUDGE   *September 1*

Here's a prediction for you to keep in mind for the general election in November. The outcome of the presidential election will not be controlled by the Catholic church, the Protestant church, and neither the Democratic nor Republican parties. The fate of John F. Kennedy and Richard Nixon will be determined by two things: Their debate on television and Nikita Khrushchev. The debate on TV is getting a big build-up and by the time the two go on the air the only people who won't be listening will be those who can't get to a TV set, and they will hear about it. Who wins that debate, who looks best to the majority of Americans, will win the election, if Nikita Khrushchev does not take a hand. Right now Nixon is running against Russia and Mr. K., not Jack Kennedy, but suppose in the last week or so Mr. K. should decide to let East Germany take over West Berlin, or suppose Mr. K. should make a war-like move in Cuba or in some other part of the world, like he did in 1956 when the Suez Canal seizure cinched the election for Ike. Suppose that Mr. K. should come out strong for Kennedy, or Nixon. Will Mr. K. intervene in the presidential election? He has not been hesitant in the past to speak out when he would get what he wanted by speaking out. Who does Mr. K. actually want elected? He has called Nixon a shoestore clerk and he has said that Kennedy's election would be bad for Russia because Kennedy is a sensible man.

Both Democrats and Republicans are now anxious for Kennedy and Nixon to meet face to face and battle it out in the TV debate. Each party feels that his man will make the best impression. If Mr. K. keeps his big mouth shut and does not create an international hostile act or aggression against the United States, the debate may well be the decisive factor in the campaign. The big question is how will Nixon stack up against Kennedy in the debate. The two men are exact opposites in looks, speech and methods. The Republicans see Nixon as the experienced debater, the in-fighter who thinks quickly. The Democrats see Kennedy as the sincere patriot who is out to save the country's foreign policy. In that debate, either one could say the wrong thing in one sentence that could ruin him. Nixon has never said the wrong thing yet; he has always said the right thing, but he has never come up against Jack Kennedy who also has never said the wrong thing. The debate could very well be the turning point in the campaign. The Democrats are confident that Kennedy will come out on top; they think he will strip Nixon's character and motives to the bone. The Republicans think Nixon will show up Kennedy as being immature and lightweight. But the American people will be the judge, and that is the way it should be.

THE COTTON PATCH GRAVES   *September 15*

The story begins on a farm three miles north of Decatur in 1916. That was the year we sold the farm and moved to a section of land in far West Texas, six miles from Tahoka in Lynn County. We shipped our household goods and farm implements in a box car. I was 14 years old, my brother Ford, 12, my brother Alf, 5, and my brother Bill, 2.

The last thing Ford and I did, after the freight car had been loaded, was to go down to what we called the Little Hill and dig up the bones of Old Sam and Old Pete, our dogs who died in preceding years. We had buried them with many a tear. We put the bones in a box and sneaked them into the box car.

When the car arrived on the siding at Tahoka, Ford and I were on hand to sneak them out. The first chance we got we buried the bones in two graves between two huge cactus plants in the pasture about a half mile from the house. We strung barbed wire around the graves and cactus. We knew which bones were which because we had put one notch on Pete's bones and two on Sam's.

We did not tell our father for several years about the bones of Old Pete and Old Sam. The next year, 1917, the year of the big drouth, we dried out in Lynn County, and traveled through the Yellow Horse Canyon and the Matador Ranch to Paducah, near where we settled on a farm at Salt Creek.

In time we all left Cottle County. I lived in Pampa 14 years, Alf and Bill batching with me until they graduated from college, married and moved away.

In 1955 Bill decided to drive to Lynn County and see the old place we abandoned in 1917. The section was nearly all cultivated. Bill told the owner about our residence there. Bill said, "Let's walk over the crop." All of a sudden he had become curious about the graves of the dogs he did not even remember, but he had heard Ford talk about them time and again.

Bill and the farmer walked through the maize. "Are you sure you are enjoying this?" the man asked. "Sure am," Bill said. "Let's go this way."

Then they came upon the small graveyard. There were the two graves, nicely mounded between the cactus that was taller than the feed crop.

The man said, "Often wondered about those two graves. Don't suppose you know anything about them. Always figured two children were buried there. We keep up the graves. My children put shells we got at Galveston on them. We keep the white fence up."

At first Bill thought he would just keep quiet, then he knew he had to tell the man about old Sam and Pete.

"Just dogs, huh," said the farmer. "Well for years we've been fools. But I'm going to leave them graves and not tell the children. I think they're kind of pretty there between them cactus. You boys must have loved them dogs a lot. Speaks a lot for a person to go to that much trouble to bury dogs."

NIXON TAKES THE LOW ROAD September 29

Why is it that Nixon can't run for any office without attacking the patriotism of his opponents, implying in the final countdown that they are traitors? He did it three times before and now he's doing it again. The man whose patriotism Nixon is now questioning is Kennedy, who was a naval hero of World War II.

The true Richard Nixon was coming to the surface last week, after being submerged since 1956. So it is apparent that he has been holding in since then, trying to convince the American people that there was a "new" Nixon, but as Senator John Kennedy slowly backed Nixon into the Republican corner of eight years of loss to the Communists and do-nothingness on the domestic scene, Richard Nixon began to fight back in the only way he knows. He began to say in campaign speeches that Kennedy is soft on Communism and will surrender to Khrushchev. That was the way he defeated Helen Douglass for his seat in the House. That was the way he talked in 1952 and in 1956 when he not only called Harry Truman a traitor, but also Ike's best friend, the late General George Marshall.

Nixon had promised that in this campaign he would travel the "high road," but it was not in him. He's got to call his loyal fellow Americans Communists, knowing that to disparage the patriotism of loyal citizens of this nation is the lowest form of campaigning.

So we will hear over and over again in this campaign that Kennedy is soft on Communism. It's just as well that Nixon has reverted back to his old self early in the campaign. It was in him to do it, but this is going to backfire on him just as the religious issue is backfiring on him, for now there is no doubt that Nixon is egging on the religious issue through his supporters like Dr. Norman Vincent Peale and Carr P. Collins of Dallas, and that the Republicans are financing the hate campaign. But to say that Kennedy is soft on Communism is like saying that the late Joe McCarthy, also a Roman Catholic, was soft on Communism. Let it also be remembered here that John Kennedy was on friendly terms with Joe McCarthy and his fight against Communism, not the persecution of innocent persons, but the real battle against Communism.

So let Nixon keep on calling Kennedy a Communist. That, too, will boomerang. For if there ever has been an enemy of Communism it has been Kennedy. Actually, Nixon is dated. For what he said 14 years ago and in 1952 and 1956 does not apply today. Nixon is dated because he can't stand up before the American people and dispute history, that America is strong and it should be.

When Nixon insinuates that Kennedy is soft on Communism it is just another way of saying that Kennedy is a traitor. Nixon knows he is not on the high road but on the low road.

SHIVERS SUPPORTS NIXON   *October 6*

The Allan Shivers administration will go down in Texas history as the most corrupt ever perpertrated on any state. At least $25 million was stolen in the land scandals. Shivers was a member of the land board. Bascom Giles went to prison, but he never squealed on anybody. It was four years ago that Shiver's political sun set forever, the day that Lyndon Johnson whipped his ears down in precinct conventions across the state. So it is not surprising that Shivers is lining up with the Nixon Republicans. Shivers is in the kind of company he appreciates and understands. It would have been disappointing if Shivers had come out for the Democratic candidate, John Kennedy. If Shivers had come out for Kennedy a lot of Democrats might have felt inclined to support Nixon. Shivers is right where he belongs. Kennedy will lose no votes on account of Shivers.

THIS QUESTION OF RELIGION

Webster's dictionary says the word "bigot" is derived from the French word meaning "hypocrite." It says that synonyms of "bigoted" are "prejudiced" and "intolerant." At any rate, the word "bigotry" has become a dirty word in the presidential campaign. It is being used to describe all citizens who are going to vote against Senator John Kennedy, the Democratic candidate for president, because he is a Catholic. So let this column point out and emphasize right now that since the beginning of the campaign, I have never used the word "bigotry" or "bigot" in this column. I have never called a person who opposes Kennedy, because he is a Catholic, a bigot, and I don't intend to. Like John Kennedy's brother Bobby Kennedy said on Face The Nation: many of the Christians who are opposing Kennedy because he is a Catholic are sincere in their belief. Bobby said these people just can't understand that Catholics as well as Protestants swear to uphold and defend the Constitution. Some Protestants actually believe that the separation of church and state is threatened. I do not believe separation of church and state would be threatened if Kennedy were elected president. The point is that many people do not oppose Kennedy, only his church, and there are others like Carr Collins of Dallas and Dr. Norman V. Peale who oppose Kennedy because they are Republicans and use the religious argument to cloak their hypocrisy.

I believe now that the election of Kennedy would guarantee the highest degree of separation of church and state that we have ever known. I do not believe John Kennedy is lying when he says that his church would not and could not pressure him. I do not believe he is lying when he said that if his faith ever became between him and the Constitution he would resign. I do not believe it ever would. I believe that Kennedy would be so scrupulous in keeping the church and state separate, we would never have any more attempts, at least while he was in office, to vote funds for Catholic schools. I think such a bill, even if passed by Congress, would meet a sudden death veto from Kennedy. I believe this because I believe Kennedy is telling the truth.

There has been persecution of Protestants in the history of the Catholic church. We've all read of the horrors of the Inquisition, and we all know of present-day persecution. But there are few Protestant churches in existence today that do not have a record of persecution at some dark period of their history, and the way I see it Protestants are now persecuting Catholics in the United States in a way that almost kills the soul. Understand, now, I do not think this is bigotry, it may be hate. It is persecution in this way: there are 40 million Catholics in the United States. During World War II, many were with me and all around me on the islands known as the Solomons. In some of the outfits I was in, Catholics outnumbered Protestants 10 to 1.

These men were ready to fight and die for their country, and many did die. A number won the Congressional Medal of Honor. Jack Kennedy was in those same islands, the commander of a PT boat which was rammed by a Japanese destroyer. He was wounded but still managed to rescue his men. Now it appears that these same people are second class citizens in that not one of the 40 million Catholics can ever be elected president of the United States. I argue that if a man is a citizen, he has a right to be president, if he is otherwise qualified, regardless of his religion. I argue that a man's religion should never be held against him in the United States. We can't segregate 40 million people and say none of them can ever be elected president because he is a Catholic. Any person who does not have all the rights of citizenship should not be called upon to fight for his country and we did not question their patriotism in World War II. And make no mistake about it, when we vote against a man because he is a Catholic we are in effect voting against his patriotism, actually saying that we do not believe he would uphold the Constitution of the United States. So what it boils down to is that 40 million Catholics are being persecuted. Their patriotism is being attacked. We are saying that every Catholic is lying when he gives the pledge of allegiance to the flag. Well, I don't believe John Kennedy is lying and I'm going to vote for him. But like Bobby Kennedy said, I am not going to condemn people who vote against Kennedy because he is a Catholic. I just wish they were better informed.

ELECTION FORECAST   *November 3*

My predictions on the outcome of the general election November 8 are:

If you vote against John Kennedy because he is a Catholic you will not only regret it the rest of your life, but you will not be able to hold your head up when the Constitution is praised.

You will eventually become ashamed because it is un-Christian, based on hate, and it is in open defiance of the Constitution which prohibits setting up a religious test for the presidency. People sooner or later become ashamed of open defiance of the Constitution and of all forms of hate.

If Texas goes Democratic, Kennedy will be elected president.

Texas is the key state. If Kennedy and Johnson carry Texas they can win the South. At this writing, Kennedy is already conceded the pivotal states of New York, Pennsylvania, Ohio, California, Michigan and perhaps Illinois. The Republicans had a chance to carry Texas until its No. 1 renegade, Allan Shivers, came out for Nixon and Lodge. The vote will be close in Texas.

I believe Texas is going to vote for Kennedy because he is the Democratic party nominee, and the nation and the world gets along better under a Democratic president. Nixon would not get to first base with a Democratic congress that holds that shifty-eyed operator in contempt because he has consistently slandered their loyalty and patriotism, as he is doing now in the campaign. He has insinuated that both Kennedy and Johnson are traitors. As The New York Times, which endorsed Kennedy, pointed out, the nation needs to move forward again and to do this the president and the congress should belong to the same party.

Nixon proved in the debates that he goes off half-cocked. He said we ought to defend Quemoy and Matsu Islands even at the cost of war. Kennedy said the islands were not worth the bones of any American boy. Ike had to come in and rescue Nixon from his impossible position. That was one of the big political mistakes Nixon made in this campaign. Nixon was the man that never made a political mistake in his 14 years of office that he could not wiggle out of as he did in the 1952 campaign when he had to explain the $18,000 in gifts he took on the side from California businessmen while he was serving as senator. The professional politicians had begun to believe that Nixon could not make a mistake, he was that tricky, but Nixon slipped on the Quemoy-Matsu issue.

Nixon's first big mistake was in agreeing to debate Kennedy on TV. It was obvious to most people that whoever won the debates would be elected. Now most political observers agree that Kennedy won. Up to the time of the debates, Kennedy's youth was an issue in the campaign, but after the first debate you never heard it mentioned again. The debates showed that Kennedy could discuss issues without getting personal and that Nixon could not. It showed that Kennedy has had the right kind of experience and Nixon has had the wrong kind. The debates showed that Kennedy is more mature, that Nixon talked like a high school debater and that Kennedy talked like FDR. Nixon tried to win points by slander. Kennedy managed to convince the people that all he has in mind is to save the nation. Nixon showed he really has no serious thoughts on foreign policy and that those he has are irresponsible. Nixon really does not know what to do about Cuba, no more than Ike does. Nixon has no more idea of what to do about Khrushchev and Russia than Ike has and Ike is impotent. Kennedy knows that the Russian and Chinese Reds are already in Cuba with their arms, planes and tanks, and Kennedy also knows that we've got to egg on the Cubans to run the Chinese and Russians out.

Cuba, Quemoy and Matsu should never have become issues in the campaign, but it was Nixon who insisted on it, thinking that he would be able to show that Kennedy is soft on Communism, for Nixon can't run a political race unless he tries to prove that his opponent is a traitor. But all these old cut-throat techniques backfired on Nixon. Kennedy had him by the jugular vein before Nixon realized that he had goofed. In fact, almost every issue Nixon pursued has backfired. The Nixon who went into the race as a master politician is now the Nixon who lost face when he refused to meet Kennedy in a fifth debate. He is the Nixon who last week was talking most of the time about Ike, hoping some of Ike's alleged popularity would rub off. Kennedy had whipped him down to such a frazzle that Nixon was hollering "Ike" every five seconds.

Kennedy made his mistakes all right, but one thing he has not done is to try and question Nixon's patriotism. In nearly every speech, Nixon insinuated that Kennedy and Johnson would sell America out to the Reds. That's the kind of man Nixon is.

But from the very beginning there was only one issue in the race. Kennedy's religion. If Kennedy had been Protestant, he wouldn't have had to campaign at all, for even the people who oppose Kennedy because of his church don't trust Nixon.

Vice President Nixon's excursions on the "low road" in the 1960 campaign have ranged from insinuations against the patriotism of his Democratic opponent to reckless scare tactics. The grim hammer and tongs specialist of past GOP campaigns comes more to the fore as the presidential contest nears its climax.

A LETTER FROM THE GREAT UNKNOWN   *December 15*

H. A. Crosby, who lives on in the hearts of his friends so strongly that it is easy to imagine him to be just away on a visit, knew for a long time that he was going to die and he made preparations for his journey.

He told many friends that he was ready for his departure. But as is so often the case, it came swiftly and mercifully to H. A. at last.

But there were things that he wanted friends and patrons of his Humble Service Station to know, and which he had to leave unsaid. He had in mind to write them all letters, but he got too sick for that. During his last days, he told his wife, Sea Willow, many times: "You will write all my friends and patrons, people who I have served in my station all these years, ever since I put it in back there in the 40's, and tell them how much I appreciated seeing them, how I liked the times when they just came around to jaw, and especially how I appreciated their business and their trust and faith in me."

Mrs. Crosby was at a loss how to send this message to all of the people whose lives touched H. A.'s. This reporter thinks this is the kind of thing that makes news. A letter from the great unknown.

We must remember that little verse:

We are such stuff
As dreams are made of
And our life is rounded
With a sleep.

YEAR 1961

JAKE LEG AND RIGHT-WINGERS   *February 9*

Back in 1929 and 1930, there were 500 people in Pampa, Tex. who had the "Jake Leg." It was caused by drinking "Jake" or Jamaica Ginger, an alcoholic beverage that came from the West Indies. If one drank enough of it, his limbs became partially paralyzed. Sometimes, just one lost weekend on Jake brought on death or Jake Leg. A Jake Leg victim sometimes had it in one leg and sometimes in both legs, and he walked like a man with wooden legs. The legs went into all sorts of contortions when the victim attempted to walk. The Jake Leg and Jake went out with prohibition, as did Canned Heat and the drinking of vanilla extract. Did you know there is more alcohol in a small bottle of vanilla than in a bottle of wine? But back to Jake. Most of those people who had the Jake Leg must have recovered or else just died off. I never see anyone any more walking as if he had the Jake Leg. But Pampa was not the only town that had Jake Leg victims. The neighboring towns of Amarillo and Borger had more victims than Pampa, and old timers here assure me that they had a number around here. Jake Leg was almost universal in the United States in the waning days of prohibition.

But what brought these morbid memories on was an Associated Press dispatch in the daily papers from Pampa. The story said that a huge streamer was strung across the main street in Pampa, a town now of 25,000, that read "Impeach Earl Warren!" The story said the city dads in Pampa made the dentist who put up the sign take it down. That was about all the story said, and it seemed odd to me that anybody in Pampa would go to that extreme. Why would Pampa get so riled up over Chief Justice Earl Warren of the U.S. Supreme Court? Now of course all this has nothing to do with Jake Leg. I just happen to remember it, that's all. The only connection I can see in it is that I always thought screwballs and oddballs drank Jake, and my first thought after reading the AP story from Pampa about Warren was that Pampa still had its oddballs.

But now I am not so sure that people in Pampa are alone in wanting to impeach Warren. For one thing, my spies over in Silsbee report that a lot of people over there are on the soap box pro and con, beating their breasts about something called the John Birch Society, but nobody seems to know exactly what it is or exactly what it espouses or condemns. The general impression seems to be that it is anti-Communist, but that could apply to almost all organizations, including the Republican and Democratic parties, all churches, clubs, lodges, and even the Village Creek Society of Thursday Night Crap Shooters and the Big Thicket Order of Stud Poker Addicts, Anonymous. Do you know anyone who is not anti-Communist?

We have been hearing about the John Birch Society for several weeks now, but have no definite information on it, so if any Silsbee readers, or Kountze readers, for that matter, know about the purpose of said Society, we would appreciate definite information on it, literature or what have you, the better to be informed.

One wonders if this Society has any connection with a fellow named Wayne Poucher who has a radio program called "Life Line." This fellow Poucher talks like a speech teacher with his vowels properly rounded and his consonants beautifully coordinated. Still it sounds as if he were putting on, as most speech teachers do. The man should have gone to Harvard if he wanted to speak good English and sound educated at the same time. His elocution sounds putonski if you have just listened to John Kennedy. The big burden of Poucher's message over the radio every night is that Communistic ideas have not only taken over the Democratic party but the Republican party as well. He exempts the late Senator Joe McCarthy and Senator Barry Goldwater of Arizona. The Kennedy program is especially obnoxious to Poucher. His technique is to cuss the government during half his program and to preach the Bible the other half, and he's not a bad preacher. Mainly, Poucher wants the government to abandon all welfare legislation, build no dams, and spend absolutely no money for the benefit of people. Practically any governmental activity you might name is Communistic to Poucher. The United Nations is a Communist front to him. Social Security, especially if tied to medical payments for the aged, came straight out of the Kremlin.

But Poucher is not the only anti-Communist radio preacher on the air. The radio is practically taken over by anti-Communist preachers. I am a radio listener after 10 o'clock at night. I roam over the dial after I go to bed, and many's the night I have gone to sleep listening to the radio preachers cuss the government and tell the world how Communistic the United States is, not card-carrying Communists, but Communistic ideas. According to them, you may be a Communist and not know it. I used to turn on the Mexican border radio stations for hillbilly music, but now these stations are taken over by anti-Communist preachers who can prove in five minutes that the U.S. is honey-combed with Communists and that you are probably one of them. About two-thirds of the people in Kountze are Reds, according to their definitions.

In my mind I'm still trying to figure out how I could start out telling about Jake Leg and that anti-Warren streamer in Pampa and wind up with the philosophy of Poucher and his pals. Is there any connection? Possibly. There could be a Jake imbibed by the mind and soul that is as pitiable as the Jake Leg seen on the streets, so incongruous that it drew laughter from spectators followed by tears of pity.

RECOGNIZABLE CABBAGE   *February 9*

I saw C. E. Clark, who lives across the street from Patterson's store in Honey Island, bringing in a load of cabbage to sell to local stores. That fellow Clark can and does grow just about everything. His cabbage, dark green heads and large, too, are easily recognizable at Williford's. They really have a taste. Mr. Clark also grows collards, turnips, watermelons, onions and cantaloupes.

THE PEACOCKS' WILD CRY   *February 16*

The most exotic, exciting living things in the community when

143

I was a boy growing up on Catlett Creek in Wise County were Uncle Charlie Cate's peacocks. I remember those peacocks as much as any other thing. We lived on a hill about a quarter of a mile on one side of Catlett Creek and Uncle Charlie lived on a rise about the same distance on the other side. Between our house and the creek was a field on the slope and in the bottom was our apple and pecan orchard. On the other side was a post oak thicket. The creek itself was shaded by huge water oak and cottonwood trees. I remember the day Uncle Charlie brought those peacocks home. Did you ever hear a peacock give its long wailing cry? It's wild and it lifts the bristles on your neck. The minute my brother Ford and I heard that peacock cry we thought it was a panther. The cry is a sort of a scream and a prolonged tenor honk combined. But the peacock gave its cry only once that time. My father said, "That must be Uncle Charlie Cate's peacocks. We'll go over there and see them, but I want you boys to let them peacocks alone. Don't you rub them or touch them and don't pull the feathers out of their tails."

There were several peahens and about three big peacocks. One of the peacocks spread his beautiful fan tail and it was the most beautiful thing I ever saw in my life. My Cousin Rowena, Uncle Charlie's wife, gave us three or four peacock tail feathers which have the satin green and gold moons on the tips. We took the feathers home and Mammy put them in the big vase on the center table in what we called "the front room," which was our parlor.

In the next few years, Ford and I got real good acquainted with those peacocks, and we did exactly what our father told us not to do. We chased those peacocks up and down that creek for hours day in and day out whenever my father would leave home to go to the Farmer's Union or to town. Once we were swimming in Cate's swimming hole and here came the peacocks. We ran to see them and those peacocks took one good look at us (we were stripped stark naked) and they flew into the big trees on the creek and began honking. After that when we would go to the creek we'd strip off and chase the peacocks and they would fly into the trees. It was something to see them fly because a peacock is heavy. Then we got to pulling tail feathers and sicking the dogs on them. We hid the feathers in the barn, way up in the hay loft

144

under the rafters.

Not long after that Pappy gave us a good licking for losing the barbed wire pinchers, and then he said, "Now I'm going to whip you for the things you do that you think I don't know about." That's when the licking really hurt and we cried for half a day. After that we would just lay naked in the creek and wait for the peacocks to come. We would wait until we heard a wagon crossing the Big Iron Bridge and then we would make a beeline for the other bridge about a half mile away and we would allow the people in the wagon to get a real fright as we lay under the bridge and honked like the peacocks. Once a man in the wagon came down under the bridge to investigate and it was our pappy and we got a licking over that.

But the thing I liked most about the peacocks was that long, screaming wild cry. Uncle Charlie kept those peacocks until he died. He was a Confederate veteran, and he played the fiddle. He lived in a huge two-story bungalow type house on the hill and it was an eighth of a mile to the front gate on the road. We used to go over there at night and he would sit there on the verandah and play "Dixie" on the fiddle. It was a verandah, mind you, not a front porch. As we grew older we quit chasing the peacocks, but we would do other things to make them holler.

I remember one Sunday morning we were all at Oak Grove Methodist Church about a half mile from Catlett Creek, and here came Thurman Cook who said that Old Blaze, that was Aunt Frances' and Aunt Dollie's mare, was in a bog hole in Catlett Creek. Well, Sunday school turned out right then and there, and the men and boys went to the creek to pull out Old Blaze who was in the quicksand up to her breast, and the women went to nearby houses, including ours, to fix dinner for the men and take it to them. There were about 20 men helping extricate Old Blaze from the bog hole, including the Cooks, the Stephens, the Harters, the Bastains, old John Tugwell, Bill Caddell, Ernest Gilliland, all my kinfolks.

Old Blaze, who had been Grandma's mare, was a pacer. She was old at this time, maybe 15 years old. She was poor with old age and no matter what one fed her she would not fatten up.

It's a real tough job to get a big horse like Old Blaze out of a bog hole. First you shovel and dig and you use ropes and then you put a block and tackle around the horse's body, and pull her out with a windlass. Well, when I got to the bog hole that Sunday morning where Old Blaze was, there in the big cottonwood trees above her was Uncle Charlie's biggest peacock and he was giving his wild cry every so often. That was the first time I ever actually saw a peacock give his cry. I did not know he had such a big mouth. I had thought he would not give his cry if anybody was looking at him. Uncle Charlie was down there and nobody tried to shoo the peacock away, and that peacock sat on that limb all afternoon and about every half hour or so it would throw back its head and give that wild lonesome cry.

That went on all afternoon until the men got Old Blaze out of the bog hole. About the middle of the afternoon, the women came and the men literally ran to put their shirts back on. They would have been embarrassed to be caught by women without a shirt on. My aunts said they were going to keep Old Blaze up in the lot and house pasture, but she got out in a few weeks and got in another bog hole in the same creek, and that was on a Saturday and they pulled her out again, and she was weak, so weak she could hardly walk because being in the quicksand sapped her strength. So they walked her up on the bank and fed her ears of corn and hay, and she ate like she was starving. They left Old Blaze there all night, but in some way during the night she got loose and went back to the creek for a drink of water, and she got in the bog hole again, this time in a really bad one and in water about two feet deep. You must understand that Catlett Creek was a creek with the water running a trickle over the sand in most places. The first time Old Blaze got in the quicksand it was in shallow water. This time her lip was in water.

Well, that Sunday morning here came my cousin John Fullingim to Sunday school with the news that Old Blaze was back in the bog hole again. And again we all went to the creek with shovels, ropes, blocks and tackles. The men worked all day until night and Old Blaze was nearly dead from drowning and being pulled, and then some men who knew a lot about horses said that Old Blaze would never live if she got out, that she was dying. So they decided to destroy her. In those days, killing with a gun was considered the cruelest method of inflicting death, probably because the War Between the States and the bloody

Indian frontier were only a few decades back. So they decided to kill Old Blaze the usual way by knocking her in the head with a single-butted axe. And since my father was the strongest man there, all looked to him, and he took the axe and told everybody to turn their heads and not watch him. He said nobody should watch when you have to kill a horse, that it was bad enough to have to kill a horse himself.

Everybody turned his head and you could hear the tremendous thud of the axe in the center of Blaze's forehead, on the white spot that gave Old Blaze her name. He just hit her once and Old Blaze shuddered all over a long time and died. Then the men cut willow limbs and completely covered Old Blaze's body, but the next day the buzzards were circling and they kept circling for days and Ford and I would hold our noses and hide in the brush along the creek bank and watch the buzzards pull at Old Blaze's remains. There was not a flood for a long time, but when it came the bones of Old Blaze washed away.

Thereafter, it seemed to me that the peacocks stayed more and more in the trees on the creek, and Uncle Charlie would go out hunting them, carrying and swishing a green willow switch he would cut first thing. The peahens were not wild like the peacocks and they would want to go home and they would let Uncle Charlie take them home, and the peacocks would follow, but every once in a while they would spread their tails to dazzle the hens and keep them from following Uncle Charlie, and Uncle Charlie would use that willow switch. Often the peacocks would give out that wild cry.

THE JOHN BIRCH SOCIETY   *February 23*

I know more about the John Birch Society now than I did the first time I brought it up in this column. Since that time, two weeks ago, I have been handed two books, one entitled *The Life of John Birch*, and the other *The Blue Book of the John Birch Society*. The first thing you should know is that the No. 1 project of the society at the present time is to get Earl

Warren, chief justice of the United States Supreme Court, impeached.

Both of the above named books were written by one Robert Welch, Jr., a 60-year-old candy manufacturer from Massachusetts. Welch is the daddy of the society. John Birch had nothing to do with the organization of the society. John Birch himself was killed in China by the Communists in 1945. At the time World War II began he was a Baptist missionary in China. He was 24 years old. He had graduated from high school and college in Georgia and then attended Southwestern Theological Seminary in Fort Worth.

I was moved and touched by the events in the life of Birch, as recounted by Welch, but I see no connection between Birch and Welch. The most you can say for these people who go around claiming that Wilson was a traitor, that FDR was in league with the Communists and that Earl Warren should be impeached is that they are deluded extremists. To illustrate: Here is a typical sentence from Welch's Blue Book, page 136. "Yet I had rather have for America, and I am convinced America would be better off with, a government of three hundred thousand officials and agents, every single one of them a thief, than a government of three million agents, with every single one of them an honest, honorable public servant. For the first group would only steal from the American economic and political system; the second group would be bound in them to destroy it."

What he's saying is that he wants no postmasters, no farm agents, no revenue agents, no Social Security agents. Welch's theories remind me somehow of the German-American Bund of Fritz Kuhn just before World War II. The trouble with Welch is he does not know Americanism from Communism. In fact, he says that the word "Americanism" has become eroded and that it does not mean anything except "collectivism." The Society wants to turn back the clock, start with the Wilson administration and "expunge" everything it doesn't like down to the present time, and it likes very little in the present American set-up. To hear the Society tell it, they are the only true, red-blooded Americans, and they would undoubtedly have to send about three-fourths of the American population to the gas chambers in order to get things just like they want them, and there is no doubt in my mind but that they would enthusiastically do just that, if they could.

But they are outdated, out-moded and out of step with the world. The world is passing them by, just as it is passing by Senator Goldwater, Governor Barnett of Mississippi, Governor Faubus of Arkansas, and the people who want to impeach Earl Warren, who I am confident interprets the law of the land as a patriotic American, not as a Communist as Birch Society critics claim.

There is nothing in the John Birch Society for a patriotic American who is concerned by the menace of disease, starvation, unemployment, lack of housing, conservation of water resources, education for all and equal opportunity for all, and a thousand other ideals that have come to mean Americanism to most of us. The aims of the John Birch Society remind me of the preacher who came in here last fall and said that he would rather have a Communist than a Catholic for president. He said Catholicism was a greater enemy than Communism, and he was sincere, too. Welch, the founder of the John Birch Society, gives the impression that he believes what he calls "eroded" Americanism is a greater danger than the Communist world.

One would think that reasonable, patriotic Americans would shun and scorn the John Birch Society, but it is sweeping the country now. It has chapters all over the United States, especially in Texas where Barry Goldwater is a hero in the Republican party. It attracts the rich and well to do first. Its public aim is to combat Communism but its real aim is to destroy Americanism as we know it.

The John Birch Society has been active in Hardin County where it has some dedicated followers. Many pieces of literature have been distributed. Earl Warren's impeachment has been demanded by a speaker at the local Lions Club.

The society has no more right to attack Warren than it has to condemn the great John Marshall, the chief justice who is credited with interpreting the Constitution to the extent that it saved the nation. Justice Holmes said that the Constitution is what the Supreme Court says it is. So what the present court says is the law of the land, and anybody who defies the Supreme Court, once it has issued a ruling, is attacking the Constitution and guilty of treason. The Warren rulings that the John Birch Society is so excited about all have to do with preservation of the rights of man. Warren simply ruled that a Communist has the same rights as you or I or anybody else.

CANE SYRUP, PREACHIN' AND THE RUNAWAY   *March 16*

One of the possessions all of my father's seven children were proud of when we were young was his molasses mill and cooking vat. We had the only molasses mill in the community and we made our own syrup as long as we lived on Catlett Creek near Decatur. After we made our syrup or maybe before, other people would bring in their ribbon cane and make their syrup. The mill was located about 100 yards from the house and the vat was nearby under some huge live oak trees. When the cane got ready to cut, my father would say one morning, "Let's go out and strip the cane." We would use pieces of board shaped like knives to knock off the long blades. Then the grown ones would cut the cane with knives and stack it in piles and then haul it in the wagon to the cane mill.

My father would build the fire under the vat when the cane mill started grinding. Usually, a boy or a girl about six or seven years old would follow the horse around the circle to hurry up the animal when he felt like lagging. The horse was hitched to a singletree that pulled the iron rollers of the mill. Two people fed the cane into the jaws. And they were careful, too. They had the example of Miss Mattie Perrin to go by. When she was a girl, she lost an arm in the iron rollers that squeezed the juice out of the cane. She was very religious and she used to get happy all alone in her house and she would shout for glory and sometimes she would run out of the house shouting as oldtime Methodists used to shout.

My father would make the syrup himself. The green cane juice would be poured in the hot end of the vat, next to the rock chimney. The tin vat had many, many partitions, all with little gates that opened and closed. My father would guide the juice from partition to partition toward the end. When the syrup reached the end it was supposed to be done enough to take off. Then it would be drained off through a spigot. It took a real master to know how to make syrup. You had to know all about the color, the temperature of the heat and what color the juice had to be in every one of the partitions. Sometimes my father would hear about a top syrup making expert and he would have him make the syrup and then stay at the vat and watch and learn, but my father was pretty good.

But all this is not what I started out to tell. My sister, Lena, was here the other day and she asked me if I remembered the day Henry Will got lost. Henry Will was about three years old at the time. When my mammy missed him, she looked under all the beds. In the smokehouse and out at the lot and the barn. Then she raised the alarm. We children began looking for Henry Will. We searched for him about 30 minutes before Lena got on the phone. People listening on the party line spread the word. The sheriff got there about an hour later. By that time, Mammy had scanned the tank in the hog pasture, and was down on Catlett Creek looking in the holes of water. She always went to the creek when any of us got lost or failed to turn up on time. She was eternally fearful we would drown. My father was searching the post oak woods near the house. I was going down the cotton rows one by one and Ford was going down the corn rows. Finally, Mrs. Stephens, who had used the mill for several years after my grandfather, Carlo Bonaparte Ball, gave it to us, went down to the mill and found Henry Will asleep in the vat. Henry Will woke up laughing. He still wakes up laughing.

That happened about the time that Alf, next to the youngest, broke his leg. My brother Ford had backed the horse he was riding up near the rail fence at the cow lot behind the big barn and told 4-year-old Alf to jump from the fence on the horse. Alf jumped as Ford told him, but so did the horse. My Uncle Shirk who was a physician came out and set the leg and put weights on it. Alf recuperated very restlessly in bed.

He was in bed in traction while the Oak Grove camp meeting tabernacle was going on about 200 yeards down a slope from our house. The camp meeting was held under a big tabernacle. Mammy had to stay home with Alf. Preaching was at 10 a.m. and at night. One still morning in August while the preacher was delivering his hour-long sermon in ringing stentorian tones everybody in the congregation and in the camps nearby could hear Alf yell as plain as day, "Mammy, bring me a glass of cold buttermilk and a hot sweet tater!" Alf actually sounded louder than the preacher who was punctuating his sermons in pretty loud tones every now and then. In a few minutes, Alf again yelled the same request. This time Mammy answered him, just as clearly. She was down at the mailbox about 50 yeards from the house, apparently waiting for John Dendrick, the mail man, to come along in his buggy. "Be quiet," Mammy yelled back. "Im listening to what the preacher is saying." Mammy in later years told me she could see no difference in listening to the sermon at the mail box than in front of a tent where many sat and listened, and the preacher always had his listeners who sat in front of their tents, swatting flies and fanning themselves, in mind, and he obligingly kept his voice raised.

But Alf did not stay quiet. He yelled again, and Mammy yelled back, "Hush, the preacher will hear you. I can't hear what he is saying for you. I'll be there in a minute." Again Alf yelled.

By that time, I was more interested in what was going on up at our house than what the preacher was saying. I glanced at my father and he apparently had been trying to get my eye. He bared his teeth and motioned me to get home and stop the dialogue. I was glad to get away because my chief interest that morning had been in swatting flies that ate at my bare legs and bare feet and in studying the hairpins in Mary Taggart's head in front of me. Later, Pappy made Alf's crutches out of pecan sprouts and Alf got to where he could almost keep up with the dogs on those crutches.

The most exciting accident that happened to me in Wise County was one twilight when I was seven or eight years old. Pappy had just got home from town. He was riding Old Gray. He took the bridle off Old Gray and told me to take him to water at the tank by the windmill but I got on Old Gray as soon as I saw my father go into the house. Old Gray was in a hurry to get to the tank and he broke into a trot. I yelled, "Whoa Gray!" and that scared him. He was a veteran of runaways, and he lit out, with me in the saddle and no bridle and it was unusual for me to ride in a saddle. We boys always rode bareback. Old Gray did not stop at the tank. He circled around the barn and lit out for the bottoms. In two minutes he was going faster than any Kentucky Derby horse you ever heard of. There's no telling how fast that horse ran. I kept yelling, "Whoa Gray," and that scared him all the more. He swooped around the Little Hill and hit the bottom and went down between a row of dead cotton stalks. It was late fall. He went clean to the back of the field and I was fearful he would try to go under the low limbs of the tall trees on the creek bank, but he turned around and headed back.

Old Gray took a different route back toward the house, this time he headed for about 40 acres of scrub oak, and I figured he would try to get me knocked off by a limb, and I was ready for the first limb. I was laying along his neck when the limb seared and scratched my back. He ran through post oak bushes and my legs were squirting blood, but I was hanging on and yelling "Whoa Gray." All of a sudden he stopped. My Pappy was right in front of him where he had jumped from behind a bush. Old Gray trembled for an hour. I was never scared. The only thing I was scared of was that I would get a beating, but I did not get one. My Pappy said, "Never yell at a horse or a man unless you have got a bridle on him."

PINE CONE   *March 30*

I saw a pine cone in the window of O. G. Smith's real estate office that measures 12 inches in height. Otis will give $5 to any one who can bring in a cone that is bigger. Otis got the cone from a long leaf pine at his place on the Honey Island road.

A "HOLD YOUR NOSE" VOTE   *April 20*

I am going to vote for Blakley but I will hold my nose while I'm doing it. I will vote for Blakley because I can stomach him more than I can stomach Republican John Tower. At least

Blakley says that he supports Kennedy's foreign policy. Tower is even opposed to that. The way I got it figured, Blakley will vote against most of Kennedy's domestic programs, but he will back the Democratic foreign program. And anyway you look at it, how the Kennedy administration deals with the god-awful mess Ike left us is more important than most of the domestic problems in this country. Just look at what we inherited from the incompetent Eisenhower administration. The Laos crisis exists because Ike and Dulles insisted on making Laos pro-western instead of neutral. The Congo crisis came to a head because we were asleep in the White House. We let Cuba slip out of the circle of friends for the same reason. Last week came the supreme humiliation when the Russians orbited a man in a space ship around the earth in an hour and 48 minutes. All that means Russia can now drop hydrogen bombs on us from space any time it wants to. "Holy" Ike and his clique were the ones who let the Soviets get ahead of us in space. Do you remember about eight years ago when the Republicans were making the people of this nation believe that the Russians were so ignorant and dumb they didn't have enough sense to make an A-bomb without stealing the secret from us? That was about the time McCarthy was in the saddle. The big trouble with the Republican propagandists was in low-rating the Russians. I wrote in this column eight years ago that the time would come that we would realize Russia did not have to steal any bomb secrets from us, that Russia was ahead.

We know now how far behind the Russians we really are, and we are behind solely because the Eisenhower administration and the fat-cat Republicans lulled us to sleep with stories of how dumb they were. Now the Kennedy administration is moving heaven and earth to catch up and we don't need a freak like Tower in the senate to throw a monkey wrench in the works everytime he votes. So I am going to the polls May 27 and vote for Blakley, as all good Democrats should, for the good of the country.

Otherwise, it will be a bitter pill to vote for Blakley who only last week got up in the senate and opposed Senator Ralph Yarborough's Padre Island bill, contending that the national seashore park on that long narrow island should be 65 miles or less in length, not 85 as the Yarborough bill calls for. In doing that,

Blakley sided in with the opportunists and speculators who want to get rich quick by gobbling up island sites. That was in character for Blakley who will vote against any bill that benefits anybody but the Big Rich. You can get ready for that. Still the danger this nation faces is not from the Blakleys of this world, but from our enemies in Russia and China. We must catch up with Russia. We must go all out to catch up. We need two senators in Washington who will support the Kennedy foreign policy.

Tower is no man to send to the senate to unify this nation. His ideals and the propaganda of the John Birch Society look alike to me. If the national crisis in this year of 1961 lies not in our domestic problems but in how soon we can grab the initiative from Russia, and it does, then Blakley is the man to send to the senate.

Thinking of the prehistoric mind of Tower, brings to mind some statistics we urge State Representative Emmett Lack, who represents Hardin County in the state legislature at Austin, to ponder well before he votes for any kind of a sales tax: Texas ranks 34th in education, ranks 38th in medical care of its citizens, ranks 42nd in the care of its aged citizens, Texas ranks 35th in classrooms, ranks 39th in research in our colleges and universities, ranks 49th in scientific research, Texas ranks 48th in the number of physicians and surgeons, based on population, but Texas ranks first in the number of John Birch Societies.

Texas ranks 49th in the number of libraries based on population and maybe that is the reason why Texans are suckers for people like Allan Shivers, Price Daniel and the Birchers. Texas ranks first in the nation in the number of Goldwater-Tower Republicans, based on population, but 47th in the number of people who buy books. Texas ranks first in the production of oil, cotton, sulphur, rice, natural gas, cattle, and first in the highest state treasury deficit in the nation. Yep, rich old Texas has the biggest state debt, the fewest doctors, among the worst schools and a population that looks upon a person who buys a hard-back book as a freak. What is the reason for all this? I'll tell you. The wealth of Texas is not taxed. The Big Rich are determined that wealth shall not be taxed, and that a sales tax shall be saddled on the rest of us. The Big Rich, year after year at Austin, have successfully lobbied our schools and colleges and even our state of mind into a sub-normal, sub-mental coma.

TO READ WIDELY, DEEPLY AND TRULY   *April 27*

The noble ambition of a group of Kountze women to found a library may turn out to be the most important project ever started here. Books, to the people who read, are the most important influence in a person's life. The books a person reads or fails to read determine what kind of success he will achieve in this life. The parent or teacher who instills in a youth the desire to read books, has already accomplished half of the job of raising him. For the person who reads books usually picks up a worthy ambition of one kind or another and if you can instill a noble ambition in a young person your worries over raising him or her are half over. Books can do this more than anything else.

Behind every successful man is usually a lifetime of good reading, for the reason that a well-read man is never a failure regardless of whether he is worth a red cent or a million. There are of course many men who have become rich who never cracked a book and who boast about it, but you will notice that the world usually does not regard these men as being successful, only rich. The lack of reading in a person, whether he is rich or poor, always shows to his disadvantage.

The best way to raise a child has always been, since Puritan days, to inspire him to read good books. You can't make him or force him, you must inspire him. You can beware of the man or woman who boasts that they never read a book, who boast that they have no time for reading.

I will admit that my reading until I went to college consisted mainly of dime novels, because the high schools I attended had no libraries to speak of, just a few encyclopedias, history and literature classics, but no novels, not even Dickens. When I was in high school, I thought that Harold Bell Wright was the greatest writer who ever lived. Somehow or another I managed to read all his books, but the only title that I can remember is *When A Man's A Man*. Once I read all the books of O. Henry I was positive that he was the greatest writer who ever lived. I remember

Fullingim his freshman year at Decatur Baptist College, 1918.

the summer I got the O. Henry books I planted a virginia creeper vine outside the window of my room and called it the O. Henry Vine, as a sort of monument to O. Henry. Then I went to the University and because my high school was not affiliated I had to take an entrance examination, and there on the campus was this great library. It came as a surprise to me. I did not know where to start. I was surprised that the works of Wright and Grey were not in the library catalogue. I never heard of the authors and titles. While in Cottle County in some way I got hold of a volume of Charles Dickens and I had liked it, even though I had to read it in a cave to keep my father from finding out. So I began to check out Charles Dickens books. That went on most of the first semester, and other students would look queerly at me, and especially the library assistants. But I was still loyal to O. Henry and Wright, and when I mentioned Wright to my English teacher, she regarded me tolerantly but with a certain resignation that I did not like. However, she suggested that I read *Anna Karenina* by Tolstoy. I have often wondered why of all the books in the library she thought of that one.

I checked it out immediately, both volumes, and for weeks I walked around like a zombie on the campus and in the Tri-Delta house where I worked. I had listened to Kate tell the story of Lena Rivers and I read slowly because I thought that I had to remember everything I read, as she did. I thought maybe I would some day have to tell the story of Anna Karenina to some person. It took me six weeks to read Anna and keep up my courses, too. But they were the most important weeks in my life. I actually finished *Anna Karenina* during the Christmas holidays. I was never the same after I read that novel. I was a changed man. I knew then why I would never again appreciate Harold Bell Wright or Longfellow or even Dickens as I had. Actually, I never read another dime novel of the Mary Holmes or Harold Bell Wright type in my life. Soon I checked out other books by Tolstoy. Then my teacher said, "You must read some other good books. There are others in the library. You are likely to begin thinking Tolstoy is the only man who can write. Check out a book by Joseph Conrad."

I promptly obeyed. Before the year was up I had read every

book written by Joseph Conrad, more than 20, I had become a Conrad devotee for life. In between I had read James Branch Cabell, Sherwood Anderson, Sinclair Lewis, Scott Fitzgerald (that was in the 1920s), but it was *Anna Karenina* that started it. It was the most important book I ever read because of the new world of reading it opened to me, and now I bless the teacher who told me to read it. I learned to read, and it was exciting and thrilling to realize that there I was only 22 years old and I had a whole lifetime of reading before me. I have never lost that attitude. It has never really made any difference to me whether I had money or clothes or cars or property. Nothing I have ever possessed could compare with the fine pleasure I have known in reading William Faulkner, J. Frank Dobie, *Moby Dick*, even William Dean Howells, Victor Hugo, Anatole France, and hundreds of others. I can now boast that I have read everything worth reading, or else I know about it. But mind you, I never really appreciated William Shakespeare until I had read, let us estimate, 10,000 books. Then he went to the head of the class and has stayed there. "First there was God, then there was Shakespeare and then there was Roosevelt." It's the books that you do not have to study in school, that is textbooks, that bring joy to reading. A forced diet is always distasteful, so the literature we are spoon-fed in high school becomes distasteful until years later.

How could I have lived without knowing the poetry of Keats, Shelley, Wordsworth, Poe, Vachel Lindsay and most of all Walt Whitman and even Amy Lowell and Robinson Jeffers and George Sterling. I know that if I picked out the single thing in my life that I have loved most it would be reading. Nothing really can touch me on account of the books I have read, not misfortune, not sickness, not poverty, not wealth, not success or failure. I have known the world of books and reading. I am not saying that everyone or anyone should be like me, or that I want them to be. All I'm saying is that good books have been the source of my ambition and my inspiration.

I have seen many men sitting on judicial benches, in governor's chairs, even in the White House, who never read, and I considered these misfits failures. I have known millionaires and multimillionaires who openly boasted that they never cracked a book in their lives, that they never read a novel or poem, and I have pitied these people. For truly, I would not exchange the memories of the books I have read for all the money that H. L. Hunt has stashed away.

Sometimes I listen to a high-salaried business executive or a bank president or a professional man, and I think, "If you had read Joseph Conrad's *The Secret Sharer* one day and *The Nigger of the Narcissis* the next and *Lord Jim* the next you would pause either in your darkening denunciations or in your platudinous plaudits, and you would see that far above and beyond the Organization Man and the Suburban Conformists is the highest human passion that comes to 'a man who has put reading at the pinnacle of all high adventures and endeavors. For if you have read widely and well, you have also thought deeply and truly, and no misfortune, no disappointment, no heartache can touch such a person."

Oh, I have not read all my life. For 18 months during World War II there were no books to read on those coconut islands, but I drew on past reading. But a strange thing happened during that time. I have never read poetry since World War II, but the memory of poetry before the war is a bright banner waving always before me.

THE DOCTOR BOOK   *May 4*

From the earliest time I can remember we had only three books in our home that my father bought. One was entitled *The Harp of Life*, a series of moral lectures that had a number of cartoon-like drawings in it. One of the illustrated chapters was the familiar story of the man who was being taken to the cemetery by his neighbors to be buried alive because he was so lazy he would not support his family. On the way to the cemetery, a neighbor offered to give him a load of corn. The man raised up out of the coffin in the wagon and asked, "Is it shelled?"

The companion book was *Mr. Worldly Man and Miss Church Member*, illustrated with Bible-like drawings. My father must have bought these two books early in this century, about 1906.

I remember when he bought our third book from a traveling book agent who sold from house to house. The book was *The Peoples' Home Library*, and it contained about 1,000 pages. It was bound in imitation black leather. From the time I was 10 years old until I was 17, I did more reading out of this book than I did out of the Bible. From the very beginning, we referred to the book as "The Doctor Book," because it gave symptoms and treatments of all the diseases that afflict man, animal and fowl. It also contained the first cooking recipes I ever saw in print, and it gave a complete description of how to make medicine from herbs. I used to read this section by the hour. We children never tired of looking at the color pictures of victims of smallpox, measles, scarlet fever and chicken pox. No one in my family ever thought of calling a doctor when any of us took sick, although we had an uncle in Decatur, just three miles away, who was a physician. We first consulted "The Doctor Book." If a cow or a horse got sick, the first thing we would do was reach for "The Doctor Book." I remember the time Old Chicken, a great frosty roan mare with huge feet, got in the cane patch and when we found her she was dying, her belly swollen like a balloon from the gas caused by the green cane. We got the book down and diagnosed her malady and knew exactly what to do. Puncture her belly with a trocar and let out the gas, and then drench her with the home remedy mentioned in the book, but it was too late and Old Chicken died. Her death depressed my father so much he stayed out at the barn for two days, only coming to the house at night.

TAXING THE WEALTH OF TEXAS   *May 18*

Let's take a look at our beloved state of Texas today, but without the rose-colored glasses of the professional Texan. Most of us grew up believing that we were more fortunate than residents of other states or nations on earth simply because we lived in Texas. That's the way we were raised, and most of us still are convinced that we could never live happily outside the borders of this great state. But there is coming a gradual awakening to Texans, as far as professional bragging is concerned. They no longer believe the hot air let off by the professional Texans, and these include newspapers, chiefly conservative, part-time Republican journals like the Beaumont Enterprise. The professional Texans also include our one-time governor, Allan Shivers, whose administration was distinguished by the theft of $25 million from the veterans land fund. Shivers has been the noisiest professional Texan, though Price Daniel has run him a close race.

The professional Texans like to say that Texas is a conservative state, that everybody is filthy rich, that it wants no federal aid of any kind, that its schools are the best, that it has the greatest resources, and that Texans are individualistic, that they actually govern themselves. That last statement is of course a myth.

The truth about the Texas state government is that the oil lobby rules Texas and has for years and nobody admits it, and there is no sign that the oil lobby's death grip in Texas is being broken.

Where is the wealth of Texas? It's in the oil and gas fields, and the sulphur mines, for without the oil and gas, Texas would be as poor as Job's turkey, but is this wealth being taxed in comparison, say, to the tax on new cars, TV sets, radios, cigarettes, beer or gasoline? No. The real wealth of Texas is not being taxed in comparison. Instead the oil lobby is spending money at Austin lobbying day and night to saddle a sales tax on the people of Texas. Will they force the sales tax down Price Daniel's throat? Daniel knows this time that he's right and the people know he's right, but the professional Texans, the oil lobby and the oil rich are going to count on the people keeping quiet. The oil lobby and the professional Texans nurture the myth that Texans are mighty individuals and bend the knee to no man, but we bent the knee to the oil lobby for a quarter of a century and are still doing it. We are spineless jelly fish when it comes to fighting back at our real masters, the oil lobby at Austin.

We will not tax their wealth, but we will let them tax the clothes we put on our backs and the food we put in our mouth. The oil companies have spent a tidy sum in recent years trying to prove to Texas they are broke, utterly broke, and brother can you spare a dime? And we have believed it. The oil lobby has actually made us believe that it's broke, but it still has enough money to finance the world's most high priced lobby at Austin. You see the oil industry is so rich that the tiniest tax would cost the oil companies millions. That's why the oil lobby can't afford to let the legislature vote even the tiniest tax on petroleum. Price Daniel is putting up a noble fight against the sales tax, but watch the oil lobby bring him to his knees.

THE LAST DAY OF SCHOOL   *May 25*

The last day of school is still a glorious event in the life of students, whether they be in the first grade or in the 12th. Last week, when the last-day-of-school fever began to stir, I remembered the last day of school at Pecan where I went my first three years. Pecan school was a one-teacher school about four and one-half miles northeast of Decatur. The school was abandoned about 25 years ago and the building was torn down shortly afterward. Now there are not that many people living in the area and much of the land is used for recreation.

I remember the last day of school during each of those three years, but the last day of the first two years stands out in my memory. My Aunt Frances Fullingim was the teacher. The last day of school was a big event. Long before the day started it was a game of wits between Aunt Frances and the larger pupils. The plan was the get to the unpainted schoolhouse first and lock out the teacher, but in each of the three years I went to Pecan, Aunt Frances won the battle. She always managed to get there first, each year earlier than the year before, and the last year she got there at 3 a.m. The first two years she took up school as usual with serious and deadly mein, and then all of a sudden, with a hoop, she cried, "School's out. We're all going on a picnic on Hale Holler."

Hale Holler was a sort of branch that meandered north from the school house which was surrounded at the back by post oak. There were a lot of possum persimmons on the creek. We would wade in the water holes and mainly just run and play games like Stealing Wood, Black Man and Stink Base. We would have dinner on the ground and we would run and play all day up and down the Holler.

But the third year was different. But as usual, on the last day of school, Aunt Frances got there first. She got up in the ceiling to await the arrival of her pupils. That was long before daybreak. Pretty soon, here we came, exulting that we had arrived before her. We posted one group of students a short distance from the school to yell back if they saw Aunt Frances coming through the woods. We posted another group to report if they saw her coming down the hill. Of course everybody walked to school including Aunt Frances who lived two and one-half miles from Pecan. We lived even farther. Some walked three and four miles and we would never think of riding.

Aunt Frances did not make her presence known until it was time to take up books, then she went to her desk on a little rostrum and began looking at papers and books. Finally one of the pupils saw her at her desk and then we all filed in without a word and took our seats. She began hearing classes. She was serious and solemn. No one protested. They were afraid to, for she was a strict disciplinarian, and she had tanned the hide and slapped the faces of the biggest boys in school. If she saw whispering going on, her favorite method of stopping it was to throw a stick of stove wood which she kept by her desk against the wall. It was up to her pupils to dodge it. Then she would make them bring the stick of wood up to the rostrum. Even the brawniest boys, and there were some big boys in that school, never knew whether she might floor them with that stick of stove wood. Whispering was rare. It was a serious offense in that school to take your eyes off your books for more than a minute. The school did not last more than six or seven months. The pupils had to stay home and help gather the crops, pick cotton and gather corn, and every minute in school counted to Aunt Frances.

She taught the last day of school that year until 4 o'clock. In previous years, there had been tearful farewells among the girls, and the boys would sit around looking wistful, but there was none the third year. It seemed the end of the world to a lot of pupils.

While I was going to Pecan, I got one of the two whippings I ever got in school. I deserved the one I got from Aunt Frances. We were playing what we called "Town Ball" in which if you struck at the ball three times and if the catcher caught it, you were out. Now attending this school, were the children of our neighbors, two German families who had come from Alsace-Lorraine. When we wanted to taunt them or make them mad we called them "Dutch." They had come to Wise County at the turn of the century to work on the courthouse, built of granite, as stone masons.

In this ball game, I was put out at second base. All the pitcher had to do was throw the ball in front of me to cross me out. I was nine years old and I yelled "Black Dutch" at the pitcher, who was a 16-year-old girl. Aunt Frances told me she was going to give me a whipping the next morning. I worried about it all night and my sisters didn't dare tell my father who would have given me another whipping. The next morning Aunt Frances sent me to Hale Holler to cut a willow switch. I brought back what was virtually a sapling. She asked me if I wanted her to beat me to death and sent me back after another switch. At recess, she whipped me with the switch until she wore it out and I cried all day. My feelings were hurt more than anything else. What made me mad was the way the "Dutch" gloated behind their big yellow-backed geographies when Aunt Frances was not looking. Oh, how I hated them that day. Of course I was young then, but that whipping may have been the reason that since then I have never made fun of people of another race.

A HUMILIATING JUSTICE   *June 1*

The political chickens finally came home to roost Saturday for the turncoats who have aided and abetted the Republican party in ruling Texas for the last 15 years, and I couldn't care less. It was a humiliating sort of justice for the so-called Democratic party that has run rough-shod over the brass-collars for 15 years. The election of John Tower as Republican senator from Texas has been in the cards for 15 years, for the politicians who have turncoated on the Democratic party were sooner or later bound to be turncoated on by the Republicans, their erstwhile bedfellows. So for weeks now we have had the astounding spectacle of these people screaming for loyal Democrats to support Blakley, a chief turncoat.

But the election figures show that the loyal Democrats either went fishing or went to the polls and voted for Tower to get revenge for the 15 years of double-crossing they suffered at the hands of Shivers, Daniel and yes, Lyndon Johnson, too. For Tower never could have won without the votes of at least some of the brass collars and liberals. Harris County is an illustration. There Tower beat Blakley two to one with the votes of vengeful brass collars and liberals. Harris County has always been a liberal stronghold.

The turncoats brought the defeat upon themselves and they deserved it. For 15 years, they spewed contempt at the brass collars and the liberals, deriding them for voting the ticket straight, making fun of them for voting for the party instead of the man. Then when one of their fellow turncoats ran against a Republican they began begging for party loyalty. It was the turn of the brass collars and liberals to laugh at the turncoats in 1952 and 1956. Oh, how the Beaumont Enterprise last week screamed to stick by the party because the worst Democrat was better than the best Republican.

The more I think of it, the more I like the way the election turned out. Tower, a radical turn-back-the-clock Republican, will go to the senate and do the expected. He will, when he can get his nose above the water, be buried on unimportant committees where he belongs. He will vote as a Republican. He will be as helpless as Congressman Bruce Alger of Dallas. He will be shunned by the Texas delegation in congress. Senator Yarborough will represent Texas and represent it well, without interference from Johnson, Shivers, Daniel or Blakley. We can expect Tower to vote against all progress and every minute item of the Kennedy program, but Blakley would have done the same. So at long last the worm has turned. The brass collars and the liberals did to the radical conservatives and turncoats what the latter have been doing to them for 15 years.

IT TAKES ALL KINDS   *June 8*

My old buddy, Richard Ward of Beaumont, druggist at the Kountze Pharmacy, is a busy young man these days, as busy as 799 ants at a picnic. In the last week he has bombarded me with a dozen pieces of mail, all in praise of the John Birch Society, the Dan Smoot report, the political views of Barry Goldwater or Tom Anderson (Farm & Ranch Magazine), or John Tower. Tower's election left him as happy as a hound dog full of potlicker. If Ward is not showing me rank partiality, one could reasonably expect that he's not passing up other citizens in his crusade to prove that "This is a republic, not a democracy; let's keep it that way." He has given me an opportunity to sign a petition against the recognition of Red China (which I did not sign, preferring to leave the decision up to Kennedy).

Ward makes some people as nervous as a long-tailed cat in a room full of rocking chairs, but I'm getting to where Ward has become so entertaining I wouldn't give a dime to see an ant eat a bale of hay, in reference to Ward, that is.

Ward has on hand a whole slew of film strips he has shown at three places, after he began running a want ad about them in The News. In addition to all this, Ward is a zealous vocal advocate of his beliefs and will get on the soap box at the drop of a pill. And nobody I've seen knows how to win an argument with Ward. The only way to save face is to hurriedly back away and then run. When Ward gets to banging into what he calls "socialism" you get the feeling you couldn't fight your way out of a paper bag, what with Ward counting out pills with his hands and ticking off American Communists in 2,000 word sentences. After listening to Ward five minutes, you get to wondering if he's as crazy as a bed bug in a hot skillet or as happy as a pig in the sunshine or as smart as a professor with nine degrees. On top of all his missionary work in behalf of John Birch and his one-man war against people he calls "socialists," Ward had time to manage John Tower's campaign here, although he lives in Beaumont and commutes to Kountze daily. Last fall, he was a devoted advocate of the candidacy of Neumann, the Beaumont Republican who ran against Jacks Brooks, and of Richard Nixon, but his heart was more in the Neumann candidacy. There are still Neumann stickers all over town. The Tower stickers were put up so expertly that they'll probably be some around when Tower runs for a second term five and one-half years from now.

As if all this could not keep a man as busy as a one-armed paper hanger with a runny nose, Ward finds time to write letters to the editors. One of his letters, which appeared recently in the Enterprise, assailed a Methodist Sunday School quarterly of the local Methodist church as preaching Communism. This made a lot of Methodists as mad as a worm in hot ashes.

Lately, Ward, knowing a good advertising medium when he sees one, has been advertising in The News, several ads per issue. One of these ads claims that this writer has written falsely about the John Birch Society. Ward leaves the impression that he's so mad if he spit on the grass it wouldn't grow for a year, but at the same time he appears to be as happy as a flea on a wet dog, when he's expounding the conservative point of view.

The other day Ward went into a local store and found some whisk brooms made in Hungary. That apparently made him as mad as a monkey in a jungle full of vines with his tail broken, because he went right back and came up with a written tirade against selling whisk brooms made in Hungary by "Communist slave labor." All of which made the store owner so mad he could chew up nails and spit out tacks.

The question now is: What does Ward do in his spare time? Well, it must take no little time to paste his two favorite slogans on the mail he sends out. They are, "Let's IMPEACH Earl Warren!" and "This Is A Republic, Not A Democray—Let's Keep It That Way." He even pasted the latter slogan on the check he sent me to pay for his printing. If Ward ever got off the John Birch Society and out of Earl Warren's hair and got into something like, say, getting an airport for Kountze, jets would probably be landing here in 30 days.

Well, it's a free country, and as the saying goes, it takes all kinds.

Ward advertises in the paper every week that I falsified the John Birch Society, when all I said, in brief, was that the John Birchers, according to both leading Republicans and Democrats, are nothing but a bunch of crackpots. But I'll add this postscript to my original comment. The way they go about fighting what they call Communism makes them the best friends of Communism in America today.

A WAGON RIDE TO THE MACHINE AGE   *June 22*

We are now living in a machine age. But our minds are back in the horse and buggy age when it comes to realizing the dangers that beset us in South America, Asia, Africa. Some of us are more concerned about the Freedom Riders in the South than we are about the leanings toward Communism in Brazil and India. Some of us are more determined to destroy democracy in America, especially in places in the South and North, than we are in trying to remove the reasons why a nation like Cuba turns to Communism. Some of us even talk about abolishing the income tax. Some of us want to go back to a loose confederation of states where every state has as much power as the federal government. We can't understand why the world hates us and we don't want to. We can't understand why a nation like Bolivia or Venezuela hates us, even though we financed the tin and oil operations in those countries that keep the people writhing in grinding poverty. We will not recognize that poverty stricken South America, Asia and Africa, all kept under the heel of a rich few for centuries, are now in revolt. They hate us because they know we have helped finance and keep their taskmasters in power, and while the whole world teeters toward Communism, we in the United States think we can ride it out in isolation. Right now, as never before, the nation is more against spending and foreign aid. When will we become aware that the world has changed from docile, subjugated have-nots to fiery, revolutionary have-nots? Will we have to be half-wiped out by Russia's rockets and nuclear bombs before we realize that the have-nots of the world are leagued against us because we have supported poverty of the masses in Bolivia and Venezuela?

Will we have to get run over before we come to? Will we be like the people who would not admit that the machine age was upon them? I was nearly grown before the machine age came into being, and I hated it. My father taught me to hate it. He hated cars and he simply would not acknowledge the invention of the radio. I did not learn to drive a car until I was 28, and I would not buy a radio until 1934. I was nearly the last person in Kountze to buy a TV set.

But I think my father and I became aware of the machine age at the same time. I was in my early teens, about 15, and he was 56. It happened on a long covered wagon trip in the summer of 1918 that took us some 300 miles from our home in Cottle County to the north Panhandle and back. And not one mile of that 300 was paved, but there were enough cars on the roads then to make a person riding in a covered wagon realize that he was behind the times. Up to that time I had lived in a world of horses and mules and wagons and team-pulled plows. I had ridden a horse to school. Everywhere we went we rode in a wagon. We had no more thought of buying a car than we had of buying an airplane, and I did not see my first airplane until 1919. Before we made this trip, I was not aware that the age of the horse and buggy was almost over. It took the trip to convince both my father and me.

There were as many horse-drawn vehicles on the road as there were cars and trucks until we reached what is now the Fort Worth-Amarillo highway. The dirt was deep on this road which was not graded, but a car would come along about every 30 minutes. We kept to the wagon ruts in the middle of the road and cars passing us had to make a new rut in the deep dirt in the ditch. At first, the horses shied at the cars but eventually got used to them, also to the long Fort Worth & Denver City trains that roared by. The highway followed the tracks.

Once we got on the high plains, we found that plowing was done by gang plows pulled by steam engines. We went on northeast to Miami, located in the gorge of the Canadian River, where we heard there was dirt fill work on the right-of-way, and we did get a week's work on the Santa Fe right-of-way, while the long troop trains filled with soldiers from Texas training camps roared by. We would stop work as these trains came through and the soldiers would crowd into the windows and wave and yell at us, "I'd sure like to trade places with you."

We left Miami and headed back south. In Donley County, near Lelia Lake, my father bought a crop from a farmer. We then drove back to Cottle County. We stayed a few days and headed back again to Donley County, about 150 miles in the same covered wagon, but this time my father brought along my brothers. It took us until the middle of November to gather the crop, pick the cotton, and head the maize. We left in a snow storm. I think my father made about $100 on the crop, not much more.

On the way, we used a different route, trying to avoid cars. It was through ranch country. My father had been over the same area in the 1880s as a cowboy on a cattle drive to Montana. He would try to figure out where the various ranches he had known were located. When we'd stop to water the teams, or when we'd meet up with another wagon or riders, he'd inquire about ranches with such names as "The Frying Pan," "The Mill Iron," "The Rocking Chair," and as the wagon rolled along, he'd try to recognize landmarks.

When we got home we began picking cotton for a neighbor whose land was sandy and which had been drenched in several freak showers that fell nowhere else. On November 11, 1918, we were picking cotton about 8 a.m. when we heard all the gin whistles blowing in Paducah about five miles away. Later in the day, we heard the Armistice had been signed.

My father tried to avoid all contact with the machine age, and to this day I also try to do the same. He yearned for the old days, even after he bought a car. He wanted to retire from it all. He wanted to go back to the open range. He wanted to repeal the 20th century, just as certain groups in the population today want to do. My father was engulfed by the machine age before he knew it, and we are going to be encompassed by the world if we don't set our sights off our own puny irritations and focus them on the world that is going to pass us by. The world has already passed the South by. Let us not permit it to pass the United States by. Let's look at the world long and steadily for a change.

HIGH SCHOOL RINGS   *October 19*

I saw the high school seniors wearing their new class rings—10 carat gold. They cost up to $32 each. Pascal Crosby, a local busi-

171

nessman, has never taken off his Kountze high school ring which he put on in the 1930's, except to have it made larger at one time. He doubts now if he could get the ring off, as it's a tight fit on his finger. He wore it all during the war.

PANTHER SIGHTED IN THICKET   *October 26*

A large panther, dark brown and weighing about 100 pounds, crossed the highway in front of J. J. Taylor, the depot agent, one afternoon last week. Mr. Taylor said the beast was holding his head high and loping, leaping about six to eight feet at a time. Mr. Taylor saw the panther cross the highway on the old Silsbee road at Village Creek.

It was not the first time the panther had been seen. Residents of the Haynes settlement had seen the panther. Mr. Taylor's first thought was that the panther was a lion that had escaped from a circus. He said the panther looked like a large female lion, except that it was dark brown.

Game warden Oian Davis said that one of the Haynes Settlement residents reported that the panther was seen at his hog pen and several out there reported they had heard the panther scream. Mr. Taylor said that it was a very dark brown and that the game warden said the panther would probably be nearly black in color after it sheds its summer fur. The hair takes a darker tinge in winter.

A number of panthers have been spotted off and on the last several years in the Big Thicket.

THE BIG RICH AND TAXES   *November 30*

About the same time that the fabulous Neiman-Marcus store of Dallas issued its restricted Christmas catalog, advertising a "wall of wine" at $5,000 to appeal to the Big Oil Rich of Texas, the Southern Regional Education Board reported that less and less is being spent for education in the South, including Texas. The South has fallen behind the rest of the nation in providing funds for college education. The board reported that 39 percent of the nation's college-age youths go to college, compared with 29 percent of those in the South, and that the annual amount appropriated for each student enrolled in public college and universities in the South was $599 ten years ago and is now only $624 compared with the nation's average of $821 ten years ago and $833 now.

The board said that financial help is needed from federal, state and local governments, and that voluntary contributions are needed from business, industry, alumni and church groups. That's what the man said and he had his facts and figures before him, and that brings up the question of how many of the Nei-man-Marcus addicts will order the "wall of wine" this year, a solid wall of fine imported wines, liquors, and champagne. Last year, Nieman-Marcus regaled the rich by offering "him" and "her" private airplanes. There are hundreds of gifts the catalog priced at from $5,000 to $50,000.

And the bragging Texans, straight from out of the pages of Edna Ferber's *Giant*, are to a man opposed to federal aid to education. They talk like Senator John Tower talked last week in Beaumont, Orange and Port Arthur. They want "local control" in education. To take it from them would be like taking a bunch of deer meat from a starving panther, that is without taxing them. And taxing them is about the only way you are going to be on equal terms with that "wall of wine" up at Neiman-Marcus.

Why are the John Birchers, the Republicans, John Tower and the Big Rich so opposed to federal aid to education? Their excuse is that it will end what they call "local control." For more than a century, the federal government has been giving federal aid to education and local control has not given up an iota of its power. There are land-grant colleges in every state in the union, all financed by the federal government, and there is no federal control over them. There are agricultural teachers in every high school in the nation, including Kountze, and federal funds pay part of their salaries and let me tell you, John Knierim and James Kelly don't have to answer to the federal government for what they teach but to the Kountze school board and the state board of education, as every teacher does. The real reason John Tower and his John Birchers and Republicans are opposed to federal aid to education is because they don't want the rank and file of people in Texas to have a college education; they want to keep them ignorant, illiterate and uninformed; they think that with an uneducated, illiterate Texas they can keep on buying their "walls of wine."

So let's quit hollering down a well and start spending more of that money that goes for the "wall of wine" on our colleges and in education. The rich don't want their oil wealth taxed to provide funds for colleges, rather they want to raise tuition in colleges, so only the rich can go to college. The education board quoted above may as well be hollering down a well as to ask for voluntary contributions for colleges and institutions from these people who buy the "wall of wine" and the "him" and "her" planes. These big rich are too busy attending cell meetings of the John Birch Society, and paying lobbyists at Austin to hold out for a sales tax to make us poor white trash pay the costs of education and state government. They are too busy attending their freedom forums and buying $100 a plate tickets to hear their darling John Tower rant against federal aid to education, President Kennedy's foreign policy and just plain democracy. Of course, these people are opposed to democracy—everybody is taxed in a democracy, and if they had to pay any more taxes they could not buy the $5,000 "wall of wine," their "him" and "her" planes, their mink and sable furs and their paintings. Last week Texas millionaires who don't know the difference between a snow scene by Grandma Moses and a "blue" by Picasso were at the big exhibit of art masterpieces in Chicago. It is now considered chic by the professional Texans, most of whom go off and brag how rich Texas is, to snap up works of art at half a million dollars each, but they don't have a dime for education, because they think that Texas colleges and universities are full of Communists teachers anyway.

Yes, a man is hollering down a well when he thinks the oil rich in Texas and industry are going to give anything to universities, and the only way we can make the real wealth of Texas pay its share is to tax it.

Texas is actually not a rich state as far as the people are concerned. There *is* fabulous wealth in Texas. It goes East to New York, Pennsylvania, New Jersey, etc. and it goes without being taxed. Those great corporations could give millions each year to Texas colleges and universities. They could, all right, but they don't. And they are the ones who inspire the jokes about Texans being so rich. Why, Texas is so poor that it had to pass a sales tax.

WALK WITH TRUTH AND BEAUTY   *December 14*

I nearly tore my house down last Saturday afternoon. I pounded on the walls, I broke a mirror, I smashed a $65 cobalt vase, I jumped up and down on the bed, I slid down the banister, and if there had been a bottle of anything in the house I would have killed it in nothing flat. The reason for all this activity was Texaco's radio broadcast of "Lucia de Lammernoor" with Joan Sutherland and Richard Tucker in the leading roles. Not since Amelita Galli-Curci have I heard a soprano like Joan, who comes from Australia. In recent years I've turned on the metropolitan opera house program in New York and seldom heard them through, but this time it was something. I've heard Maria Callas, whose voice is like quicksilver in a tube; I was thinking that I never would be moved again, but with the sextet my hair began to stand on end, and in Lucia's mad scene in the second act, brother I got with it. My sister Virginia Simms and I had her children and Dee regarding us with consternation, as we reacted wild-eyed and weeping with ecstasy to the voice of Joan which surrounded us and went through us. It was just what I needed in this world of non-everything: non-poetry, non-painting, non-fiction, non-music, not to mention nonsense. For a time I was a Birchite or a conservative, radical Republican wanting to go back to the 19th century in which the prefix "non" preceded only the word "sense." Poetry was poetry, painting was painting, fiction was fiction, and music was music. Now, fiction is only sex, painting is only for other painters, poetry is not for reading but for psychology. But better times are coming. I know it. I wouldn't have dared to write like this during the Ike years, or even the Truman years or the FDR years, but with our great president John F. Kennedy bringing the cellist Pablo Casals to the White House and Jacqueline bringing beauty to the White House in antiques and John Kennedy, the first president since Thomas Jefferson, openly admitting that he is a devotee of beauty, beauty in the abstract, I actually don't feel like an oddball in getting worked up over one of the greatest sopranos I ever heard. If the truth were known, I'd bet that John Kennedy and Jacqueline both were listening to Joan sing "Lucia." With a man in the White House of whom 78 percent of the people approve, we might shake off this "non" business that has come to shackle us. We may again, even in the shadow of the Tomb, walk with truth and beauty. I feel so grateful for Joan's and Tucker's singing that for the next three weeks I'm going to buy Texaco gasoline. As I said, with Kennedy setting the example, we might all again see the beautiful things of life. If you ask me, I think that Joan is aware of the new feeling in the country and is rising to feed it. And come next Saturday afternoon, I'm going to be glued to the radio broadcast of "Das Rhinegold."

YEAR ▌1962

THE DON YARBOROUGH, CONNALLY PRIMARY *February 1*

Texans who don't like the present sales tax and who don't want it increased or extended to cover groceries are going to elect Don Yarborough (no relation to Senator Ralph Yarborough) governor of Texas. And there are enough Texans in that category to put him in the governor's mansion, despite the pleas of Lyndon Johnson and Price Daniel.

The people of Texas gave Price Daniel a third term as governor of Texas because he promised everything high and holy that he would never accept a sales tax, but Price had got into the habit of turncoating on the people. He did it in the last session of the legislature. Don Yarborough is the only candidate in the race who cares a whit for the people of Texas. He is the only one who is talking to the people: the others are talking to Brown-Root Corp., to the Texas Manufacturers Assn., to the sales tax lobbyists and to the Big Rich who are rolling with glee because the poor folks of Texas are paying the sales taxes they ought to pay; they have the wealth but it is not being taxed.

Will Wilson daily lambasts John Connally, the Lyndon Johnson candidate. Connally is talking to the John Birchers and the radical conservative Republicans, who he wants back in the Democratic party. In fact, Connally's major mission is to keep the Democrats who vote Republican in the Democratic party, and to keep Texas lined up for Lyndon Johnson in 1968. In brief, Connally's mission for Lyndon is to keep Texas from being a two-party state. Connally is not even going to mention the sales tax in his campaign. You'll have to guess at what he means. But Connally, as governor, would rapidly sign into a law a sales tax on groceries. John Connally learned to toady to the rich when he was manager of Sid Richardson's vast billion-dollar holdings in Texas. He will not bat an eye in opposition to increasing the present sales tax or extending its coverage. As for Don Yarborough, he not only would veto any extension of the sales tax, but he will fight to repeal it. That's the No. 1 plank in his platform. Texans who believe in justice and fairness will have to vote for Yarborough. They won't be able to swallow Connally or Will Wilson.

Connally has done the dirty work for Lyndon Johnson; he has carried the syrup and distilled the vinegar in state Democratic conventions. He has toadied to the big rich; he palavers of unity in Texas, meaning that he wants the John Birchers to come back into the party and give up their notion of making Texas a two-party state. The reason Connally wants this is because if the John Birchers stay in the party then he and Lyndon and Price and Shivers and the sales tax lobbyists can keep on running Texas as they have ever since Jimmy Allred was governor.

I guarantee you that if Don Yarborough is elected governor, there will be the biggest public horse-whipping of lobbyists and sycophants for Daniel and Connally that ever took place in Austin.

Don't let the syrupy talk for unity by Connally fool you. He's as hard as nails underneath. He knows who's putting up the money to finance his campaign and he knows he's going to listen to them first. And don't let that false, synthetic crusade talk of Will Wilson impress you. He'll tell you who he's against (Daniel and Connally) but he won't tell you what he's for—he never has and he never will.

Don Yarborough is the kind of a Democrat that James Stephen Hogg was, that President Kennedy is. He is simply a no-handle Democrat, as Sam Rayburn described himself. The moderate Texas Democrats like to call that kind of a Democrat, if he is running for office in Texas, "an extreme liberal," but if he is running for president his liberalism doesn't bother them. But Don Yarborough will bother them; he has never turncoated on the Democratic party; he didn't support Ike and he didn't support Nixon, and to such radical conservatives anybody who voted for FDR, Truman, Stevenson, Kennedy right down the line is an extremist. So don't let the radical, right-wing talk that Yarborough is an extremist throw you. Any consistent Democrat is an extremist to them.

HEN FOR RENT? *February 15*

I saw Mrs. Jeanette Smith and she would like to borrow, rent, lease, either on her premises or somebody else's, a setting hen. She has a dozen duck eggs given to her by her next door neighbor, George Yeo. She lives on Williford Road, the third house east from the Printer. Will somebody hatch the eggs for her or loan her a setting hen?

WE NEED TWO YARBOROUGHS

Now comes that old master of the turncoat, Price Daniel saying that after three terms as attorney general, three terms as governor and 11 sessions of the legislature, including eight special sessions (that cost $8 million), he wants another term as governor to finish his program. At the rate he has moved in the last five years, it would take him three more terms and eight more special sessions to get his so-called programs enacted. While not admitting that his influence with the legislature has been lower than any governor's within memory, he gives you a hint how low it was in the last special session when he complains that he could not even get the legislature to appropriate $100,000 to repair the hurricane-damaged San Jacinto monument. Now everybody wants the monument repaired, even the legislature wanted to vote the money, but what did Price do? He slipped in a garage for employes that the legislature wouldn't swallow. The monument is one of the excuses Price gave for asking for another term.

But let's go back to 1960 when he ran for his sixth term. His alibi then was, "If you will elect me governor again, I'll huff and I'll puff and I'll blow the sales tax down," and the people, taking him at his word, believed him. Even I tried to believe him. But Daniel, true to his turncoat nature, at the end sided in with the sales tax lobbyists and saddled the sales tax on the people of Texas. His reward was the statewide TV hookup in which he announced for another term, else where did he get all the money to pay for the hookup—not from the people who pay the sales tax.

You ask me what's so ridiculous about a sales tax in Texas? I'll tell you, so bend down an ear. Here in Texas we are nine million bragging Texans, bragging that we have more millionaires, more oil wells, more bales of cotton, more Cadillacs, more mink coats, more "him" and "her" planes than any state in the Union. We brag that not only are we the richest state, but that all you have to do to prove it is drive for hours down the millionaire streets of Houston and Dallas, and go to Midland where they brag that 9 out of 10 are millionaires and all belong to the John Birch Society. We brag that we have all the wealth and what do we do, tax it? No. We saddle a tax on the two million people in Texas on relief, who draw pensions and old age assistance and social security. We make them pay the taxes. We tax poverty, not wealth, and Don Yarborough knows all this.

SMALL BUSINESSMEN AND POLITICS   *March 29*

My main interest this year in politics is in Don Yarborough's race for governor, and this year my interest is not the same as in previous years. I'm for Yarborough for governor because he's the only candidate who has the courage to say publicly what thousands of small businessmen all over Texas know in their hearts to be true—namely, that they are being squeezed to death by the monopolistic practices of huge, out-of-state corporations. This year I'm voting for Yarborough not because he is a brass collar Democrat, not because he is a liberal Democrat, but because I'm a small businessman and I know that if he's not elected and a sales tax on groceries is levied on the people, it's going to hurt all small businesses.

For almost 20 years now, merchants in small towns, up and down main street, have been voting for the candidate they considered stable, the conservative candidate, and he has usually been elected. The average small town businessman likes to think of himself as stable and conservative and so he has voted for the Coke Stevensons, the Allan Shiverses and the Price Daniels, and he has almost voted himself into bankruptcy. It's like Birdwell says, "I feel that I've had all the 'cheese' I can stand; now all I want to do is get out of the trap."

What the small businessman has not realized in his support of the Shiverses and Daniels and Ben Ramseys is that these candidates belong to the monopolistic, big business, out-of-state corporations that are making it hard for him to stay in business. The Daniels and Shiverses were elected by big business and financed by them and they owe their first allegiance to them. The present governor does not owe the small businessman anything, but he does owe allegiance to the men who pay for his TV time. A sales tax was wanted by the out-of-state corporations and that's what they got. I'm not saying that Don Yarborough will be able to repeal the present sales tax but I'm saying that if he is elected he will stop a sales tax on groceries and will remove inequities in the present sales tax, and I am saying that as governor the small businessman will have it better.

If Don Yarborough is elected, he will be beholden to the small businessman and the average citizen because that is where his money is coming from. So it is not surprising that his greatest opposition is coming from the lobbyists who saddled the sales tax on merchants and consumers.

THE BIG THICKET AND BIG GOVERNMENT   *April 5*

Why do Governor Price Daniel, the Beaumont newspapers, and assorted Republicans and John Birchers hate the federal government so much? I refer to Daniel's long, drawn-out warning recently that if the state did not pre-empt a good-sized chunk of land in the Big Thicket for a park, the federal government would. Daniel may not have realized it, but he sounded exactly like the John Birchers when he said that the federal government is the last thing we want in the Big Thicket.

Let's go into that a moment. The big difference between the federal government and the state taking a chunk of the Big Thicket and making it into a park would be that if the United States did it, we'd have a park that people from the other 49 states would know about and visit. It would be developed right, because the Interior Department is expert at the job.

Daniel appeared struck with sheer terror when he clamored melodramatically that the reason he proposed a Big Thicket state park now was because the terrible federal government, headed by that terrible President Kennedy, was going to preempt wildernesses across the nation and turn them into natural park wildernesses, and the awful thing about it, he hissed, is that any wilderness the government makes into a national park is going to stay exactly the way it is, except more so as time goes on.

He said the awful, landgrabbing federal government would have the Thicket exactly as it is, with no roads or trails. Well, what's wrong with that? For weeks, people in this area have been preaching that the best thing to do is to leave the Thicket as it is, and that to develop it would be to destroy the very thing we wish to preserve.

Well, let me tell you, when Daniel said that, he talked me right into believing that a federal wilderness in the Thicket would be better than any of Daniels' halfbaked plans. I say halfbaked, because his publicity agents at first led you to believe that he was going to exterminate Hardin County with a 400,000 acre park. Then he said 5,000, then 10,000, then 20,000, then he said what he would do is just form a Big Thicket Association, and appoint a committee to study tourist possibilities and make recommendations.

If the only way we can keep bulldozers out of the Thicket, and keep the state from destroying it, is to let the federal government take a chunk, brother, I'm ready for the federal government.

THE DOG CATCHER'S CANDIDATE   April 12

There is one big thing about John Connally's candidacy for governor that worries me. He has been able to set up organizations in 225 counties in Texas, he has spent more money for printing, billboards and advertising than all the other candidates combined and he is spending more cash for TV and radio time than all of the other candidates put together. He has four telephones in Fort Worth headquarters that costs $900 a month each. All of this costs lots of money. Where is John Connally getting his money? He doesn't say, and I did not ask him when he was in Kountze the other day, because he had already given a hint in his remarks. He told the dozen or so people at the fire hall that before he became Secretary of the Navy, he managed the billion-dollar estate of Sid Richardson and he had been associated with big money during most of his career. I got the impression that a lot of this money rubbed off on Connally when he announced for governor.

Now I am not worried or concerned that Connally is a friend of Lyndon Johnson, but where he gets the money to run for governor gives me a cold chill. In politics, a candidate's first obligation is to the people who finance his campaign. If his money comes from the people, his first obligation is to the people. If it comes from the big rich, his first obligation is to big corporations. No candidate can truthfully say that he will be governor for "the people" if his campaign is financed by the Big Rich.

I know where Don Yarborough's money is coming from. It is truly coming from the people. When Yarborough was in Kountze, he took up a collection and the first person to make a donation, the first man to walk out of the crowd and put a dollar in the hat, was "Red" Williams, the dogcatcher. That was symbolic of Yarborough's interest in the people and of his appeal. He is getting his money from the people. Wherever he goes he takes up a collection and that's how he's running for governor. Connally can't say that, because the people simply don't have the kind of money he is spending in his campaign. I listened carefully to Connally at the fire hall, and not once did he say that he would be a governor of the people.

I studied Connally very carefully while he was talking and answering questions. Connally stands in awe of money, more than anything else. He has absolute faith in money. He believes that it can do anything, and that's why Connally is so confident he's going to be in the runoff. He has the same look in his eyes that multimillionaire Bill Blakley had, and Blakley is still trying to figure out why, with all the money he spent, he couldn't beat Ralph Yarborough or Tower for senator.

Connally and Blakley have that same confidence that money can buy an office. Connally is a handsome man, in his dark blue suit with the last vest button undone. He has dark hair with a little gray at the temples, and he is a tall man. But his eyes are those of a man who has handled millions of dollars for other people and he has handled it well, so the eyes have come to have the hard look of hard money. There is something sinister about Connally when he starts telling you about how he handled the Sid Richardson millions.

For governor, I'll take the man who runs his campaign on the donation from the town dogcatcher. I'll take the man who hugs the dogcatcher just as fervently as he hugs the Democratic Hardin County chairman, whose father happens to be a millionaire. I'm proud that "Red" Williams, the dogcatcher, was Yarborough's first contributor here.

DEMOCRATIC PRIMARY   June 14

The sickness that afflicts most of the daily newspapers in Texas was never more evident than in the runoff campaign. This sickness is the daily press' devotion to special interest corporations and monopolies and its hatred of small business, workers, the aged, indigent and what it refers to as "liberals and labor." These daily newspapers, all of which supported Connally, have carped and complained for years that they are opposed to pitting "class against class," labor against industry, the poor against the rich, but that's just what they have been doing for 30 years. If there is a class division in Texas, the newspapers can be blamed, for the people they turn against in every election, roughly grouped together as the working class, have few printed organs of communication. They are voiceless in Texas as far as the printed page is concerned.

The essence of democracy is the majority vote of the people. Yet, daily newspapers in Texas for 30 years have ignored the majority vote. They support one thing and the majority vote supports another. That ought to make the Texas daily press stop and consider their tyrannical position, but it never has. FDR always carried Texas with nearly every daily newspaper opposing him, Kennedy won Texas with the press against him. Senator Ralph Yarborough won election with the daily press fighting him tooth and toenail, and even today his name is barred from mention in many dailies, unless it is treated in a derogatory manner. In the runoff, every daily newspaper in the state opposed Don Yarborough. It was the people against the press.

Isn't it time for newspapers to quit prostrating themselves before big money? How can they preach democracy when they ignore it?

LUTHER TIPPIN'S SOUL   *June 21*

The other day when I was writing a column, I remembered Luther Tippin, a Negro who worked as a farm hand and handyman for my father from the time I could remember until I was 14. We were living three miles northeast of Decatur in Wise County where both my parents were born. We made a living off this farm, raising cotton, corn and oats, but the money crop was cotton and there was not much money.

Luther Tippin was half-white and had blue eyes. Everybody knew who his aristocratic white father was. Because of his light yellow skin, Luther had to be very careful how he acted around white people. Remember this was only 45 years after the slaves were freed.

Luther had to be more humble and ingratiating before white people than other Negroes of darker shades. White people thought that a Negro with white blood in him would try to act white. Luther worked for white people, but he did not hang around them. When he walked from town to our place, he would cut through pastures and woods.

At that time, in the first decade of this century, there were not more than 50 Negroes in Decatur and all were either former slaves or children of former slaves. They worked in town for the rich or the well-to-do. Luther worked for the Waggoners when he wasn't working for us, and the Waggoners are still the richest family in North Texas. When Luther died he was working for the Waggoners in Vernon, and there was security for a Negro in working for the rich in those days. It was a sort of protection.

Luther was the only Negro we knew for years. He would go

home to his mother's house in the small Negro section of Decatur on Saturday night. He loved an ebony-black woman named Hector Mae, but he had trouble there, what kind I don't know, but he drank a lot and went on sprees. And sometimes we would not see him for weeks. When Old Matt, a mare we had, foaled a mare colt, my father named the colt Hector Mae and Luther acted as if he liked that, but you could never tell. He acted as if he liked a lot of things. Another time Old Matt foaled a mare mule colt and my father named her Maude after his brother's wife. This seemed to please Luther.

Luther often brought a quart bottle of whiskey from town on a weekend and hid it some place in the barn or about the barn where my father wouldn't find it. My father was a strict prohibitionist and voted for prohibitionists when they ran for office. He always voted against "Farmer" Jim Ferguson because Ferguson was a Wet. My father knew that Luther drank and he probably didn't like it, I don't remember. But Luther always had a job at our place after he had gone on drinking sprees in Decatur or in Fort Worth, which was 40 miles south. I don't think my father held Luther's drinking against him. I can see now that Luther had to live with the knowledge that he was half white and that his own father was one of the town's leading citizens, and that he had to abase himself every time he was noticed by a white person.

Luther every now and then mentioned the fact that he admired black Negroes, and one got the idea that he wished he was black. Later on Luther worked at a wagon yard in Decatur and we would see him there, and he was always friendly. I remember the candy he would bring us when we were little.

There was no feeling of equality between us. We were taught to believe we were better than Negroes. I can remember my father speaking scornfully of President Theodore Roosevelt because he ate with a Negro in the White House, but now I think the contempt in his voice was due more to the fact that Teddy Roosevelt was a Republican than to the fact that he ate with a Negro.

When we finished eating a meal, my mother would clear the table except for the victuals and she would set a plate for Luther nearest the door which happened to be at the head of the table where my father sat. Then she would call Luther who was waiting outside, and he would eat by himself, and if we children lingered at the table or in the room, we would be sharply told to get out of the kitchen and let Luther eat. That was the way he wanted it.

Luther had an odor of pipe and chewing tobacco, and where he slept on a cot in the hay loft the same odor was strong. It was a musky odor. He chewed Brown Mule tobacco, but he did not dip snuff, and he did not smoke cigarettes, most of which then were Prince Alberts which you rolled yourself. Luther liked horses and he said he liked to go to sleep with the sound of the horses below him in their stalls, chomping on corn and hay.

In those days, many people pretended to believe that Negroes did not have a soul. I have heard people refer to male Negroes as bucks and females as mares. I never heard them express an opinion as to whether a Negro who was half white had a soul, but I know now that Luther had a great soul.

Luther was a great help to my mother. When my father was gone from home, she was scared to stay in the house alone, even though she had five, six or seven young children in the house with her. Then Luther would come from the barn and sleep on the back porch. He would build the fire in the kitchen stove for her and he helped her all he could.

Luther also had a 21-jewel solid gold watch that he kept in a chamois skin bag, but he always knew what time it was without looking at his watch. We'd be hoeing cotton or corn along beside him, and would ask him what time it was, and he could tell you almost to the minute, and then we'd insist on looking at the watch, and slowly Luther would take the chamois bag out of his overall pocket and show us that the time was just what he said it was.

Luther was a tall, slender Negro and he did not sweat as much as my father who would get wringing wet with lathering sweat. Luther sweated but never through the watch pocket.

I wish Luther were still living and that I could talk to him again.

THE LOVE & WRATH OF OLD MATT   September 27

Pappy bought old Matt from Matt Clark long before I was born and he named her Matt. He always named his horses, dogs and even fowls after people that he both liked and disliked, that he held in honor or dishonor. A person whose name my father had given to one of his animals never knew how he stood in my father's opinion and affections. He named both a mare mule and a Jersey cow after Aunt Maude. He named old Pete, a white dog with brindle spots that we had for thirteen years, after one of his best friends. He named one of old Matt's colts Hector Mae, after the wife of Luther, a yellow Negro who worked for my father on and off for 20 years. He named a strawberry roan mare for his sister, Dolly. Mammy, a timid, retiring and conscientious woman, would reluctantly protest my father's habit of naming livestock after relatives and neighbors. She subtly imparted the feeling to her children that it was not proper, and we never mentioned the names of the animals around the people after whom they were named.

Pappy would invest in his animals and fowls the characteristics of the people after whom they were named. He used to say to old Matt, "You're just as stubborn as old Matt Clark," and to Hector Mae, "Now don't start puttin' on your hifalutin' airs around here; you're not going to feel so frisky tonight after I ride you all day." It got so that we were thinking that the people whose names he gave to our livestock and poultry had traits of character identical to those of the animals, chickens, turkeys and geese that were their namesakes.

Old Matt, when she was a 3-year-old, was the best trotter in the county and won the championship at the county fair, but I can't remember when she was that young. She was losing her teeth the first time Pappy opened her mouth and showed me how to tell the age of a horse by looking at the teeth. I know that he loved old Matt more than any horse he ever owned, and he owned hundreds of horses in his life-time, but he did not love her so much that he didn't lose his temper once and attempt to beat her. Old Matt had a stall of her own in the barn. She would never share it with another horse, although the stalls were built for two horses. One of the first things I remember my father saying to

188

me was that old Matt was such a she-devil that she wouldn't let any other horse eat in the same stall with her, but he would chuckle as he said it, and I knew that he was rather proud of her picayunishness, as he called it. So we children were proud of it, too.

Old Matt's heels were in the air the second another horse or mule even so much as looked in the door of her stall. It was next to the corn crib, and she was always the first one fed. When old Matt began to get really old we shelled the corn and soaked it for her. Pappy always fed old Matt until we boys got old enough to do the chores. Even then he'd try to make it a point to feed her. When we fed her she didn't like it; we never gave her her ten ears of corn that she didn't lay back her ears, toss her head and paw at the manger which held her feed box. Her ill temper lasted throughout the feeding. If the horses in the next stall whinnied or looked gluttonously at her fastidious nibbling, as they always did, she would let fly a hoof in their direction; a hoof not intended to hit the partition but flourished to let us and the other horses know that she could shatter it any time. Worse than that, she wouldn't eat all of her corn when anybody except Pappy fed her. She'd take several bites out of each ear and leave the rest. We saved these half-eaten ears only one time to show to Pappy. We hoped that he would starve her for a while, but he humiliated us right before her by feeding the ears to her by hand. Old Matt ate them nickering and neighing as if she were starved to death; her indignant glances at us implied that we were double-dyed villains.

"What did you do to this corn before you gave it to her, wet on it?" Pappy said to infuriate us further. He laughed at our fury, saying, "Good old girl," over and over.

The day that old Matt lost her temper completely my father lost his completely. We had fed her and she had acted as usual. We all were sitting at the dinner table when we heard a noise in the barn that sounded as if a demolition squad were at work on it. "That's old Matt—I mean Matt—kicking at Dollie; she's really going into conniption fits this time," I said. He never allowed us to call her "old" Matt in front of him. Right away he began blaming her fractiousness on us. "You probably did something to her feed," he accused. "Did you clean the chicken manure out of her trough?" "Yes sir, and her manure, too." Ford said.

Just then we heard timbers crashing, and Pappy lost his temper. His grey eyes clouded to a bluish purple and the pupils danced in a glaring expanse of white; his nostrils flared and trembled. He lunged from his seat at the head of our long dining table. He kicked old Pete who was sitting on his haunches behind him waiting for Pappy to throw him some morsel over his shoulder. As Pappy left the house on the run he allowed the screen door of the porch to slam, a first-degree crime in our household. Ford and I ran behind him, but at a safe distance. Mammy, as scared as Pappy was mad, followed us to the door.

"Oh, he'll kill her! I know he will. When he goes to hit her, grab the rail and hang on!" she pleaded. On the way to the barn, which was about a hundred yards from the house, he tore a thick branch from the mulberry tree and trimmed it as he went. "I'm going to teach her a lesson once and for all," he threatened between clenched teeth. Old Matt and Dollie were kicking at each other when Pappy reached the barn.

The partition had already been kicked down. It was obvious that Dollie had refused to be intimidated any longer by old Matt. Ford and I knew that when old Matt had let fly a scornful hoof at Dollie she had retaliated in kind. Pappy, bareheaded and furious, stood at the door of the stall and yelled, "You God-blasted old Campbellite!," Pappy's only oath and epithet, and reserved for occasions when he gave vent to superlative anger. He attempted to flail her hindquarters with a mulberry limb. He wasn't able to hit her but once. She had seen him as he stepped through the door of her stall, and just as he let go with the limb she started to nicker, but the blow stifled the whinny, and left a welt on her chestnut skin.

The effect of the lick on old Matt was terrible. Her eyes expanded to the size of white saucers with blue apples sticking to them and her nostrils looked like caves. She kicked sideways at my father with one leg and missed. He had to dodge and run out of the stall to avoid both hind hoofs which old Matt aimed at him as soon as she maneuvered into kicking position. As Pappy backed through the stall door he slammed it shut. She kicked it down a second afterward, then she methodically kicked down the side of the barn which formed the outside of her manger and feeding trough. In demolishing the latter, she had her head toward the door of the stall, and Pappy swiped at her a few times with the limb, but we knew that he was not trying to hit her. As old Matt's wrath increased, his decreased, and soon he was chuckling, spent by his anger, but he regarded my brother and me with distrust and distaste. He still placed part of the blame on us. He ordered us to go back to the house and finish eating our dinner. He stood outside the stall and watched us. We kept looking back until he yelled, "Get in that house and be quick about it!" We peeped through the window at him. We saw him throw the mulberry limb as far into the hog pasture beyond the windmill as he could send it. Then we saw him extend a hand and say loudly but gently, "Whoa, Matt! Old Girl! Whoa, Matt!" Then he went into the stall.

Pappy did not come back to the house until supper, and we were afraid to go near the barn that night to do the chores. The partition had been rebuilt, and all the boards old Matt had kicked out had been nailed back in place, but it hadn't taken him six hours to do that. Old Matt was curried and brushed until one could see his reflection in her coat, and Pappy was sitting in the manger watching her eat. "Feed the rest of the stock," he ordered, "and get a move on you!" He never mentioned the incident again and we were afraid to, but, and this is the truth if I ever told it, old Matt never kicked at Dollie after that.

Old Matt must have given my father a dozen colts in the 27 years that he owned her. Three or four of these colts were mules of which Maude was one. The others were either mare or horse colts. When she began to foal Pappy never allowed any of his sons, let alone any of his daughters, or his wife, to come near the barn. Pappy wanted Luther present but nobody else. Luther slept in a cleared space in the barn loft. He usually had a quart of whisky hid somewhere about the barn, and he'd tell us that if we ever came across it not to tell "old man Alf."

My father was a strict prohibitionist, and I never saw him take but one drink in his life, and that was one night when Ford and I were peeping through the crack of old Matt's stall, watching the foaling. I consider now that Pappy may have taken as many as two drinks on such occasions and occasions equally as important. One time while we were on a fishing trip over on

Denton Creek, an uncle of mine handed him a quart bottle. Pappy took a big drink, but before he swallowed it he looked down at Ford and me and then spit part of it out. "That's awful," he said, making a face. "It would kill you."

Luther always celebrated to the extent of a bottle when old Matt foaled. We knew that because when we'd ransack the barn the next morning we could never find the bottle, and we always knew where he kept the bottle. The morning after a foaling, Pappy would rouse us out of bed at daylight and yell, "Come out here you lazy no-accounts and look at Matt's new colt!"

The winter old Matt was 26 years old she got so poor that one could count her ribs. Pappy said she would pick up and fatten out when spring came and she could get some green grass. Spring came and old Matt fattened out only a little. She would still bring in the horses every morning from the pasture after my father yelled, "Quoap Matt! Quoap Matt!," just as she had done ever since I could remember. But she didn't toss her head and start for the barn on the run; her long red tail didn't fan out, but hung limp. Her ears pointed forward as of old, but her bangs didn't blow back from her blazed face. She would nicker louder than ever, but it was pitiful to hear. She would attempt to run, but her gait would be only a series of stumbles. We had been feeding her bran and shorts for years, but that summer she would eat very little of it. She'd hold it in her mouth until she got to the water tank, and then she'd rinse it out and mess up the tank. She just didn't have an appetite, and she looked worse every day.

We tried keeping her in the horse lot, and we strung a shade over a corner of it, but she got down and couldn't get up. We tailed her up and turned her loose to pasture again. Within a month she was skin and bones, and we had to tail her up every day.

One hot morning in August she didn't head the horses in from the pasture. They followed Hector Mae who was then about ten years old. Old Matt hadn't come in when we had finished breakfast.

"Matt's down somewhere. Go tail her up, and take a bucket of water and some bran with you."

"She won't eat it," I protested. "She won't eat bran."

"Do as I tell you," Pappy ordered. "And you'd better take some brown sugar with you if your Mammy has any in the kitchen."

We found old Matt down in the Bone Yard in the corner of the pasture where we dragged all dead animals. It was about a mile from the house. She was stretched out, head to the ground, tail thrown back and a small pile of manure, measly and hard under it. Seeing her we thought at first that she was dead; then, we saw that one eye was open and full of life. We saw, when we raised her, that the other eye was filmed with dirt, red and watery. We tailed her up. Hoot at the tail, Ford and Alf at the flanks, and I at the head. We stood her on her feet, but her hoofs caved under. She would make no effort to stand. We shoved the water half way up to her eyes, but she wouldn't open her mouth; she wouldn't even snort. Her teeth, the few that were left, were clenched and her lower lip hung away. Her eyes closed when we shoved the bran bucket under her mouth. She wouldn't even taste the sugar. We held her up for a long time reckoning that she was cramped and that when the blood got to circulating she would take hold. After thirty minutes we gave out and she crumpled to the ground. We went back to the house to tell Pappy.

"She's going to die," he said. His tone was the voice of goodbye. "Else she never would have gone to the Bone Yard. Let her lay where she is; don't move her; she doesn't want to be moved. And don't try to tail her up again. Poor old thing, I reckon she knew when her time came."

"Go saddle up Hector Mae for me. I'm going to town." He looked at me.

"The rest of you boys go over there and stay with Matt until she dies. Keep the flies and ants off her. Take the wagon sheet and build a fly over her and don't leave. Understand? Don't leave her. Take a bale of hay and spread it evenly under her."

The first thing he said when he came home late that night was, "Is Matt dead yet?" "No," said Mammy, "the boys are over there with her."

The next day he sat on the back porch and looked in the direction of the Bone Yard which he couldn't see on account of the rise across the canyon, but he wouldn't move a step in that direction. He nearly lost his temper when Mammy said at noon, "Why don't you go over there and see her?"

193

"You shut up and keep out of this," he answered. "I know what I'm doing. Matt was the smartest horse I ever had. She even had enough sense to go to the Bone Yard when her time came. Reckon she didn't want to be dragged over there behind a wagon as she's seen all the others. I'm not going over there. She doesn't want me over there or she never would have gone."

Mammy said he just sat there all day, and that once in a while he'd hum a snatch of "I'm Going Home to Die No More" which was the hymn they sung at Ma's (his mother's) funeral. He hummed that hymn all his life when he was sad, and all his children still have the same habit. Even now I never hum it that a feeling of utter woe and desolation doesn't engulf me.

We boys were making out fine over in the Bone Yard. One of us would go to the house for our meals which Mammy packed into a big water bucket, and we took turns about going down to the well for a jug of water. We drew up a system of eight hour shifts in which two of us at a time fought the flies and ants off old Matt. While two were on duty the other two could sleep, read, hunt or just fool around. We'd broken open two bales of hay, one for old Matt's bed and the other to spread under our quilts. We spread a wagon sheet over it all for shade to make it cooler. We made our bed right next to old Matt's so we could reach over and fight off the flies and ants with mops made of broom weeds. We sneaked the Victrola with all the Hawaiian records out of the house while Mammy and the girls weren't looking.

We built a big fire the first night, but when Pappy saw it he sent word over by one of my sisters to "put out that fire," and that if we lit another he'd tan our hides. We got around that by building a fire in the canyon about a hundred yards back of the boneyard. There we fried rabbits that Hoot killed during the day across the canyon. The third day Alf and Hoot had a big fight over who was going to get grub at noon. Ford sided in with Hoot and I with Alf and we all had a knock-down-and-drag-out fight. Then Ford and I made up and made them go after it.

That night, the four Walker boys, each of whom matched one of our ages came down from their place two miles up the canyon, and we played poker with matches. The card game also ended in a fight and the fight ended in a draw. That morning about 4 o'clock old Matt began breathing heavily; sometimes she wouldn't breathe at all, but she'd always catch her breath. We decided to give her water forcibly. Alf held her mouth open and Hoot poured water down it, but it did no good, the water just ran out of her nose. We thought she couldn't live through the day but she did.

The fourth morning we knew old Matt was going to die because the buzzards began circling high over us. They couldn't see her for the wagon sheet, but they knew she was there. It made us mad and sad at the same time. Hoot wanted to shoot them with his .22 but we knew that Pappy would give us all a good licking if we let him. He didn't believe in killing buzzards and besides there was a law against it. He went back to shooting at the prairie dogs. We were beginning to wish that she would die and get it over with. By the fourth day sitting up with her was beginning to get old.

Old Matt died that morning about ten o'clock. She just raised her head a little and tried to nicker, but she died before she got half of it out. She kicked about five times and pawed the ground a little with all four feet. Her bony, shrunken hips jerked spasmodically, then she trembled all over and stiffened. Seeing her die thus frightened us, and saddened us anew. I ran to the crest of the rise and yelled as loudly as I could, "Matt's dead!". I could see Pappy sitting on the back porch, and I knew that he couldn't hear me. He waved for me to come in.

The night the Walker boys sat up with us we had decided that maybe Pappy would want to bury her, but that was unheard of in our country. The Walker boys said people in Kentucky buried their fine race horses when they died. We knew that if Pappy buried old Matt people would say that he was balmy, but we hoped he would so we could brag that we had a horse so fine we buried it when it died. We were still talking about burying old Matt after she died. We left Hoot and Alf to keep buzzards off her, and took part of the stuff with us and went to the house. We immediately brought up the subject of burying old Matt.

"Are you crazy?" he said. "Go back and tell those boys to come in and bring the rest of that stuff. When you get back you can wash your Mammy's quilts you messed up."

The buzzards began settling as soon as we got out of sight.

Late that afternoon Pappy came in from a walk over the fields.

He talked about the cattle and the crops for a while. Finally, he asked Alf, and he tried to speak casually but the attempt unsteadied his voice, "Did Matt act as if she were conscious before she died? Did she do anything when she died?"

Alfred Fullingim

Mahala Fullingim

❧

TACTICS FOR A TWO-PARTY STATE   *October 11*

Democrats can take this old saying of the Negro race to heart when pondering whether to vote for John Connally in November: "Come here, black child, stay away from the poor white trash, they'll lick the 'lasses off your biscuit and then call you niggah!

In the past we've let the Republicans and anti-Democrats in the Texas Democratic party lick the 'lasses off our biscuit in November and then call us Red and betray our platform. We've elected them in November and then repented as they passed a sales tax, filled the insane asylums with poor folks who are not insane but who have no place to go, wrecked the oil industry for drillers and roughnecks, placed the colleges and universities in the hands of radical, right wing conservatives, and to cap it all voted for Republican presidents.

Make no mistake about it, if we elect John Connally who has never held an elective office, it will be Shivers and his crowd who will benefit. The "party unity" Connally talks about will be the unity of the old Shivers forces. Connally and the big rich corporations don't pay their fair share of the taxes and forced the sales tax on Texans. They will run Texas as they did in the Shivers administration. The brass collar Democrat will still have his biscuit but there will be no 'lasses on it.

Our job in November is to smoke out the Republicans from the Democratic party by defeating Connally, for we don't have a Democratic party in Texas in control of Democrats. We have a party which bears the name of our party but which is controlled by enemies. Shivers hasn't voted for a Democrat since 1952, and it was Shivers who gave Connally the 25,000 votes that defeated Don Yarborough in the run-off.

For 30 years, the anti-Democrats have been trying to make a Republican party, and if Connally is elected in November they will have succeeded. They have fought the New Deal, the Fair Deal and the New Frontier. What they want is a Republican party with a Democratic label. They want the Texas Democratic party to be what the Republican party is nationally. In Texas, these anti-Democrats are the No. 1 enemy of the party and their present leader is Connally with Shivers at his right hand, Daniel at his left, the Big Rich corporations at his back, and the humble, long suffering brass collar Democrats on the floor at his feet, ready to kiss the Connally foot in November.

What we need in Texas is Democrats in the party who vote for Democratic candidates for president, and Republicans who vote for Republican candidates. That means a two-party state. If a person can't vote for a Democratic candidate for president he should be in the Republican party. And that's why and where Shivers and Connally and their pals should be and the only thing that is holding them from being out and out Republicans is the brass collar Democrat whose vote they get and then betray. The only possible way of forcing these anti-Democrats who are in charge of Connally's campaign will be to join up with Republican Jack Cox and leave the Democratic party to the so-called Democrats.

Connally has perpetuated a fraud upon the party and no Democrat should uphold him in it by voting for him. The deception that he practices is that he fails to represent the goals of the national party. He represents those who are opposed to Democratic party aims. He was elected in the main by Republican-oriented, self-interest groups which paid his way to buy the vote in San Antonio. Instead of upholding the national Democratic platform he attacked the brass collar Democrats as Reds. We should not vote for a man who charges that the entire traditional Democratic party in Texas is Red. Connally himself voiced that lie by innuendo in a dozen speeches in which he said that Eastern "radicals" had come into Texas in the governor's campaign last summer.

Our first duty as Democrats is to preserve the party, not to vote for a man who is hell bent on destroying it. We know that it would be in the best interest of the Democratic party to purge the party of anti-Democrats and force them to join the Republican party. For if Cox were elected governor, wouldn't it be reasonable to assume that by 1964, he will have lured most of the anti-Democrats in Texas, who provided the majority that nominated Connally, into the Republican party? Cox would be preferable to Connally as governor only because Democrats could unite in opposing him in the legislature on measures inimical to the people, and Republicans could unite in supporting Cox. That alone would separate the Democrats from the Republicans. The anti-Democrats could support Cox, forcing potential Republicans who nominated Connally to join the Republican party, thus making it a two-party state, and leaving control of the Democratic party in traditional hands.

YEAR 1963

The Texas State legislature has been in session at Austin for
three weeks now and the pattern of action or lack of action to
come is beginning to become clear. The outstanding personality
is not going to be the governor, John Connally, but a dedicated
servant of the corporate powers of the state, the speaker of the
House, Byron Tunnell of Tyler. The first appointment of Connally, three members to the University of Texas Board of Re-
gents, indicates that Connally is not going to appoint John Birchers as did his predecessors, Daniel and Shivers. Connally is out
to take over the brass collar Democrats, liberals, Mexicans,
Negroes and all of us poor white trash. He's out to swallow us up.
So many rank and file conservatives have bolted to the GOP that
the Big Money candidates are no longer able to treat our side like
Shivers did throughout his long political career, and as Daniel
did in 1952 and 1956.

Connally and his Establishment have got to get the liberal,
labor, Latin, Negro, brass-collar and poor white votes. So Connally is out to try and con us. And this is the great danger. It has
now become apparent that Tunnell is going to try to do in the
House what Ben Ramsey did so long in the Senate as lieutenant
governor and presiding Senate officer. Tunnell will try to destroy any attempt to pass liberal legislation that would benefit
anyone except the corporate interests. He is the most dangerous
man from the standpoint of the peoples' interest the house has
had in recent decades.

It looks as if Tunnell will be Connally's hatchet man, the man
Connally can hide behind. So Connally is not going to be an easy
target. Connally is not the least interested in the semantics of
liberalism vs. conservatism. He is only interested in retaining
control of Texas state government through the instrument of
the one-party system. Connally's establishment aren't Birchers

and fanatics. They are the suave, sophisticated corporate-executive types, and when they, in the past, had to use Shivers' tactics to beat us, they used Shivers' tactics; but with so many conservatives bolted to the GOP primaries, the Shivers-type tactics no longer worked so the establishment came up with Connally. His tactics are sweet talk, big promises, and efforts to placate our side of the fence, while retaining the one-party system and the corporation government which it makes possible.

If you had to pinpoint Connally you could call him a "modern Republican." That's essentially what the establishment is, "modern Republican." They go for the rhetoric of governmental structural reform; they like the language of modernization and progress, and they abhor fanaticism. They are the corporate-executive types, not Birch screwballs. It is going to be a real challenge to the people who feel the sales tax is unfair, the people who want more aid for the aged, who want no increase in college tuition, to prevent Connally from destroying the liberal movement with sweetness and light. But the kind of people who voted for President Kennedy and Franklin Roosevelt ought to be aware of something for good: that Connally is not a New Frontier Democrat. If anything, his type of "business-progressivism" is a form of modern Republicanism. He is not an easy attack target now that he's in office and my greatest regret is that we didn't beat him last year. For he is going to be more dangerous to Texas than either Shivers or Daniel.

THE GHOST ROAD *March 28*

Mrs. W. E. Ayres who lives at Bragg in the old hotel on the Santa Fe railroad a dozen or so miles west of Kountze was here last Friday to pay for her subscription, and when she left Charlie Stappenbeck of Houston, who was in the printing shop installing a press, said, "You know, that little old lady is remarkable. You don't meet people like her often. She must have been here a good half hour and she stood there by that table and in all that time she never complained once. You heard her say that she had a stroke and that her speech is a little effected by it, but she never recited her ills and woes nor complained one time.

"A lot of times you meet elderly people," Charlie went on, "and if they are not cussin' the government, they are cussin' somebody who did them dirt, to hear them tell it. But that little old woman, just five feet tall, was wonderful. I could listen to her all day."

A lot of people know Mrs. Ayres, who has lived at Bragg 54 years. She is a native of North Carolina and came with her husband to Bragg in 1908. He was a station agent on the Santa Fe there. The trains used to stop at Bragg, where Mrs. Ayres operated the hotel and dining room and was famous for her cooking. There used to be considerable switching facilities at Bragg. A spur railroad ran southwest to Saratoga, but long ago that track was removed and the roadbed became the famous Bragg ghost road where strange balls of light move up and down the road. Periodically, they arouse much interest.

The most recent renewal of interest in the Bragg light was several years ago when thousands drove up and down the dusty road hoping to see the "ghost" light. Mrs. Ayres is confident that the light is a reflection of car lights from the Saratoga end of the road; she believes that cars traveling on the Saratoga-Votaw road reflect their lights down the Bragg road. However, she concedes that the light could be gases from the swampy terrain near Bragg.

"Many's the time," she said, "I have seen jack o'lanterns-luminous gas rising in balls from the earth, all over the place, in a low spot near my home."

Many people say that the lights were seen before the invention of automobiles. Geologists from Houston and Beaumont have said that the light is caused by gases rising from the Big Thicket swamp. The Bragg "ghost" road runs as straight as an arrow through the heart of the Thicket. It is one of the most picturesque roads in the Thicket, with tree branches meeting overhead and flowers of the Thicket shining the length of the road.

DOG SURVIVES 24 DAYS IN WELL   *April 4*

Sissie, a Walker hound, survived 24 days in a 14-foot well by eating almost every scrap of a 10-point buck that fell into the well with her. The hound, owned by J. O. Hicks of Silsbee, was rescued by Sam Collier, Negro, the last day of the squirrel season when he was hunting squirrels.

Sam Collier heard a hound baying when he parked his car near the old square well. He went out into the piney woods and killed five squirrels and when he returned he heard the hound again. This time he remembered he once lost a dog in a well and he went to the well and looked in. He saw the hound and went after help, a rope and a chain, and fished the dog out. He had a pretty good idea that the hound belonged to some of the Hickses.

Mr. Hicks, owner of Sissie, figured that she was hanging on to the big buck when he lunged into the well. During the 24 days Sissie picked the deer carcass clean, and Mr. Hicks, who was in the News office last week, said she was in good shape. He figured Sissie got a drink of water now and then when it rained and water ran into the well. Mr. Hicks lost Sissie the Saturday before Christmas when he was hunting between Spurger and Town Bluff. A short time after he took her into the piney woods she jumped. That was the last he saw of her.

When Sam Collier found her, the buck's antlers were caught under some roots in the well. Else, he figures the buck would have stomped and horned Sissie to death. Sam sold the antler rack to a Beaumont man for $20, said Mr. Hicks. Mr. Hicks said there are eight open wells in that vicinity and when hunters lose dogs they might look into these wells.

Mr. Hicks said that after he lost Sissie he lost all his spirit to hunt; she was a good homing dog and he knew something had happened to her. He hunted her every day for weeks, and he said he had no spirit to hunt any game with her gone. Once while hunting Sissie, he saw Bozie Newman parked on the side of the road and stopped to ask him if he had seen her. The well Sissie was in was only a few hundred feet from the spot.

SICKENING OPPRESSION IN BIRMINGHAM   *May 9*

It's hard to believe that what's going on in Alabama, Georgia and Mississippi is not taking place in Communist countries like Red China, Hungary, East Germany, anywhere but not in the United States. For in Birmingham, Alabama, police are sicking ferocious police dogs on citizens, jailing hundreds of children, some of them first graders, maiming women and teenagers with the crushing force of powerful water hoses, while some white policemen are screaming in glee, "Watch them niggers run when we sicked the dogs on 'em!"

It's hard to believe this sickening oppression is taking place in the United States of America. Freedom? There is no freedom for the Negro in Birmingham. The inhuman treatment being given the Negro in Birmingham matches any tales of torture that have come out of Communist police states. Why? All this to prevent peaceable marching to the city hall in Birmingham to ask for the vote and to register to vote. But Alabama, Georgia and Mississippi do not want to give the Negro the vote. It will do these inhuman acts of cruelty to deny the Negro his legal right to vote, guaranteed to him by the Constitution, for those states are defying the Constitution and they are flying in the face of Christianity. These states do not recognize that the Negro is a free man. He is no longer a slave. He has a right to parade and picket. He has a right to march to city hall. You can parade and picket before the White House in Washington, D. C. It is your right as a free citizen, but the Negroes in Birmingham can't march to the city hall to register to vote. The city of Birmingham is digging its own grave in dealing out misery, cruelty and injustice to children, women, teenagers, anybody just so they are black. Freedom to vote will eventually come to the South.

John Kennedy does not have to send an army to Alabama, for that state stands condemned before the entire world. The persecution of the Negro in Birmingham is for all the world to see and look on in horror as the police urge the ferocious dogs to bite women and children, all to keep them from picketing for the right to vote. Public opinion will eventually bring Alabama to its knees.

In Alabama these days anyone who does not enjoy seeing giant dogs sicked on Negroes, who does not enjoy seeing people knocked out and maimed with crushing streams of water, who protests the shooting in the back of a marcher at night on a lonely road, anyone who does not approve of all this is called a nigger lover. And what's so wrong with that? In my books, you are a patriotic American if you love all the people in it. You can't hate a fourth of them.

THE POOR FOLKS' ORGANIZATION   *May 30*

Back a few years ago when Harry Truman was President, so the story goes, he and wife, Bess, and daughter, Margaret, went walking through the White House grounds one Sunday afternoon. Ole Harry, with the practiced eye of a Missouri farmer, looked around and said to his wife and daughter, "This grass sure does need some manure."

Margaret turned to Bess and said, "Oh, mother, can't you make him say fertilizer instead of manure." Bess looked at her daughter and said wistfully, "It's taken me 20 years to get him to say manure." It's going to take me 20 years before I'll even say manure to this "unity and harmony" line of hog-wash which the Johnson-Connally-Corporation clique is trying to peddle to the real Democrats of Texas.

Do you know why John Connally, Byron Skelton, Eugene Locke and the other servants of the Establishment which LBJ and the Corporation dominate are so strong for "unity and harmony?" It's because their political house, the one-party system, is about to come tumbling down and they are trying desperately to save it for a few more years.

The establishment, the big corporations, big city banks, major oil companies and utilities which have used the one-party system to control Texas Government and the Texas Democratic Party for 30 years hasn't got many votes. Sure, they've got lots of newspapers, lots of money, lots of power and influence, but doggone few votes. Not many just plain folks deep in their heart took to Lyndon Johnson, John Connally, Jim Wright, Ben Ramsey, Preston Smith, Byron Tunnell and other corporation government pretty boys as their political heroes.

Fact of the matter is, there are just two really effective precinct organizations in Texas which are based on pure idealism and devotion to principle. One of them is the Poor Folks' Organization—the folks in all 254 Texas counties who go all-out for Ralph Yarborough because he stands for government of, by, and for the people. These are the same folks who came within 25,000 votes of putting Don Yarborough into the Governor's mansion over the opposition of the Dallas Morning News, the Dallas banks and insurance companies and corporations, the Houston Post, the Houston Chronicle, and the whole dadblame corporate power structure.

The other great body of political combat troops belongs to John Tower and Jack Cox. These are the Republicans, nuts, screwballs, status seekers in suburbia, and people who want to repeal the 20th century because they can't understand it and think it's costing them money. This motley crew used to vote for Allan Shivers in the Democratic primary and they used to be the only big voting bloc which LBJ could count on to maintain corporation government. But with Tower's election all these people began moving into the Republican primary, where they belong.

Poor Lyndon, poor Connally; ain't nobody left in the Texas Democratic party who really loves them anymore. The Republicans have finally joined the Texas Republican party, and they can't be counted on to keep corporation government entrenched like they used to when they voted in the Democratic primaries.

Lyndon and Connally are about to lose control of the political power structure which they erected for the corporate power structure. Doesn't that just bring tears to your eyes? It's about to drive the Dallas Morning News nuts. You see, the Dallas News is not really a Birch rag. It's really just a mouthpiece for the establishment. It has to spout that daily stream of anti-20th century editorials in order to build up its credit with the nuts and status seekers who populate the Dallas area. Then when Connally opposes Don Yarborough it tries to call in this credit and editorializes in favor of Connally and other corporation-government candidates. But with the coming of the two-party system the heat is on the corporation journals. They've got to sound conservative enough in their daily editorials (or, in the case of The Houston Chronicle, liberal enough) to keep their readers happy, and at the same time convince them that Connally and Johnson and Preston Smith and Ben Ramsey deserve their votes.

We don't want to unify with the Texas Democratic party as it now exists, because us Po' folks are on the threshold of taking it over and rebuilding it completely so that it will resemble the national Democratic party. Heck, there's less than a dozen real Yarborough Democrats on the state Democratic executive committee. Its chairman is a corporation lawyer; its secretary is a corporation lawyer; and its vice chairman is a daughter of one of the Browns of Brown & Root. Great bunch of Democrats, eh?

One night in April of 1957 when Ralph Yarborough was first elected to the U. S. Senate (despite LBJ's efforts to gut him) he stood up on a table in his state headquarters in Austin and told the crowd that his was just the first of many victories which the people would win in Texas. Ralph was right. That victory made the Po' folks—the white Po' folks, the black Po' folks, the brown Po' folks, the Po' folks with a union card and the Po' folks with a plow—look to Ralph Yarborough as their champion because he stands for the principles of the national Democratic party.

Under the leadership of Ralph Yarborough the Po' folks are about to reclaim the Texas Democratic party; we're about to elect many other public officials to replace the corporation stooges which the one-party system has foisted upon us during these past years. LBJ and Connally know this. And when you get right down to the Brown and Root of it all, that's why they and their henchmen are so diligently preaching "unity and harmony." That's the only way they can possibly maintain corporation government and corporation control of the Texas Democratic party for a few more years.

Why, you know Lyndon and Connally are so scared that they've even started to give the Po' folks a few crumbs off the table. Lyndon quakes in his Neiman-Marcus boots every time he remembers that Don Yarborough came within 25,000 votes of beating Connally. And he starts to quake all over when he thinks about the cinch reelection of Ralph Yarborough next year. He starts to quaking and shaking and then he starts to spur on his boys to shout "unity and harmony" a little louder. It's the only hope they've got, and if it doesn't work then LBJ and corporation control of the Texas Democratic party are gone forever.

These are the reasons it'll take me at least 20 years to believe that "unity and harmony" have the same vitamin-giving aroma as a good, honest truckload of sweet-smelling Hardin County manure.

Watch out for anyone who tries to tell you that the Texas Democratic party needs "unity and harmony." He's either a poor guy who just doesn't understand the forces of change at work in Texas politics or else he's a political manure salesman.

THE ALL-TIME CLASSIC ERROR

Mrs. Cecil Overstreet and I had another good laugh about the crazy turn a want ad she had put in the News took after the Printer took it over the phone while a job press was running.

Mrs. Overstreet was advertising a pair of parakeets for sale, but the way it came out in the want ad was "a pair of teeth for sale." That was the News' all-time classic error. This time Mrs. Overstreet was in to announce that the annual Gardner picnic will be held Sunday at the roadside park at Warren, and we hope we don't make any mistakes in announcing it.

A PINE FARM OR BIG THICKET WILDERNESS?   June 27

Now that the eventual extinction of the Big Thicket appears not only possible but highly probable, the time has come to make a realistic, scientific evaluation of the storied Thicket. We need to know if the Big Thicket is worth preserving, not only as a treasure trove of flora and fauna, but as a tourist attraction. We need to separate sentimental considerations from the economic facts of life. We talk aimlessly about preserving the Big Thicket, its fauna and flora, but we do not know exactly why we talk that way, except that it is a pet subject of newspaper columnists and nature lovers.

The time has come to decide whether it would be economically sound to preserve the Thicket. That is, to set aside thousands of acres to keep intact a natural wilderness. The question is, do we want the Big Thicket to stay as it is, or do we want to destroy the hardwood growing in it, and transform it into a profit-producing pine forest. There is a compelling reason why we must make a decision soon about the future of the Big Thicket. Land taxes have been increasing for years and are going to continue to increase. That means one thing: the land companies have got to realize a profit from the land, and if they are going to do that they have to grow more pine timber in the Thicket.

In order to grow more pine timber in the Thicket, the underbrush and hardwood must be destroyed so that pine can spring up and grow. The big land companies, about a half dozen in number, and some individuals who own the Thicket, all know this. They know that in order to make their land produce a profit in timber they must kill out hardwood and produce pines. Cy Williams believes that from now on more and more Thicket land owners are going to do as he did this month: spray his Thicket land from the air and kill out the underbrush and hardwood. Cy Williams says that the land in the heart of the Big Thicket must produce a greater profit in pine timber in order for the owners to keep on paying higher and higher taxes and also make a profit out of growing timber.

Cy Williams was only resolving an economic necessity when he killed the hardwood growth in a section of tight-eye Thicket. He said he had to make his land produce more revenue from timber and to do this he had to kill out the hardwood so the profitable pines could take root. Now, Cy Williams is not a sentimental man. He is a sawmill man and a timber man, and he has a hard eye when it comes to making a dollar, either a fast or a slow buck. He has several thousand acres in Hardin County, and he looks upon that land solely as a producer of revenue. He does not look upon the Big Thicket with sentimental postures. He sees the Thicket as a place seething with mosquitoes, briars, snakes, bugs, intolerable heat—a place where no one in his right mind would go for a picnic, or hike, or camp, to look for rare plants or bird-watch. But here I am trying to tell you about Cy Williams. You know him. He lived here for years and ran the sawmill. But Cy Williams did not acquire his land in Hardin County for sentimental reasons. And the same can be said for Kirby Lumber Corporation, Nona Mills, East Texas Pulp & Paper Company, Champion and the other big land companies which own 85 percent of the land in Hardin County. Sooner or later, it now appears that these companies are going to consider doing what Cy Williams did—kill the brush and the hardwood trees that give the Big Thicket its name, for there can not be a Big Thicket with only pines growing in it.

Spraying the Thicket with deadly poisons will mean the end of the Thicket as we know it and the odd thing about it is that we may like it better that way. That is the thing we've got to find out.

Now various people, notably Joe Combs, Price Daniel, Lance Rosier and others have talked about preserving the Thicket. Price Daniel wants to make it into a park, and so does his pal, Lance. Joe Combs inclines to the idea of keeping the Thicket intact without benefit of a park.

We have always opposed building a park in the Thicket and still do, for the best way to destroy the Big Thicket would be to try to develop it. The only logical way to preserve the Thicket would be to keep it in its wilderness state, and that was our argument two years ago when we went against Price on his idea of a Big Thicket park with trails, campsites, and roads. For once you attempt to build roads, paths, trails, or camp sites in the vastnesses of the Thicket, you would destroy that which we want to keep intact: the wilderness state. But it begins to look now as if the argument we put up two years ago, that is to let the land companies keep and preserve the Thicket because they are the best custodians, will not pan out. For if the land companies consider plans to spray it with the deadly poisons to kill out the very thing that makes the Thicket, then we must make the decision: Do we want to preserve it or turn it into a pine forest?

Let's get down to cases and quit the sentimental talk. If we decide that we want to turn the Thicket into a pine forest for the economic benefit of the county, then let's give Cy Williams a pat on the back. But if we find out that it is vitally necessary to preserve the Thicket for the good of Hardin County, then let's sue hell out of somebody every time they loft a spray gun in a helicopter. If we decide that we want to keep the Thicket as it is as a tourist attraction, let's get the Thicket designated as a wilderness area and ignore all talk of government encroachment and socialistic spending and of course we would have to ignore the gas erupting from that fountain of radical right wing conservatism, Senator John Tower, who would likely oppose it.

In brief, let's make up our mind if we want to keep the Thicket. Now is the time; let's put up or shut up.

THE BIRMINGHAM TRAGEDY

The inflammatory statements of Governor George Wallace of Alabama and his defiance of the law of the land can be blamed for the death of the four children in the Birmingham Negro church bombing. He can be blamed for the death of the two Negro boys shot by white police and white teenagers on the street Sunday, for the governor was the leader in flouting the law. Now he offers a reward, but he doesn't mean it. There have been 22 bombings of Negro homes and churches in Alabama and not a single arrest made. The governor does not want any arrests or convictions and that goes for the mayor who shed crocodile tears. Now a federal judge wants to indict. Let him start by indicting the governor, the brutal Birmingham police and the mayor.

SILLY TO CRY   *July 17*

Finally old "Red" Williams, the town dogcatcher, just sat down with the little girls at the elementary school and cried, remembering all the heart-breaking letters he received from them. This all happened after "Red," true to his word, picked up all the stray, untagged dogs he could lay a hand on. Then he was told about the little brown female dog at the elementary school.

He came to find out that the little dog had been adopted by a group of small girls, and when they learned that "Red" had picked up their little brown dog, they sat down and penned him these letters:

Dear Dogcatcher,

If we get our dog back we will buy him a collar. If you don't know which dog I am talking about it's the one you got today at school. Please do not shoot him. Please do not shoot him.

> *From: Sue, Debbie,*
> *Sandy, Frances, Carol,*
> *Mary, Beth, Kath.*

Dear Mr. Williams:

I am one of the many that was crying this morning when you got Brownie. The first time we saw her we started feeding her and that's the way it all happened. Every time something had happened to her we tried to help her any way we could. She was brown and we are Girl Scouts, so we named her Brownie. If we get her a collar and you give her the shots she needs, may we have her back, Please! Please!

One of The Sad Ones

Dear Red Williams,

I know you know my daddy. He is Ben Williams. I am one of the girls who came to say goodbye to the dog. I know it was silly of me to cry, but the dog was kind to us. I am not mad at you but will you keep good care of the dog. For me. Please. We all love him. Do not kill him.

Love always,

Suzanne Williams

When "Red" read the letters he beat it to the office of Principal James Heaton, Jr., his eyes awash, clutching the letters. The soft-hearted "Red" wanted to do something. The dog was in the pound, but he was not going to kill her, not after all those tears and letters. Mr. Heaton said he would give a dollar toward buying her a tag and getting her vaccinated and spayed and "Red" gulped that he too would gladly give a dollar and then the Printer, when he read the letters, gave a dollar, but they need a few more, so if you want to help save the dog for the little girls, call up Mr. Heaton and see if he has enough money.

LBJ LINES UP TROOPS FOR KENNEDY VISIT   October 10

Fifteen years ago in the summer of 1948, I spent considerable time, money and sweat campaigning in the post oak belt of central Texas for Lyndon Johnson who was running against Coke Stevenson for the U.S. Senate. My newspaper (which was about the smallest weekly newspaper in Texas) was one of three papers in Texas that supported Johnson. I remember on election day, Odis Henry and I made a swing in the car down as far as Cameron making noise for Lyndon. I voted for Johnson when he ran for reelection in 1954. The next time I went all out for Lyndon was when he had his big feud early in 1953 with Shivers. They came out of the Big Thicket to back Lyndon in that showdown. The sun that set on Shivers that day has never risen. The last time I went all out for Lyndon was when he was a candidate for vice president in 1960. I shall go all out again for his candidacy. If President Kennedy wants him on the ticket, that suits me. But in between these various campaigns of his, I could have cheerfully and enthusiastically planted a political hatchet in his back.

These days Lyndon talks like a New Frontiersman when he makes his speeches. There's nothing wrong with his speeches. There was nothing wrong with his speeches in Beaumont and at Jack Brooks' farm in Jasper County on his recent visit. He even said he favored the controversial public accommodations section of the President's civil rights bill. He supported the President's program in his speeches. What else can you ask of the vice president?

But that's all on the surface. Below the surface, Lyndon Johnson digs at U.S. Senator Ralph Yarborough. He tries to be the Democratic senator from Texas. He aids and abets his protege governor, John Connally, who is making about the same kind of governor that Shivers made. How can Lyndon stand up for Connally when the latter opposes the President and acts more like a Republican than a Democrat? Now, since we are asking questions, why did Johnson come to Southeast Texas at this time? To line up the troops for Connally? Partly. He knows that if Connally gets beat next May he, LBJ might as well drown out the fire and call the dogs as far as his political influence is concerned, even though Houston got the Space Center and Fort Worth the contract to build the super plane, the TFX. But mainly Lyndon came to line up the troops for Lyndon, to improve his own image —he's thinking of 1964 and he knows that President Kennedy is coming to Texas next month to see if Connally and Lyndon have been lying to him. Connally told the President last week that he would have a hard time in Texas in 1964. This writer thinks that Connally is going to have a harder time next May than Kennedy is going to have in November. Both Lyndon and John are already trying to ride in on the coattails of JFK, and he had better know it.

Now to my way of thinking, both Senator Yarborough and Don Yarborough are better Democrats than John Connally, and since both Connally and Johnson are out to gut the Yarboroughs,

I couldn't work up enough enthusiasm for Johnson to hightail it down to Beaumont to welcome Lyndon.

So the best way the vice president could improve his image in Texas would be to cease and desist from trying to be the Democratic senator from Texas and to change over and deal the same kind of misery to Senator John (Useless) Tower that he has been giving Senator Yarborough. He could improve his image by breaking bread once in a while with both the Yarboroughs and their supporters, instead of wining and dining with Shivercrats and Connally.

STEVENSON SPITTING INCIDENT IN DALLAS   October 31

During the presidential campaign in 1960, an unruly gang of Dallasites surrounded and jostled Lyndon and Lady Bird Johnson and wound up spitting on them. Since then, Dallas has got what it soundly deserved; it has lost one government agency after another and still hasn't got its new federal building. The other day another typical mob of Dallasites hit Adlai Stevenson over the head with a placard and spit on him and a policeman who was trying to guard him. The John Birch-loving Dallas Morning News has created the climate that has inspired such uncivilized behavior. The Dallas Morning News is in the same position as Governor Wallace of Alabama who continually shouts the racist hate that results in bombings. Stevenson, former governor of Illinois and twice candidate for president of the United States, is the Ambassador to the United Nations. In that sense, the Hate-America-First hoodlums in Dallas were insulting the President. It doesn't matter that a packed house gave Stevenson several standing ovations. The minority had its way. The Dallas News by railing day in and day out for years at such figures as FDR, Woodrow Wilson, Eleanor Roosevelt, the Kennedys and American foreign policy set the stage for the election of Bruce Alger who acts more like a member of the Black Hand than a member of Congress. The News also can claim credit for the election of John (Useless) Tower, who weakly reproved the spitters. Tower is not going to say anything strong enough to

213

offend his John Birch gang in Dallas.

CONNALLY FIGHTS REDISTRICTING

Governor Connally of Texas could not have been more petty, political or demagogic than when he accused federal judges of playing Republican politics when they ordered congressional redistricting. Connally says that he is going to fight the decision; he says that the two federal judges, appointed by Eisenhower, were playing politics. So instead of calling the legislature into special session to redistrict the state's 23 congressional districts (at a cost of $400,000; his estimate of the cost of a special legislative session) he is going to spend money to fight the decision in the Supreme Court. Connally knows that the population of some districts is half that of others. He also knows that only this year, a three-panel federal court ordered Alabama, Tennessee and Georgia to redistrict, and that Florida came under the same ruling.

Now why would Connally take the attitude he has chosen to take, that of claiming that federal judges play politics? When he knows that their decision is just and right? Connally is desperately trying to build himself into a popular image that will guarantee his reelection next year when Don Yarborough is expected to run against him again, and Connally is using the tactics of the governor of Alabama to create that image. Like Wallace, Connally is trying to stand in the doorway. Thus far, Connally has been governor nearly a year, and there's nothing in his record he can point to. He came off second best with the most reactionary legislature, inspired by Preston Smith and Byron Tunnell, Texas ever had.

Do not think that Connally did not deliberately make the rank and file of Negroes and Mexicans mad at him in recent months. That was all a part of his notion of creating the kind of image he wants. He made labor mad at him for the same reason. He has had a fuss with Lyndon Johnson, his godfather. He sensed that Lyndon is losing friends and influence in Texas and Connally was one of the first to desert Johnson's sinking ship, but that is the kind of man he is; you'd have thought that after all Lyndon did for Connally, Connally would have stayed loyal, but of course, he is doing Lyndon as Lyndon has done others.

Well, how could all this tie in with Connally's attack on the federal judges? Connally senses that as in Alabama and Mississippi there is a segment of the population, including the very rich, who are against government period, and another group known in Georgia as "red necks," in Oklahoma as "okies," in Texas as "poor white trash," whose political credo is bigotry. In Texas there is a big group of Big Rich, John Birchers, radical right wing conservatives, the corporate structure, whose allegiance Connally would like to have. Then there is another group of bigots who live by racial hate. Hell is not going to be hot enough for this group, which at present is small, but which Connally wants to build up to screaming mob size. He wants to build up a big group of fascists who hate Mexicans, Negroes and poor white trash, like they have in Alabama and Mississippi. Connally senses that this group is increasing and it is. The fact is that nowadays you can find church people who have become racists in the last two years. But Connally, whether he is conscious of it or not, is not aiming at that group. He is aiming at the group that never darkens the door of a church, the wildcat gang, the nonconformists to society and the civilizing influences. His appeal is to those who really don't want to be civilized, to those who prefer the law of the jungle, the mob, the secret attack, the night rider, those who love to be against something, rather than for something.

Will Connally get by with it? It's a big gamble he is taking. Actually Connally appears convinced that Kennedy has lost Texas and he is going on that assumption; he thinks it's going to be "Bury" Goldwater for the GOP and that he will have to make like Goldwater.

OF DEATH, COFFINS & FUNERALS   *November 14*

I have not read the new best-selling book, *The American Way of Death*, but I have read a lot about it and heard it discussed several times on TV.

Long ago, I began to have my own ideas about funerals and burials. The modern ways of putting corpses away for keeps have all happened in my lifetime. I have seen undertakers become morticians. I have seen the cost of funerals soar from a basic low of $7.50 to a minimum of $500 in some places.

I remember the first funeral I ever attended. It was for Hubert Gilliland, who was about 14 years old. He was kicked in the stomach by a horse and he died without the medical attention he would have had today. There was no hospital in Wise County; the closest one was at Fort Worth. It was about 1911 and there were no cars. I went with my father to the Gilliland home the day of the funeral. The Gillilands lived on one of those white rocky hills in Wise County, where the first houses were built, the better to enable the first settlers to see marauding Comanches. Hubert was in a cedar coffin, or it may have been a pine box. It looked like cedar. It cost about $50 to bury Hubert. He was not embalmed before burial. I grew up believing that no one was embalmed unless he was shipped by train to his burial place. I thought that was the law, but it may not have been.

I did not go to many funerals when I was a boy, but my parents went. I went to the funeral of my grandmother, Virginia Fullingim. She was buried in a black coffin, a board box covered with black cloth. They brought the coffin out of her home on top of another white hill and the neighbors put her in it. When I did not go to a funeral and other members of my family went, the first question I would ask was, "Did they take on much? (meaning the survivors). Did anybody jump into the grave and want to be buried with him? How many flowers were there?" And those questions haven't changed fundamentally since then.

My great-grandfather on my mother's side had his own coffin built years before he died. He kept it in the ceiling. Others of the same generation also built their coffins and stored them away until their time came.

Many present residents of Kountze can also remember when all coffins were hammered together right here in town. There was no undertaking parlor and no embalmer here. As soon as someone died, the dead person's relatives or friends would call up carpenters and they would build the coffin. Al Mounce once told me that when he lived in Cherokee County he helped build two coffins.

As for me, I am a lover of wood that is not painted or varnished, but wood in which you can see the natural grain, and I think that a coffin made out of cypress and stained a driftwood color or given a clear coat of varnish would be prettier than any coffin I have seen in years. Cypress is one of my favorite woods and if I could find somebody to build me a coffin out of cypress, I'd order one right now. I just know that my coffin is going to cost more than anybody else's. My coffin is going to have to be 81 inches long, because that is the length of my bed and when I scrooch down in my bed it is not long enough for my 6 feet, 5 inches. I think I could get such a coffin built for $100 by a cabinet maker, $200 anyway, maybe less.

Mr. Miller at the hardwood mill was telling me about candy-stripped gum—that should make a beautiful coffin, but I think that cypress would be my favorite. I am almost sure that I had rather be buried in a coffin made out of cypress or candy-striped gum by, say, Charles Daniel or Carter Work, or Jack Jordan or Ed Carrier, than put away in a plywood box covered with fake velvet.

PRESIDENT KENNEDY IS DEAD *November 28*

The mayor of Dallas, a city now universally acclaimed as the hate capital of the world, said over TV while he frantically sucked a cigarette, that it could happen any place, that nobody could point the finger of blame or shame at Dallas, but that is exactly what everybody is doing and with good cause. For the hate has been building up for years in Dallas, under the leadership of The Dallas Morning News, General Edwin Walker, Lifeline, H. L. Hunt and Dan Smoot. The hate that spewed out on Lyndon and Lady Bird Johnson in 1960 and Adlai Stevenson a few weeks ago finally brought death to both the President and his slayer. The mayor of Dallas said it could have happened anywhere, but could it have? Could it have happened at any place but Dallas?

The defiant attitude of Dallas was best reflected on TV by District Attorney Henry Wade at his news conference. The attitude he presented to the world was that of a surly, resentful man who just couldn't care less. He seemed to be resentful that he even had to tell the world why he thought Oswald was the murderer. The Dallas News in an editorial Sunday said that it was time to get back to "normal living," normal hating, that is. Undoubtedly, there were many who were glad that Oswald was slain, but most responsible people regretted it. Most people wanted to know why Oswald murdered the President, and most believed that he would eventually confess, but that hope died forever with the bullet fired into his bowels by a Dallas super-patriot.

At first, it seemed unbearable that NBC and CBS had nothing on the screen for three days but the tragedy, but gradually one began to see that the continuous coverage of the story from every angle was the best way to prepare the nation to get used to the death of President Kennedy and to get used to the new president, Lyndon B. Johnson. I believe Johnson will try to carry out the Kennedy program of civil rights, tax cut and medicare. If he does, he will be the next Democratic nominee and the next president. If he does not try to put the Kennedy program on the statute books, he will never be nominated. As for me, I'm supporting the President on the basis of his pledge to carry out the Kennedy program.

We all heard over and over on TV that the entire nation is to blame for the assassination, and that we must get rid of the hate that has come to possess us. Of course, every man is going to say that, "There is no hate in me. I hate nobody. It is in everybody else, but it's not in me," but it's likely that the person who says that has a backlog of hate that could qualify him for residence in Dallas.

Take the governors of Alabama and Mississippi, for instance. They both came to Washington and both decried the "cowardly" assassination on TV, but in their own state nobody has been punished for the ambush assassination of Medgar Evers and the bombing deaths of the children in a church. The governors called those killings dastardly and cowardly, but they refuse to even try to punish the murderers. So one raises the question that was never asked on TV: Will the shocking murder of the President lessen the hate, will it bring the hate-mongers to repentance, will pangs of conscience smite those who have hated? Will they suddenly discover they have a conscience? The TV panels and commentators prayed and hoped the President's death might in some way prick that conscience, but I say it won't. Oh, they may take off their cars all those "Kill the Kennedy Klan" signs I saw in Dallas two weeks ago, but they'll think up some other new hate slogan. Assassination came natural to Dallas. They had gained fame by spitting on Lady Bird and hitting Adlai over the head with a placard. There are some who take slogans literally. The trouble in Dallas was that the stable minds incited the unstable minds to violence. It was no accident that Oswald chose the hate-Kennedy capital of the world as the place in which to murder the President. It was an ideal setting for him.

It was like a member of the family had died. It will take a long time to get used to the idea that President John Kennedy is in his grave at Arlington cemetery. It seems incredible that he is dead. I do believe though that since he was a martyr to the cause of what President Johnson called "making the free free," America's final tribute to John F. Kennedy will be the adoption of his program, and the awakening of consciences. As so many TV commentators said, America feels guilty about John Kennedy. All of us feel in some way responsible. All of us feel we have been lacking. For Kennedy's program was neither Democratic nor Republican, liberal nor conservative, but something each mind's conscience had to decide.

AM I A HATER, TOO? *December 5*

I am going to quit spelling Barry Goldwater's name as I have been spelling it in this column: "Bury Goldwater." And I have taken those Goldwater stickers off my car, and the reason that I'm going to try to quit hating the John Birchers and radical, right wing Republicans as much as I have, is because by hating them it puts me in the same class with them. I'm going to have to admit that I have been harboring pure D hate. I'm even going to try to quit hating Allan Shivers, and Governors Wallace and Barnett. All the commentators and President Johnson now say that what is wrong with the country is hate. President John Kennedy said that many times before he was murdered. And I'm even going to try to quit hating Dallas and that is a big concession. I am not promising I'm going to get rid of all my hate; I may fail. Right now I feel like the time just before I was getting ready to go on a diet: Just one more big meal, just one more good stuffing, just one more orgy of gluttony, and I would be ready to start. Right now I feel as if I will be ready to quit hating Birchers and radical, right wingers if I could just let loose and give them one more good cussin'.

Birdwell was in here and so was John Blair and they told me I was full of hate and they didn't come at the same time, so I know it was not premeditated, and they pointed to the "Bury" signs on my car and said that was as bad as Dallas where they distributed on the day Kennedy was murdered a mess of handbills showing the picture of John F. Kennedy with the caption, "WANTED FOR TREASON!" Now of course John Blair did not promise not to tell any more of those anti-Kennedy and anti-Negro jokes he used to be so chuck full of.

According to them, I am the biggest hater in Kountze, but if I am, then I'm going to reform right now and sit down and try to reason with the John Birchers. But what about them? Are they going to try to reform and quit hating presidents, or are they going to take up on President Johnson where they left off on Kennedy? It looks like old John and Bird ought to try to convince the Birchers they ought to quit hating, too. I've already seen some hate letters in the Houston Post against Johnson, and I believe that the Birchers are just laying low for a decent time to pass before they let loose on President Johnson. Now don't start throwing up to me that I have been cussing Lyndon Johnson. For I have and recently, too. But I call upon you also to remember that I was the first writer to suggest that he would make a good president, and Lyndon Johnson wrote me a letter to that effect. I also call upon you to remember how I was one of those here who swamped the supporters of Shivers in that big showdown a few years ago. The headline in the Kountze News after that voting shoot-out in the old courthouse was prophetic: It said: "Sun sets on Shivers and rises on Lyndon Johnson." So I have both praised and cussed Johnson, but from now on he is the

Democratic President of the United States and as long as he pushes the program of John Fitzgerald Kennedy, as he has promised he would, I'm backing President Johnson.

John Blair, who never in his life voted for a Democratic candidate for president, said he was disappointed in this column last week because I laid the blame on Dallas. He said I could have done better. He said I should have blamed Communism instead of the Dallas spitters and slappers and shovers and pushers. But what I was really blaming and what he did not choose to see, was the hate climate of Dallas, which John said I was a match for.

Now for a word of praise where praise is due, and I refer to the commentators of NBC and CBS to whom I listened for three long days. They had a touch of greatness in the way they presented the murder and burial of President Kennedy and the other events. It got to where they sounded like your own conscience; they sounded like oracles of sympathy, wisdom and understanding. Men of both NBC and CBS were equally great. They as much as anyone else made the sordid events a morality lesson, a morality play. They rose to the great opportunity they had to avoid sensation and circus aspects. They kept the American people from being demagogues, and ever and always they preached against hate and intolerance. When anyone in the future lists the shortcomings of TV, I shall remember the great example set by the NBC and CBS commentators. They made TV truly great for the first time.

They were our own conscience, our own hopes and our fears, our great heart-aching grief. I think they said what they felt the dead president wanted them to say, what the new President had in mind. The voice we could not hear any more was theirs those three heartbreaking days.

YEAR 1964

TO BE HATED BY THE RIGHT PEOPLE   *January 2*

I just couldn't make myself do it. So I had no Christmas tree and no home decorations at all, though I had all the lights on hand.

I usually send out many Christmas greeting cards to practically anyone who I figure will not sue or assault me, but this Christmas I did not send out a single Merry Christmas to anyone. It was just not in me to do it, and it came to me a day or so ago why. I'm not even beginning to get over the death of President Kennedy. I avoid all TV programs in which I figure they will show his face. When I hear that voice again, I know that my grief is as poignant as ever. Dee is even worse than I. He was for Kennedy before I was, and since then his utter loyalty and devotion to the Kennedy program has never wavered, and of course mine never did either. I marvel at the greatness of John Fitzgerald Kennedy, and especially his courage. When it seemed that he might be defeated for a second term on account of his civil rights stand and his insistence on medicare based on social security, he never hesitated. He pushed harder than ever for them, and he made not the slightest compromise and there was no foot-dragging. Why do I think he will be ranked as a president as great as Lincoln? Because like Lincoln he was hated by the right people—the bigots, the racists, the greedy-guts and the professional patriots. Did you ever stop to think that Lincoln became the greatest American of the 19th century, even though he was hated by even more people than those who hated Kennedy? The bigots and the racists also hated Lincoln.

For weeks after the assassination, I was angry, frustrated and vengeful (I'm still that), but now I'm beginning to be only grief stricken. But my big hope is our new president. It will be his nature to want to compromise a little, though he has done none of that yet. One thing he's doing that Kennedy did not do is keep books on right wing, radical conservatives like John Dowdy of Crockett who never voted for a single Kennedy bill and who voted as if he hated the president. I can see signs that Lyndon will get Dowdy in a bind one of these days, and force that radical conservative to vote like a Democrat for a change. Kennedy did not keep any books on any congressman, and he let them get away with murder, but that was the noble nature of Kennedy. The character of the president taught me one thing. It is important to be hated by the right people—the Dowdys, the Wallaces, the Barnetts, the John Birchers, the radical, right wing conservatives, the H. L. Hunts, the Dan Smoots, the racists and the bigots.

I VISIT MY PSYCHIATRIST *January 9*

1963 was so memorably tragic that when New Year's Day came around I could not muster up any enthusiasm for 1964. The blackeyed peas had a whang to them, or maybe it was just the bitter taste that has been in my mouth since November 22. But I could not rid myself of the feeling of impending doom that has possessed me since Dallas, even though I rejoiced in the way Tony Crosby and the Longhorns crushed Navy in the Cotton Bowl, and it is my unblushing opinion that any Southwest conference team could mop up on Navy.

On January 2 it came to me what I ought to do. I ought to go around and sit a spell with old G. B. Richardson at his TV shop. He was just what I needed. He put the old spizzerinktum back in me. He got to telling me about his hideaway 30 miles from here up in Polk County on Double A Lakes. G. B. described how the smaller lakes were frozen over and how the ducks and the geese swoop down on them every now and then. He talked about Chester and Minnie, and about the good food they are serving at the cafe, and all of a sudden I became aware that come the latter part of February the bass will be jumping a foot high in those lakes, and then I thought: Why wait; why not go up there now, this weekend and get away from it all. It was a bright thought and I felt better, picturing the cabins in the pines and the brilliant January moonlight on the lakes. And I said, G. B. tell me more, tell me how the trees look, how the air feels, how the sun hits the ice, tell me about the birds and the animals up there. Tell me about that old hunter who hangs around, old what's-his-name who goes hunting every day? And G. B. did. I tell you, G. B. ought to charge a psychiatrist's fee for what he did to me.

I came back to the shop and there were two or three candidates ready to announce, and I treated each one as if I was going to vote for him alone, which is the proper way to treat a candidate. One of them asked me if I was sick. No, I said. Well, has somebody left you a fortune, he asked in utter disbelief as he regarded my courteous demeanor. No, I said, I've just been to see my psychiatrist. Well, said he, don't get out of the habit.

A BEFITTING MANNER *January 16*

Goat McDonald's cat, Pat, died last week and Goat buried him in a manner befitting the high regard he held for the cat. Goat, the local barber, went to the cabinet shop and had a coffin built. The coffin was no mere box, but was according to the style of coffins built for human beings. Goat took the coffin home and put Pat in it and held the funeral service in his back yard and buried Pat. The man who came in here telling the News about it said that Goat has a heart in him as big as that coffin.

I CAN'T ATTACK CONNALLY *February 13*

This column is getting irate letters from supporters of Don Yarborough over the state who said the events connected with the wounding of Governor John Connally have nothing to do with the present race. And of course it doesn't, but it has to do with the President of the United States and his actions regarding Texas since he became President. I think it is useless and futile for Yarborough to run this year because I believe that people want to back the President and they believe he wants Connally elected governor. I believe that even Hardin County which voted 5 to 1 for Don Yarborough in 1962 will vote for Connally this year.

The way I see it people are not spoiling to unseat Connally. First they feel a sympathy for him and second they identify him with Johnson. I have not a word of criticism to say against Don Yarborough. In fact, I can think of more praise-worthy things to say about him than I can of Connally, but I don't believe this is his year. I'll holler for Don in 1966 if he runs, and I hope he does, and I will not hold it against him if he runs this year, but there is something in me that says, "Lay off John Connally." I may be wrong in believing that my mood is the mood of the majority in Hardin County, but every time I sit down to fight Connally at this Linotype, my mind goes back to Dallas, then to the rotunda of the national capitol and finally to a grave at Arlington cemetery where an eternal flame is burning. No, I can't attack Connally. And I want to be with the President.

JUST LIKE I DO   *February 27*

Birdwell saw a woman laughing fit to kill as she looked at the gourd display in the window of his store last week. He went out and asked her what was so funny, and she told him this story: "I once knew a man in the old days who stopped at a house to get a drink. He went to the dug well where a woman was drawing a bucket of water. She was wearing a bonnet that hid most of her face. When she had drawn the water she handed the man a gourd dipper full of water, and then the man saw her face. She had snuff all around her mouth and it was dripping off her chin and running down the corners of her mouth, and the man held the gourd dipper full of water in his hand, wondering where she drank from, but he knew he had to drink it, and he finally decided to tilt it up and drink out of the handle end. Then the woman began laughing. 'I'll say!' she said, 'You drink water just like I do, right out of the end of the handle.'"

THE BEAUTY OF TWO SIDES FIGHTING   *March 5*

The other day I saw this 50-year-old copy of the "Hardin

County News" which was published in Kountze for at least 25 years around the turn of the century. Most of the front page of this particular issue was taken up with two letters, written by two close relatives and both prominent citizens of Kountze who were public officials. The letters were strong denunciations of their political enemies. One of the letter writers had taken part in a political shooting scrape with his political enemies and he and his relative published the long letters to explain how and why the shooting took place and to describe in detail how low-down and mean their enemies were, and how just and righteous they were. It was clear from the letters that there were two factions in town and had been for years. All the people connected with that feud are dead now, but their deaths did not stop the political fights.

I mention this only because the other day an obviously self-righteous woman, who was also indignant, complained that Kountze about 10 years ago used to be sweetness and love, and then I remembered that about that time there was a mayoralty race and this very woman kept telling me, "How you gonna vote? You can't stay on the fence. You got to get on one side or the other."

You can still hear stories about the big church fights that happened years ago when a preacher would draw a line on the floor and those who would not cross over to the side of the preacher would march right out the front door. For years there were feuding families in politics here and this went on for decades, with knock down and drag out fights. Feuding in politics is nothing new in Kountze, Silsbee, Saratoga, Sour Lake or any place in Hardin or Tyler counties or any other county I know about. It's been going on since the year one. Each one tries to convince the voter that on his side are all the Good Guys and on the other side are all the Bad Guys. I rather suspect that the people who complain the loudest about the political bickering and battling now going on in the county, really mean that they deplore it because it's just that right now they don't happen to be in the thick of the fight. They've probably been antagonists in some mighty interesting hair-pulling and nose-biting contests themselves. Political brawling is nothing new in Hardin County. It's been going on since somebody burned down the courthouse at Old Hardin so they could build a new one in Kountze. Don't think that Hardin

226

County is in a class by itself. There are always two elements in a community, town or county, a law-abiding element and a lawless element, and some members of each group belong to both. Personally, I have found that it pays to follow leaders who believe in and practice Christianity, who regularly attend and support churches. You can't trust everybody who goes to church, but you can trust most of them for they are more likely to have a conscience and heed it. But be he churchgoer or not, the person who quotes the Bible to achieve political ends will bear watching.

No matter where you live you will find two sides fighting it out. I have come to the conclusion that where there ceases to be two sides, where there ceases to be a war between the law-abiding and the lawless, a dictator has taken over. There is only one side in Russia, only one side in Red China, only one side in Cuba. As long as one side is able to carry on a fight, we have nothing to fear, it's only when somebody has grabbed absolute power that it's bad. It's when one man seeks to be the dictator that we must rise up and slap him down.

COURSING A BEE TO A TREE   *May 28*

I heard that the most knowledgeable man on bees who ever lived in Hardin County was Mitchell Gandy of Honey Island. It is said that Mr. Gandy was an expert in coursing a bee, that is following a bee to his tree. Mr. Gandy in his day probably found and cut more bee trees than any other person. In those days, when a person found a bee tree he carved his initials on it and that was his tree and no one else touched it. Mr. Gandy was the father of 14 children.

MUSIC IN YOUR SOUL   *June 4*

There are times in a person's lifetime when he needs music more than he does at other times. Not every person, perhaps, but most people. Some people don't need music at all. They can do without it very well, but in retaliation, I'm going to quote you

Shakespeare on the kind of people who don't need music: "The man who has no music in his soul or is not moved by a concord of sweet sounds is fit for treasons, stratagems and spoils . . . the motions of his soul are black as night, his affections dark as Erebus . . . mark the music." (If I have quoted the bard correctly from memory.)

I have needed music most of my life, but less in the last ten years than in any other period—probably due to TV. I have an electric Baldwin concert organ and I bet I don't average playing it once a month.

The time when I needed music the most was from the age of 22 to 40, and that period covered the years of the great Depression and about eight years before, but if by that statement you think that the Depression began on a certain date you are wrong. There was always a Depression on the farm where I was brought up. There was always a depression on the farm before the New Deal of Franklin Delano Roosevelt.

The kind of music I needed in the late 1920s and in the 1930s was what is known by some as classical music but which, in my own mind, I thought of as Beautiful Music. Every so often I had to have my appetite for Chopin, Mozart, Liszt, Beethoven, Wagner, Brahms and a slew of other composers of the 18th and 19th centuries, assuaged and satisfied. I went to great lengths, at times, to do this. For instance, in the winter of 1926 I followed Paderewski, the great pianist, from Dallas to New Orleans, to Atlanta, to Jacksonville, Florida, and to Miami by freight train, and in each city I attended his piano concerts. Another person I followed on tour one time was Madame Amelita Galli-Curci, the soprano of pure voice.

In the 1930s, I was the close friend of a woman, May Foreman Carr, who taught piano, and she was a good pianist. She played Chopin and Mozart to suit me. Sometimes she would sit down at the piano, with me sitting in a rocking chair, rocking, and she would play all night. It was pure beauty and I had John Keats' credo then: "Beauty is truth, truth beauty; that is all ye know on earth and all ye need to know." Nobody ever gave me as much beauty as May Foreman Carr, and it went on for 10 years.

World War II broke it up, and during the war I never had any music, and I never had a great need for it. I never had any need for poetry, either. On the ship, Portuguese sailors from Rhode Island would play the accordion. I would run across hillbillies from the south and Texas who played hillbilly music.

The 1940s and early 1950s was my hillbilly music period. The Grand Ole Opry. The Louisiana Hayride. Bob Wills. Ernest Tubb and the early Eddie Arnold. Old Hank Williams. It was then I grew to like the 1920 songs of Jimmy Rodgers, whom I despised in the 1920s. In the 1940s I became infatuated with hillbilly music. And that's where Jack Neil came in. Radio Station KTRM was the best hillbilly music station in the area from 1949 to 1952. I never turned KTRM off. Jack Neil and his announcers were moving with the tide and I was with them all day in the shop and at home. I did not own a TV until 1957. But with the ascension of Holy Ike in 1953, hillbilly music was on its way out. I was not ready for it to fold, but then again I was not ready for the Democratic regime to fold. I am seldom ready for things I have grown used to to fold. I wasn't even ready for prohibition to go: I had learned to like home brew.

As I said in the last ten years I have not needed music as I did in the 1920s and 1930s. My hillbilly period began to fade after I wrote The Book and that may have been the reason for it after all. I have gone to Beaumont at times to hear the personality performers like Van Cliburn, Bob Wills, Hank Williams. But it was not like listening to Galli-Curci or Paderewski or Esther Johnson, who could play Mozart better than anyone I had heard up to that time, 1934.

Once or twice a year, I'll turn on the grand opera on Saturday afternoon, and it will seem like the old days with Grace Sutherlin and Leontyne Price, the Hattiesville, Mississippi, Negro woman who has become the greatest soprano of this decade, and I have jumped up and run around the house twice so great was my appreciation and excitement, but then somebody calls about a want ad or cusses me out on the phone or just rings and hangs up when I answer. But despite it all, I still don't need the great music as I once did and that worries me. I don't need hillbilly, either. The so-called folk music is synthetic. Maybe it's the cares of life's busy day, but I would not want to become a man who has no music in his soul . . . mark the music.

LET'S HAVE GOLDWATER IN '64 *July 9*

Does it make any difference to you whether the Republicans nominate Goldwater or Scranton for president? President Johnson can take either one of them, but still I have a hankering for the Republicans to nominate Barry just to prove once and for all that the radical, right wing conservatives are not as numerous as they think they are. To read their letters in the Beaumont Enterprise, the Houston Post and the Dallas Morning News, you'd think they dominate the earth. How they love to pen letters to the papers!

It's time for them to see where they stand, even if it wrecks the Republican party, and if they do I will shed no tears. It's time for the nation to find out just how many fanatics, John Birchers, Gordon McLendons, Governor Wallaces, General Walkers, it has. There may be more than we think, and if there is we need to know the worst, and we need to know in 1964. You have read in the daily papers that our European allies are stunned that the Republicans would even consider nominating a Neanderthal, Ice Age throw-back like Goldwater, but if the GOP can do it, let it do it. If the Republicans can come up with Goldwater late this month, to the dismay of England, West Germany, Italy, France, then why try to stop them?

If you have an idiot in the family there's no use telling him to get under the bed when company is coming. Put him right out on the front porch and let him slobber and gibber and run off at the mouth where everybody can see him, and know the worst right off and what to expect. Once the nation and the world knows just where Barry stands, the better off we will be. Let's get Goldwater and the John Birchers out of our system once and for all, and the only way to do it is for the Republicans to nominate him for president. And if the American people should elect Goldwater president over Lyndon Johnson it's time for us to know that, too.

However, if Goldwater loses like the Gallup Poll says he will, then let the right wing extremists keep their big mouths shut and start supporting the Constitution for a change, for the Constitution is exactly what the Supreme Court says it is, as Justice Holmes used to say. If Goldwater gets skunked, it'll be time to quit waving all flags except the Stars and Stripes. Maybe if Goldwater gets the licking the polls say he would get, the extremists who follow him will see the light and come back into the Union.

If old Barry can get enough votes to be elected, it's time the world knew it and it's time we ourselves realize how many extremists we have in the United States. In addition to the Hate-America-First, Hate-the-U.N., Hate-the-Supreme-Court contingent, who else would vote for Goldwater? Maybe more than we think. Would those who are frustrated on account of Vietnam, foreign aid and civil rights, all be inclined to vote for Goldwater? Then how about those who can't accept the fact that both Russia and the United States have enough nuclear bombs and weapons to kill every living thing on this planet? Will they let that horrible thought influence them to vote in pure anger for Goldwater? Would those who hate Koons, Kikes and Katholic people who blah-blah for the Ku Klux Klan, Negro haters and union haters go down the line with Barry? That could mean a lot of people. But the United States needs to know in 1964 just how many misled and misguided people it has. The only way we can find out is to put Goldwater on the ticket.

Only a jaded, weary, desperate fanatic wants to impeach the Supreme Court, abolish the U.N., repeal the income tax, wipe out social security, invade Cuba and give army field generals the say so as to whether nuclear weapons should be used against an enemy. So let the GOP put Barry on the ticket. Let's have it in 1964. Let's see where we stand.

THE GOLDWATER CANDIDACY   *July 23*

The hero of the Republican convention as far as I was concerned was Governor Nelson Rockefeller. His speech telling off the John Birchers was the best part of the convention. The Birchers among the delegates booed him continuously and in so doing showed the stripe down their backs. It was easy to see that there were few Republicans among the delegates, but hundreds of Birchers and their sympathizers. Rockefeller is the man who should have been nominated.

"Bury" Goldwater's speech was a declaration of war, not on poverty, illiteracy, disease, the things the Democrats fight, but against life as it is in America today. Goldwater is out to destroy Communism—even if we get destroyed in the process. He said he was through talking with Communists. His was a fearful speech to me. It frightened me. The man is truly a fanatic, as his speech proved. Go ahead and vote for him because you don't like the Civil Rights bill, but be ready for all out war under Goldwater.

Just before Barry Goldwater, the idol of the John Birchers and Texas Republicans and racists, was nominated Republican candidate for president, he name-called President Lyndon B. Johnson as the biggest faker and phony in the United States today and was applauded by Senator John Tower and General Walker. Does this personal attack on the President of the United States indicate the kind of character assassination the darling of the right wing radicals intends to use in the campaign ahead? If it does, then let him have at it. Johnson and the Democrats do not have to launch a personal attack on Goldwater. All they have to do is rub it in on the voters what Barry Goldwater has been preaching for years, and never let the voters forget for a moment that here are some of the crackpot ideas that Goldwater would like to put into effect if he were elected president. He has opposed distribution of surplus food commodities for the needy. He has opposed giving surplus food commodities to school lunch rooms, about half of the food used by the school lunch rooms. He favors instant war. An invasion of Cuba and allowing generals in the field to use nuclear weapons as they see fit; he talks of going to war against the Communists every time they cross us. He would have gone to war if necessary to keep Russia from building the wall in Berlin. Now he wants to use nuclear bombs in Vietnam. He has opposed social security, income taxes, old age pensions and medicare.

Goldwater says he does not approve of the John Birchers, but his foreign and economic beliefs are exactly like theirs, and anyone who watched the convention in San Francisco and did not come to the conclusion that the Birchers were the Goldwater delegates, for the most part, must be naive indeed.

You can vote for Goldwater because he voted against civil

rights, but you will also be voting against many of the things you regard as the necessities of life, like old age assistance, social security, surplus commodities, hospitals, school lunches and dams. Think it over, friend, before you decide to vote yourself into the poor house.

THE CHILDREN KNOW   *August 13*

J. Frank Dobie wrote a book called *The Mustangs* that was more than a documented history of the horses of the plains and prairies. The book was, one discovered, about freedom, not the kind of freedom the John Birchers rant about, but the kind of freedom the mustangs knew, and Dobie managed to teach the meaning of true freedom throughout the book. It was the kind of book to live by and live with, and I have not known many books like that in my lifetime.

I go back to Faulkner and to Conrad the way I go back to *The Mustangs*, when I want corroboration of the true meaning of freedom. I tell you, it was a book to live with. So in 1953, when I moved into this tin building, there were these 12 feet high walls on each side and the white ceiling, and the walls are of sheetrock over two-inch boards, and I prevailed upon my brother-in-law, Tom Simms, to paint me a mural about Dobie's mustangs. I told Tom I wanted him to illustrate Dobie's mustangs in a mural, but he wouldn't read the book. He did look at the drawings, but Tom wouldn't read the book, and for weeks I told him about it and read portions of it to him, but I doubt if he listened, for Tom knows about horses of all kinds. He has spent much of his life drawing horses and the rest drawing pictures of Jesus and he never gets the two mixed, but before he began painting the mural he seemed to get the feeling of freedom that Dobie taught so unobtrusively. Tom Simms painted the murals, 4½ feet high and 50 feet long, and it took him three months. That mural may be the most important single thing in Kountze, and Tom Simms may be the most important man, so don't put too much emphasis on that wild look he has, and the wild way his hair waves, but you had better believe those hell-fire sermons he preaches. I have never met Frank Dobie but Bertha Dobie, his wife, was here one day last year, and she saw the murals, but I had a feeling that she was not too much impressed, but I know what I know: That if I can spot greatness in Mozart, in Faulkner, in Dobie, in Conrad, surely I can know when I see it on a wall.

Anyway, I have Dobie's mustangs under my eyes all the time. I cannot tell you how much they have meant to me, not because they are paintings, but because they are connected with the mustangs. I know they can stand alone without the Dobie connection by the way children look at them. They have been on the wall for 11 years, and I consider that they are there for my edification. I'll admit that at first I thought that I had it here for the enjoyment of the public. I figured it would be an asset to the shop and I wanted all to see the murals. Finally, I became aware that only other painters and children would raise their eyes to the murals. Children know what it's about. It is the first thing they see when they come into the shop, and they don't want to leave until they have seen it all. Children are always concerned with freedom and they recognize what's in the mustangs' manes, eyes, nostrils, hooves, tails and marvelous muscles; they know what it has to do with. Some adults don't care about the true freedom which they have shaped into something else that passes for freedom; you hear it in the big talk of bosses and also in the big talk of union bosses, and you hear it from the Birchers, too. Some of these people have been forced to adopt current prejudices that pass for freedom. But the children know. After a while you get used to a mural and for days it's just there; then all of a sudden you look at it, and Dobie's mustangs come back.

I know about the kind of freedom he writes about. It will be with me to the day I die. I believe that in learning about mustangs, Dobie learned more about the earth they trod and about their pursuers and about the function of all creatures with calcium bones and water-soaked bodies that came out of the sea billions of eons ago and finally walked on the land.

When Frank Dobie walks down that lonesome valley, he will have become aware that like the mustangs and the grass, he must become a part of the earth again, something we all must become reconciled to.

234

ST. JOHN, THE EXEMPT *December 3*

Every time I think about Governor John Connally I become so sad I could cry if some hillbilly were around to play "Precious Memories" on the steel guitar, for Governor Connally has become so inextricably linked with the assassination only sadness comes when one thinks of him. Connally is fast becoming St. John the Exempt, exempt from criticism, from politics, from anything mundane. We see his tears on TV recalling the assassination, and we weep with him. We read his speeches delivered in Florida and they read like he's a changed man. Yes, yes every time I think of John Connally I become sad, because what I fear is that now, no matter what happens in the legislature next year, Connally would get by with it. He has already become St. John, and we have had a couple of saints in recent years, Saint Ike and St. Edgar Hoover. But does John Connally want to become a saint like Ike and Edgar? If he doesn't, he'd better move fast.

So I am going to tell John Connally how to avoid being the saint he's sure to be and how to win a place in history outside of his role in the assassination. I want to say that I once addressed this same plea to Price Daniel, assuring him that he would go down in history books as a great governor, but he paid me no mind, and I want you, John Connally, to look at Price Daniel's scant two lines in history. But Governor, I'm going to get in on the ground floor with my plea, for that is really what it is. I appeal to you, John Connally, to say that you will veto a sales tax on groceries if Byron Tunnell and his lobbyists can pass it with the help of Lieutenant Governor Smith. I also plead with you to say before the session starts you will veto any college tuition raises. But most of all I want you to say that you will veto a sales tax on groceries if the legislature passes such a bill.

The reason I'm worried is because I think the big lobbyists in cooperation with Speaker Tunnell and Smith are right now drafting a sales tax on groceries. Maybe they have it down in black and white. I don't think it will do any good to threaten you, John Connally, for if you were to run again, I'd probably vote for you, because I feel so sad when I think about you. I don't think browbeating, coercion or ranting and raving against you will do any good. That is the reason I'm getting down on my knees to beg you to say right now to those scheming oppressors of the poor, Tunnell and Smith, that you will veto any sales tax on groceries they send you. By the way, John Connally, while I think of it, why didn't you ever acknowledge that you got those fancy long-handled gourds Harris Fender of Tyler talked me out of? He said you would write me a letter that you got the gourds and liked them, but I have heard no word from you or him, but if he ever comes back to Hardin County with a carpetbag full of bonds to sell, him and me are going to fist city over them gourds he said he was going to give you and that you ignored—beware of a gourd grower scorned.

But back to the governor who is in peril of becoming Saint John. Nobody could beat Connally. He could be governor for the next 10, 15 or 20 years, but he would only be a saint. Connally might even be president. He could be the senator to replace "Peewee" Tower. But the point is that I don't want to look upon Connally as a saint; I don't want to feel sad when I think of him. I want either to be mad as a wet hen at him or to fight flatfooted for him. I don't want him to be a non-governor as St. Ike was a non-president. We have a lot of non-things these days, non-books, non-music, and non-art and non-people, but what we need less than anything is a non-governor, and I plead with John Connally to read Dr. Cotner's biography of James S. Hogg again. Hogg was for the people.

I'm kinda rambling here as I sit at this Linotype, but this St. John the Exempt thing has a lot of facets, as the head shrinkers say. I wonder what Don Yarborough would think if he knew I really voted for Connally, even thought I penned editorial after editorial against Connally and in favor of Don. I got to inquiring around and that's what all my friends did. I think that even our State Representative Emmett Lack did, too. Truth was when I got to the polls and saw John's name the Big Sadness engulfed me. I actually felt a surge of satisfaction when I finally voted for Connally.

Now that threats are out, the only thing we can do is to appeal to Connally to not forget us poor white trash whose purses would suffer the most as a result of the sales tax. And governor, you have been in Kountze. Right in front of the Kountze News, and you have seen this sheet iron building, and you looked east toward what our late beloved Dr. Anderson used to call Fly Blow and you saw the kind of poverty your mentor, Lyndon Johnson, talks about, and I want you to ask yourself whether you really want us poor poverty-stricken wretches to pay a sales tax on groceries? As of now, governor, you are going down in history as the man who was shot in John Kennedy's assassination, but people will not quite remember your name. I can't think of a single thing the history books could pick up either for or against you that could give you more than a couple of lines in history. Neither the people nor the Lobbyists can brag now. Both were given to cussing you before the assassination.

But governor, by taking a firm stand against a sales tax on groceries, you could go down in history and I wouldn't have to go on feeling so sad, and you would miss being a saint. I would feel like fighting for you, and it's a cinch that you would get at least a page in the history books instead of two lines, and somebody in the year 2040 might even write a biography of you.

Especially, governor, if you inspired the legislature to pass a corporation tax and a state income tax to meet our constantly increasing expenditures. We need both, governor, but that sales tax on groceries would be murder. Don't let them do it.

YEAR 1965

First I heard President Johnson's inaugural speech over the radio in this shop, then over TV and then I read the complete text of it, twice, in The Houston Post. The speech grows on you. Already, I have come to look on it as a blueprint for this generation, under Johnson. I would like to see it printed on fine paper suitable for framing, like JFK's was. I would take down the Kennedy inaugural speech and hang the Johnson speech in its place —not that Kennedy's speech suffers in comparison, not that the Kennedy speech is, in my mind, incomparable, but because Johnson is our leader now. It's what Johnson says and does that we will live by.

The President said these fine words straight from the heart, without rhetoric, but they sounded like Lincoln's Gettysburg address: "In a land of wealth, families must not live in hopeless poverty . . . children must not go hungry . . . Neighbors must not suffer and die untended . . . Young people must be taught to read and write . . . waste of our resources is the enemy . . . Let us reject any among us who seek to reopen old wounds and rekindle old hatreds . . . Justice requires us to remember: when any citizen denies his fellow, saying his color is not mine or his beliefs are different, in that moment he betrays America, though his forebears created the nation."

The above quotes are, in a nutshell, what Johnson means when he speaks of the Great Society. For the President was saying that poverty must go, and that medicare must become a fact, that the nation must see to it that the people become educated, that every opportunity that is open to the white man must be open to the red man, the black man, and the yellow man. Later the president said, "But we have no promise from God that our greatness will endure."

We Americans always believe that God is on our side, but now most of us are quite sure that He was not on the side of the South in the Confederate war, else we would have won. We were wrong then and we are still wrong when we try to embrace the aim of the Lost Cause.

Bearing all this in mind, the playing of "Dixie" 73 times by the South Carolina band in the parade left me cold, ashamed and resentful. The Confederate flags carried by the marchers from some Southern states seemed out of place, seemed like trying to reopen old wounds and rekindle old hatreds. Now I grew up on "Dixie." It was the big song of my childhood. Until World War II, no martial air ever thrilled me as much as "Dixie." Both of my grandfathers were in the Confederate armies. They had cousins, uncles, brothers following the Stars and Bars. None of my kinfolks wanted to hide out in the woods to keep from going. They believed in the Cause. Uncle Joshua Reeves fought under Lee and Jackson, Uncle Jess Fullingim fought under E. Johnston before Atlanta. During my first three years in school, my teacher was Aunt Frances Fullingim in the one-room school on Pecan creek. She taught us fierce loyalty to the Lost Cause. Before 1961, I wanted to celebrate the 100th anniversary of the Civil War, but when the anniversary of Bull Run came, I was sick of trying to reopen old wounds, trying to rekindle old hatreds. Now I live in 1965, not 1865.

Now I pledge allegiance to the flag of the United States, and to the Republic for which it stands, one nation, under God, with liberty and justice for all. No more liking "Dixie" better than I do the Star Spangled Banner, no more running up or waving the Confederate flag. It took World War II in which I served four years to teach me that in order to play the Star Spangled Banner on the piano you must use both the white and black keys. The Texas flag is a matter of pride, but I pledge no allegiance to it, only to the Star Spangled Banner.

A FOREIGNER AT HOME

A Negro man came up to the counter in the post office and asked Mrs. Kathleen Reeves for "one of the cards."

"What kind of card?" asked Kathleen.

"An ailin' card," said the man.

"Oh, you mean an alien card," Mrs. Reeves said, bearing in mind that all aliens had to register before December 31, and that here it was well into January.

"Do you want it for yourself?"

"Yessum."

"Where are you from?" Mrs. Reeves asked.

"From Lufkin. Born and raised in Lufkin," answered the man.

"Then you don't need an alien card," Mrs. Reeves began.

"But I'm feelin' pretty bad, and I want the government to know that I'm pretty sick. Ain't I suppose to get an ailin' card and tell 'em I'm sick? I heard you are supposed to get one of them ailin' cards and register if you are ailin'."

"No," said Mrs. Reeves. "You are not supposed to fill out an alien card unless you were born in a foreign country and are not a citizen of the United States. An alien is a foreigner."

"Oh, I see now. Excuse me."

LOST BROTHERS REUNITED   *February 11*

Walter Ganus of Kountze and Conrad Ganus of Vidor were reunited recently with a brother they had not seen for 50 years. The family was separated in 1914 and three of the children were adopted out. They lost track of one another. A family by the name of Rowland adopted the brother whose name is now Hugh Rowland. He had been trying to locate his brothers since he retired from 31 year's service in the Navy and Marines. He located Walter and called on January 30 from Mobile, Alabama. He arrived in Kountze and stayed until last Thursday. It was a dream come true.

STILLBORN INFANTS ABANDONED IN WOODS

The bodies of two stillborn infant boys were found in a paper sack in a pasteboard box on the banks of Village Creek Sunday afternoon on Highway 327. The Sheriff's Department is continuing an investigation. It is believed that the infants were white. County Attorney Dwayne Overstreet said a pathologist's report indicated that the infants had been stillborn Saturday night. The bodies were found by Adolphus Lewis shortly before 2 p.m. Sunday. Judge C. A. Kimball, justice of the peace, held an inquest but said he is withholding a verdict pending completion of the pathologist's report. Bodies of the twin boys were taken to Farmer's Funeral Home in Silsbee.

BODER, THE LAUGHING INFIDEL   *March 4*

After I mentioned Paducah, Texas, in this column last week, I got to thinking about way out there in Cottle County, and then I began remembering how life was on Salt Creek, six miles southwest of Paducah in the 1920's. I remembered Boder Walker, who was our closest neighbor. Boder nearly always had a dip of snuff in his mouth, as did his wife, also.

The Walkers had six boys and one girl. They had one son named Debs and that name tells a whole lot about Boder Walker. For Boder was a socialist and he named Debs after Eugene V. Debs, the great Chicago lawyer who ran for president on the socialist ticket several times. Boder subscribed to The Fort Worth Star-Telegram. We lived a mile from the Star route and Boder would always be waiting for the mailman when he came by the box at about 3 p.m. He would read the Telegram all the way home, walking slowly. I was for William Jennings Bryan and Boder was for Debs. I was for Bryan not because I did not believe in evolution or believed the Bible literally as Bryan said he did, but because Bryan made his "Cross of Gold" speech and because he was a Democrat. Boder thought that I had not learned much in my two years in the university because I defended Bryan.

Boder also read Bob Ingersoll, the infidel, and Brann, the iconoclast, who carried on a feud with Baylor University. But the Star-Telegram was Boder's big pastime. It would take him five hours to read everything in it.

Boder kept all his possessions in a huge humpbacked trunk in his bedroom, including his Ingersoll books. Now we used to go up to the Walkers to play 42. One time during the summer, we went up there and during the 42 game, Boder said to his youngest son, Durward, who was named for the hero of *Lena Rivers*, a novel that came out serially every six years in the Dallas Semi-Weekly Farm News, "Durward take this here key and unlock my trunk and get out that big watermelon and let's open it." Boder didn't trust those boys of his out of his sight, and he said any man was a fool who would trust any boy out of his sight.

After the Walker children quit school, they were on their own. Boder didn't want them hanging around. They had to go out and get jobs. Since none of them graduated from high school, they were on their own young in life. Boder had a loud explosive laugh; it didn't fool his sons. They knew he meant business. You could hear Boder laughing a half mile. His laugh began with a great shout, and it occurred like clockwork during any conversation he was in. It didn't matter whether there was anything to laugh at or not. A laugh like that is called a nervous laugh nowadays, but Boder was not nervous. Boder simply laughed at the whole human race and he liked to do it often. I think that if Boder had not decided that he would laugh at the human race, he would have been compelled to be an assassin. Neither did he plan his laughter. Just about every five minutes he would see something explosively funny about the human race, the plight of humanity or of animals to laugh about. In a sense, the laugh was cruel and derisive, but it was full of genuine enjoyment.

I always thought that Boder wanted to be an infidel like Ingersoll. It was plain he shared the skeptical view on immortality that Debs professed to have. I never did hear Boder come out and say flatfooted that he was an infidel, and nobody else ever did, but Boder did not spend any time inside churches. Once in a great while he would go to church, walking two miles from his house to Salt Creek school house. But Boder never would go inside. He would sit outside, squatted on his heels, or leaning up against the house. There he would talk to other men in the community who would bring their wives and children to church but never would go inside. Boder was not a whittler; he always carried a whet rock with him and when he sat on his heels or haunches or whiled away the time talking, he would whet his pocket knife which had five blades, one six inches long. He would whet the pocket knife for hours, every once in a while laughing, and if he was outside the school house we would hear him and punch each other. If Boder could catch what the preacher was saying he would comment on it unflatteringly. He cussed preachers as much as he cussed politicians.

We had our church and Sunday school at Salt Creek school house in the afternoon. It would begin at 2 o'clock and last until 4 p.m. It was nearly always Sunday school because the preacher didn't come often. My father organized and founded the Salt Creek Methodist Church which met in the school house. Boder was a violent man at heart, but he played 42 and he laughed and kept watermelons in his trunk from his greedy boys. He was a violent man, and he had no way to let off steam. Once at Salt Creek school house, in the cistern house, I saw him slap a beginning Methodist preacher because the preacher said he had heard that Woodrow Wilson, who was then president, was dying of syphillis. My father tried hard to be a good man. Boder did not try to be anything except a man who never lost his temper.

At Sunday school, we would sing at least a dozen songs and sometimes I would play the organ. I think that Boder liked the singing. But I am sure that the reason he came to church was not to hear singing or preaching either, but only to see and visit the neighbors and cuss everybody but Jim Ferguson and Eugene V. Debs, and quote you The Star-Telegram word for word. Boder walked nearly every place he went, even to town, unless he had to buy groceries, then he drove his mules hitched to the wagon. Sometimes he would put on a black suit, tie and white shirt, and sometimes he would wear his blue overalls.

Boder's oldest son was an Assembly of God preacher and he was a favorite subject of conversation with Boder who was inordinately proud of his son and proud that he was a preacher. The son still lived back in Montague County but ever so often he and his family would come out to visit the Walkers and this was a big day for them. The son was a true evangelist, and he always "talked" to his father about conversion. Boder would put up a big argument and quote Bob Ingersoll, and when Boder got to that point, the son would drop to his knees and pray fearful prayers that would make you tremble.

By today's standards, the Walkers and the Fullingims lived in utter poverty. We had no bathroom, just the canyon below the house; no running water, we hauled our drinking water on a sled in a barrel from a well in the canyon; we never went to a movie, we went to town maybe twice a month, and we had no car. We did have a phonograph, and we read books, and we had an organ. We thought we were pretty well to do, even if we went to town in a wagon. We owned our land, 320 acres, and we talked in our family about sunsets and sunrises as people nowadays talk about TV shows.

When I came back from the university after my second year, Boder wanted to know what I had learned. I could not tell him, but he asked many questions, and he would argue with me. I would take him books to read but I doubt if he read them. He was not interested in novels or poetry. He had troubles in mind enough without borrowing any from men of imagination.

I never lived in Paducah after 1927 and I don't know what happened to the Walkers, but I bet I could guess. I would say that they left that land of sun, sandstorms and harsh winds and went back to Nocona, and that before he died, Boder was converted by his son, the preacher.

LBJ AND NEGRO VOTING RIGHTS *March 18*

Since the column below was written last Thursday President Johnson has asked Congress to pass a law guaranteeing that all Negroes in the South be registered to vote, with the appointment of federal registrars if necessary.

In doing this, he knew a mighty howl would of course go up in the South, but let 'em howl. I, for one, am tired of seeing brutal and sadistic sheriffs and patrolmen terrorize Negroes in inhuman ways. It makes the blood boil to see burly Alabama officers of the law pour tear gas into a crowd of Negroes, stick them with electric cattle prods and beat them to the ground with clubs. The Alabamans and some of the rest of the Southerners will scream look how terrible they are being treated, but what have they been doing to the Negro for 100 years since a four-year Civil War won the black man the right to vote?

Let's not kid ourselves. We all know that justice is a mockery in both Alabama and Mississippi and in Georgia, where the Negro is concerned. It has got to the point that about the only one who goes to the electric chair is the black man. It is maintained mainly for his benefit. Yet, the homes and churches of the Negro are burned and bombed and no one is punished. Grand juries even refuse to indict white murderers of a Negro. Mississippi has not yet indicted anyone for the murder of the two white men who were shot and killed last summer. Mississippi officials know who did it, all right. The whole world knows who did it. The murderers of those two white men sit back and chortle and make vulgar, crude jokes as they throw their weight around. One of the suspected killers is an officer of the law. Yes, it is time to let Alabama, Georgia, and Mississippi know the might and the right of the federal government.

The Negro has been voting in Hardin County about 75 years. It is true that during much of that time, his vote has been bought and paid for, for maybe a little cash, maybe a bottle of liquor or maybe a threat or a favor or a promise. It is true that there are people in Hardin County who can still vote the Negro, but whole blocs of white people can also be voted for a favor, a threat, a bottle of liquor. But at least the Negro can vote, and we are better off for it, and Alabama and Mississippi would be better off if they would let the Negro vote. We must also bear in mind that there is an increasing number of Negro voters whose vote can't be bought, coerced, threatened, whose vote is not for sale to anyone. They vote as they please. They may get fired or persecuted but they still vote as they please.

The picture of the burly Alabama deputy wiping the blood off his billy club and saying, "I got just one good lick at her before she ran into the church," and the picture of another deputy beating a Negro woman on the breasts with a club, leaves one with the feeling that President Johnson is not going to let it happen again.

Some Southerners may rail against the so-called "outside agitators," that is the white preachers, nuns and priests from the North who marched with the Selma Negroes, but we all can see now that the Negro in Alabama and Mississippi would be no nearer the ballot box now than they were this time 100 years ago if it had not been for the marches, and President Johnson knows that.

⊂⊖⊃

RECOLLECTIONS OF KILRAINE   *April 8*

Nearly all the friends and cronies of his youth are gone. Carter Hart at 82 has outlived most of his generation. He is one of the few men still living, if not the only one, who hunted in the Big Thicket with Ben and Bud Hooks, Ben Lilly and others whose names are already in the history books. I went down Saturday to see Carter Hart, to talk to him about Kilraine, a Negro who lived here 50 years ago, and I immediately realized that we ought to be talking about Carter Hart who was born at Village Mills and has lived in this community continuously. Mr. Hart seems to be in good health. He is a heavy man, and he has trouble getting out of his easy chair, but once he gets on his feet there is nothing feeble about him. Most of all, his mind and memory are as fresh as you want.

I went to his house to find out some things about Kilraine, the master roper and bronc buster. Kilraine was mainly a dog man. He had his own hounds and he went on hunts with the Hookses, Mr. Hart and that gang. "Kill," as others have told me, could rope any foot of a horse. You could name the foot and he would rope it. But Kilraine, though he was an expert roper and dog man, was a poor shot and he never hunted bear.

Jack Flowers says that Kilraine was the only Negro who could go to Saratoga and spend the entire day there, and all day he would be surrounded by hilarious audiences, as Kilraine acted out his funny stories. Both Mr. Hart and Charlie Roberts say that Kilraine was what they use to call a "white man's Negro" meaning that his actions were designed to suit white men. He would put on shows for their benefit, telling stories to amuse them. Hart said that Kilraine came down here from Jefferson County where he had worked for Langham and other cattlemen in the early part of this century. Kilraine had served a term in the pen in Jefferson County for cattle theft. He was still liked by the big cattlemen down there and one of them gave him a handmade pair of bits which had silver mountings on them. Hart keeps these bits, now rusty, in a drawer in his desk in his house. The fact that Kilraine gave the bits to Hart should indicate what Kilraine thought of Hart.

Mr. Hart told about the biggest bear he ever killed in the Big Thicket. Both Ben and Bud said they thought it was the biggest bear ever killed in this area. Mr. Hart and helpers skinned it, cut it into quarters and brought it to Kountze and weighed it. They weighed the hide, head, quarters and all, and it all weighed over 600 pounds. Mr. Hart said the Big Thicket bear ate just about what a hog eats, and some of them ate hogs.

Kilraine is remembered here as a master of dogs, hounds, horses, and hunting, and as one of the most popular and exciting residents here between 1895 and 1918. Kilraine, who probably got his nickname from Jake Kilraine, a famous bare-knuckle fighter of that time, took care of the dogs and the drives at the famous Ben Hooks camp in the Big Thicket during the annual Hooks fall hunt. In Kountze, Kilraine always had a pack of his own dogs, honed to a fine hunting ability.

Glover Prince said that he and Kilraine and the dogs, about 25, slept in the same room on cold nights on a hunt. He said Kilraine always took off his hat when talking to white people, and was a picture of humility.

Goat McDonald said that Kilraine came here when a wild west show broke up in Houston. The show had played in Mexico City and down there Kilraine bulldogged a Mexican fighting bull, the vicious kind, grabbed the animal's nose between his teeth and held him, and that the Mexicans almost mobbed him for it. Prince says that Kilraine came from Houston with a number of Germans who worked in the sawmill at Old Olive for Olive Sternenberger. The Germans' graves are still out there with German lettering on the grave stones.

When Kilraine made dog bread, Prince said, he built a fire under a black wash pot, filled it about half full of water, added coons and any other meat or bones he had, and boiled it for hours and then added meal and bran and sometimes shorts and stirred like the blazes. Then he let it set and later cut it up.

Gus Hooks says that Kilraine always made the Ben Hooks fall hunt. Prince said that one time a fellow named Banker, who really was a banker, went to a Ben Hooks hunt and was put on a stand to wait for deer. Kilraine was in charge of the drive and saw the bear when the dogs jumped it. The bear lit out straight for Banker's stand, with Kilraine in hot pursuit to get to Banker before the bear did. Banker saw the bear coming and got hunting fright and went up a small tree, or tried to. When Kilraine got there Banker thought that Kilraine did it on purpose and held his gun on Kilraine and was threatening to shoot him any minute when Uncle Ben Hooks also hurried up, but only after he had killed the small bear that had come his way. Kilraine was down on his knees begging for his life.

MORE ON KILRAINE   April 8

Dear Mr. Editor:

You asked me if I knew "Kilraine" (Johnny Williams). Of course my answer was yes. I came to Kountze in 1906 and Kilraine was here then. Carter Hart and Carl Richardson know more about him than I. Kilraine was no ordinary Negro. He was ordinary in appearance, ordinary in size, maybe 5'6" or 7", 140 to 150 pounds, but he was not ordinary in many other respects. He was known as a great deer hunter, but strange as it may seem Kilraine never killed a deer that I know of, but that did not detract from his cheer and enthusiasm when others did. He was known to holler to his driving partner, "Here they go; shoot, shoot" while he sat on his horse and watched them go. Kilraine rode a saddle with pockets built in it and he carried his shot gun shells in these pockets. Some of them years old. I've been told you would find squirrel shot and a mixture of all sizes of buck shot in those pockets and I do not think Kilraine ever noticed what kind he put in his gun. He wasn't going to shoot anyway.

His joy was in putting the deer to running and the hounds bawling out. He was known widely as a storyteller, and he was one of the best, and an actor all thrown together. His stories were nearly always told at the fire when the guests were just drinking and relaxing after the hunt. He never volunteered to entertain, but did not hold back or hesitate when someone would ask him about "Big John" and the bear fight, or any of his many campfire stories.

The most valuable gift of Kilraine was his personality. Simple, un-

adulterated friendliness and cheerfulness. He had no enemies and he liked everybody. He was the only Negro I know of that was welcome in Saratoga in those days, and those days ended more than 30 years ago. I did not realize he had been dead so long until upon reflection.

As stated before, I first knew him in 1906 upon my arrival in Kountze, but it was several years later before I really got to know him. My first few years here was fox hunting with such fellows as Uncle Bud Hooks, Bryant Coe, Carter Hart, Carl Richardson, Tom and Jack Dies, and Judge D. F. Singleton. Then I took up deer hunting and Kilraine and I were closely associated in that sport as long as he lived. I could talk and talk relating tales, incidents and experiences. But I believe we all overlooked the real personality of our colored friend. He was a fine, inoffensive man and he liked everybody, just people, and naturally he was liked in return.

One of his stories that always brought a laugh was about Mr. Fletcher, who did not trust himself or Kilraine to find their way back to camp after a certain drive, so when they came to a fork in the road Mr. Fletcher got down and put an old cow head pointing down the road they were to take on their return. Some of his friends noted this action, so after Mr. Fletcher and Kilraine rode on they got down and switched the head to point wrong. Finally upon their return to the spot, Kilraine wanted to ignore the cow head and take the road, but Mr. Fletcher had no doubt, because he had marked it. Mr. Fletcher's idea prevailed and a long ride ended in a dead end. This story was usually told in the presence of Mr. Fletcher and he would tell about the big argument between himself and Kilraine. And everybody would have a big laugh.

A friend asked what Kilraine did besides hunt. That gave me another thought. He was just a handy man, always had a wagon and team and did hauling; he was called on when a bad horse needed riding; he was called on when a wild steer, horse or cow needed to be roped. And there was always time out when a hunt was on.

Kilraine was a very remarkable, friendly and unassuming Negro man we all liked and thought a lot of.

(Signed)   J. A. McKim, Sr.

YARBOROUGH ALWAYS BACKS THE PEOPLE   *May 20*

Texas has never had a senator like Ralph Yarborough, for the senior senator from Texas has always unfailingly voted for the people. He is deaf to the pressures of special interests and lobbyists. His first thought is for the great masses of Texans and Americans, their education and welfare. There is no way to corrupt Senator Yarborough and his voting record proves it; there is no way for advocates of prejudice, bigotry, greed or favoritism to get to him. I can think of great senators Texas has had, among them Sam Houston and John Reagan, and Yarborough reminds me most of them. Like Reagan, Yarborough's ear is attuned to the deeds, desires, and aspirations of the great masses. What brings this on is Yarborough's vote to ban the poll tax in states that have the poll tax as a qualification for voting. In casting his vote, Yarborough did not go along with the President who said that it may be unconstitutional, but how could banning the poll tax be unconstitutional, if that portion of the civil rights bill that eliminates literacy tests for voting is constitutional? The bill abolishes literacy tests. The quickest way to give the vote to most voters in the state is to abolish the poll tax. Texas may be the worst victim of the poll tax when you consider that a greater percentage of Negroes than whites vote. Why is that? Latin Americans and poor whites are the ones who are being denied the vote.

Most of those simply don't have the money in January to buy a poll tax. I know a lot of people who are so broke in January they can't afford to buy a poll tax. I applaud Senator Yarborough for voting to abolish the poll tax as the quickest way to give the vote to all. I can see why John Connally has not gone on the warpath against the poll tax. Connally wants the people to give him a four-year term. If too many Latin Americans and poor whites voted they would possibly deny him.

The only people Yarborough has to fear are the wealthy purveyors of stories like the lie that he was bribed by Billy Sol Estes. The Dallas Morning News spawned that lie. The special interests never want a man like Yarborough in office. He does not toady to them. Connally has yet to favor one single bill that will place a tax burden on those most able to pay. A four-year term for Connally would wreck our school system, would take control of state government completely out of the hands of the people and perpetuate it in the hands of lobbyists and big industrialists.

THAT LOOK IN HIS FACE   *May 27*

I saw this boy who looked to be about 16 or 17, and he was already taking the place of his father who died recently. There was that serious look on his face, and the grief and sense of loss were in the face and he was doing for his mother. It's a responsible row that boy has to hoe, but he will do it.

~~

MORE ON KILRAINE   *July 8*

Forty years ago, Oscar Marshall, a longtime member of the Kountze city council, integrated baseball in Kountze and nobody thought anything about it, but Leon Barlow, a big wheel now in the stevedore union in San Francisco, tells about it in the following in his own words in a letter to Goat McDonald.

Leon was writing about Kilraine's baseball team in 1926. He said that the team played Woodville in Kountze. Present were Oscar Marshall and D. Q. Creel. "That Sunday, our catcher," wrote Leon, "was Son Pears. He got hurt and Mr. Oscar Marshall caught the 7th, 8th, and 9th innings for Kilraine and we won 5-3."

Goat asked Oscar about that the other day and Oscar remembered it. "Just trying to help the boys out and nobody thought a thing about it."

"I was Kilraine's manager and secretary in 1925," wrote Barlow. "Our ball club played Prairie View College. We had Mr. Jim Daniel's truck to go in, Robert Hooks' Ford car, Archie Arline's Ford, and Ralph Brackin's Ford. Ray Toliver and Alton Creel went with us so we could get through Saratoga safely." Saratoga used to have up signs that said, "Negro don't let the sun set on you in Saratoga." Saratoga has no Negroes to this day, though Kilraine was always welcome there because he was such a comic and storyteller.

"James Berry, a close associate of Kilraine's, should know where he is buried, also Charlie Arline, Judge Bevil and Carl Richardson, Sr." Barlow wrote in his letter to Goat.

Barlow made good in San Francisco. He is head of the big

and powerful stevedore union. He has numerous relatives in Kountze.

THE CHANGE IN CONNALLY   *August 19*

Governor Connally is becoming more politically overbearing and obnoxious all the time. He now sets himself up as an authority on the morals and purposes of people. I have never heard one word against the Farmers Union except that it did not support Shivers and Daniel, but here lately Connally said no to the people of 13 Texas counties that wanted the Union to sponsor a job corps project, and as a consequence the 13 counties do not have any project at all and the economy of those counties will have to do without several million dollars they otherwise might have got.

A great change has come over Connally since the assassination. Remember how we all felt so sorry for him and how he never failed to act maimed and look stricken, but since he was elected the second time he has become arrogant and haughty. If he says it, he thinks it's so. He may be the favorite of President Johnson, but for the life of me I can not see what Lyndon sees in Connally who has signed into law, and plotted and obtained its passage, an act that will enable every school pupil to go up to a teacher and say, "Teacher you beg us not to smoke, but you get paid in cigarette tax money." A slogan of the Texas public school system might well be, "Smoke more cancer sticks and educate more children." Connally plotted the law and passed it and if that is not the essence of hypocrisy, then show me the stuff it is made of. As it is now, the teachers of this state get most of their pay from beer, cigarette and liquor taxes. That puts the teachers in a wretched position to teach children, don't you think?

CROSSROAD CAMPAIGN FUNDS?   *September 30*

The way John Connally, Waggoner Carr, Preston Smith and Secretary of State Martin Dies announced for the four highest elective offices in Texas, that is announced as a slate, indicates the total depravity of the political establishment which has run Texas since Allan Shivers showed them how it was done. That establishment is composed of all the big corporations and their lobbyists. They not only control the legislature but they are the only ones that have money to finance state political campaigns. You won't hear any squawking from these four about shortage of campaign funds. They will have all they need. That is part of the deal. If anybody runs against these four, they will have to raise campaign funds at the crossroads.

The establishment never contributed a dime to the Yarborough campaigns, and that is why he is still paying off campaign debts. If you are naive enough to believe that the millions these four will spend to get elected comes from anybody except the big rich who have their way in the legislature, then you can go to the foot of the class.

Both Carr and Smith wanted to run for governor. Well, why didn't they? It takes money to run for a state office, and Connally is the man who tells the establishment who to give the dollars to. They had to run as Connally directed or not run at all. It's all for one and one for all with those four men. Connally had made up his mind not to run if the senate were not increased by eight to 31, but the establishment really got worked up over that; it saw that it now needs Connally more than ever. It assured Connally that the cash would be forthcoming to brainwash the people of Texas to vote for the four-year term in November. Connally hesitated but he finally gave in. So you can look for a big snow job to get you to vote for the four-year term. The Establishment also decided it would need Connally more than ever if the four-year term scheme doesn't get approved. With that kind of a revolt from the people, they decided Connally might even have an opponent in 1966, and that the likes of Smith and Carr running for governor could easily go under so they insisted Connally run and he says he will.

The American people are dedicated to the belief that the most taxes should be paid by people of property and money, that those who make the most money should pay the most taxes. The Texas taxing system does not operate on that basis. In Texas, those least able to pay, pay the most taxes. The special interests, the corporations and the Big Rich in Texas who put these four men up to run, pay less taxes, comparatively, than old age pensioners, small town businessmen, workers and all of us poor white trash in general.

ᴄᴈ◡

CITIZENSHIP & THE KKK   *November 4*

It's 30 miles to Woodville, 30 miles from Woodville to Livingston, 40 miles from there to Huntsville, and 25 miles up the highway to Madisonville where 1,300 persons attended a Ku Klux Klan rally in a cow pasture the other night. About half wore KKK robes, according to the Associated Press. Most responsible citizens of that community probably realize now that they need a KKK like they need a hole in the head. When the thing first started, they probably laughed and ridiculed the KKKs as a bunch of kooks, as responsible citizens did in Alabama, Mississippi, South Carolina, Georgia, and Florida, where now a KKK robe is a passport to commit murder, arson, mayhem and bombings. Responsible citizens are not laughing now at Madisonville, and they are afraid to frown.

That Klan meeting 125 miles from here is too close for comfort. For if Madisonville has one, you can put it down that there are KKKs in Huntsville and Livingston. They will become missionaries and will try to evangelize their neighbors. Maybe they already have contacts in Hardin County.

What is a responsible citizen? That's a good question. You could probably add to or take from any definition you might hear. My definition of a responsible citizen is one who upholds law and order, who does not belittle his fellow man, who believes in obeying all laws, not just some, who will not get up in a public place and make an inflammatory speech against any race or religion, who will not say to a neighbor, "You want your daughter to sit in a classroom with Negroes" who will speak out when bigotry, race hatred, religious prejudice and scorn for the laws of the land is preached by demagogues. A responsible citizen will speak out against the KKK which tries to take the law into its own hands.

Now I don't think the KKK could ever gain a foothold in Har-

din County. There are not enough potential Klansmen here.
There was back in the 1920s. Today only wild-eyed radicals flock
to join it.

BALD CYPRESS

PART THREE
1966–1975

YEAR 1966

An old-time patriotic speech was soul-stirring and inspiring. I used to hear them from 1912 through the early 1920s.

What the old-time patriotic orator did was to praise everything. He'd start in with the Declaration of Independence, ramble through the Constitution, single out each member of the Supreme Court, list all the heroes of the Texas and American revolutions and of the Civil War. He lauded everything in sight in the past and present. He never had a word of criticism about the government, and the last thing he would do would be to toast the flag, and what he would do was paraphrase the words of the World War I song, "She's a grand old flag and she never shall drag, but forever in triumph shall wave. She's the emblem of the land I love, the home of the free and the brave, every heart beats true to the red, white and blue. . . ."

In 1966 the old-time patriotic speech has gone the way of the Model T and so has old-time patriotism. Nowadays, it depends on who's making the speech. If the orator is from the South he will tell you that Martin Luther King is a Communist and so are all the other Negro leaders who want to vote as they please in Alabama and Mississippi. If the orator is a beatnik or a follower of Senators Fullbright and Morse he will tell you that we have no business in Vietnam and should never have sent troops to the Dominican Republic. No Speaker is content to merely wave the flag nowadays. Everybody is finding fault with LBJ. The Great Society, the New Frontier and the New Deal are fighting words to millions of Americans.

Every night, if you want to, you can turn to almost any radio station and hear that the Communist takeover is near at hand, for night radio has become monopolized by radical right wingers, radical preachers, all chanting the alleged Communist menace. They tell gruesome stories that rival James Bond escapades. There are the talk programs which go on for hours; in these, little old ladies in tennis shoes get on the phone and repeat the John Birch news letters which attack the government, the Supreme Court, the United Nations and LBJ.

An old-time patriotic speech which concentrated on praising Democracy (a bad word to the radio orators), the government, "our great president," would stick out like a sore thumb. Every night literally tens of thousands of words are devoted to attacking the very institutions the old-time patriotic orators praised. All you hear is bad; you hear nothing good about the government, the Supreme Court, the President, even the armed forces.

It would be nice for a change to hear that our armed forces are defending the nation's future in Vietnam, and that our fighting men are great, even if 50 per cent of the men in combat are Negroes, and another 15 per cent are Latin Americans and poor whites from the South. For the first time in the history of this nation Negro casualties outnumber white.

The reason there are more Negroes and Latins in the armed forces is that they have trouble finding jobs, fewer go to college, whereas the colleges are bulging with white draft-exempt students. Then there is absolute equality in the army. The colored man in the armed forces can do anything the white man does, whereas he cannot at home. The old myth that the colored man was not a good soldier has been exploded. During World War II, soldiers of Mexican descent from Texas and the Southwest, including California, were outstanding. There were more petty officers from among this group than white. More Mexican-Americans won the Congressional Medal of Honor in World War II, based on number, than any other ethnic group. It was an old saying in World War II that the Latin stayed a private as long as he was in the United States, but that he was made a sergeant the minute he landed on foreign soil because of his bravery.

It would be nice to hear some patriotic orator give Martin Luther King his just dues, for King is no more of a Communist than you are. King wants only one thing: civil rights for his race. I applauded when I heard James Meredith say over TV that white supremacy must be destroyed, and it must, for there is no such thing as white supremacy except in the minds of some people who still think the Negro should be a slave. I could sympathize with the Negroes massed on the grounds of the state capital at Jackson when they burned the Confederate flag which has become a hate-the-Negro symbol. The way it turns out usually is that the 1966 people who wave the Confederate flag and violently oppose civil rights for the Negro had ancestors who were hiding out in the woods in the 1860s to keep from fighting for that flag.

When I read the death roll of the Vietnam war and see it top-heavy with names like Lopez and Garcia and Franklin Delano Jones, then I realize that it takes both the white and black keys on the piano to play the Star Spangled Banner. I first heard that remark, made by a Negro army officer, July 4, 1943 on a Pacific Island.

I would like to hear a patriotic orator praise the Supreme Court, the United Nations, the Congress, the President, the Armed Forces. I believe in the court; I believe that Warren is as great as justice as were Roger Taney and Oliver W. Holmes. I believe that if the world is ever to achieve peace it will be through the United Nations. I want to believe that every president we have ever had conscientiously acted and made decisions under the oath he took. I believe LBJ is now doing what he thinks he must do, and that what he has done was because the oath he took compelled him to do it.

FREEDOMS THAT SHOULD BE LOST   *August 4*

Every so often somebody comes in here and complains that we are losing our freedoms. Just giving them away. Every day. Then you read the daily papers and you see the same thing on their editorial pages. There is not a big city in the United States that is not right now moving heaven and earth trying to milk the federal treasury for stupendous sums of money, and daily papers in those cities are egging them on and at the same time decrying the loss of freedom! Columns and columns of letters from people who write as if they were living chained in a black hole and subsisting on bread and water moan the loss of freedom. You pick up the morning paper and there are the radical right wing columnists, Drummond, Buckley, Chamberlain, you name 'em, all chanting the loss of freedom. The only time the daily press in Texas ever points with pride is when it is bragging on Texas' right to work law, and Texas has more destitute, dependent children than any state in the Union except Alabama and Mississippi.

So what I would like to do is ask all these perpetual gripers just what freedoms they have lost, freedoms that their fathers or their grandfathers had. What freedoms are they losing every day. Just name them. Don't be bashful, be specific. Get right down to the lick log and put up or shut up. All right, what freedoms have they lost?

Let's quit beating around the bush and answer for them. Let's name some of the so-called freedoms they have lost that seem to be hurting them most. They can no longer use the Bible in schools to propagate their particular brand of denominationalism, and impose their religion on children. They assert their belief in separation of church and state as guaranteed by the Constitution, but they insist on teaching religion in schools. They expect teachers to teach the Bible and they won't even send their children to Sunday school. They have abandoned family prayer, but they expect the school to do the job they or their church should do. The home and the church are the places to teach the Bible, not the school.

They complain unceasingly of federal control, but they go to Washington instead of Austin to get money for every improvement. They want the money without any strings attached. They want bridges, dams, deep water ports, medical centers from the federal government. They oppose state income taxes, corporation taxes, higher taxes on natural resources, hogtieing the state from paying higher teacher salaries, and building more schools. They preach states rights to no end and refuse to give their own state any right. Then when the state is unable or unwilling to provide the improvements its citizens demand, they go to the Federal government.

We have lost some freedom. We have lost the freedom to discriminate against any American. We have lost the freedom to deny any American the right to attend any school of his choice, or to keep any American out of any hospital built with federal funds.

We have lost the freedom to segregate the armed forces. We have lost the freedom to keep anyone in economic slavery. We have lost the freedom to deny anyone the vote. We have lost the freedom to make the Negro bend the knee, bow down, to cow him to get off the sidewalk. Is that the kind of freedom we have lost that is burning us up?

The truth is that no white in America has lost any freedom, but because the Negro has gained some that have been long overdue him, some of us think that we have lost part of ours, and that is true.

We are now engaged in a great struggle to alleviate poverty. Many feel that Texas, being one of the richest states in the union, should have better schools, should not lead the nation in the number of poverty-stricken families, but as usual, our leaders are waiting for the federal government to take over, and at the same time screaming that we are giving away our freedoms. But when old age pension checks and social security checks started going out to the aged, we lost a freedom, and that was the freedom to die destitute.

NEWSPAPERMEN & NOVELS   *August 11*

I got to thinking about my 40 years as a newspaperman, the last 20 years as a newspaperman-printer. I made a mistake by studying journalism at the University. What I always have had, since I was 10 years old, was an ambition to write fiction. I thought I could learn to write well if I studied journalism and became a newspaperman. What I did not know was that if you worked for a newspaper you would have time for nothing but journalism.

There are hundreds of newspapermen in the same boat as I. They all wanted to write the Great American Novel, and they all ended up newspapermen and nothing more. There are some who made it, but none of them made it while connected with a newspaper. Ernest Hemingway started out working for newspapers, but not for long, but then I have never liked Hemingway. To me he is just a writer of super feature stories. To me, there is only one great writer of fiction that America has produced: William Faulkner. Nobody else can compare with him.

I did some pretty good writing in the navy, and that was when I learned that if writing is in you it will come out if you don't waste all your energy in writing for newspapers. Still I am a frustrated writer. I never did master a style, in fact I never did create one. What I wanted to write was literature, but I never began to accomplish it. I had several hindrances that are part of my nature. First, I am a sentimentalist, and try though I did, I could not keep sentimentality out of my writing. Now I am not talking about newspaper and column writing. I am talking about creative writing. And between the time I started out trying to write creatively, between the 1920s and the 1960s, fiction styles changed violently several times. By the time I became familiar with one it was out of date and a new one would take its place. What I didn't have in me was the ability to create my own timeless style. One thing you can't write in the 1960s is anything that is sentimental. But I, at the age of 64, I am irrepressible when it comes to writing. I'm still at it. Still trying to write a book that people would like to read. But I'll probably never get around to writing that book. But I can assure you that it was a rare month indeed in the last 40 years in which I did not plan at least one general interest book, one novel, one epic poem.

The only way to write is to sit down at the typewriter and begin. That's my trouble. I use up all my passion to write, writing up what kind of a trip somebody had in Arizona, what Martha Laird cooked for Christmas dinner, but I am not griping. I am satisfied but not content. After 40 years I know what I like most. I like people.

I love people because they go on trips, cook big dinners, catch fish, get married, get divorced, get rich or stay poor. I am always looking for the story in every person, and I think every person has a story.

When I first started out in the newspaper business, I thought that the big stories were about fires and crimes, as I had been taught, and I used to chase fires like mad. Then there were the political and business stories, and I liked the political stories best. But since I have been in Kountze I like people stories, what they do, what they think, what they eat, what they talk about.

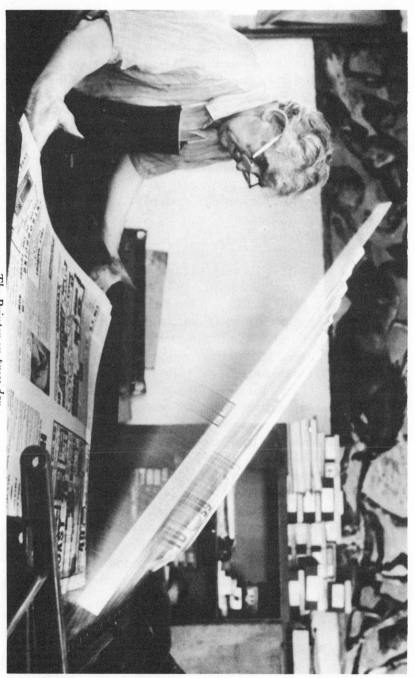

The Printer on press day.

COLLEGE DEGREES & CARROT PICKERS   *September 22*

Probably every column I write makes a lot of people mad, but before I go any further I warn you that this one is going to make more people mad than usual. It's on account of the subjects I'm going to take up, Robert Kennedy and John Connally. If you can't abide Kennedy, then don't read any further. I don't want to be blamed for any ulcer you might acquire. If you like John Connally, then stop right here, period.

First's let's take up the persnickety doings of Connally lately, and in particular what his apologists called his "confrontation" with the Valley vegetable workers' march on Austin. A "confrontation," that's what The Dallas Morning News called it, as if Connally were confronting a dragon. According to the Dallas News, which is always egging on radical right wing haters, the governor declined to call a special session to raise stoop labor in the carrot patches to $1.25 per hour, and he told the marchers from the Valley, led by a Catholic priest and a Houston Baptist preacher, that he would not dignify their march by showing up at Austin on Labor Day. This confrontation took place near New Braunfels on the highway. With the governor were Attorney General Waggoner Carr and House Speaker Ben Barnes who let the governor do their talking for them. Now what the Dallas News glories in is what it said Connally told the Mexican-Americans. Connally said, "What the migrant workers need most is education." Now wasn't that a smart thing to say? It was so smart it was dumb; what would anybody with a degree be doing yanking carrots out of the ground and picking up cantaloupes? The governor allowed as how the field worker is disappearing on account of mechanical pickers. And we agree. But they haven't disappeared yet, and St. John also should know that they are not going to disappear in the Rio Grande Valley as long as people can hire illiterate Mexican-Americans to pick for a dollar a day, as they have been doing. Nobody with a degree is going to pull up onions or chop the heads off cabbage roots.

We agree that the harvest of farm crops is becoming mechanized. But it's not completely yet. Who is going to do it until it does? The gist of St. John's advice was "go to college and quit messin' with mush melons." That's another sample of the remarkable education theories which his 22 education commissioners have come up with in the last four years.

So the governor did not show up at Austin on Labor Day when the valley marchers arrived at the capitol, but 25,000 other persons did, including John Connally's brother who at the last minute fell in behind Senator Ralph Yarborough and marched the last four blocks with the horny-handed stoop workers. The papers kept saying that Connally had another engagement, but they never said where he was. I'd like a report on that.

Those people marched 400 miles, walked all the way from the Valley to Austin, just to get $1.25 an hour for their backbreaking stoop labor, and the governor should have walked the last mile with the marchers. Personally, I don't think the marchers had any reasonable ground for asking for a special session of the legislature. A special session should concern the entire state, but you have to sympathize with them. The governor, by motoring down there in his Cadillac, was like some big wheel with a degree and lots of dough going out to Pigeon Roost Prairie and telling the pulpwood cutters that they should go to college. It's beside the point if there were labor organizers or organized labor back of the march. The point was that these people were telling the whole state they don't make $1.25 an hour and they think they should. What's the governor got against somebody making a dollar and a quarter an hour?

St. John boycotted the Labor Day meeting but Bobby Kennedy didn't and lawdy how I love that man! If you want to know exactly why Bobby is leading the Gallup poll over LBJ, I'll tell you. There's no doubt in the people's mind that Bobby is for them first, last and always. Bobby is on the right side of every issue. Bobby isn't playing footsie with the fat cats, the racists, the hawks and doves, and then acting as if he were on the side of "Koons, Kikes and Katholics," too. Bobby sent a telegram to the marchers telling them that he was with them.

I salute Senator Yarborough who is not ashamed to walk beside a wet-back, a pulpwood cutter or a melon handler. Senator Yarborough does not think that the point is whether they have any education or not. He would not turn up his nose and tell an uneducated person that if they want to make more money then go to college, or else be satisfied with rice and gravy, $3 a day and an aching back. Senator Yarborough has a great compassion for a human being, as did John F. Kennedy. Senator Yarborough is always thinking of how to raise the economic status of the poor, knowing, as did Lincoln, that we will have them with us always. He also knows that everybody can't get a college degree, as Connally seems to desire, and that just because a man doesn't go to college he shouldn't be forced to live in abject poverty.

THE DEMOCRATIC PARTY & TEXAS   *October 6*

I do not class myself as either a liberal or a conservative, and I am shocked when people refer to me as either. I am only a Democrat who believes in the principles of the national Democratic party. I voted for John Davis, for Al Smith, for FDR, Truman, Adlai Stevenson, Kennedy and LBJ.

Those of us who have a feeling of loyalty and love for our national Democratic party, and nothing but contempt for the state Democratic party of Texas, are, in reality, loyal to the principles which the national Democratic party upholds.

When special interests diametrically opposed to those national party principles seize control of the Democratic party in any county or in any state, as they have in Texas, we are not bound to follow a suicidal course of continuing loyalty to a party which opposes our principles. When a political party upholds those principles it merits our loyalty. But owe no loyalty to a name, or to a nostalgic memory, or to any special interests which may dominate our state's Democratic party.

Arthur Schlesinger, Jr., tells us in his best-selling book about his years in the White House, *A Thousand Days*, that John Kennedy once confronted a situation in Massachusetts which was similar in several respects to that which Democrats in Texas now face. They were discussing the Massachusetts senate race that year, and Kennedy was disturbed about the sorry state of the state party, and the even sorrier state of its nominee for the U.S. senate against the incumbent Republican.

These were the words of John Kennedy: "Sometimes party loyalty asks too much."

Schlesinger says that Kennedy spoke gloomily about the Massachusetts Democratic party, and then said, "Nothing can be done until it is beaten, badly beaten. Then there will be a chance for rebuilding."

In Texas we must beat and rebuild. For we have no state Democratic party, dedicated to national principles, in Texas. In Texas, many Texas congressmen, state senators, state representatives, all of whom say they are Democrats, are nothing more than lackeys for the major oil companies, the larger insurance companies and every big business special interest group, which is really the Republican party in progressive states.

We want every one to understand why it is that you and I, who toiled for Roosevelt and Truman, the noble Adlai Stevenson, Kennedy and LBJ, are outcasts in the Democratic party of Texas.

Do you understand how it can be that those who turncoated on Stevenson and Truman and even Kennedy and the principles of the Democratic party, and I am referring to people like Allan Shivers and Price Daniel? Do you understand how it can be that they have usurped control of the Democratic party in our state?

During primary campaigns we are attacked and smeared and called names and we are kicked out of conventions, or our delegate strength is diluted, and we have no voice in the formulation of party politics and writing of state platforms. Our candidates are tarred and feathered by the press, and beaten in the primary. You can well remember then we called ourselves Loyalists, meaning loyal Democrats, and scorn and contempt was heaped upon us by those who screamed, "I like Ike" and who are now beating their breasts and emptying their money bags for Waggoner Carr. Now we are called upon to be party loyalists and to vote for the corporation stooges. Do you remember when Representative Jim Wright went on TV earlier this year and asked for donations for the U.S. Senate. Oh, he got thousands of dollars in $10 checks like the one I sent him, but John Connally had already sacked up the big money for Waggoner Carr, the kind of big money that Wright could not contest.

Please pardon us, if we have the impression that St. John Connally, Shivers and Carr don't really want us around at all, until they need our votes against the Republicans in the November general election. How did we get into this sad situation? We got into it because Texas suffers from the one-party system, which has made Texas the personal property of corporations which control our state government. Progressive states like California, Oregon and Wisconsin have fully developed two-party systems, in which Carr and his friends vote in the Republican primary, and we vote in the Democratic primary. But in the one-party states of the South everybody votes in the Democratic primary, even though there are millions of Republican-thinking voters in the South, and especially in Texas.

Loyal Texas Democrats, and I mean loyal to the principles of the national Democratic party, are outnumbered in our own party's primary, and we haven't controlled the machinery of the Democratic party in Texas since James Stephen Hogg and James Allred. Mr. Carr and his friends control it. Thus, it is the one-party system which chains Texas to political bondage by the forces of corporation government. In most two-party states, Democrats sometimes lose elections to Republicans but adherents of the national party always remain in the majority within our own Democratic party. But not in Texas. No. Here we always lose in the primary and we don't have a say in our own historic party. In a two-party state, Democrats who espouse the principles of the national party always have control, but not in Texas.

MINGLING WITH THE OUTSIDE WORLD   *November 10*

During October I made plane trips to Fort Worth, Dallas and Austin, but don't get excited. Liberal Democrats of Texas paid my fare each trip. They got the money from contributors all over Texas. I took these trips to make speeches for the two-party system. I gave virtually the same speech at each place. At Fort Worth I addressed the Tarrant County Democratic Women's Club and debated a fellow named Morris who told the women to vote the ticket straight and for Waggoner Carr.

At Dallas, I spoke at the student union building at Southern Methodist University, and it was the first time I had been at a university in 40 years, and I was disappointed that the students didn't look as they did in 1925, the year I graduated. Students at the University of Texas, where I spoke October 27, and at SMU wore long hair and the girls wore short skirts, but I found out about the long haired boys. They wash that hair every day. That eased me, because that is exactly what I would do if I had long hair. A bunch of tired liberals were my hosts at Dallas, and they met the plane and took me to a Chinese cafe where I ate Chinese food, but what I liked best was the green tea.

But back to my trips. At Austin, I had the best time and the most varied experiences. Understand, I was not overjoyed to be making all these trips. I considered it a duty, to spread the word that John Tower should be elected to keep Ralph Yarborough powerful, not helpless, in Washington, and to build up a two-party system in Texas. I was not endorsing Tower. I never did get up a head of steam except when I made the speech at Austin in the Student Union building to about 1,400 Democrats.

There I debated State Senator "Babe" Schwartz of Galveston. Somebody from Hardin County had called him up (you can guess who) and told him that I was a racist and a radical right wing conservative. He challenged me to prove that I was not a racist.

I answered, "It was in 1952 when Adlai Stevenson was running for president that I got religion and ceased to be a segregationist. It was in 1954 that they began calling me a nigger-lover. When did they begin calling you a nigger-lover?" There were a number of Negro students in the audience and they jumped up and led a wild applause. The Young Democrats sponsored the debate, and as it turned out, 80 per cent of those present were for Tower, and they were all Young Democrats. I then told them that if Senator Schwartz were running against Waggoner Carr I would vote for him; he has supported Yarborough all these years, fought Carr's segregationist bills, and filibustered against the pet schemes of Shivers, Daniel and Connally, including the four-year term for governor. He has been one of the best legislators in Austin. I don't see why the Young Democrats at the University wanted me to speak since all had made up their minds anyway to vote for Tower.

I saw in Austin that the style in neckties for men has changed, just when I got me the kind of black silk narrow necktie, the kind I've been hunting for two years. They are now wearing wide neckties, not real wide like the Mods wear, but wide, and also thick.

When I was in Scholz' beer garden in Austin, I ate a hamburger that was made like those at the Top Half. In the airports, you get hamburgers with meat in them and nothing else. If you ask for lettuce that costs you 10 cents extra, and so does a slice of tomato. Hamburgers can cost from 75 cents to a dollar. The hamburgers in Galloway's are 25 cents, and had everything, but still are not as good as Kountze's best. When I go on trips, I eat only hamburgers all day long and I feel like I'm celebrating.

During World War II, I flew across all the oceans, seas, gulfs, that you can name and every time I got into a plane I wondered, but I wouldn't say I was scared, and I was not scared on these trips, but I showed how corny and country I was by buying $30,000 worth of insurance for every trip and sending the policy back to Dee. The weather was cloudy every trip and we flew above the overcast except on the trip to Austin and I could look down and figure that the winding river I saw was the Colorado. Otherwise, on the plane, I read, and swallowed (to unstuff my ears). The time passes slowly on a plane.

I made all these trips on Friday, else I never could have got off from work. I want to assure you that I did not try to put on the dog while away from home. At Austin it became necessary for me to say to my audience that I worked in a tin building and had ink under my fingernails and I put up my hands to show them.

It was really the first time I had mingled with the outside world in 15 years, except that one time I went down to the country club at Beaumont with George Kirkpatrick, Sr., and those men looked down their nose at me. I met a lot of people, mostly with long hair, but learned that those long haired boys and platinum-haired, short-skirted girls, are ahead of the university students of 1925—way ahead intellectually. And they are responsible, thoughtful and concerned about the state, nation and world.

OLD-TIME MEDICINE

As far as doctors and hospitals are concerned I have never got out of doing the way I was brought up in during my youth. I never go to a doctor unless I'm half scared to death, and that is usually caused by somebody I've been talking to: somebody who warns me over and over that I'd better go to a doctor.

Now doctors were a dime a dozen in my family when I was growing up. The nearest doctor was Uncle "Shirk" Fullingim who was three miles away. I had other uncles who were doctors. We had seven children in our family. If we had broken bones and a high fever my parents couldn't break, the doctor was called in.

As for medicine, we had three stand-bys that we used for all diseases: Syrup of Figs, Oxidene and Watkins Liniment. This Oxidene was something. It came in a bottle and was dark brown and had the bitterest taste. I remember there was a picture of a Chinese dragon or some kind of horrible lizard on it. I think that we took it to ward off malaria, fever and chills, although there was no malaria in that country. But also I think we took it as a sort of tonic to tone up the system. Anyway, if we felt bad, my father would dose us with Oxidene.

But the cure-all was Watkins Liniment. We would take that for bad colds, stomach ache or anything else. We would put it in water and drink it with a little sugar in the water. This liniment tasted like liquid fire. We would also put it on cuts, bruises and doctor the horses with it. Right now you couldn't pay me to take a dose of it, but back there, it seemed the right thing to do.

The only times, up to the time I was 14 years old, that I remember the doctor coming to our house was when my mother gave birth to a child, when we had the measles, and when I fell out of a tree. I had been warned not to climb trees, and that's just what I did, and I fell about 14 feet to the ground. I broke a bone in my hip joint but did not know it, and I did not tell my folks for fear of getting a whipping. One day about three weeks later I blacked out and stayed out for a week. Now bear in mind there were a total of nine in my family and for my first 14 years I don't think the doctor was at our house for anything but births.

So I never go to the doctor unless I think that my time has

273

come, and then I rush in screaming that I'm done for.

AMERICA DOES NOT LIKE THE VIETNAM WAR

This is the day after the general election and I have been thinking what's the significance of it, nationally. I don't want to comment just yet on the Tower victory, because it does not appear as important as what happened in California and New York and in between. This election seemed to say that America does not like the war in Vietnam, that it will support the President's will to fight it, but that it believes we have no business in Vietnam. All of the opposition in the election is traceable to the war: both the white backlash and inflation. If it had not been for the war and Stokely Carmichael there would have been no backlash. It all started with the war. We have got a bear by the tail in that war.

So once again, the Republicans are profiting politically by something they started. You will remember that it was Holy Ike who first sent Americans to Vietnam; it was Ike who made the promises, who took the first step. Actually, Ike ought to be made to come back and take charge of it now. But the Republicans got rich in the election last Tuesday by laying blame on the Democrats, laying the blame for something they started.

If Lyndon Johnson doesn't shake us out of that war by some miracle, they'll beat him as sure as shootin' for president in 1968, and you know who'll beat him. A good prediction is: Ronald Reagan, governor-elect of California, will be the Republican nominee for president, and that senator-elect Brooke of Massachusetts will be the vice-presidential nominee. That would be the smartest move the Republicans ever made. They would get all the conservative votes and also the Negro vote. They'd lose the South, but they always did anyway. From Florida and South Carolina to Texas, the racists would have a field day, they would rant and rave, but the big cities would go Republican. Reagan and Brooke could win even if the war is over and we have won it which we are not going to do the way we are now fighting it, but if the war is not over by 1969, a cross-eyed Chinaman from San

Francisco and an Apache Indian from the Painted Desert could beat Johnson and Humphrey. The only Democrat the Republicans can't beat is Robert Kennedy who is hated by the same people who hated his brother.

I predict that Johnson will somehow or other get us out of Vietnam pronto; he sees the handwriting on the wall. I feel sorry for Johnson; he's been a good President; he is doing in Vietnam only what he had to do; what he did was cut and dried. But now with about 50 new conservative Republicans in the U.S. House of Representatives, the Great Society has come to a halt. No more open housing. No more social legislation. It would take two years right now for Johnson to regain his popularity if the war were over this minute.

So we shall see what kind of a man Lyndon Johnson is. Will he be like Harry Truman who set his jaw and fought the Chinese in Korea and fired the insulting General MacArthur who should have been court-martialed, or will LBJ give in. I hope he doesn't give an inch, but we can soon tell if the election has been a political persuader.

I said I hope LBJ stays and fights, but at the same time I don't believe in war, and that sounds like Richard Nixon, doesn't it. We've got no business fighting that war the way it's being fought.

So LBJ, better start trying to make a deal to get out of Vietnam the best way he can, if he wants to be re-elected in 1968.

YEAR 1967

RACCOON MEAT FOR SALE   *February 2*

If you like coon, and many people do, you can buy it across the counter at Moore's Super Market for 38 cents a pound. That is in season, which is now. As far as the News can find out, Kountze is the only place in East Texas where coons are sold like any other meat at a store.

"Hub" Moore buys the coons from a trapper up around Segno, whose last name is Cain. Alice Crow in Moore's market says that the coons weigh from 2½ to 8 pounds dressed and that one weighed 12 pounds, the biggest brought in.

Sometimes the trapper brings in 18 fresh coons dressed, and the most he brought in at one time was 36. People on both sides of the track stand in line to snap up the coons which are delicious barbecued, baked or stewed. Jack Flowers used to trap coons every winter and he'd sell the dressed coons locally. But now there are not many coon trappers around.

BLOODHOUND SEARCHES FOR LOVE

After a manhunt that had some comical angles, two men were arrested Friday and Saturday, and charged with burglary in connection with the looting of schools at Colmesneil, Fred, Spurger, and West Hardin near Saratoga. They were also charged in connection with breaking into the Chester State Bank.

One of the comedy of errors was related by one of the alleged burglars. He told County Attorney Dwayne Overstreet that he had fled all night from one of the hound dogs Sheriff H. O. Overstreet had assembled to hunt him and the other man accused of breaking into West Hardin school. The 42-year-old suspect from Woodville said that after fleeing from the baying hounds all night, he sat down by a tree in the woods near Batson, completely given out.

He said that all at once he felt something cold on his neck, and that he became unwound and nearly went to pieces. He said he looked around and there was the hound that had chased him all night. Then he discovered the hound just wanted to be loved, and he patted the hound and scratched his ears, and the hound meekly followed him into Batson, where he was finally arrested by officers of the Hardin County Sheriff's Department.

BREATHE DEEP & LOOK & REVEL IN SPRING   *March 2*

The Windwood correspondent reports in this issue that the mayhaws are blooming. Not only are the mayhaws blooming, but also the pear trees and plum trees.

I'm ready for spring. I never thought much about it until last Thursday when there was a heavy frost, and all of a sudden I was ready for spring. I looked at the redbud trees near my house and in front of the shop and there was not a bud in sight. The buds are there all right, but they look weeks away. Still the plum trees are beginning to bloom, and in another week they'll look like white clouds adrift.

I was almost ready for spring back in January when my Reuter's 1967 Spring Seed Catalogue came from New Orleans showing in full color on the cover page the Burpee Hybrid Cucumber No. 26, the Mainerock Hybrid Cantaloupe, the New Giant Swiss Pansy, the Blaze Climbing Rose. I read that catalogue for weeks and looked at it almost every day and have decided that I will plant gourds again, also okra, banana cantaloupes, Tiny Tim, Yellow Pear Tomatoes, squash, and I think I'll use 8-8-8 fertilizer.

I'd like to see Village Creek on a tear (pronounced "tare"), not a big one, mind you, but a tear anyway. That Village Creek, with its thousands of springs running down slopes and banks shaded by cypress, dogwood, beech, oak, gum, magnolia, cherry, elm; that Village Creek of the cool unpolluted water. Yes, I'm ready for spring's azaleas. There's nothing more satisfying to look at than blooming azaleas. They can do solace to the soul of man. But the holly does not know that it's spring, and camelias don't either. The later are still blooming, and holly is loaded with red berries, as if it thought it was December. That worries me. I have never seen holly berries hang so long.

Yes, I hope to tell you I'm ready for spring. I'm ready for Dee to catch me a big mess of perch, and I'm ready to go down to that spring below Alf's house on Village Creek and stick my head, all of it, down in that cool spring and look at the green moss on the bottom and drink deep, and then turn over without even wiping the water out of my eyes, and look up through that mass of leaves to the sunbeams, and listen to the soothing bird calls.

I'm ready for the mockingbirds to sing all day and on moonlight nights. I'm ready for the prettiest sight on earth to open. Springtime in Hardin County. It's opening now, and it will seem that every week is finer and more beautiful than the last. All these blooms will come within the next two months, not to mention the petunias, the pansies, the violets, the blue bonnets, and the thousands of wild flowers that will clog the Big Thicket and crowd roads in every direction. This spring I'm going to revel in it all again; I'm going out every day and breathe deep and look and look. And I'm going to like it more than ever.

THE NEGRO SOLDIER & BLACK POWER   *May 11*

The other day 27 boys left Liberty for the induction center at Houston. Out of that 27, 24 were Negroes, so I don't blame Cassius Clay for complaining that Negroes are getting a raw deal in the draft, but I condemn Clay for saying he will not take an oath to defend his country.

I remember way back in the '30s and '40s that the same people who are now beating the drums for George Wallace were then saying that the United States would never let the Negro be a front line fighter, that the Negro couldn't fight in a battle, didn't have enough sense to; they would get rattled, all of which was racist talk of the most vile sort. Yet, I heard many a person, some of them in Kountze, say it just wasn't in a Negro's makeup to be a good soldier. Well, it has come about that the Negro is doing his full share in the lines in Vietnam. He is fighting intelligently and brilliantly. His morale is high. He knows what he is fighting for. Yet Wallace is still preaching racist hate, and you have never heard George Wallace admit that the Negro is fighting as well as the white man in Vietnam. How brave is Wallace himself? Did you see him cower and tremble on TV the other night in Concord, New Hampshire, when some students demonstrated against his racism. The patriotic bravery of the Negro in the Vietnam war denies the truth of all the hatred Wallace has preached for years.

The same people who once were all wrapped up in the John Birch Society are now giving their silly rebel yells for George Wallace and flying their stupid Confederate flag for him. Lyndon Johnson may not be elected president of the United States again, maybe he doesn't deserve to be, but Wallace is the last dying effort of the phony states righters. He, too, will pass away, along with the Birchers, the Ku Kluxers, the Black Muslims, for they are just as phony as Wallace. The white man and the black man must live as brothers in the land of the free and the home of the brave. I think that what Stokely Carmichael, who gave birth to the phrase, "black power," had in mind at first was to make the Negro proud that he is black, to make him quit trying to be a white man, and that was a good idea, but it got lost in the shuffle. There is no reason that a black man should not be proud that he is black, just as the red man is proud that he is red, as the yellow man is proud that he is yellow, no reason at all except among some white men who want to argue that only the white man can be proud of the color of his skin.

Clay has a right to demand there should be Negroes on all draft boards. There should be a Negro on the draft board at Liberty, since most of the men now being drafted in Southeast Texas are Negroes. Where I part company with Carmichael, Cassius Clay and Martin Luther King is when they start preaching defiance against the draft. To me those three are no better than Wallace when he encourages church-burning and murder of Negroes in Alabama. They all four should be put in adjoining cells, facing each other for the duration; then maybe they could get all the talk out of their system.

Of course, I don't mean that last statement. You don't put people in jail for expressing an opinion, or shouldn't. Let them rant and rave for or against the war. The extreme hawks are just as bad as the extreme doves.

FAITH, ELECTIONS & ICE CREAM   *July 6*

The other day we got a letter from Barnetta who lives at Alvord near Decatur in Wise County, and I remembered that of all my cousins I had more rapport with her than any of the others.

"I go to the Assembly of God on Wednesday night (we don't have anything at the Methodist church)", she wrote. "Their preacher has a little boy, 3 and a girl, 5. Last night that little boy looked me right in the face and said, 'Cook a chocolate cake.' I said, 'Well I am going to cook Kenny a chocolate cake,' and Cathy said, 'What about me? I told him to say it.' The preacher is just a boy and he has such a sweet wife. It does me good to go there when I kneel in that altar and hear praying all around me. Well, it is a good place to be."

After reading that letter I sat in my house and remembered how it was on election day from about 1910 until 1916 when we moved from Wise County to Lynn County. My father would go to town and stay all day and half the night, and so would Uncle Gus, Barnetta's father. My father and Uncle Gus were usually on opposite sides. Uncle Gus was a Jim Ferguson man and my father wasn't. On election day here would come my cousins and Aunt Meg and stay all day. They'd come in a buggy. We'd start feeding the milch cows as soon as my father left and take food to them all day so they would give lots of milk that night. Then in the afternoon, my two oldest sisters, Estelle and Lena, would hitch up a team to the hack or wagon and drive to Decatur, a distance of three miles. That would be the last Saturday in July. They would have a bunch of old quilts and gunny sacks in the wagon.

They'd go straight to the ice plant and buy 100 pounds of ice for 35 cents. They'd go up and down back streets so Uncle Gus and my father would not see them. They'd wrap the ice in the quilts and sacks and drive home and let me tell you that after they made the trip they felt as you would feel now after returning from a trip to Dallas. They felt as if they had made a long trip.

In the meantime, Ford, Barnetta, Lucille and I would pen the cows and Mammy and Aunt Meg would milk them. Just about the time the girls got home from town with the ice, our mothers would have had two cakes baked and the ice cream mixture fixed, and that mixture was something. Then we'd start turning the freezer and keep on turning until the handles would not move. Then we'd let the freezer set for an hour.

We had already decided in monumental fusses and battle who would get the mixer when they pulled it out of the freezer with gobs of ice cream clinging to it. All the kids would beg the lucky one for a lick. When we'd get them licked clean, we'd start on the ice cream and cake, and by that time here would come Dolly Priviett, a neighbor who lived across the branch, with her sons, Clyde and Charlie near the age of Ford and me.

About 9:30, all would be gone and we would be either stuffed or sick and sleeping on a pallet on the back porch. Along about 2 a.m. here would come my father by himself, and Uncle Gus later, and both of them would be mad, my father because Jim Ferguson got elected again and Uncle Gus because one of his local candidates got beat. Uncle Gus would rouse up his kids and Aunt Meg and they'd go home.

I think that Barnetta has made a success of her life, and particularly in determining what is worth doing in life. Greater than anything is her faith. She grew up in a church where the presence of faith was attested to by shouting and fervent praying at the altar and in the grove meetings. You may not know it but the modern Assembly of God Church is in certain respects like the Methodist church of the 19th century and the early part of the 20th. I can understand how Barnetta feels reassured praying with the Assembly of Godders on Wednesday night and attending the Methodist church on Sundays. I would give everything I own right this minute if I had the faith that Barnetta has.

RACE RIOTS & SEPARATE WORLDS   August 10

The United States is the only nation of its kind that ever existed, the only nation which ever had its unique freedom, the only nation in which everybody can own firearms, the only nation where freedom to think, demonstrate or express opinions verbally or in writing is absolute, the only nation which has unlimited free enterprise, the freest most democratic nation that ever existed.

So don't despair of our country when a Negro rebellion in Detroit sets 1000 fires going at once, burning unchecked. We all know this is criminal. We will deal with this in time; it is our nature to repay violence with violence. We had no idea that the Negro and white criminals in our big cities would try to burn America to ashes, but now that we know we will begin to deal with it. That is the way we have done things in America. We will probably resort to excesses of revenge and punishment as we did with the American Indian, but we will stop it.

We had thought that we could integrate with the Negro, and in the main we can, but we did not understand people like Rap Brown and Stokely Carmichael, but now that we do, we will crush what is known as Black Power, because it will be necessary. We understand now that those Negroes who are imprisoned forever in the filth of ghettos must be released, and we will gradually do that, too, but we will stop the burnings and the Rap Browns and the Carmichaels.

I am not ashamed this happened in the United States. We have become what we are through violence, fire and death, the high point being the Civil War, and the Indian Wars, and countless feuds, killings and devastation on the frontiers. Detroit and Newark and Watts happened because America is the freest nation that ever existed. America runs to excesses because Americans have unlimited freedom, and the thing to remember is that the majority conscience triumphs in this country. It always has. The majority rule is what makes us free. It is Democracy.

I saw the first line of an editorial in the Baptist Standard, "Hang Your Head In Shame, America," commenting upon the racial burnings and killings. I am not ashamed of Detroit and Newark, for I know that could happen only in free America, and

I will predict now that it will never happen again. America won't let it. We have learned that just as all whites aren't criminals, neither are all blacks. The Negroes will help us punish the black and white arsonists. We will eventually run the Carmichaels, the Black Power maniacs, the Black Muslims into the ground, just as we ran the Ku Kluxers to nothingness. The great majority of the Negroes will help us because the great majority want brotherhood. When you think of the arsonists and looters in Detroit, also think of the Negro boys and the American boys of Mexican and Puerto Rican descent who are in the majority in Vietnam, at least on the casualty lists. Anybody who can go over there and fight that unwanted war, that stinking, costly war, that war we should never have got into, and still uphold the reasons we have to fight it, still present a heroic example to the world, is my brother and he is integrated in my heart and soul, and I don't want him living in a world of his own, as Carmichael does. I want him living in and enjoying my world.

DREAMS & EARLY STORIES   *August 24*

Recently, I began to remember the Arkansas phase of the Fullingim family up in Wise County. It was probably going on before I can remember, but when I became aware of it the year was probably 1911 or 1912. When I was a child my father took two or three papers. One was Holland's magazine, one was Home and State, which I think was a prohibition paper, and one was The Semi-Weekly Farm News, published on Tuesday and Friday by The Dallas Morning News. It cost only a dollar a year, and if that seems cheap, let me assure you that that dollar was harder to raise than $10 today. The paper was usually about eight pages and had no display ads, but it had a half page of want ads, and these ads were largely of farms for sale in Texas, Oklahoma, Arkansas, Louisiana, New Mexico and other states.

Our mouths would literally drool as we read those Arkansas farm ads. They would go something like this: "Farm for sale in beautiful foothills of Ozark mountains, 160 acres, crossed by gurgling streams, pure water, fruit trees, apricots, cherry, apple, pecan, pear, 100 acres in cultivation, rich sandy loam; you can make your own living off the land; also 14 sheep, 6 horses, 4 mules, 5 milch cows, 14 hogs, 40 Rhode Island red chickens, and five-room house, surrounded by lilacs, roses, wild persimmon and wild plums; big barn and chicken house; $3,000 cash."

Once or twice, my father would get interested in the ads from New Mexico, but he was afraid of drought out there. He had contempt for Oklahoma. He always called it the Indian Territory, and I believe his dislike for Oklahoma was based on the raids the Comanches made from their reservations into North Texas when he was a boy. He was born in 1862 in Wise County in a log cabin, on top of a high hill. All houses were built on tops of hills in Wise County so their occupants could see the Indians coming. When the Huff family of eight was massacred and scalped a few miles from my grandparents place, everybody moved out of the sticks to the hills. In 1925, when I told my father I was going to the University of Oklahoma he said, "You won't learn anything in the Indian Territory, up there amongst them gut-sucking Indians."

Another reason I think my father didn't like Oklahoma was because his brother, Uncle Cates, who I never saw, disappeared when he went in to the Indian Territory to make the Run.

My father finally left Wise County in 1916, but we went west, not east to Arkansas. We rode the train two days and nights, but I am sure that my father would have preferred to go in a covered wagon, driving all our stock, cattle, horses and mules, and swinging the chickens under the wagons in coops, and cooking out of Dutch ovens. I would have preferred that, too, but we all got our first train ride 400 miles to Tahoka in Lynn County on the South Plains.

Now I can see that my father played with the idea of living on a fruitful farm in Arkansas that had everything. My father was of the west. He left Wise County in his early youth and went west. He wound up working on cattle ranches in Montana 10 years, eating from chuck wagons. He lived there in the day when the cowboy was king, from 1880 to 1890. He came back to Wise County wearing a buffalo hide coat, to a farm on which the cash crop was cotton. He tilled the soil and fought the boll weevil, but I think he always yearned for the old west. He came back from the Montana ranges at the age of 31, mainly to marry my mother and to be near his mother, but I think he was unhappy at farming, although he never said so.

We stopped taking the Semi-Weekly Farm News when we left Wise County in 1916. I can look back now on some of the most enjoyable reading I ever had in that paper. They would run a sentimental, romantic novel serially, and we would anxiously await each installment. Books then were scarce and if there was a book in the community everyone would read it. These books would now be called "dime novels," but we looked upon them as the best literature.

Before I started reading books I used to listen to my Cousin Kate Fullingim tell the story after she had read the book. It would take her all day, if we were hoeing cotton or corn. My sister, Lena, and I would listen spellbound; we would cry when she did and cuss when she did, but Kate was always careful to make us cry first because that was considered a test of one's story-telling ability. Kate told us the novel *Maggie Miller* by Mary Holmes and *St. Elmo* by Augusta Evans. She would start in at the first page and leave nothing out. She would quote the dialogue throughout the book with proper inflection, and she was not a bad actor.

Sometimes she would say, "If you don't hurry up and catch up with me, Uncle Alf will get all over us, and you'd better get all that Johnson grass, dig it up by the roots like he says, don't cut it off, and quit leanin' on your hoe," for both Lena and I were hoe-leaners, with one bare foot at the knee and leaning on the hoe, especially when Kate would get to the exciting parts. We would forget to hoe and just listen, and she would scold us. We'd always be behind Kate, just work enough so we could keep within earshot. I remember when Kate told us the novel *Thorn Among Roses*.

It took Kate nearly all week to tell us that book while we were hoeing Johnson grass in Catlett Creek bottom. She told it differently. She used their tone of voice. She sneered when they sneered, shouted when they shouted, wept when they wept; whatever the adjective Kate put the action to the word. The way she played the part of the villain made us hate Jim. Lena and I cried the last two chapters when the girl died, and finally Kate

Archer Fullingim and sister, Virginia, with cotton sacks in 1922.

got to crying with us.

The first book I read serially in the Semi-Weekly Farm News was *Lena Rivers*. Kate had already told us that book twice, but we still read every installment, and I can say right now that no book has excited me as much as *Lena Rivers*, except maybe *Gone With The Wind*, or *Lord Jim*. Don't remind me that *Lena Rivers* is trash. I know it, but it was the first book I ever read.

WHAT ABOUT LBJ IN '68? *November 9*

I am addicted to reading the radical right wing conservative editorial page of the Dallas Morning News, which is the leading hate-monger in the hate capital of the world. I don't believe a word of what I read and it never could convince me, but I read it to learn what the enemy is thinking and doing, even though it makes my blood boil and gives me heartburn. The other day one of the Dallas News columnists answered what he called the four most important political questions in Washington, and they all have to do with Texas because Texas in 1968 will be the most important political state. What's worrying the Democrats is whether LBJ can carry Texas.

Could Johnson carry Texas tomorrow? That is only half a question. What you have to know is what other names would be on the ballot. The only way Johnson could carry Texas tomorrow would be for his name to be the only one on the ballot. I have seen many people who every time the Vietnam War is mentioned say, "I'll vote for anybody but Johnson, except Reagan or Nixon." Johnson could carry Texas in 1968 if he wins or ends the war next year, but if he doesn't his name is mud, but not because of the war. That may sound contradictory, but if he ends the war they'd vote for him as a reward; if he didn't they'd vote against him because they don't trust Johnson.

The four questions didn't mention any Kennedy, but I will. A Kennedy, either Bobby or Ed, could roll up a big yes vote in Texas. You put the word out that a Kennedy would replace Johnson as presidential candidate and you'd see a record registration of poor whites, Negroes and Latin Americans, and of the people who would vote for a Kennedy regardless. Now how about Reagan, Nixon and Rockefeller. I never hear anyone admitting that he would vote for Reagan, though they are still plenty of die-hard Nixon people around who know that Nixon almost carried Texas in 1960, but Nixon could never carry Texas and neither could Reagan. They are worse hawks than Johnson. I predicted that Reagan would be the 1968 Republican presidential candidate when he was elected governor. I still believe he will be. Johnson will be safe in Texas if his opponent is either Reagan or Nixon. Every day I hear more people say that they would vote for Rockefeller if they had the chance. I don't know how it happened but Rocky is slowly but surely taking over the John Kennedy image in Texas. For some reason, JFK's mantle has fallen upon Rockefeller. Why? LBJ has waged the war in an underhanded manner. People who cuss Johnson dislike him because he has come to mean deception, trickery, double-dealing. It doesn't help when they read that he has piled up a $12 million fortune since he became senator in 1948. It rubs the wrong way that he is doing the same thing in Vietnam, only more so, that he said Goldwater should not do.

Why are so many Texans now for Rocky? Because they see Rocky as frank and above board, the exact opposite of the way they see LBJ. Rocky is a hawk on Vietnam, same as LBJ, but they trust Rocky and they don't LBJ.

What issue is hurting Johnson the most in Texas? I've already told you, personal dislike for him. Most Texans don't hold the war or civil rights against him; they don't like inflation but they are being tranquilized by fantastically high wages that enables them to buy everything from diamonds to cabin cruisers. The civil rights thing that devastated the cities this year is not Johnson's fault, neither are the peace demonstrations and the hippies. People don't get mad about civil rights until they hear George Wallace on TV, so Wallace has in his corner the dregs of the John Birch Society and the Ku Klux Klan, including the ultra right wing conservatives. If Johnson were to start acting like Harry Truman for a change, giving his critics hell and telling the real facts about the war and America, as old Harry did, LBJ might infuse some enthusiasm and patriotism into the Democrats, even the demonstrators. LBJ needs to talk, long, loud and often and mad, to get a lot of people on his side again, but he never will do it by letting Rusk and McNamara speak his piece. The thing that nearly everybody holds against Johnson is their belief that he covers up and avoids telling the stark truth.

WATCHING THE SOARING BUZZARDS   *November 16*

I have been remembering every now and then for the last week how I used to watch buzzards in Cottle County where I grew up, and I find myself wanting to go back out there to watch them again. We lived there from 1917 to 1928, on a cotton farm six miles southeast of Paducah. An arroyo or small canyon ran right behind our house. This canyon had wild plum thickets all up and down it. This canyon ran into Salt Creek just across our fence line. Salt Creek ran at the bottom of a mile-wide maze of "breaks." It was a miniature Grand Canyon, with all its colors and formations, but on a tiny scale. Salt Creek didn't run except when a rise was on. It had small holes of water every now and then and the water was salty.

Our cotton field was on a flat, plateau-like elevation overlooking Salt Creek Canyon. In the fall, we'd be picking cotton by sunup. I had a strong back in those days, and although I wore knee pads, most of the time I was on my feet and stooped over. At noon, we'd rest an hour, and that's when I became a buzzard-watcher. Sometimes we would take our lunch to the field and sometimes my poor Mammy would bring it to us. If she did it was cornbread and beans or peas, but what I remember was the fried peaches. Oh, how Mammy could cook those pies. When I ate, I'd get on top of the cotton wagon or pile, which ever it was, and lean back and face toward the canyon and the buzzards. At first I was not aware that I was a buzzard-watcher; but I knew I was when I began to look forward to it. When cotton picking was over and I was driving a four-horse team to a riding middle-buster, I would watch buzzards when I could take my eye off the team. In the summer, when I was hoeing Johnson grass I would lean on my hoe and watch the buzzards. I was a great hoeleaner, too. Sometimes, when I had nothing to do I would go down to

Salt Creek Canyon, climb a big cottonwood tree and watch the buzzards.

It's now time to say that there were always patches of buzzards flying over the canyon. I would hold my breath when a buzzard, hundreds of feet above the ground, would seem to be motionless. I knew it wouldn't fall but I'd hold my breath anyway. Then the buzzard would slant a wing and sail downward, wings motionless; then it would flap its wings lazily, effortlessly and soar to a height and there rest again motionless. That far away the buzzards were free, beautiful, and I envied them. I saw buzzards close up, too. I would hide near a dead cow or a dead horse or a dead coyote or just a dead prairie dog, and watch them. I have seen their red naked heads which are poked eagerly into the filth they feed on. Their heads are free of feathers, so the purifying rays of the sun can kill bacteria clinging there. Their eyes have a transparent nictitating membrane that covers the eye and keeps it clean and moist. Internally, the vulture's digestive system is capable of destroying, instead of harboring, bacteria that would make other creatures deathly ill.

What I liked most to do in my buzzard-watching period was watch the buzzards soar endless hours over a stricken creature that would be approached only when death was evident. The buzzard has unbelievably keen sight and it sees things with striking clarity. It uses both eyes and smell to tell when the creature it is circling dies. The moment death comes, the buzzards fly down and because their beak is weak, begin their meal at the eyes or the anus. From a cave in a cliff, overlooking the place where old Matt died, I watched the buzzards begin on her the moment she died and old Matt was a long time dying. For a day she did not move a muscle, but was in a coma, but the buzzards knew when she died.

My big dream is to retire and become a beachcomber up and down the coast between High Island and Padre Island, but I would take time off to go back to Cottle County to watch the buzzards soar over Salt Creek Canyon.

YEAR 1968

I never thought I would see the day in Texas when the conservatives of this state, led by John Connally, would regard Vice President Hubert Humphrey as conservative. Until he was elected vice president, Hubert was looked upon by King John Connally, Allan Shivers and their crowd as a radical left-winger. Now when they compare Hubert with Senators McCarthy and Bobby Kennedy, Hubert looks like Goldwater. But I predict that the attitude of the Shivercrats and Connally-followers is flexible, depending on orders from LBJ. If he says Hubert, it will be Hubert. LBJ hasn't said yet, but he will, just give him time.

I felt kind of sorry for LBJ while he was making that speech, saying he was going to back down in Vietnam and wasn't going to run for president. I remember when Roosevelt died. I was stationed at Banana River, Florida (now Cape Kennedy). Watching LBJ on TV was like watching a man dying. It was agonizing to watch a man backtrack as he did. I think he meant every word he said, though, and was not angling for a draft, and I also believe that he would never have bowed out of the presidential race if someone had known his secret and broadcast it before LBJ had a chance to tell it. What he did was okay with me. He had fouled up fighting the war and fouled up running the country. He quit because he knew he could not win, and that was smart, but just look what we have on our hands now in the Democratic party. We have Bobby, who a year ago I hoped would be president but who now nauseates me. We have McCarthy, who I don't understand even a little bit. I don't want either one of them for president, and Hubert is about as inspiring as a turnip. George Wallace is a racist, and I'd just as soon vote for the Ku Klux Klan. On top of all that Nixon looms as the Republican nominee, and I would not vote for Nixon under any circumstances. I just wouldn't. There is a chance that Rockefeller may get the nomination. If he does, that would suit me, but I may not have to vote for him in preference to Bobby, Hubert or McCarthy. For I hope that a dark horse, now not in the spotlight, will be the Democratic nominee, though off-hand I can't give an example.

The White House reports that never before has a president received so many telegrams, all asking that he reconsider his decision not to seek or accept the nomination. Isn't that asking the President to increase his credibility gap, since the prevailing opinion is that the President can't tell the truth no matter what?

"I WAS A NEGRO"   *April 18*

A local businessman was over in Saratoga (where no Negro has ever lived) the day they buried Martin Luther King and he was greeted by a male resident who informed him, "We've closed up for the funeral." I have heard a lot of griping the last few days because TV was turned over to the King march and funeral for several days, but every derogatory word I have heard about King cut deep, and I'll tell you why. King belonged to the Negroes, they believed in him, they loved him, and they revered him, and I respect them because they are human beings and Americans.

For two days I was a Negro. I was black and was in Memphis and Atlanta. I was in the march in Memphis and marched behind the mules and wagon carrying the coffin in Atlanta. I repeat, I was a black man, and I was full of sorrow because of the death of Dr. King. I'm not going to tell you what I thought while I was a Negro, because you white people wouldn't want to hear it, but I want to tell you whiteys and honkeys something. You ought to be black for a couple of days just to see what it's like, and then you'll understand why you ought not to have griped so much because the funeral was monopolizing TV. It would do you good to be a Negro for a couple of days.

I was reading the other day that compared to World War II and the Korean War, there are practically no psychos in the armed forces in Vietnam, that is, very few soldiers suffer mental breakdowns. One reason is that the armed forces are top-heavy with Negroes and Mexican-Americans and men of Puerto Rican descent, and that they know exactly what they are fighting for:

the United States, not against this or that or for this or that, just for the United States of America. My country right or wrong, but my country. When we think of the "boys" in Vietnam and write these poems that are printed in papers about them, we've got to realize that they are not all white. The reports from Vietnam say the Negro soldiers in Vietnam grieved for Martin Luther King. I grieve for him, too.

HATTIE WILLIAMS IS PRAYING   *April 25*

I went down to get my tamales at the intersection north of the C. L. Sowell Lumber Company last Friday and the tamale woman, Mrs. Hattie Williams, wasn't in sight. I was afraid she might be sick and I went to her house. I didn't see her but I could hear her praying inside, and I did see her husband Willie Williams who plows up gardens with that aged mule he has. Willie said that Hattie was on a seven-day fast for the Lord, drinking only water, but praying night and day for sinful people to love each other and to repent for their sins. Willie said that people are shooting and cutting up each other. He said we are all going to be punished and here on earth, too, for the devilment we do, permit or inspire. Willie is staying close around the house during the fast, and his carefully tended yard is full of blooming roses and other blossoming flowers. Once Hattie Williams, in a town north of here, sold enough tamales to build a church for the Lord. There are people who say, including Dee, that nobody makes better tamales than Hattie, who can quote you the Bible all day and never run out. While I stood outside the gate talking to Willie whose hair looks like curly steel shavings, I could hear Hattie on the inside talking with her Lord. Willie said she would be back at the tamale stand next Friday.

MAMMY AND THE CONVERSION   *May 30*

The first Methodist preacher I ever knew who was interested in saving people, their character, their bodies, their welfare, their peace of mind, as well as saving their souls was Gaston Foote who is now pastor of the First Methodist Church in Fort Worth, in preference to being a bishop. He is probably one of the two greatest preachers in Texas. The other is the pastor of the First Methodist Church in Houston, Reverend Allen.

When I knew Gaston, he was pastor of the Methodist church in Pampa. He was intensely interested in the affairs of the community. People looked to him for leadership. Now a block from the church was a liquor store. The owner was a woman who had had a sensational past in oil field boom towns. She was also a beautiful woman. She got to attending the Methodist church and sitting in the balcony. Now the liquor store was next to the post office, and Gaston Foote spoke to everyone, and he would pass the time of day with anyone, saint or sinner. The woman, aware that Gaston was kind to her, and did not condemn her, thought she would like to hear him preach. She thought, as did I and a lot of people, that Gaston was the greatest preacher ever. One day she told Gaston that she wanted to join the church, and he said fine, and that she did not have to sit in the balcony.

The Sunday she joined, she sat on the main floor on the back seat. When Gaston gave the call, she left her seat and walked slowly down the aisle toward the front. I was sitting about halfway, but I heard and smelled her coming. She was wearing rustling silks, satins, furs and expensive perfume. Diamonds flashed from her fingers, her throat and her ears. She was dressed fit to kill.

Afterward, I asked her why she wore all the finery and perfume. She told me she liked to dress up for church. She liked to wear fine clothes, why everything she wore that Sunday came straight from New York and Paris. Now the Methodist church at Pampa was loaded with millionaires who had got rich off oil. But these people did not dress up. They had been living from hand to mouth for years before the oil was struck, and they looked it. They bought their clothes at the Montgomery Ward Store in Pampa or at J. C. Penney's. They all sat near the front, and they gave big money to the church and acted as if they owned it.

The woman was the only joiner that morning. When she got to the altar, she broke into tears of repentance which streaked her rouge and her mascara. You could tell she was truly repentant. I am sure that Gaston had told her that owning a liquor store would not keep anyone from being a Christian. The poor woman had probably long ago become resigned to the fact that because she was a bootlegger and a prostitute during prohibition, and the owner of a liquor store afterward, that she was automatically consigned to hell and the devil.

I could tell that the old-timers in the church, including the rich ones, were shocked that the woman had the "nerve" to join "our" church. You could cut the holier-than-thou atmosphere with a knife. The Big Rich sitting near the front were affronted and offended. I might say here that among those offended was a woman and a man who had lived together for 20 years or more without benefit of clergy but who gave money to the church like mad.

After the song, Gaston asked the congregation to welcome the woman into the church. Now my mother, known to me and all who knew her as "Mammy," sat on the fourth row near the front every Sunday, and I mean every Sunday, would always wait until a number had gone up to welcome the new members and then she would go so she would not be conspicuous. Mammy welcomed them into the church whether she knew them or not, just as she attended all funerals at the church regardless. As for me, I never went forward to shake hands with anybody unless I knew them. The choir was singing almost in a whisper and there was shocked silence in the congregation as they stared at the woman.

That morning, Mammy waited but nobody came forward to welcome the woman in the church. I saw Mammy turn around and look at the congregation. Her eyes met the eye of a woman friend who shook her head at Mammy, but Mammy got up slowly, and I was afraid she was going to faint because she had fainting spells under strain and stress and I started to go down there and help her, but her eyes caught mine and her eyes flashed. She then walked to the altar and hugged the woman who was still dabbing at her eyes with her bejeweled hands, and her perfume, pushed by body heat, was wafting out. Mammy patted the woman on the back as she hugged her, and then Mammy started crying with her. Then Mammy took her arms from around the woman and faced the audience, and her eyes were full of tears, and so were mine, and I think that if Gaston had ever wept he would have cried that day, but Gaston was not a weeping man, he was a doing man. Gaston was watching Mammy, and I thought he was going to hug her, but he restrained himself and patted her on the shoulder as he took her hands.

When we got in the car, Mammy asked why nobody came to shake hands with the woman, and then she asked who the woman was. I told her. "She's a good Christian woman," Mammy said.

BOBBY KENNEDY IS DEAD   *June 13*

I watched the Bobby Kennedy funeral from beginning to end just as I watched his brother John's four years ago, and Martin Luther King's recently, and it all seemed hopeless and discouraging until Edward Kennedy, now the only surviving son, gave his eulogy for Bobby. When Edward read the speech Bobby gave in South Africa, it occurred to me that perhaps the people who couldn't stand Bobby, including me at times, had misjudged and underestimated him, that we had just looked at his long hair and ignored his words.

Now I'm for Edward, for I believe he has the best characteristics of both Bobby and John without their faults, though as of now I can't recall any faults that John actually had. Edward Kennedy was the one hopeful, optimistic force that came out of that sad funeral.

I wonder if the reason Bobby was so bitterly hated by some was because he was held in such adulation by the Negroes, but I don't think that was the reason. His looks rubbed a lot of people the wrong way, also his voice. The Dallas News and the Enterprise hated him worse than anybody I know. They cussed him so much that I was beginning to be for him.

Now there are two Kennedy martyrs, and, like John, Bobby will win over his enemies, even in death. His words will keep coming back, and all we have said in condemnation of him will be as chaff in the wind. He has won more in death than he ever could win in life, as his brother did before him.

It wasn't like it was before, but it was worse in ways that had nothing to do with grief, which was my main reaction after Dallas. This time people all of a sudden are worrying if murder and assassination haven't become a habit with us, when it's been a habit with us all along. In the last several years, it seems, we just assassinate Kennedys and Negroes. I've never seen the figures on the many, many Negro churches that have been burned in Alabama and Mississippi, or how many Negroes have been shot dead, but they would be impressive. The TV talkers kept saying we murdered 6,000 last year with guns and Great Britain only 30. In England it is against the law to possess guns. You could deduce from that that every American is to blame for every murder because we don't have any gun laws. Bobby had not breathed his last before the National Rifle Association was on the air warning that "gun nuts" were again trying to take our guns away from us.

We blame Russia for Oswald and now we are blaming Jordan for Sirhan. So we are not going to face the truth about our uncontrolled guns. We are going to alibi, rationalize, make excuses, blame the other fellow and pass the buck. We barbecued the Negro for a century, and then he got freedom and put to use all he had learned from us. We formed mobs to lynch him, and when he got our foot off his neck, he formed mobs to march and burn, baby burn. He knew that the most telling way to make us holler was to hit our pocketbook. It needs to be pointed out at this time that the white man who assassinated Evers has gone free and that nobody in the South has been convicted in the scores of assassinations and burnings in the last few years. Where do you think the northern Negro got the idea for burning anyway? They got it from the whites burning Negro churches in the South.

Now we say we are not surprised that Bobby got killed, considering all the rioting in the streets, the looting and the burning, and we holler for law enforcement, forgetting that for a century we showed how to take the law into our own hands. Lynching was against the law, but for a hundred years we broke the law and murdered and burned. We taught him how to break the law.

Are we going to learn anything from Bobby's murder except to brag that it was a dirty foreigner who done it? It may be too late for us to reform. We've killed too many. There will not be an anti-gun law that will amount to anything. If there is, we will evade it as we evade all laws. The same day Bobby was shot he pointed out that the six richest men in America pay no income tax at all.

When Martin Luther King was assassinated, Bobby Kennedy said, "If you live by the sword, you die by the sword," and that's what we are going to keep on doing.

VIETNAM AND THE PENTAGON   *August 15*

The last time we mentioned the Vietnam War in this column, we said, line up all our troops, planes, tanks, rockets, battleships and march into North Vietnam and take the country, including old Ho Chi Minh. Either do that or get out. Now we've been talking peace for two months. I know now that we are never going to try to win that war, so I say get out. Get out and leave the country as fast as we can. It's not worth it. I have a terrible fear that the military-industrial complex of Pentagon and munitions makers want to keep this war going, and are going to keep it going. Too many plane makers, rocket tycoons and bullet capitalists are getting rich off this war. They want the inflation to continue, and it is going to continue if we don't stop this war, and I mean now. We are not going to try to win it, so I say get out. Inflation is wrecking everybody except the billionaires who supply the armed forces. What we need is a little deflation. The war is costing $75 billion a year; and a big part of the nation is living off jobs making rockets, planes and guns. Can our economy stand up without fighting a war? Let's find out quick. We have heard the Republicans and we have heard Wallace and both want that war to go on as usual. Maybe the Democrats will finally get some sense in their heads. The Pentagon and the munition makers are ruling and ruining this country.

CONVENTIONS OFFER STALE POLITICS   *September 5*

Reaction to both the Democratic and Republican conventions seems to have resulted in an increase in Wallace's already impressive strength in Hardin County. Thoughtful and responsible citizens I have known and respected for many years told me that after the Republicans had nominated Nixon they were going to hold off on committing themselves to a candidate until after the Democrats meet at Chicago. Over this weekend, some have told me they will vote for Wallace. They don't see him as a racist. General frustration and a yearning to be rid of the stale and conventional politics of both major parties accounts for much of Wallace's support.

Personally, I don't cuss Wallace as much as I did before Chicago. I used to say that I could never look a black man in the eye if I should vote for Wallace, but I don't say that any more. I understand why so many around here, especially working and labor people, are for Wallace. They feel toward the Democrats and Republicans like I feel toward the Connally and Smith Democrats. If they are disgusted with both Democrats and Republicans at Washington, they should be doubly disgusted with the LBJ hierarchy, including Preston, Connally and Ben Barnes at Austin, and they should vote for Eggers for governor. Look at what two-timing Smith is doing. He says he's voting for Humphrey, but he wants the Wallace people to vote for him. Nothing would give this state the good house cleaning it so badly needs in Austin than the election of a Republican governor. If we are going to clean house, let's not neglect our own state. The election of Paul Eggers would plant Texas in the column of states which have a two-party system, and that would do more for good government and honest politics in Texas than anything else.

This is the first time that after a Democratic convention I am not whooping and hollering for the nominee. I can't vote for Richard Nixon, but as of this moment I have little enthusiasm for Hubert Humphrey. Lyndon has done what he swore up and down four years ago he would not do, fight a major land war in Vietnam, and the Democrats did at Fort Chicago what George Wallace swears he will do if elected: crack the skulls of all dissenters.

299

For the first time I heard the Vietnam War really debated. My sympathy was with the minority, known as the doves. The debate was an eye-opener. I learned that we spend $82 million a day on a war we will never win, and that's why I'm against it. If the convention reflects the opinion of our country, then 40 per cent of our population wants to stop the war. That's the way the convention voted. The hawks are fond of calling the doves liberals, leftists, Communists, kooks and hippies but I saw none of those on the floor. They were loyal, conscientious American citizens.

There was only one issue at that convention, the war, and there is only one issue in the nation today, the war. The convention settled nothing. There will be no unity in this nation until the war stops. It looks like we are going to have a long bloody wait here at home before the war ends, what with Nixon, Humphrey and Wallace all determined to keep on killing and spending.

As for Connally, he was the biggest loser at Chicago. He revealed himself to the world as a racist conservative. He ranted and raved for keeping the unit rule and he was snowed under. The convention showed what it thought of him when more than 40 per cent of the delegates voted to kick out his puppet delegation and substitute and integrate a group including Senator Yarborough. Connally almost wept over this repudiation.

A STAR SPANGLED SALUTE   September 12

I never said anything about it, but the one thing I enjoyed most about the Democratic convention at Chicago was Aretha Franklin's good vocal rendition of the Star Spangled Banner. She is what they call a Soul Singer, but that is just another word for soulful singing. Aretha learned to sing in a church where she was a vocalist, as did Leontyne Price of Hattiesburg, Mississippi, the finest living grand opera soprano. Aretha sang the national anthem as Sister Vestal Goodman (TV Gospel Jubilee) sings "When He Reached Down His Hand For Me." Goose pimples came all over me; she sang it as if it were a Christmas hymn, and it thrilled me so that I stood right up there in my living room and saluted that TV flag. This Aretha Franklin is a big woman and her voice roars with feeling. None of this puny singing of the National Anthem from her. It was the most thrilling, touching and moving rendition of the anthem I ever heard.

Then the other day here came a letter with a clipping of a column in it, from a paper at some place called Kerens, Texas, and this Kerens editor was making fun of the way Aretha sang the Star Spangled Banner. He said it was disgusting and a lot of other things. I felt like getting in my car and driving 90 miles an hour to Kerens and whipping that editor. He should be ashamed of himself. What seemed to bug him more than anything else was that Aretha got mixed up in the song. At one time she said, "O say can you see" when she should have said, "O say does that star spangled banner still wave," or something like that. That was pure dee nit-pickin' with that editor. I'll bet that he can't recite more than one verse of the Star Spangled Banner, if he can recite one. The trouble with that Kerens scribe is that he's wallowing in prejudice. He'd probably find fault with Leontyne Price, too.

You don't hear many church songs sung with feeling these days, but I can remember when a camp meeting rendition of "The Unclouded Day" would turn on the shouters. That's the way Aretha sang the Banner.

If that editor had ever heard my Uncle Jess Fullingim, my cousin Alma Bell, Simp Privitt, and my Uncle Row Fullingim sing "Palms of Victory" at the Oak Grove camp meetings, he'd see how it fired up the congregation. I tell you one thing, Mr. Kerens editor, if I wanted to make a charge against the Viet Cong, I'd choose to hear first Aretha's version of the Star Spangled Banner. I don't want any puny version from the likes of Anita Bryant or Frank Sinatra. If I can't get Aretha, I'd take Kate Smith, Miss Price, or Mahalia Jackson (except that she sings only sacred songs). Then next I'd take Richard Tucker, or Glen Campbell or Charley Pride. If there ever was a wet blanket killjoy it's that Kerens editor.

HHH MY KIND OF DEMOCRAT September 19

For the past five years I have not even pretended to vote every time for the Democrat. I learned in the '50s from Shivers, Daniel, Connally, et al, who went to the Democratic convention at Chicago swearing loyalty and then came home and renounced it, that party loyalty is for suckers. So I have no criticism for the Democrats who are going to vote for Wallace and Nixon. I voted for Tower last time, hoping it would help promote a two-party system in Texas. It didn't. I'm voting for Paul Eggers, the Republican, this time hoping that he will be elected and that a two-party system might result. For only when radical conservatives start voting in the primary with their fellow-traveling Republicans will we have a two-party state.

I've made up my mind to vote for Humphrey because he is and has been my kind of Democrat for 20 years. I think that HHH is about to get Tricky Nixon in a corner. HHH is not acting like LBJ. He is acting like he's his own man. I can't vote for Nixon under any circumstances. I remember what he said when he got beat for governor of California. He was mad and sore and he said he would never run again. I can't vote for Wallace because to me he acts like a super police chief, and I think any vote for Wallace will be wasted. The surest way to elect HHH though is to vote for Wallace and throw the election into the House of Representatives where Democrats will vote for HHH and elect him.

The war is the key to all our problems: rioting, crime, high prices, too high wages and not enough help.

STAND UP AGAINST THOSE WHO HATE October 31

I am beginning to get worked up over the presidential election; I am becoming enthusiastic about Hubert Humphrey. I look around me and I see people on social security and drawing medicare; I see commodities being distributed at the courthouse; I see children at the school getting milk free and eating food that came from the federal government. I see everybody working who wants to work. I see the highest union wages ever in the history of this nation, and I see prosperity that has never been equaled, and I give the Democratic party all the credit, and I note that HHH voted for all of it and Nixon voted against all of it.

Some people are scared enough to believe that law and order have gone to pot in this country, but I'm not. I know that among white people there are a few hippies, and that they have their counterpart among the Negroes, but that the overwhelming majority of both whites and blacks are law-abiding. So I am not going to be scared into voting for George Wallace. Some say, "Stand Up for America," and many of those who are saying it have managed to stay out of Vietnam. Blacks and whites who are not voting for Wallace are standing up for America.

I, too, say stand up for America. I say stand up against racism. Stand up against the new hate. Stand up against cringing fear of most of the human race. Stand up against cruelty. Stand up against those who say that America is sick, sick, sick, and that to get our country well we must crack skulls. Stand up against those who would keep people in the ghetto back streets of America. Stand up against those who arouse the young to hate the old and vice-versa, the white to hate the black. Stand up against those who would make this country a police state. For if you stand against these things, you will stand up for America, and you will be standing up with Hubert Humphrey.

As for Nixon, I don't trust him, period. I don't trust the Republican party, and I have 100 years of history to convince me that I shouldn't. But you can trust the Democratic party.

What I want most of all is to bring the war in Vietnam to a close, and I believe HHH can do it quicker and better than Nixon or Wallace.

Besides all that, this time I'm voting strictly for my pocketbook and you better, too.

THE BURDEN HAS BEEN LIFTED *November 14*

The great burden that has been riding on the over-loaded

back of the Democratic party has been lifted. In that way it was a distinct relief that Richard Nixon was elected president, for the burden of the war, the revolt of youth and the students, the revolt of the ghettos and the struggle of minorities to attain justice, had become almost intolerable. The Democratic party had become thoroughly discredited. It had failed mainly because of the Vietnam War which was the basic cause of all our woes.

I am feeling almost relieved that now it's up to Nixon to achieve what the 29 million who voted for Nixon and the 10 million who voted for Wallace wanted: law and order, and solution of the war, for Nixon and Wallace talked much alike on the basic issues. Nixon was just not as specific as Wallace was. Both said about the same thing on law and order and Vietnam.

I believed that Humphrey would have succeeded where LBJ, the joint chiefs, and the Pentagon failed, but it would have been difficult. The Wallaceites, most of whom are Democrats as it turned out, were as thoroughly disgusted with the Democratic party as the McCarthyites, though the two groups despised each other. The Democratic party was in a wretched condition. Chicago proved that. Defeat at the polls was probably the only thing that could ever help it recover from Chicago.

I want to give LBJ all the credit he deserves for passing medicare, civil rights, the peace corps, for his stand on Israel and for the space accomplishments. The Vietnam War simply belittled every good thing that he did. People still have great faith in the Democratic party. Now the Democrats can start rebuilding on the heritage of Roosevelt, Truman and Kennedy.

Another aspect of the election that pleases me is that for the first time in 30 years Texas is cut off from Washington. We have no pipeline to the White House. Nobody now can sit in the seat of power in Washington and aid and abet the conservative establishment in Texas, as did LBJ. We will get along better in Texas without support for John Connally. The one person in Texas who benefitted most from the election was Senator Ralph Yarborough who went all out for HHH, while Connally grudgingly assisted. It will be easier now for us to elect a Republican governor next time if our liberal candidate loses in the primary. It is significant that Paul Eggers got more Republican votes for governor than any Democrat in the past. I am glad that there will be nobody in the seat of power in Washington who can control this state as it has been for 30 years.

Nixon got off to a bad start. The first thing he said after he was elected was that his first job would be to unite the country. That sounded like a politician, not a statesman. Unity to Nixon means getting everybody on his side. He's going to find out that there will be no unity in this country until we get out of Vietnam, until he stops spending $100 million a day in Vietnam. There will be no unity in this country as long as there are black ghettos.

LESSONS AT PECAN SCHOOL   *November 21*

Every time I eat some of the wild persimmons off the tree in the D. T. Sharp's yard in Kountze, I think of Pecan School which flourished for 50 years five miles east of Decatur in Wise County. Not that there were any persimmons right at the school; there were only post oak trees in the pasture back of the school house, a rather thick woods for that county. The persimmons were up in Hale Holler, named for my Uncle John Hale, first sheriff of Wise County, who was among the first to settle there.

The seven-month school would begin along in October, and early in November the teacher, Aunt Frances Fullingim, my father's youngest sister, would turn out school at noon on a Friday afternoon and take us on a trip to Hale Holler which would become rocky and hilly after about a mile. The persimmon trees up there were thick and loaded. I never saw a persimmon until I was seven years old, and I saw them first in rocky Hale Holler. I thought I had never tasted anything as wonderful as those persimmons.

Aunt Frances was a stern teacher, but on the picnic, she laughed, scuffled, hollered and ran with the rest of us, but we always knew she was the teacher. She was a strict disciplinarian in school; she never tolerated any sass or cutting up. When she punished a student, if he was small, say under 12, she sent him to cut the willow switch from the branch near the school, with which she whipped him before the whole school. If he didn't have a knife and had to borrow one, she'd give him extra licks, figuring he was lying. If he was one of the bigger boys or girls she'd throw a chunk of wood at him, and she used various tricks to keep him from dodging.

Aunt Frances taught from the first grade through the eighth, and she would have taught higher grades, if necessary. If anyone wanted to go any higher than the eighth, he would ride a horse to Decatur, but they usually quit school in the eighth grade. She would start hearing lessons in the first grade. She would say, "First grade, rise, pass." The four or five in the first grade lined up in a row in front of the teacher and stood throughout the recitation. In some classes, older pupils were allowed to march to a long bench in front of the teacher and sit, but when they recited, they had to stand. If a pupil did not know his lesson, Aunt Frances would say, "Go back to your seat and study some more and don't look up once, or I'll send you after a switch." You didn't look up.

You had to keep your nose in a book in that school, with one exception, and that was when the seventh grade history class came up to recite. Then there was a sort of understanding between teacher and the rest of the pupils that they could listen when a war was being talked about, and history was nothing but wars. Aunt Frances was fascinating while teaching history, especially Civil War history. When I was seven years old I used to sit back with my mouth open and eyes wide as she described the bloody details of the battle of Chancellorsville. Everybody cried, even Aunt Frances, when she described the tragic death of General Stonewall Jackson.

Some Friday afternoons we would have a program. Some of the older girls would declaim a poem. I still remember my sister, Estelle, declaiming, "O, why should the spirit of mortal be proud, like a swift-fleeting meteor or a fast-flying cloud, a flash of the light, a break of the wave, man passes from life to rest in the grave." All the big girls, we called them big, but none was over 15, would declaim with emotional gestures. The more gestures they gave, the more we were impressed. The big boys would sit in the back of the room and want to snigger, but we were afraid of Aunt Frances and that stack of wood which she would come and stand by at intervals. Then you could hear a pin drop.

On some Friday afternoons, we would have a spelling match,

306

and a lot of times this would last all afternoon. If there was one thing Aunt Frances couldn't stand, it was a poor speller. There were simply none in Pecan School. They learned to spell by sound and syllable. Right now I am almost sure I could spell down anybody in Kountze. My mother was a champion speller at old Cold Springs School.

We ate lunch from dinner buckets, mostly syrup buckets, but some had straw baskets. I can still see that small woven basket Aunt Frances carried. I thought it was the most elegant basket I ever saw. We carried our dinner in one bucket, and I had to eat with my two sisters, and they'd eat with other girls. I remember us all sitting in a corner of the school house at the back, and a girl named Jewel Cook was eating cooked prunes. All of a sudden I said, "Jewel look up at the sky and you can see stars," and when she looked I scooped up her prunes and stuffed them in my mouth. She accused everyone but me. I swallowed the prune seeds and my sisters told me that when they came out they'd tear me to pieces. I was scared for a week.

A short distance from the school house was a white church. It was the Cumberland Presbyterian Church. None of the boys and girls ever went inside that church. Aunt Frances would have skinned them alive and they'd have got it worse when they got home. That was another rule that was strictly followed: if a kid got a whipping, he'd bribe his brothers and sisters not to tell on him, like I did when I got that big whipping from Aunt Frances for calling a German girl "Dutch." That was the worst insult you could hand the Germans around there. For a month I was a slave to my sisters who threatened to tell on me if I didn't mind them.

Aunt Frances cut through the woods in walking to school, a distance of about two miles. In the spring, she would pick wild flowers along the path and bring them to school. The greatest thrill I had in school during those three years was to go home with her and spend the night. She lived with my grandma and Aunt Dollie and my two cousins, Kate and John, in a house that was started in 1858.

I owe my early ambition to Pecan School. We studied, in the first, second and third grades, the *Art Literature Reader*. It had excerpts of great poems and passages from great literature. We had to memorize a selection every day. Everybody had to memorize or take a whipping. I remember a girl reciting Whittier's "Snowbound." Only the other day, part of something I memorized at Pecan came to me. "O sun and skies of June and flowers of June together, you cannot rival for one hour October's bright blue weather," and from another, "The robin and the wren have flown and from the shrubs the jay and from the wood top calls the crow through all the gloomy day."

YOUNG & ON THE FARM December 19

The other day I was down at Hardin Memorial Hospital eating a jumbo hamburger and I sat down at a table with Booksie Mathews. Before me was nearly a full glass of ice tea, already sugared and lemoned, and I asked whose ice tea was that, and Booksie said it was Joan's, the cook. I yelled out, "Joan, can I have the rest of your iced tea," and she laughed and said yes, and a bunch of nurses at another table had a shocked expression on their faces, for to drink after anybody nowadays is unthinkable. Then Booksie and I got to reminiscing about how it was when we were young and on the farm.

I remembered that when we all went to the field out in Cottle County in the 1920s, we carried a waterbag full of water which we either hung on something or put it in the shade of a clump of Johnson grass. The wind blowing on the bag kept it cool. We all drank out of the bag without a dipper or a cup. Booksie recalled that at home there was a water bucket with a gourd dipper. Everybody drank out of the dipper. Then we remembered that we all washed out of the same wash pan and dried on the same cottonsack towel, and that towel really got dirty, but it always came out clean from the wash pot where it boiled in a foam of home-made soap.

Then I remembered about our breakfast on the farm. It consisted of big biscuits, syrup and butter, real soft butter. The six kids of us at home could almost clean up a gallon of syrup a meal. Another thing we ate lots of was blackeyed peas. We grew 'em, and Booksie remembered that we would put them while dry in sacks, and when we thrashed them we'd beat the sacks with flat boards, turning the sack over and over until all the peas were out of the hulls; then we'd "wind" 'em. That is, we'd spread out a wagon sheet and hold a bucket of peas higher than our head and let the wind blow the chaff away and the peas fall on the sheet. Then we'd put the peas in a large box in the barn, and stick a bottle of High Lifer down in it to keep the weevils away.

Another thing we did in our family was lower the milk and butter down in the well to keep cool, and we would always put the watermelons in the horse tank to cool. So I said, "Booksie, tell me something. How in the world did we manage to avoid fatal diseases drinking after each other, wiping on the same towel and soaking watermelons in the horse tanks? It's a wonder we all survived those days on the farm, and I'll tell you something Booksie, people then dipped snuff and chawed tobacco and we'd drink right after them out of the water bag or the jug and think nothing of it, but at least we'd always wipe off the mouth of the jug or bag if we had to drink after a snuff dipper or a tobacco chewer. How come, Booksie, we didn't catch all kinds of plagues?"

THE GREATEST CHRISTMAS GIFT

I almost got the Christmas spirit last week setting Birdwell's ad. That was the durndest ad I ever set. He copied it out of the Center paper, but our ad looked better than the Center paper's. But what almost gave me the spirit were the many Christmas gifts old Bird advertised, but like I said I didn't quite get it and I knew exactly what to do.

I had to go back in memory to the time I was 10 years old. That was 56 years ago. We were living at Decatur, and we had a lot of huge pecan trees down in the bottom, and we went there to pick pecans and earn our Christmas money. On Christmas eve I went to town with 50 cents in my pocket, and I had in mind to buy only one present, and that would be for my mother. I have bought a lot of presents since then; but even now that present that I bought my Mammy that cost 50 cents was the greatest present I ever bought. Just thinking of it now gives me the Christmas spirit. I went into all the stores in Decatur that Christmas eve, seeing how I could spend the fifty cents. I wound up in the biggest one called Perkins & Timberlake. There I bought the scarf. It was of pure silk; white with blue flowers on it and it was six feet long and about 20 inches wide. It cost exactly fifty cents, and the scarf was the prettiest thing I ever saw. I would not tell any of my brothers and sisters what I had bought because I knew they would tell.

That night we went to the Christmas tree at Oak Grove Methodist Church, as we went every Christmas, and I put the scarf under the tree and put my mother's name on it. The tree was a live oak with small green heart-shaped leaves. I waited anxiously for Santa Claus to call out Mammy's name and finally he did; and I got to watch my dear Mammy open the package, and her blue eyes glisten, and that was the first time I ever knew the Christmas spirit. It always comes back to me when I think of that scarf, for the spirit of Christmas is giving, but you just can't give, you have to give as I did when I was 10 years old. You have to give because you love, for loving is giving.

YEAR 1969

They say that you can know a person if you know what he reads. I thought of that again today and began wondering what sort of a person I am. It's a disturbing thought when you get to wondering what sort of person you are. You are likely to come up with surprising findings. In my research on this subject I made a list of all the things I have read recently, hoping to get a clue as to how I am at the age of 67. So let's explore it together; you will have as much information as I have and you can probably make deductions as good as I can.

I spend a lot of time reading newspapers, but I don't consider that real reading. It's like shaving or taking a bath, something you have to do. Just because you read the newspapers every day does not make you a person who reads. When it comes to magazines, I read The Texas Observer, Harper's, the Atlantic Monthly, and I have for years. I am a periodic reader of Time and Life. I take The New Republic, True West, True Frontier, and Gourmet magazine, which I subscribed to one time when a boy came to my house who was raising money to go to college, or so he said. He also talked me into subscribing to Venture which is a magazine for rich world travelers.

The last book I ordered from Cokesbury's in Dallas was *African Genesis* which I am now reading. And the book cost $7.95, but I justify my big book expense by saying that I don't spend over $75 a year for clothes (and I durn sure look it, too) and I never drink whiskey any more and have cut down on beer to about two cans a week. *African Genesis* advances the theory that Man came from the killer apes along the equator in Africa and from there he spread out all over the world. If that is true the first man was black. Since Moore's Super Market went out of the paperback book selling business, I have no place to buy books locally, so I spend my extra cash on books I see advertised. I buy them all from Cokesbury Book Store in Dallas. The next to the last book

I got from there was called *The Hundred Yard War*, and it was about pro football, but it was a disappointment. I have read all of John Updike I want to. I never want to read another book like *Valley of the Dolls*, because I have lived long enough to know that the telling of one sex affair after another is like telling dirty jokes, but not half as funny. Most of the novels written now are sex books and they are all alike. You read one and you've read them all. There is not too much difference between Updike and Philip Roth, both of whom are boring.

I never did care much for Ernest Hemingway, who is quite passé now. My old favorites in the 1920's and 1930's were John Steinbeck, Willa Cather, Vachel Lindsay and Carl Sandburg; but I now appear to have a lasting passion for Joseph Conrad and William Faulkner, the latter I regard as America's greatest novelist, and I wish he had not passed away. Faulkner is the master. There was both comedy and tragedy in the American South and he plumbed its depths. I still read the books of J. Frank Dobie for he was the first Texan to convince the world Texans can write. Since then I have enjoyed Larry McMurtry and William Humphrey, Texas writers. But since the novel has become nothing but meaningless gymnastics in sexual orgasms, and I eschew paying out good money to read experiences I have already read, the novel does not mean as much to me anymore. When you read a novel and after you have finished reading it, if you remember the bedroom episodes rather than the personality and intelligence of the characters then you have wasted your time, and I hope that my good friends Alfred A. Knopf and Angus Wilson realize this. That is a digression I had not intended. What I want to say is that now I reach for the non-fiction books, especially on politics, economics, the frontier, the old west. Last year, I bought books about the Matador Ranch, the White Deer Land Company, Charles Goodnight, Jesus Christ, and LBJ, who has become a tragic figure. He's strictly out of "King Lear" or "King John" or "Hamlet," but don't mistake me. If Othello was a villain so is LBJ. The trouble is that nobody can make up his mind whether LBJ is a villain or a hero or maybe a fool. The most telling clue we have about LBJ is that when he went to the Senate in 1948 he was broke and when he left the White House in 1969 he was worth $13 million.

When I was 18 years old I wanted to be a poet and I wrote poetry, but it must not have been very good because I could never sell the few pieces I submitted for publication, but I wrote lots of poetry before I was 35 years old and some between the age of 34 and 41, but not after that. I have written sonnets galore, and a trunkful of ballads. The last poem I wrote was a ballad about Guadalcanal and I wrote it during the war, but that war took all the poetry out of me. Since then I have scarcely read a poem, let alone written one, though I didn't mind it so much when I heard Johnny Cash, the hillbilly singer, read "The Ballad of the Harp Weaver" over TV last Christmas.

To recapitulate: I don't read poetry, and sex novels bore me; I read biographies, history, historical magazines and opinion magazines. I don't read Life and Time now, but have in the past.

I read every night and nearly all day Saturday and Sunday between chores. Reading has been the biggest single thing in my life and still is. I'd buy a book before I would buy a pair of shoes. I'd even skip a meal to buy a book, if I had to.

I like Conrad, Faulkner, Dobie, Humphrey and others like them. I read a Shakespeare play three or four times a year and realize then that I have been wasting my time in reading sex books. Although poetry is now out of my ken, all the lines of poetry I have read in the past keep reciting themselves in my mind. If you want to know what else I read that list would not include Readers Digest. Reading it is like eating straw.

So now that you know what I read and what I don't read, what kind of a man am I? If you have any clues let me know because I still am not positive I know who I am or why. Socrates said, "Know thyself," and that's the biggest order ever given to man. When I was young and very poor, I stole books. I would steal them out of libraries and I still have some books I stole out of libraries, but I haven't stolen a book in 40 years, not counting a book I "procured" from the U.S. Navy.

Some of you people are going to say, he's not mentioned the Bible yet. I'm coming to it. I have read the Bible seven times, and now I had rather hear it read than read it myself. I don't like to read something in the Bible that I have read over and over because I don't read the Bible for pastime.

THE SMITH-BARNES LEGISLATURE   *June 26*

Preston Smith cut down Ben Barnes and Gus Mutscher to tadpole size in vetoing their one-year appropriation bill which they tried to stuff down his throat knowing it was as phony as a $3 bill. I have not been a Smith man, but he was right in vetoing that bill. Now the Legislature is going to have to meet in special session and raise the tax money, and the governor should realize that it's time to slap some taxes on Texas corporation profits.

Ben Barnes, who entered the Texas Legislature broke and penniless, but with his hand out a few years ago when he was still in his twenties, is now a rich man. He is an influence peddler deluxe and first on his list is Ben Barnes, not the people of Texas. This is the man who wants to run against Senator Ralph Yarborough next time around. The senator is still a poor man although he has been in the senate almost as long as LBJ was, and LBJ came out of Washington worth $17 million. Maybe Ben is trying to break the LBJ record. Ben is a young man, but he is a wheeler dealer. He wasn't in the legislature long before he began to make connections with important people. He began to acquire an interest in this and that over the state.

Ben has the backing of the wheeler-dealer lobbyists at Austin; and they turn things his way, secure in the knowledge that he is not going to touch oil, utilities, gas, sulphur or corporation earnings, when he starts hunting for tax money. Ben will do them right. He will slap a sales tax on everything but groceries and he'd like to do that, and he will tax cigarettes to the limit, 11¢ now; and he has drawn that other disgusting Austin character, Gus Mutscher of Brenham, speaker of the house, along with him. It took quite a bit of arm twisting to make Gus go along with him, all Gus had to do was look at the financial assets Ben has piled up since he hit Austin broke and Gus, what with a new wife in town, and a former Miss America at that, thought, what the heck, I wanna live like Ben Barnes and LBJ.

The Dallas News which is the conscienceless, snaggle-toothed harlot for the corporation lobbyists, John Birchers, Kennedy haters and war mongers, is singing the praises of Ben against the people. Ben himself tries to play liberal; he fooled along with the liberal crowd this year in order to cut Preston Smith's throat, and he may have done that but I'll tell you this: Preston is great compared to Ben. Everything Ben did in the recent session of the legislature was aimed at wounding Smith who stood up under it. Some of the state's liberals were foolish enough to go along with Barnes and they'll regret that.

For I've got my ear to the ground and the noise I hear tells me that Ben Barnes has come along too fast, piled up too much wealth too quick and that he could not beat either Smith or Yarborough next go-around, because the people of Texas are going to find out about Ben before then.

A NATION OF GOD & VIOLENCE   *July 17*

The other day a person handed me a coin about the size of the old dollar, and one side was stamped, "God, Guns and Guts," and on the other, "Let's keep all three." The people who put out that coin probably just put in God because it began with a "G" and to make the slogan appear as if it had his blessing. But do you suppose that God is all that much for guns? Somewhere in the Bible it says that if you live by the sword you die by the sword. I just can't believe that God has put his stamp of approval on guns. I know that the National Rifle Association would like for you to believe it; but somehow it sticks in my craw. Every week in the United States more than 200 people are killed by guns, more than are killed in the Vietnam War, and we glorify the gun. If you really want to stir up a wasp nest, just mention registration of guns to certain people.

I can't figure out the guts part of the slogan on the coin. It's not very specific just to say "Let's keep our guts." Of course the genius who thought up the slogan for the coin was not referring to the guts that are in your belly, but that old do or die spirit. Guts to ram your head against a brick wall. Guts to fight for guns. It all sounded pretty violent. But what the heck. The United States is a nation of violence. We have always lived by violence and we will probably die by it, and it's probably too late to change now. So let's keep the guns and guts, and get more of them, and then lay it all on God.

The United States had its beginning at Jamestown and Plymouth Rock early in the 1600's. We spent the next 250 years slaughtering the Indians so we could take their land away from them. We said they were savages and godless and didn't know how to use the land. It took us 275 years to rob the Indians of their land, but we finally made it, but the Indians put up a pretty good fight against us. They fought back with guns they got from white men, and their guts were superb.

In the meantime we were having trouble with the Negroes. As soon as the nation was founded men with guns and guts, men who quoted the Bible much as the Red Chinese now quote the thoughts of Mao Tse-tung, began raiding Africa for slaves. But the mean old Yankee North was jealous. They didn't want us to have our slaves. Nary one. They also had guts and guns and they also could quote God in volume. The mean old Yankees said we are going to free your slaves, and the South said, no, you are not. So there was a big war of guns, guts and God. Both said God was on their side. What did the churches do while all this was going on? I just know for certain what the Methodist church did. I'm a Methodist. When the Civil War broke out the Methodists down south said, you're wrong, Damn Yankees. We believe in slavery, so we are going to separate from you and for the next hundred years there was a Methodist Church, South. You see many of the big slave owners were Methodists. Did you know that people in the south were taught that the Negro had no soul, that he was like a mule or a cow? I myself have known Southerners who lived during that time who said that the Negro had no soul. My father who was born in 1862 never referred to Negroes as human beings. He called males "bucks" and females "mares." He learned all this from the Civil War generation. The churches not only did not try to correct this attitude, but they condoned it. I can remember when white folks used to debate in back country school houses on the subject, "Does a Negro have a soul."

Northern guns and guts won the Civil War, of course, aided, they claimed, by God. But the Indians were still around, and as soon as the war was over we really took care of the Indians. About that time there were 70 million buffalo roaming the great plains of Texas, Colorado, Oklahoma, Kansas and New Mexico, mostly in Texas. So our men with guns and guts said, you ain't

seen nothin' yet, and they took their Sharps rifles and built tri-
pods to hold them and surrounded the buffalo on the Texas
plains. The guns would get hot but they had a boy handy to keep
pouring water on the red hot artillery. In two years, it was almost
as hard to find a buffalo as it is now to find a whooping crane.
Guns and guts had triumphed again. About the time the buffalo bones began whitening on the plains, the people we called
the "niggers" started acting like they didn't want to stay in their
place. Now everybody in those days knew exactly what his place
was. He was to keep out of the white man's way, stay in his shacks
in "nigger town," stay out of the white man's part of town unless
he was up there to buy something at the white man's store. The
people we called the "niggers" did not want to stay in the place
the white man had hemmed them up in, so the men with guts
and guns organized the hooded Ku Klux Klan which burned,
tarred and feathered, beat up and sometimes emasculated the
Negro under the banner of the Cross of Jesus Christ. It still
marches off to burn and raze and terrorize under the Cross of
God. You will note that we Americans may be violent but we always like to take God along with us, as well as guts and guns. An
era ended when Ike appointed Warren to the Supreme Court
and he began ordering complete integration. The black man
now has the nerve to think he can go to school, eat and live any
place any white man does. So it takes guns and guts, and God,
all three, to cope with that kind of thinking. For 200 years the
white man had the black man as his slave. Then the black man
was freed and for the next 100 years the white man lynched the
Negro, burned him out, beat him up every chance he got, and
told him to keep his place which was out of the white man's sight.
In the 1960's when the Negro began acting up again, the
righteously indignant people of the South burned more than
400 Negro churches alone. Then the Negro, taught how to kill
and burn for 300 years by the white man, started burning back.
They burned down Los Angeles, they burned down Detroit,
they burned down Philadelphia and they are continuing to burn.
They holler, "Burn, baby, burn," and throw their gasoline
bottles.

And that's not all they had the nerve to do. Here recently, one
James Foreman has gone around to all the churches asking for

317

$500 million in "reparations" for aiding, abetting and upholding the crimes committed by people with guts and guns against the Negro for the last 300 years. They went before the Methodist conference in Texas asking for reparations and they got turned down flat. Why the Methodists had nothing to do with dooming Negroes to the ghetto! All the Methodists did was tell the Confederate soldiers; "God is on our side, take your guns and guts and go out and kill the damn Yankees so we can keep the Negro in his place which is slavery."

I don't know about the Jews, Roman Catholics or Baptist but I think the Methodist Church South owes the Negroes about $100 million in reparations. For when you get down to the lick-log, the churches are responsible for the moral and religious beliefs of its members and if they aren't, who is? Until I was 12 years old I never missed Sunday school, a sermon or a revival at Oak Grove Methodist church. I believed that the Negro was an animal and had no soul, because that was the way I learned it. The churches for 300 years never recognized that the Negro had a soul. They aided and abetted the doctrine that the Negro should be kept in his place which was really slavery before and after the Civil War. So the churches are more responsible than any other body for the ghettos, and they should now in good conscience admit and help pay for it.

Some of the things the blacks want to do with that $500 million are to spend $200 million for a southern land bank and $130 million to establish a black university in the South.

But some of our guns have misfired lately, like the tank the army has spent $10 million to build and every time it fires it kills everybody in the tank, but last week the Pentagon which runs in guns and whole tubs of guts say they are going to keep on building it. We continue to spend billions on useless weapons. In spite of all that, there is getting to be a lot of opposition to taking Hamburger Hill one day, with heavy loss of life, abandoning it the next, taking it again the next and so on. Our fine boys in Vietnam seem to have plenty of guts, including Negroes, Mexicans and Puerto Ricans who make up 30 per cent of the fighters in Vietnam, but they don't have all the guns they want at times.

I feel for those boys in Vietnam, especially when I think it's all likely to be in vain. Nixon, like LBJ, isn't going to try to win, so we are going to have to pull out, and that will be the signal for Hanoi to take over South Vietnam, Laos, Cambodia and Thailand. That won't be so bad. A lot of people over there have got rich off the war and we will undoubtedly give them time to pull out, to draw their American dollars out of Swiss banks.

THE SILENT MAJORITY AND VIETNAM   *November 20*

All you could hear about last week was what Nixon calls the Great Silent Majority, but by week's end it turned out that the GSM were just Republicans, radicals of the right, John Birchers and war hawks who really want us to stay in Vietnam. Useless John Tower came to Beaumont and begged for patience. The proof that GSM propaganda is only Republican strategy lies in Useless John's remarks to the Big Rich of Beaumont in the Camelot Room of the Royal Coach Inn (a travesty on the memory of John Kennedy since his name is the only one associated with Camelot). Why didn't Useless John implore patience when poor old LBJ was being crucified? Where was the GSM then? Tricky Dick has thought up the GSM only to look good before the American people.

Nixon has wrapped himself in the flag, as have all his supporters who are now calling everybody traitors and Communists if they are not for staying in Vietnam until the South Vietnamese can take over, but it won't work. Truth is the South Vietnamese will never be able to take over the fighting. Useless John now says we've got to hold on to Cambodia, Laos and Thailand regardless. So you see what Nixon and old Big Mouth Spiro Agnew are tryin to do is convince the American people that we can't get out of Southeast Asia.

Oh, but Useless John, Tricky Dick and Sputtering Spiro are big patriots now and everyone who disagrees with them is a traitor and I note the Young Republicans at Lamar University are sounding off for staying in Vietnam. I would just like to ask those draft dodging Republicans at Lamar one question: If they are so all-fired hot for this war, why ain't they in uniform, instead of going to college to evade the draft? Also what about Nixon's son-in-law, David Eisenhower? He's 22. Why isn't he in uniform? Why isn't he in Vietnam? At least both of LBJ's sons-in-law went to Vietnam. What about Spiro's boy? I notice that people who don't have anybody in Vietnam are mighty big patriots, and especially those who were draft dodgers in World War II, but you ask the mothers of the boys in Vietnam, and you ask the boys who come back and they will tell you that the South Vietnamese don't care who wins as long as we bring over food and supplies that they can steal and sell on the Black Market. I say that South Vietnam has proved over and over that it's not worth saving and doesn't want to be saved. Who is the George Washington of South Vietnam? Ho Chi Minh, the now dead dictator of North Vietnam. All the Saigon buzzards want is our money, and they are getting that at the rate of $1 billion a month.

MAI LAI: CHARGE THE WAR HAWKS   *December 4*

One time in the dim past, a past most of us now want to forget, but it was less than 100 years ago, our army massacred a whole village of Indians, defenseless men, women and children, shot them down as they ran and cowered and tried to hide. You remember that story: It used to be on TV often but now it's something we as a nation want to forget, but here in March of 1968 we did it again. We slaughtered a whole village of South Vietnamese, and now the brazen, lying Pentagon is trying to find a goat. They are trying to find somebody to hang it on. They have arrested an officer and a sergeant, but who is to blame? Certainly not the men who did the killing; they were only taking orders; if you have ever been a member of the armed forces you know that you don't do anything unless you get the order and then you obey the order regardless of what it is. So I'm like that mother in Ohio: the army made a murderer of her son. The last people on earth who should be tried are those boys who are forced to shoot down the villagers.

The real war criminals are in the Pentagon and the people who got us into this war and are keeping us in it. One of the soldiers who was quoted as saying that he shot down 10 of the massacred villagers said that he wouldn't go back to Vietnam because those people don't want us over there. Our boys and our officers thought that all the people in that village were Viet Cong who the day before had murdered our soldiers. They wanted revenge and you can't blame them. The Viet Cong controlled that village and they would have killed our boys again.

All charges against our people should be dropped immediately, and if any are filed they should be against General Westmoreland who is now throwing up his hands in holy horror, along with LBJ, and saying he knew nothing about it. Well, if he didn't he had no business being in command of 500,000 U.S. troops in Vietnam. He's trying to pass the buck, and it's likely he will succeed. Drop the charges immediately against the men who did the shooting. They were only obeying orders. That incident proves that we are in the wrong war, that we've got no business over there, where you can't tell friend from foe, where the people themselves don't want freedom; they want the U.S. to keep on spending a billion dollars a month over there, so they can steal half of it. Don't forget the No. 1 hero in South Vietnam is still Ho Chi Minh.

We Americans have always prided ourselves on being a humane people and far different from the Germans who massacred six million Jews during World War II. We choose to forget how we burned Negroes at the stake and massacred Indians, forgetting that the Indians were here before we were and that we brought the Negroes here in chains. We have always congratulated ourselves on being above savages, and after World War II we tried German after German for the atrocities they committed. We also tried and put to death Japanese for their treatment of prisoners, and right now we are itching to get hold of the North Koreans who tortured and beat up the men of the Pueblo, but now we have committed an atrocity, and the brazen lying Pentagon wants somebody to suffer for it, but I say that nothing should be done at all. Just write it off as a part of a war we should never have got into.

I demand that the charges against Lieutenant Calley and the others be dropped, and that if anybody is going to be charged file them against all those war hawks in the Congress, the Pentagon and LBJ, not against those boys who were only following orders. You see we have the same alibi that the Germans and Japanese had, "We only followed orders." My sympathy is not with the South Vietnamese, but with those men now back in the states and out of the army who say they can't sleep because they keep thinking of the children and mothers they shot to death in that massacre. Those ex-soldiers are the ones who have my sympathy.

Meanwhile, the Pentagon continues to spread scare stories about what the Russians and Chinese will do to us if we cut one cent off their inflated budget, and they are getting the money and we are believing their propaganda, with the help of Senator Stennis and Congressman Mendel Rivers, who stays drunk three-fourths of the time, but is the Pentagon's stooge as chairman of the House Armed Forces committee. Don't charge those soldiers, slap them instead on Stennis, Rivers, et al.

Get the picture once and for all. We now have 450,000 boys in Vietnam, half of whom are smoking marijuana, it is said; the army is talking about establishing regulated houses of prostitution in order to keep venereal disease down. Our boys don't know friend from foe; they can't fight to win; just go out and kill and be killed. They are being exploited by the black market; they face vicious temptations that they never heard of in the States; they have no faith in the South Vietnamese people; the South Viet army deserts and runs away from a fight. Worst of all we can never win. So let's leave.

An example of the character of the South Vietnamese can be seen in the declarations of the officers of their army who say that no one was massacred, that the villagers made it up, this in the face of testimony from our boys who shot them down. The Pentagon and the war hawks are now criticizing the TV networks for uncovering the massacre and quoting the soldiers. Naturally, the Pentagon wants all its sins buried. It doesn't want anything known about its generals who work for the arms makers, or about the navy's stupidity in allowing the Pueblo ever to set forth without protection. The networks are doing their job. Let the boys tell all; I want nothing buried by the Pentagon, and if a single one of those soldiers involved in the massacre is convicted, I want them to shoot Stennis, Rivers, et al, first.

ON DEATH AND YOUTH   *December 11*

I was going to write a final column this week about my brother, Henry Will, who died, but it's too early and I start crying again. I keep seeing him when he was 16 and living with me in Pampa, Texas, and yodeling Jimmy Rodgers' songs and playing the guitar. And company would come and I'd say, Henry Will, play and sing for these people, and then I'd say, now isn't he the most wonderful child you ever saw? And of course they had to agree, and Alf and Virginia would be sitting there nodding and applauding. You see, he was the baby of the family.

There's one thing we've got to stop in this country and that is alienating and condemning our youth. In past generations youth has been criticized and low-rated but never to the extent that we are doing it today. In the 1920s, the flappers, with their jelly beans and their coonskin coats, attracted wails that the young generation was going to the dogs. The young generation during the depression was docile and silent. Now we have a generation of youth who are thinking, they want a piece of the action, so to speak. They want a hand in running this world. They think they can avoid some of the mistakes their fathers and grandfathers made. We've got to deal with them. We've got to communicate with them; we've got to recognize them, long hair, demonstrations, sideburns, miniskirts, their four-letter expletives and all. The other night Nixon said that eight million young people in America are smoking marijuana; he said until he found that out he wanted to put them in jail but now he doesn't know what to do, but that he knows jail is not the answer. Most of the elderly I know want to put all demonstrators in jail. The only youth they think is worth a durn are those in Vietnam.

Sputtering Spiro has not helped the situation any. His daughter wanted to demonstrate for peace but he wouldn't let her leave the house. Spiro may be the idol of the Great Silent Majority, as Nixon claims, but he is looked upon as an incredible idiot by youth. Spiro may be making a big hit with the silent majority, but not with the youth of today, and the youth of today will be running this country in the 1980s and 1990s.

Personally, I think they are right about a lot of things we are condemning them for. First, there is the matter of the hair and the sideburns. You don't hear men objecting to miniskirts but they are far more revolutionary than long hair. At least two years ago I quit getting excited about long hair. Joe Namath made a believer of me. Marijuana is something else, but now that eight million are smoking it and if it's as bad as they say, Nixon ought to start an exhaustive study to find out exactly why our kids are smoking it, and what the effects are. Evidently our youth don't think the effects are as bad as pictured.

There's one thing about youth that I like very much. They are all conservationists and they talk ecology constantly. Do you know what ecology means? If you don't you better find out. My dictionary says that ecology is "biology dealing with the mutual relationships between organisms and their environment." Ecologists claim that when you dam up a river or a creek you change the environment, or when you kill out all the hardwood as the timber companies seem to favor, you destroy bird, plant and animal life.

Another thing the young people are going for is anti-pollution. The main fight now against air and water pollution is being made by long-haired students. As they say, that's their bag, and they are studying it in college. When they get out, backed by their scientific knowledge, we may not take pollution as casually as we do now, and I say hasten the day. Of course, youth began changing long before the Vietnam war began to bleed us. The first big sign of it was the Peace Corps. Here were educated young volunteering to work for nothing in foreign countries, and I mean educated youth of high moral character. No missionaries, freaks or kooks, but youth who wanted their lives to mean something, who wanted something out of life besides a car, a color TV and a good job. Now a lot of young people are like that; they scorn the image of the typical do-gooder who belongs to committees and is president of this civic group or that. They see people as the human race, each person a human being, nothing more. They don't care if Jesus Christ was black or white, or if a person is black, brown, yellow, red. They see the world as the astronauts saw it, just a green globe isolated out there in space teeming with life, one world and one people.

The most noticeable flagwavers today are those people who seem to know exactly what our forefathers had in mind when they wrote the Constitution. Usually these people, who wrap themselves securely in the flag and denounce youth and all demonstrators and are safely well-to-do, should be reminded every so often that the young, not the middle aged and not the old, instigated and fought the Revolutionary War. They had a few old men like Benjamin Franklin and John Randolph to back them up, but let it be remembered by our patriots that in the South 75 per cent of the rich planters were loyal to England, even George Washington was opposed to separating from England until July 4, 1776, and then he had his doubts. The long-haired radicals who fought our revolution in spite of the safely rich were people like Thomas Jefferson, James Madison, the Adamses, all of whom were under 30, and let us remember that even though Spiro now says the East is full of effete snobs, the New England states, Virginia and the Middle Atlantic states furnished the manpower and ideas for that war, and wrote the Constitution which to the safely rich of that day was more radical than anything our youth have done to date.

GOODNIGHT, CHET; GOODNIGHT, DAVID   December 18

For years I have been turning on Huntley and Brinkley for the 5:30 evening news. If the phone rang between 5:30 and 6 p.m. I wouldn't answer it. If anybody knocked on the door I'd say come in and sit down and don't say nothin' cause I'm listening to the news. I have taken Chet's and David's version of the news as gospel. They suited me to a T though sometimes I would decide that they were radical, rightwing conservatives and hated all Democrats, but they seemed to have a sense of humor, and to a man who lives in a town whose slogan is "The Town With a Sense of Humor," that means a lot.

But sputtering Spiro has rocked me. Now I've got a hang-up about Chet and David. I have watched them closely to see if they editorialize; and I am glad to report that I have cleared them of that charge. Also, I am satisfied with their choice of news. I want to know everything there is to know about the Vietnam War, I want to get all the dirt on the cover-up Pentagon, and I want to know every move that Richard Nixon makes, so I can't fault H&B on their choice of news.

Still about a week ago, I began to have a dissatisfied feeling after the H&B broadcast ended. I couldn't put my finger on it. It took me nearly a week to find out what was wrong. What I don't like is the way H&B say good night to each other. David, most of the time, has the last story and it's usually a human interest story pointing up the follies of mankind, like Ecclesiastes, vanity all is vanity. Then David says, "Good night, Chet," and there is a sort of mocking lilt in his voice. Or is it? His eyebrows lift ever so slightly, and the corners of his mouth turn up. He has a Mona Lisa smile on his face that is enigmatic. Is he making fun of us violent Americans? What does that Mona Lisa smile mean?

Then there's Chet. When the camera turns on Chet again, he has those spectacles in his hand and he lifts them to the temple in a sort of hopeless gesture, and the corners of his mouth turns up like David's and Chet's smile is tolerant and seems to say, "Lord what fools we mortals be." (From Shakespeare's "Midsummer Night's Dream." There is a statue of Puck, who uttered that truth, in front of the Folger Memorial Shakespeare Library in Washington, D.C.) Now what I'm getting at is that I want Spiro to investigate the way H&B say good night to each other, and I want him to go on national TV and tell us what sinister influences he sees in the good night scene. I am sure that he and Nixon and their writers can come up with some expletives that can even outdo Effete Snobs. For instance, only last night David was telling all about Erskine Caldwell's *Tobacco Road* in Georgia, and showed Caldwell walking up to a ramshackle building and reading a portion of *Tobacco Road*. Right after that David said good night in that lilting voice and Mona Lisa smile. Do you reckon that David is trying to remind us that Georgia still has all that poor white trash, that the Georgia rednecks are the kind of people Spiro and Nixon are trying to please the most? Shame on you David, I hope sputtering Spiro goes up and down your back with a rake for this.

The excuse for this *Tobacco Road* segment is that Georgia wants to change the name of Tobacco Road and H&B didn't say what they wanted to change it to, but I presume it would be something like Cherokee Rose Lane.

Then, before that, H&B showed Congressman Mendel Rivers of South Carolina in such a way that you could see his whiskey nose and they let him carry on in that shinning voice of his so that the picture you got of Rivers was not at all flattering. Spiro ought to jump on that like a duck on a June bug. He could get a lot of mileage out of that one. During the broadcast, H&B and their staff reported on the tax bill which some congressman characterized as "this thing," on the claims and counter claims of Arabs and Israelis, and I couldn't tell whether H&B are for the Jews or the Arabs, nor what kind of tax bill they want nor whether they are pro or anti Black Panther, but I am sure Sputtering Spiro can, but I want to give Agitatin' Agnew a hint. The answer lies in the way H&B say good night to each other, the enigmatic look on their faces, the tone of their voices. Spiro, that's the key to the whole H&B broadcast. So Spiro you get your writers and your Madison Avenue boys who make up Tricky Dickey and coach his every move on TV and break down that H&B good night and accompanying looks and tones. That's the climax on their broadcast. Without it their program would mean nothing, so Spiro hop to it and let us know. Get with it boy, you've got your work cut out for you.

YARBOROUGH, YOUTH AND NIXON   *December 25*

Gordon Baxter's column of December 11 has both mystified and infuriated some readers. You will remember he commented on Spiro, EasTex and Ollie Crawford and a proposed Village Creek dam. This is a quote from a letter to the News: "I just read Baxter's column . . . and I feel disoriented once again. His back-handed compliment to EasTex and Kirby was a little puzzling; in any case I think the companies who do make antipollution and conservation efforts should be applauded, no matter how self-serving their reasons . . ."

I was infuriated by the column, not because of what he said for or against timber company types or the Village Creek dam, but by this quote from his column: "Archer sounded just like Ralph

Yarborough, gagging at the speaker, missing the speech." I did not see that sentence until I read proof on it and I have been burning up ever since. I don't mind the slam at me; I am called worse than that every Wednesday (two weeks ago two telephone callers informed me that I was a lyin' SOB) but what I resent is Baxter's reference to Yarborough.

Now every time Baxter jumps on me and I answer back he gets mad, but this time I don't care if he does. I'm not going to let his bad-mouthing of Senator Yarborough go unanswered. To begin with I'm going to quote a little Shakespeare to Baxter: "Blow, blow thou bitter wind, thou art not so unkind as man's ingratitude," and I'm referring to the red carpet the senator laid out for him every time Baxter went to Washington. Baxter can say that because when he accepts favors from a person that is no sign he has to support him politically. In my books you do not ask favors from a politician you are going to stab in the back. I wouldn't give Useless John Tower or Sputtering Spiro Agnew or Tricky Dickey the sweat off my backside; and furthermore I would not ask them for any favor either. If I were going to bad-mouth somebody I would take no favors from him. For 17 years I fought Shivers, Daniel and St. John Connally, and during all that time they never allowed me to print a single amendment, though every county seat paper in Texas got them but me. I figure I lost about $3,000 as a result of my editorials against those three. I'm still agin 'em, because I figure all three of them will fight Yarborough next year, and vote for Republican George Bush if the latter hasn't got any more sense to run against Yarborough, because the senator is going to win.

They talk about George Bush, the senator's prospective 1972 opponent, being young at 44. He'll never be as young as the senator who happens to be 66. Bush was an old man at 21, or else he never would have espoused the lousy Republican causes he has. Yarborough is young because he has young ideas, he understands youth, as well as the old and the poor. Bush is already an old man because he talks like one. If Bush is planning to run on his youth, he better have more to offer than Madison Avenue facials and hairdos, and that coat slung over his shoulders. You never realize just how old he is and how youthful Yarborough is until you hear them talk.

I'd rather listen to some youthful views than those of some people now in their 40s and 50s and up; also those ever present experts in their 30s. These people can tell you how it was in World War I and World War II. But I'd rather listen to the younger generation, and most of them in college, too, who say, "Yes, yes, yes, man you know all about patriotism. You won World War II and the cold war and the Korean War, but where have you got us. The scientists complain every day that in less than 50 years we will literally starve to death in world-wide famine, we are about to smother to death in garbage and pollution. Yes, you have fixed it up nice for us. We have stark, killing hunger in the United States. We spend most of our income on killing people in foreign wars. Get lost, man, and let's get with really saving this country instead of killing it as you appear determined to do."

Don't talk to me of Agnew and Nixon; I'm with the young who want to save this world from itself, not blow it up or smother it to death.

You say, but I'm against those damn demonstrators. Everything we ever got in this country was through demonstrations. Did you know that in 1776 the safe souls in America, the Agnew and Nixon types, looked upon Patrick Henry as Agnew looks upon the Black Panthers? What we need in this country is more demonstrations, not less, more long hair and thicker sideburns and less squares who want the country to continue on its present merry way to a living death in garbage, pollution and famine.

YEAR 1970

THE INFINITE UNIVERSE MAKES US ONE   *January 8*

Suddenly we saw the earth in 1969, and that vision may be the most important event of this century. Not the fact that we walked on the moon, mind you, but the fact that we saw the blue planet spinning like a top in an infinite and limitless universe. There it was, just one world, one little world hanging in space, surrounded by a million planets. We saw the earth as it was televised from the Apollo space ship and it was beautiful. The earth, bathed in a shield of oxygen that comes from the greenery and wetness on this earth. But once the source of the oxygen is stifled and cut off by pollution, the earth will be just like the moon. The earth is little more than that; it is still just a rock 6,000 miles thick covered with a comparatively thin layer of soil which we scratch to make a living, which gives us our oxygen to sustain life.

So we saw the lonely earth hanging there in space, but we could not see what was happening on the planet in the TV picture, but we know what is happening. Still that vision changes our lives. We will not realize it for decades maybe, but it is beginning to show up in little intimations. The smart people of this world are no longer worried about nuclear threats or ideologies, but about how we can control the birth rate to avoid famine. These will be the big issues of the latter part of this century.

John Kennedy was not able to do much while President, but look what he started. It was JFK who said we would walk on the moon before 1970, and he started NASA. We can thank JFK finally for our vision of the earth. In that Apollo picture you can't see the horrors in Vietnam, in Russia, in Africa, all over the world, yes, even in the United States, but that vision makes us here on earth, one people, all human beings who must love all life and this earth to survive.

"ARCHIBUS" COURTS A SWEETHEART   *January 22*

The other day Wiley and I got into a long conversation in the snack room at the hospital here and it turns out that Wiley is a native of Cottle County where I grew up. He's absolutely the first person I ever saw who came from Cottle County, of which Paducah is the county seat. We did not know each other in Paducah but we knew the same people.

But this is not a lesson in geography. The only reason I'm writing it is because of one remark Wiley Ellis said to me in the snack bar. He said, "My mother's best friend was your old girl friend, Oma." I haven't blushed in 40 years but I know that I must have turned a little pink when he said that. For if Oma will now say that she was my old girl friend, I could kick myself. I had no idea that Oma Irons had any feeling but scorn and dislike for me when I was worshipping the ground she walked on at the age of 16. Oma was blonde and she was both popular and smart. In high school she did not go with anybody, but she would go down to the Zana Theater stage and dance with her group, and I would stand at the back in the darkness and look on. This dancing was frowned on by everybody and the fact that some of the students did it was considered daring. All that year when I had this feeling toward Oma, I never said one word to her face. I kept thinking how could anyone so beautiful and smart even look at me. When she looked at me I would turn my head and blush and she would laugh and she would tell her best friend, Pearl Campbell, and they would see my red ears and both would giggle and point and everybody else would laugh. They and others in the class would make me miserable by calling me "Archibus"; we studied Latin and "ibus" is a plural suffix of the Latin verb.

This attitude I had toward Oma was disturbing, but I had other worries. For about a year I was convinced that I had tuberculosis; not that I coughed or had fever; I could run a mile and never get out of breath, but I was thin. I was 6 feet, 3 inches tall and weighed about 130 pounds. I was all legs. I read an ad in some magazine, probably the Comfort, that the way to cure tuberculosis was to drink the strippings when you milked the cows. The strippings were the last milk the cow gave, what she was holding up for her calf. It was supposed to be the richest. I drank

331

these strippings out at the barn every morning when I milked, but none of my family ever caught me doing it. I just did not want to die of tuberculosis. I don't remember if I gained weight but I'm sure that I did. Another worry that plagued me was that I had pimples on my face, and I imagined that they were as repulsive to people, especially to Oma, as they were to me. I had these pimples for six years or more and they always made me feel as if people got one look at me and would think, "What a repulsive sight." I could do nothing about the pimples, except be seen as often as possible with my best friend, Houston Barrett, who had no pimples and who went with girls and was popular with them. Houston and his brother Bill drove a Model T to school from their farm on Buck Creek. I rode a horse to school; the round trip was 14 miles, but I would ride down to the post office at noon with Houston in the Model T. One time he made me drive it and when I got to the post office I said, "Whoa," as I would have to a team of horses, and Houston laughed his head off as the T stopped by the sidewalk. I didn't put on the brake, just hollered "Whoa" like an idiot.

There was another thing that worried me. I wasn't certain that I was not "afflicted." There was a man in our community about 35 years old who was sort of mentally retarded, but I never heard that phrase then. Everbody said he was weak minded. One time my father told me that the man was clabber-headed because he abused himself. He called it "self-abuse." What he meant was masturbation, but he would never use that word. That scared me so that I virtually tied my hands behind me when I went to bed. At times I was sure that I had already become like the man. It didn't impress me at all that I was making straight A's in school and could speak Latin better than Vera McGown who had what they called a "pony," which was a translation of the book, which she kept hid from the teacher. It was several years before I would admit that I hadn't suffered mental damage before I was 16. Then I was sensitive about riding the horse to school. I would ride the back streets. I had one pair of pants, one pair of shoes and a couple of shirts, a cap, and a coat, but I probably looked as well as other boys but I just knew that I was the gawkiest, ugliest, worst dressed boy in school.

On top of all this there was Oma. Then Houston Barrett (who

332

later became a bookkeeper) discovered my secret. He guessed I was stuck on Oma and he highly approved. He nagged me to ask her for a date, but I could not face Oma and ask her for a date. There was another thing about me that was repellent. I stuttered. I am sure that if I ever had to say one simple sentence to Oma Irons I never would have got the words out. I could barely recite in class. I would choke up and my mouth would make speaking movements but no words would come. Then everybody would laugh and I would turn red from head to toe and my body would burn up and I would get physically weak. Houston Barrett couldn't make me face Oma Irons and talk to her, but he talked me into calling her on the phone, and I had talked on phones.

One day I called Oma with Houston standing by telling me what to say. Finally I got out what I had rehearsed for two days. What I said was, "Can I take you to the picture show?" Oma laughed, silvery and gaily, and I started blushing. Then she said "Go with you, Archibus, you've got a nerve even asking me. Nothin' doin'," and she hung up and I slunk away and told Houston Barrett to go get to hell away from me and he laughed, too. It took me at least three days to get over Oma and I never thought of her again as a girl friend. So if she remembers me as a girl friend of mine, that is news to me. After about 10 years, though, I began to remember Oma Irons as the girl I liked best, as the most beautiful, even after I found out she married.

It could mean something though, that the next girl I had a crush on was also named Oma. That romance lasted a whole summer, until I went away to the university. Then she married a bootlegger.

WHAT IS THE DEFINITION OF FRIENDSHIP?   *February 5*

The great minds of this lonely planet have always been concerned with friendship. Aristotle, Plato and Homer wrote about friendship. Then came Shakespeare and he had more to say about it than anyone. In our own civilization, Ralph Waldo Emerson had his say. Friendship has meant different things to different minds, and to great minds, too. So I will not go into any set definition of friendship. I will not even say whether I agree with Emerson or Aristotle, but I will always say that I agree with Shakespeare and cannot be wrong because the whole world agrees with Shakespeare. In our day, each man has his own idea of what friendship is, and what is required to be friends. There is a saying that the only way to have a friend is to be one, but how do you know how to be a friend? What does it require? I only know what my idea of friendship is, and I am not even clear on that point.

I got to thinking about friendship Monday after Gene and Ann Worley left. Gene has been a friend for 35 years. I first knew him in the Panhandle when he was 24 and a state legislator; he campaigned in a Model T when he was elected to Congress and I was for him; and we went through quite a lot. He was a favorite of FDR and Harry Truman, who in 1949 appointed Gene to the U.S. Court of Customs and Patent Appeals of which he is chief justice. Gene is now in bad health, and he is taking medication under Dr. De Bakey at Methodist Hospital in Houston, but he came over here for a day.

So when Gene left I got to thinking about friends. Have I made any friends in Kountze the 20 years I have been here, I asked myself, and I got to thinking of different people. There is nobody in Kountze I now dislike, nobody I would not treat friendly, but have I any friends? In those 20 years have I made any friends? I am not sure, but I know one for certain, Rocky Richardson. I think if I went to Rocky and said, "Rocky, I've burned down the church and they are going to run me out of town," he would say, "Oh, no they're not. If you burned down the church, you had a good reason."

I had another friend in Pampa by the name of Morris Pollard; he was a welder and his wife is named Ickie; he is dead now, but he was a friend, and his wife still is. I have another friend in Clovis, New Mexico, by the name of Dee Blythe. He is now a district judge, but I am sure he is my friend, even after knowing him 40 years. I have another friend I met in the Navy, Scott Miller, who lives in Youngstown, Ohio. I think if I were to get on the phone and say, "Scott, are you my friend? he would say, "Yes of course, what the hell do you want now?" I have another at Bushland, Texas, in the Panhandle, name of Odis Henry who I am sure is the kind of person I define as a friend.

So what do you expect of a friend? Favors? Money? What? Really none of those. Friendship to me is the exhilaration of realizing that a person shines and glows when you think of him. All these people I have named are not young and I will avoid no friendship with the young. I have known and helped the young and they have called me friend, but I have let it go at that. Still I see a young person now and then who shines and silently I think of them as golden and inspiring.

What do I require of friends? I don't know. What do they require of me? I don't know. But I do know that if I am a friend I must be ready to give up everything I have for a friend, but all the time confident that I won't be required to do it. Of course I am thinking that I am sure that it will never be necessary for Rocky to value my friendship more than he values being police chief and fire chief. I would like to say I have many friends, but I know I have not. What I have named is just about the crop with the exception of one golden friend whose name I shall not call.

One thing I told Ann Worley while they were here. I said, "Ann when you go back to the Panhandle (they live in Wheeler County at Shamrock) go down to Sweetwater Creek in Wheeler County in the Panhandle of Texas, and say, 'I bring you greetings from Archer Fullingim who now lives in the Big Thicket country and has a love affair going with a creek that is called Village Creek which he says is the most beautiful creek on earth, but Sweetwater Creek, he still loves you; he still remembers your hackberry trees, your sands, your grapevines, your water holes, your birds, and he told me to say hello to you, Sweetwater Creek in Wheeler County. Archer has not forgotten you and he still loves you.' " Ann promised me she would say those very words to Sweetwater Creek in the Panhandle.

As for Gene, I am grateful that he came and caused me to think about friendship, and my last word is that I am sure now what friendship is. It's just the feeling you have when you think of your friends. The glow that you get. It's certainly not what you can do for them, or they can do for you, though I am sure you must be prepared to give up even life itself for a real friend, and the Bible as expected is the final authority on friendship. It talks about the greater love that no man has than he lay down his life for a friend.

I have said that Shakespeare said it best in comedies and tragedies, "Much Ado About Nothing" and "Julius Caesar," and in the sonnets, so let us quote a sonnet from Shakespeare that my friend Billy Mounts gave me 30 years ago.

> *When in disgrace with fortune and men's eyes,*
> *I all alone beweep my outcast state,*
> *And trouble deaf heaven with my bootless cries,*
> *And look upon myself and curse my fate,*
> *Wishing me like to one more rich in hope,*
> *Featured like him, like him with friends possessed,*
> *Desiring this man's art and that man's scope,*
> *With what I most enjoy contented least;*
> *Yet in these thoughts myself almost despising,*
> *Happily I think on thee, and then my state,*
> *Like to the lark at break of day arising,*
> *From sullen earth, sings hymns at heaven's gate;*
> *For thy sweet love remembered such wealth brings,*
> *That then I scorn to change my state with King's.*

INTEGRATION & FRIENDSHIP   *February 19*

We can be proud of Kountze when we read what is going on at Center, Burkeville and, judging by a letter in the Beaumont Enterprise, Vidor. A Vidor woman wrote: "My children will never go to a school in the Negro section of town under any circumstances, U.S. Supreme Court or no U.S. Supreme Court." The same thing has blasted Center and Burkeville to pieces. I wish those people of those communities would come to Kountze and see how sensibly and peacefully we did it. We didn't have the money, just like they don't have it, to build another school, so we used Carver. No sweat. No trouble. We don't even call it the Quarters any more, but North Kountze. We can pat ourselves on the head. That was one time we lived up to our slogan, "The Town With A Sense of Humor." Humor is a good thing to have when you face the inevitable. This is the second year that the junior high has been in its present location. It has worked out fine; far better than going into debt with higher taxes for a new school. Kountze has had lulus in school fights in the past, but we can be proud of our record in solving this problem. We can be proud of our administrators, our school board, our teachers and our citizenry. Some noted Southern politicians wouldn't like it, but I think that the Man who said, "Come unto me all ye that labor and are heavy laden and I will give you rest" would approve.

This column has received more comment on the friendship article than any I ever wrote. That was the column in which I listed making only one friend in Kountze in 20 years, Rocky Richardson, and now I find out that Rocky didn't even read it. He's too busy with that truck line and he sleeps half the time down at Richardson Supply. After analyzing myself for a week, I have decided that maybe I have made more than one friend in Kountze in 20 years but hesitated to advertise it, for fear of denial.

I had a letter from an old time friend of World War II days, Little Tex Warner who now lives at Iraan. One time Warner and I bought a bottle of scotch, paid $40 for it from a flier who flew it back from Australia. Warner and I started drinking it and wound up so sick we just lay down in an abandoned tent and puked and puked and let the mosquitoes eat us and we didn't even feel them. I suspect that was about the last drink Warner ever had. But what I started to quote was a part of Warner's letter. He wrote: "I was about half teed off when you listed your friends. Ford (my brother who also lives at Iraan and is an acquaintance of the Warners) said he had read that with interest too. We both agreed that was a smart listing of that secret friend. Then I got to thinking later on and I don't think your paper's large enough to list all your friends."

I had a letter from the person Warner described as the "secret friend." I described this friend in the column as the "golden friend." Here is an excerpt from the letter: "Your feelings about friends are similar to mine . . . if I like a person I am friendly . . . It's funny I can think of a dozen things I want to tell you, but when I sit down to write it, I can never think of it . . . the best movie I've seen in a long time is "The Lion in Winter."

Thanks, golden friend, for the letter.

⤳

THE SILENT MAJORITY
& THE LONG-HAIRED YOUTH   *March 26*

It probably won't do any good but I'm going to suggest that the so-called Great Silent Majority, if there is any such thing, the squares, and generally speaking those over 29 years of age, get off the backs of the young people and take a good look at themselves. Most men who are no longer young and take pride in their crew cuts have fallen into the habit of ignoring their shortcomings by railing and ranting against long hair, demonstrators, rioters, pot smokers, lumping them all into a mass of undesirables. They seem to think if they keep up the barrage against long hair they can draw attention away from their miserable failures.

And what are those failures that are now afflicting not only the United States but every country in the world? Let's look at a few of them. For years, we have strewn the highway with beer cans and all kinds of litter, we have polluted our streams, endangered wildlife species, and every six months we cut down forests that approximate the size of the state of Rhode Island. In Hardin County, we have supinely and gutlessly stood by and watched the destruction of the Big Thicket which is our greatest natural resource.

Nationally, we have suddenly discovered that the trains are gone, the plumbing doesn't work, there are no repair men, the electricity goes off in blackouts, repairs for our electric gadgets and appliances are harder and harder to get, our planes are bigger than our airports and our whole prosperity is based on war and killing people. We have discovered that if you own a home and draw social security, you will have to sell the house to pay city, school and county taxes.

And what is our reaction to all this? We cuss long hair, strikers and demonstrators. Anybody who has long hair is immoral, illegal and a Red. It gives us a big kick to cuss long hair; it has become the national pastime, and the silliest we ever had. I have heard so much railing against long hair by some of our self-acclaimed patriots, that long hair has become a symbol of better days for me. If those long-haired kids are in revolt against the inefficiency of America, the war complex, the destruction of natural resources, then I'm for them. You didn't see any squares down there on the beaches of the Gulf of Mexico below Louisiana wiping oil off ducks and birds, did you? You saw the longhairs. Those flowing oil slicks, destroying oyster beds, shrimp, waterfowl, birds and beaches, worse than Santa Barbara, are the heritage the squares of this world are giving the younger generation. Five oil gushers covering the Gulf and they can't shut them off!

The governor of Georgia, that Maddox fellow who flourished axe handles to keep blacks out of his cafe before he was elected governor, wept openly and copiously the other day when he told about his son being charged with burglary in Atlanta, and it showed a picture of his son who had a crew cut. Maddox wailed, "Oh, I don't know what I did wrong. I did everything to raise him right." Yes, he set a good example of lawbreaking for the boy. He openly and joyfully violated the Constitution of the United States because the Constitution is exactly what the Supreme Court says it is. He urged his people to defy the Supreme Court and the laws of the United States. He upheld brutality and inferior treatment of a minority race. Now he wonders how his boy went wrong.

When you consider that the cost of one airplane the defense department is trying to build, about $75,000,000, would build three medical schools, or wipe out the ghettos and slums of every city in Texas, or build a new high school in every district in Texas, it may be that our greatest failure since World War II has been to base our entire economy on war and defense. Also what good is it to go to the moon, if we destroy our earth? The scientists of doom say that over population and pollution will destroy this earth by the beginning of the 21st century, if we don't do something.

The way I see it, the youth of this country are in rebellion against the mess we have created; they want to change it; they want to end pollution and control the birth rate. I thank God that they are not as benign as we are, that they are not as tolerant of the dangers to our existence as we are, that they are in revolt against the failures of their parents. So it's time for us to quit railing against long hair as symptomatic of drug addition, demonstrations, and it's time for us to really find out why youth demonstrate, and if we actually want to continue what they are demonstrating against: foul-ups in everything from Internal Revenue on down, a government that owes its prosperity to killing people thousands of miles from home. It's time we decide if we are really against the ideals of the demonstrators.

AMERICA IS THE GOOD AND THE BAD — *April 23*

The other day I was part of a captive audience before a speaker who for 10 minutes made statements, every one of which began, "I'm fed up with," and he was fed up with a lot. He was fed up with the Supreme Court, long hair, pot, rioters, welfare, even Martin Luther King. Well, it took him about 10 minutes to recite the list. I am sure that there are many, many things he likes about this country, but he didn't name one. When he got through, I felt like asking him if he was fed up with miniskirts, too. Several weeks previous I was reading in Life about people who in disgust have left the USA for Australia. They were also fed up. I don't know why, but coming back to the shop after that speech I thought of a song that was sung in World War I in 1918 and I burst into the shop singing it at the top of my voice:

> *If you don't like your Uncle Sammy*
> *If you don't like the red white and blue*
> *Then go back to the land from where you came*
> *Whatever be its name*
> *But don't be ungrateful to me*
> *If you don't like the stars in Old Glory*
> *Then don't be like the cur in the story*
> *Don't bite the hand that's feeding you.*

Now having said all that, it follows that I must tell you what I like about this country, what I am not fed up with, what I'm proud of, what I like in the present American scene. America is still the land of the free and the home of the brave, the Four Freedoms, and the Bill of Rights which our Supreme Court protects. We can demonstrate and we can strike. I am proud of our labor unions and our chambers of commerce, because they balance each other nicely. There is nothing in Kountze itself that I'm fed up with. I enjoy our schools. I am proud that we integrated without trouble. The whole community benefitted by it. I don't like to think of myself as an East Texan, or a Texan or a Southerner, but as an American. When I learn about other countries I know that America is the greatest on earth, and that what has made it great are the people, and we have been and still are a violent people, and I am proud of that, for I know that only through violence can justice be achieved. That's our history. We had to destroy the Indians and their cultures to create this nation; we had to kill a million Americans to preserve it. I am proud of our government, our congress. I am proud of our youth, whether long-haired or short-haired, and I sympathize with them when they demand a more meaningful education. Their demonstrations and sit-ins may seem criminal to older heads, but what they are achieving is what America has needed a long time. Justice has never been attained in America without violence so civil disobedience does not worry me, because our history is a long story of civil disobedience.

We are now in the throes of a war, pollution, inflation, overpopulation and worst of all we are in bondage to the perpetuation of war to maintain our economy, but I am optimistic that we shall finally shed the war and solve our problems.

We are becoming more humane year by year. Nobody has died in the electric chair, gas chamber or on the gallows in the U.S. in eight years. I am proud that we are spending money on education, on surplus commodities, on dependent children. I am proud that we have Medicare and Social Security. It would seem that the income tax is an unbearable burden; but when it really becomes unbearable, Americans will refuse to pay until everybody is taxed some and alike. The taxpayers will strike if they have to. The crime wave does not worry me too much because I know that what's causing it is economic injustice, the war, and that when social and economic injustices are corrected, crime will lessen. I think that America is moving along the same line that started in 1776 when the great majority of people were fed up with the revolutionaries. Don't be discouraged, the American scene is more normal than some think.

You see, America is Martin Luther King, it is the Negro, it is minority races, it is long hair as well as miniskirts, it is welfare and the Supreme Court, and a whole lot of things people are fed up with, like Indians, lynchings and crime. You have to take the good with the bad and there's one way you can change what you don't like, and that is vote. Personally, I'm fed up with people who are fed up.

TIMES & MINDS CHANGE   *July 2*

Twenty years ago I was a rank segregationist; I really thought the Negro race was inferior. Now I know that it isn't. I know that Negroes are Americans in every way, and I know they have just as much intelligence as the white man and are not half afraid of hard work. In 1950, I believed that integration would never work; now I know that it will. I get down on my knees every day and thank the good Lord for John Fitzgerald Kennedy, who changed my whole life.

Five years ago, I was for the war in Vietnam. Now I know that it is tearing this nation apart, it is the cause of inflation, riots, crime, you name it. It is a war. We have 400,000 troops (still!) in Vietnam and Cambodia who are hated and despised by the natives, and who are killing, burning, frying, bombing and destroying in a country that means nothing to us. We all know that the minute we leave the North Vietnamese will take over, so why not leave now? Russia is glad we are there because we are spending ourselves to death and dividing our country. Russia has wanted us in Vietnam all the time. Nixon says, "Now let me make this perfectly clear," and he makes nothing clear. They brag about going into Cambodia to save lives, but our death rate increases, the Cambodians are killed like flies, the country destroyed, and the enemy has now spread all over Cambodia and we are following in planes to bomb him.

A lot of change has been forced on us, so I can't take credit for changing my views. A man can't boast that he has changed his mind on education, the moon, segregation. Events change our minds for us. Of course there are still some miserable, frustrated souls in the world who will not accept change no matter what, even if they choke to death. They are our pollutionists, our Big Thicket destroyers.

❧

POLITICAL FEUDS & THE YARBOROUGH DEFEAT   *July 23*

It always worries me when somebody hands me a compliment. I'd much rather be cussed than praised. Any editor who likes to be praised all the time needs to be took down a notch or two, and any editor who just loves to print letters which agree with him is a conceited ass. As for me, I love to get letters that cuss me black and blue, but I don't like to get critical letters from Baxter. They do something to me. Here a while back I got a letter I wouldn't print. The reason was the letter said, "A copy of this letter goes to _____" and another paper was named. If somebody wants to write a letter to this paper, well and good, but don't send the same letter at the same time to another paper. That burns me up. Another reason why I didn't print the letter was because about two weeks before I got it the person who wrote it came in this print shop and ordered, "Don't ever put my name in your paper again." Mad over politics. I promised I wouldn't, so even if the letter hadn't been addressed to two papers, what was I supposed to do?

What brought all this on, was that I received through the mail a framed plaque that says, "The credit belongs to the man who is actually in the arena, whose face is marred by dust and sweat and blood . . . who knows the great enthusiasms, the great devotion; who spends himself in a worthy cause; who at the best knows in the end the triumph of high achievement . . . and . . . if he fails, at least fails while daring greatly, so that his place shall never be with those cold and timid souls who know neither victory nor defeat—John Fitzgerald Kennedy." The plaque was sent from Austin by a friend who is in politics.

I probably deserve every word on the plaque, and JFK's words are not necessarily complimentary. It's always a painful thing to get bloodied in politics, whether you win or lose, especially if you operate a small-town newspaper where you lose ads if some of your local advertisers are not on your side, like it was in the recent primaries. But the paper lived over it and the advertisers who get mad at you are also losers.

The day after Senator Yarborough got beat, I got a letter from a woman in Silsbee who said she knew how awful I must feel, and she was the only member of her family to vote for Yarborough. When I read that I got so mad at her that I felt better. Imagine living with a family who voted against Yarborough! I'd have poisoned them long before the primary! But seriously the day is going to come soon when the people who Yarborough helped the most, the poor, the black, the sick, the aged, who let him down in the election this year, are going to miss him, because every health bill, every education bill, every social security raise, every medicare bill, every GI bill, every civil rights bill passed in the Congress since Kennedy was murdered in Dallas, had Yarborough's name on it.

Bentsen was elected on the basis of three major lies: that Yarborough was a peace demonstrator and marched in a parade, a despicable lie; that Yarborough was against prayer, Yarborough a devoted Baptist, a Christian man if there ever was one and who relies on prayer; and the other lie, that he had no right to vote against the confirmation of Supreme Court nominee Carswell, who lied to the senate judiciary committee and admitted it.

Bentsen was doing exactly what his pals, LBJ, Connally and Shivers, sitting in the back room, told him to do. Bentsen is far to the right of Bush; so far in fact, that Bush seems like a Democrat compared with Bentsen.

MY HAIR REVERTS TO NATURAL COLOR   *October 1*

I'm having trouble with Doc Selman. He won't give me a chance to answer his questions. He just keeps on talking. The other morning in the cafe, he asked me if I was wearing a wig or something. He said my hair didn't look right. He's not the only man that's asked if I am wearing a wig. Nope. My hair has reverted back to its natural color, with the aid of a bottle that barber Don Smith sells me for $2. I've used four bottles to date. All you have to do is rub a little in the hair every day, and it gradually takes out all the gray, and I had plenty before Don told me about this bottle. Then I started to grow sideburns, but I may have to cut them off if they turn out gray.

AT THE KENNEDY MEMORIAL   *October 15*

I had this expense-paid trip to Dallas proposition and I took it, but don't think I would have taken it if I hadn't got a chance to see something that I've been waiting to see since it was completed. The memorial to John Kennedy built over a parking lot about 200 yards east of where he was assassinated. When I saw it a hard cold wind was blowing and I had no coat, but I went inside it and got the feeling of it, the whole mad city of Dallas shut out of it, a loneliness, and yet a communion. This memorial consists of two doors at the ends of a square created by four concrete walls rising about 20 feet, with no roof and open at the bottom. In the center of the space is a black marble square with JFK's name on it. A New York engineer designed it. It's set in the center of a whole block and surrounded by the thickest and greenest grass I ever saw. Small oak trees line the sidewalks. The monument was paid for by public subscription. As time goes on it will become precious.

I got into only one argument while I was in Dallas and going up there. I didn't even fuss with Ollie Crawford when I saw him. I suggested that we have our pictures taken shaking hands. Ollie has two kids at SMU, and one is studying journalism. The only argument I had was with a fellow who said, "Here is the way I am about niggers. They have to prove themselves to me." "Prove themselves?" I said. "Every person has to prove himself, regardless of color, but no black, brown, red or yellow man on this little earth has to prove himself in order to qualify as a human being. A white man who believes a Negro has to prove himself in order to merit his love is a freak."

AN HONORABLE MAN   *December 3*

I saw Minyard Riley who is a custodian at the courthouse and he passed his 62nd birthday the middle of November. The thing about Minyard that arouses one's admiration is that he is an honorable man, in a day when the word does not have the meaning it used to have when people said he's an honorable man when they wanted to pay a man the highest compliment.

THE DEAD ARE WITH US ALWAYS

It doesn't take Thanksgiving for a person to be thankful. Thankfulness can come every day. It's only on Thanksgiving that we are reminded. A friend of mine called up Thanksgiving morning and asked, "Who was it that wrote that most men live lives of quiet desperation." I thought it was Emerson, but I'm not certain, but I used to know exactly who wrote it and where. It was a thing I read in my youth, and it didn't mean much because although I was always desperate in my youth, it was not a thing that curbed my enthusiasm. So if we are desperate most of the time, what have we got to be thankful for? And who to thank? We can be thankful, not that we have food to eat, and material necessities, but that we have sympathy, compassion, a love for our fellow man, for I have learned that the most important thing on earth is not the appearance of goodness but actually being good, and that our only hope in this world is to love one another, regardless of race, creed, color, or long hair, with tolerance, sympathy and compassion. I have the feeling that the Lord God does not care one whit about our long-winded prayers, for he is watching what we do, say and think.

I am thankful mostly for the things that are free, the trees, the creeks and the breeze. Did you read that letter that Frank Boston wrote to The News recently? He said I have found the word that the wind whispers, I have found what's on the wind. It was probably the most important letter ever written this newspaper. I read it over and over, and apparently others did, too, because people have written about it and have come in and talked about it. Frank is a young man of 20 and he has the Holy Ghost and talks in tongues.

The way we act and carry on in this life is the open page that pictures whether we have true gratitude. As Shakespeare wrote:

"To be or not to be: That is the question. Whether it is nobler in the mind to suffer the slings and arrows of outrageous fortune or to take arms against a sea of troubles, and by opposing them to die, to sleep; to sleep, perchance to dream: ay, there's the rub; for in that sleep of death what dreams may come, when we have shuffled off this mortal coil, must give pause; there's the respect that makes calamity of so long life; for those who would bear the whip and scorns of time, the oppressor's wrong, the proud man's contumely, the pangs of despised love, the law's delay, the insolence of office, and the spurns that patient merit of the unworthy takes, when he himself might his quietus make with a bare bodkin? Who would fardels bear, to grunt and sweat under a weary life, but that the dread of something after death, the undiscover'd country from whose bourne no traveller returns, puzzles the will, and makes us rather bear those ills we have than fly to others that we know not of?"

The trouble with Hamlet was that he was thinking solely of himself, bent on avenging his father's death, which is not un-natural, but he had not learned that the dead are with us always, as well as the living. "Pink" Wiggins, "Speck" Crosby, J. P. Blessing, Kermit Carrier, all on my street. They are still with us. They are everywhere. At football games, basketball games, at church. The dead are with us always, and that is why we learn not to grieve.

FROM KENNEDY TO NIXON   *December 17*

It came to me the other day that everything in this country started going sour the day President John Kennedy was killed seven years ago. Up to that time, if you remember, everybody was rejoicing in the way the country was going, all except a few John Birchers, The Dallas Morning News and other right wing papers, and a good portion of the population of Dallas. The college kids were innocent. There was no marijuana problem, no riots; we had not discovered pollution. Shoulder length hair had not appeared on the scene. Remember how it was in Kountze. Everybody was optimistic. We had a Santa Claus that year, and everybody is so mad this year that they are not even going to have a Santa Claus, or that was what Dudley Keith said at the Lions Club. Makes me want to dress up as Santa myself.

As soon as Kennedy was murdered by a madman a wave of hate swept the world. People still call Dallas the hate capital of the world after reading a typical editorial page in the Dallas News. The assassination brought out the worst in us. The Negroes began rioting and burning, youth began cussing the establishment and when they found out that long hair infuriated their elders they didn't cut it until they could sit on it, so to speak. It was as if the murder triggered rebellion, hate and revolution. Then the people learned that Lyndon Johnson had accumulated $17 million while he was in the House, Senate and White House, and they had only scorn for him, even though he had passed Kennedy's civil rights program. Youth hated him and most of the population despised him.

In King Arthur's day, Camelot was the seat of the palace and knighthood. The knights fought only for ideals. Camelot was a place of romance, fascination and beauty. They had begun to call Washington Camelot while JFK yet lived. But after he lay under the eternal flame, and Lyndon's pet war in Vietnam began killing off 40,000 boys and wounding seven times that many, youth began to hate LBJ with such intensity that he could move outside the White House only to West Point, army and navy bases and Texas.

A dream ended with the JFK murder. The world sank deeper into depression and hate with the murder of Martin Luther King and Robert Kennedy. The world, particularly the U.S., yearns for a return of the Kennedy days and would even gladly elect Ted Kennedy president, but he wants no part of it; he wants to live. No matter where you go now, you only hear expressions of hate.

Nixon has not brought us together. He has just made it worse. Agnew is the hero of a lot of haters, and George Wallace is still the hero of many, but they are admired because they attack, because they too, hate.

YEAR 1971

What's ahead for Kountze, Texas, the nation and the world for 1971? To know the answer you'll have to tune in Garner Ted Armstrong on the radio. He will start out by telling you he can predict exactly what is going to take place, but when he finishes he will have told you nothing. He's made more suckers out of the American people than anybody in my memory except "Goat Gland" Brinkley of the 1930s. Personally, I believe things are going to get worse before they get better.

We are going to have to pay more car insurance, and Texans deserve to pay it. They voted in vast numbers for Preston Smith and Ben Barnes, and Lloyd Bentsen, so let's hear no painful yelps from them. Unemployment is going to increase and the only way prices are going to go down is that there will be no money to buy the goods. Pollution will not lessen one bit and we will continue to destroy the environment. Everybody will say quit using DDT, but their answer will be the same as those who object to saving the Thicket: we've got to make a living.

I predict some good things will happen in 1971. People are going to start listening to youth and college professors who started all the talk to end pollution and improve the environment. Spiro Agnew's star will go down. He can't get by with bad-mouthing the media, the press, youth, colleges, Democrats and everybody except racists and law 'n order fanatics who are usually in the lead of those breaking the law. We will know by the middle of the year if Nixon's popularity will be so low that like LBJ he can't run for president again. The Texas legislature will do its best to slap a sales tax on groceries and if you are not on your toes that's what will happen. The aged and the poor are going to get the dirty end of the stick at Austin. They deserve it. Instead of voting their pocketbook and kicking out Smith and Barnes, they voted against colleges, long hair, marijuana, and they voted for J. Edgar Hoover, Spiro Agnew and Lloyd Bentsen. Now they can take their medicine.

The Vietnam War will continue, and Melvin Laird, defense secretary, and Nixon will keep on telling lies about how we are winning. Six months ago Nixon invaded Cambodia to save it, but Reds now control three-fourths of Cambodia. The minute we start pulling out of Southeast Asia in force, the Reds will take over. Every time Nixon pulls out troops he sends more back to take their place.

Here's the score card on our record in Vietnam: we have destroyed a big part of the vegetation in the country, killed, maimed and poisoned thousands of civilians, dropped more bombs than we did in World War II, and kept the big rich in office who will never give land to the peasants as promised. We have lost nearly 50,000 men and have veterans hospitals full of 300,000 wounded, many of them basket cases. We are now in the ridiculous position of trying soldiers for the crime of killing the enemy, for the enemy in Vietnam can be and often is women and children. Half of our youth are draft dodgers and the rest are in Vietnam either because they are not white or because they are not in college. Mexicans, Blacks, Puerto Ricans are in the majority in Vietnam, but not in the United States. The war is going to drag on through 1971 about like it is now. Nixon will want to bring all the boys home, but the Pentagon and the munitions makers are in control in Washington. Even Congress is afraid to disobey the Pentagon.

It is no secret that most of the residents of west Hardin County think little or nothing of saving the Big Thicket. They'd just as soon it be leveled. You can talk and preach all day and they'll tell you the woods are for sawmills and hunting and nothing else. It's useless to tell them if we saved the Thicket, minus roads, development, concessions, just an untouched forest, left alone, that our economy would increase five times what it is now, that thousands upon thousands would seek the cool recesses of the Thicket, just to tramp it, just to sleep in it, just to walk in it. When you tell them that you are just wasting your time and breath.

If we don't save it, 50 years from now their present children will be saying to their grandchildren, well, there's a tree up around Segno, I'm going to take you to see it.

PUT MAMA'S TOMBSTONE AT HER GRAVE   *February 18*

The Eason name is one of the most honorable in Southeast Texas and has been since the first white people came. The Easons were and still are individualistic. Mostly they do what they feel like doing, like "Barefoot" Eason, as he is called, and his wife Lizzie, who has been dead these past ten years.

The News wants to set the record straight about a lot of talk that has been going on about a tombstone. Two of the Eason boys had to go to jail in Kountze after they did what they felt they had to do.

After Mrs. Eason died, the Eason children ordered a monument for their mother's grave near the Caney Head community where the Easons live. The monument cost a whole lot more than they thought it ought to cost and for that reason and others they did not pay out the monument. So it sat by the road facing the street over at Silsbee. Under her name was a phrase carved in stone, "Mother Of 13 Children." The Eason boys told the owner of the tombstone yard they thought it was disrespectful to their mother to see the stone by the street and they asked him to move it or turn it around. They said he wouldn't do it. So one night about two weeks ago, they loaded the tombstone in a pick-up truck and took it to Frank's Branch Cemetery and sat it at the head of their mother's grave.

The monument man called the Sheriff and deputies found the stone at the head of the grave. They moved the stone back to the monument yard in Silsbee. They also charged two of the Eason boys with theft and jailed them. One made bond but the other did not get out until last week.

It seems a rather tragic story, doesn't it? Some may say the News shouldn't have printed it, but the News believes that Mrs. Eason would have wanted it printed. She thought the world of all of her boys, and she would have understood putting the stone at her grave. She had a great sense of humor as well as a lot of intelligence. At any rate, she had enough sense not to wear shoes.

DREAMING OF THE IVORY-BILL WOODPECKER

For the last five years, I have had an ambition that I wanted to realize before too many more years go by. I never thought about death until this year, although there's nothing wrong with me and I work just as hard as ever, even at one year this side of 70. My greatest ambition is to see an ivory-bill woodpecker in the 70s and to hear its song. I have the recorded song of the ivory-bill on a record, and I want to hear that call. I know there are still ivory-bills in the Big Thicket. Neal Wright has seen them. Other people have said they saw them.

This passion to see an ivory-bill has become almost a mania with me. To me, it's like climbing Mt. Everest is to mountain climbers. I have been in the cypress swamps of the Thicket where the ivory-bills are supposed to be and that's why I have developed such a great love and admiration for cypress trees. I think that I would be content if I could see an ivory-bill, but I never will be until I do.

I had it all planned out last year how I would see the ivory-bill. First I would buy a camper from Alf, but of course I was not going to take the camper back into the Thicket. I was going to park it on a passable road and go from there in a Jeep or boat to a spot where the ivory-bill is supposed to be. I was going to retire from this newspaper, and look for the ivory-bill until I found it. I figured I'd have to stay weeks upon weeks in the Thicket but that in the end I would find it.

I have pictured it so much, nearly every day the scene comes to me. I am staying in a tent next to a cypress swamp in the depths of the Thicket. I'm watching and waiting. The only sounds I hear are those of birds and insects. When I hear the drum-drum-drum of a woodpecker on a nearby tree I move carefully and noiselessly. I wake up of a morning and hear the thrushes, the hundred kinds of cheep-cheeps. Do you know that some birds literally scream? I can listen to them all day, and that's what I do. During the day I walk endlessly and ceaselessly, looking, watching and waiting. For weeks. I move to another place. I have gone into the Thicket in April, the nesting period, knowing that the ivory-bill covers a wide area, ranging from place to place. Knowing that an ivory-bill may be here one week and the next week in Louisiana. By the end of June, I have pitched my tent in five different spots, but still no ivory-bill. Then one morning I hear that sound. Unlike any bird sound. It's plaintive, it's supernatural, it's the most beautiful sound on earth but I lay still. I am sleeping outside under the kind of mosquito netting I slept under on those coconut islands in the South Pacific. I put on my glasses. There are two ivory-bills building a nest in a big hole in the cypress tree. I lay there for hours, afraid to move and scare them away.

THE VIETNAM WAR IS AN ATROCITY   *April 15*

All this came to mind as I was drinking coffee and eating breakfast in Mary's Cafe. George Kirkpatrick, Sr. was sitting at the table eating breakfast when I came in. George brought up World War II and talked about it some minutes before he left. Of course, we have never fought a war like Vietnam, and it's impossible for World War II veterans to try to understand Vietnam. We had strong and certain discipline, no let-down. There was no such thing as atrocities committed by Americans, atrocities such as My Lai were committed only by the enemy.

It was not the atrocities that Americans have committed in this war. They were expected; it's the war itself that is an atrocity. We should never have got in it, and neither Republicans nor Democrats can blame the other. Ike sent in the first advisers and LBJ escalated it, and Nixon is too slow. We can see now that Senator Fulbright was right from the beginning. We all believe that the minute we leave the Reds will take over, so why delay in leaving? Why not now?

I never will forget the day I got back. I had flown from Pearl Harbor to San Francisco. I was wearing faded clothes. I had to write the Pampa bank for money to buy new clothes. I thought people would look at me and see that I had been gone two years but nobody did, and I was glad. I really didn't want to talk to anybody. I just kept thinking of that world I left behind on the islands and the new one was hard to get used to. All the women wore artificial flowers in their hair.

Everything was unreal, even when I got on a Santa Fe passenger train and rode it straight through to Pampa. I knew that the war had changed my life but I didn't know exactly how. The war was the biggest thing in my life. Everything else became smaller. So it must be tough on the men who come back from Vietnam; we don't treat 'em right; they are unwept, unhonored and unsung. That Vietnam War just shouldn't have happened. What we have done to our young people is an awful thing. Those who went and those who didn't. That war is an evil thing.

THE LIEUTENANT CALLEY VERDICT   *April 22*

Richard Nixon has made the whole Calley affair look rascally and contemptible, because Nixon has dealt with it politically, not militarily, not honestly, but as if it were a political problem. When Nixon decided that the American people were up in arms over the verdict which gave Calley prison, he misunderstood what the American people were thinking and made Calley a hero, which he is not. Nobody denies that Calley shot down the South Vietnamese, nobody denies that if he killed innocent civilians he murdered them. What the American people were up in arms about was not that Calley mowed down South Vietnamese, but that they tried the wrong man. After World War II we tried the Japanese and Nazi generals and executed them. We said that the men at the top were at fault. Now we are saying the opposite, that the generals are not at fault. That's what angered the American people. Three years ago when the My Lai massacre occurred, LBJ was commander in chief of the army.

What Nixon must have sensed but ignored was that the people are up in arms about this war, the way it is fought, the lying LBJ and Nixon have done about it. They are finally seeing that the war produced Calley. So when Nixon saw that the American people were in an angry flap over it, Nixon played politics, just like he has played politics with inflation, unemployment, ecology, education and all the other major issues that he has meddled in, all to our disadvantage.

The last thing on earth that Calley should be is a hero. The

American people should never make a man who shot down innocent civilians in an evil war, heroic. Calley did nothing heroic. He does not rate being a hero, even though George Wallace, governor of Alabama, and Lester Maddox, lieutenant governor of Georgia, would like to make him a hero.

The effect of the president's two actions, beating the army to the draw in taking Calley out of the stockade and then announcing that he will have the final say in deciding what will happen to Calley, was to make the long trial seem useless and to tell the army what it had done was useless, and that regardless of what the court decided he would free Calley in the end. Calley should be freed in the end, but not for the reason being put forth. Useless John Tower, Texas' right wing, radical conservative, no good senator, hit the nail on the head when he said there is a lot of political mileage to be made out of Nixon's Calley decisions.

WHO OWNS THE BIG THICKET? *August 5*

While interviewing Pete Gunter on TV on channel 6 the other day, a questioner asked why the Big Thicket Association would pick a man so far from the Big Thicket as the BTA president. He also asked Pete about bringing in "outsiders" to help stop the hardwood cutting. I'd like to answer those questions in my own way, although Pete did a good job, saying that saving the Thicket is a matter of state and national concern. Pete did not go into the outsider business.

First, let us be aware who the No. 1 outsiders are in the Big Thicket. They are not members of the Sierra clubs in Dallas, Houston or San Francisco; they are not the 500 members of the BTA who live outside Hardin County. They are the owners of the Thicket. And just who owns the Thicket? Nobody who lives in Hardin County, nobody that lives solely in Texas. If you want to buy into the Big Thicket you've got to buy it off the stock exchange in New York. For the corporations that decide the fate of the Thicket are based in New York and Chicago. We have had them here so long we do not realize that absentee landlords in the form of giant corporations own the Thicket. The decision to clearcut the Thicket was made in New York and passed on down the line. For years the five or six corporations that own the Thicket used selective cutting. They did not cut the brush, or destroy young hardwood. But the prime purpose of a corporation is to make profits, for a corporation has stockholders that demand a profit. Those stockholders live in every state in the union, though most of them never heard of the Big Thicket. Until World War II, none of the land companies, or oil companies for that matter, paid taxes to amount to anything in Hardin County. Taxes began to rise in the 1950s as people began to demand roads and all the services Hardin County has instituted in the last 23 years. When Fletcher Richardson became county judge in 1948, the valuation of Hardin County was less than $12 million. Five years later it was $50 million. Oil had gone scot free of taxation in the county for half a century. Now the land companies are taxed on the basis of from $18 to $25 per acre valuation, and they say that's too much. They say they can't keep on paying taxes. In fact, they don't want to pay any taxes at all on their land, only on their production.

You can take for granted though that the corporations that own the Thicket are making a profit, and that profit goes to the thousands of stockholders all over the nation, from New York to St Louis and Chicago. Still, if we permit these absentee landowners to destroy the Thicket, as they have set out to do, we will be destroying our heritage, the finest thing we have, our greatest resource. If we let these absentee landlords destroy the Thicket, then goodbye hunting. It will be worse than it was in the early '30s when there wasn't a deer between the Red River and the Gulf of Mexico. Worst of all, if the Thicket's unique ecological system is finally destroyed, gone will be what brings naturalists here from all over the nation.

The land companies know exactly where the Big Thicket is; it's what they are feverishly cutting every day. Not in 40 years has so much pine and hardwood been cut as today in the Thicket. Ten times as many heavily loaded log trucks are coming east on the Kountze and Saratoga road as in any summer in the last 30 years. The companies are feverishly cutting the logs, and you may ask the question why? The answer seems clear; if the companies clearcut the Thicket, that is, level it, bulldoze down the hardwood and brush and burn it, then when the national park bill gets in Congress the companies can say, what Thicket are you talking about? There is no Big Thicket. We have leveled it, chewed it up, spit it out and burned it. There is nothing left to save. That's the reason the highways are choked with heavily loaded log trucks.

REAL PROGRESS & THE WORST POLLUTER   *August 19*

Nobody really believes industry any more, especially after such an edition as the Beaumont Enterprise's progress edition. Humble gets on NBC TV at 5:30 and tells how it is not polluting, when all the time the viewers know that although Humble is not lying in what it says, it is not telling the whole truth and that in truth it is polluting. Humble has one series of ads telling how it is helping the Eskimos in Alaska by melting the ice and digging oil wells. Look at all we are doing for the Eskimos. Yeah, look. The truth is that the Eskimos and their reindeer have been getting along fine on the tundras for the Lord knows how many years. No Eskimos on relief. No sweat, no trouble at all in Lapland. Now the oil companies are destroying the tundra environment and bragging about it. That is reminiscent of how we Americans took care of our American Indians. Pushed them off into rainless reservations and barren lands, but when oil was discovered on these barren lands, the oil companies somehow got their hands on it. So believe nothing you see on TV about how Humble is fixing it up fine for the Eskimos in Alaska, or the Cajuns in Louisiana, for that matter.

Funny thing, but all these ads and this "progress edition" sounds just like Richard Nixon who invents something sensational to do every week in order to get our minds off Vietnam, off inflation, off employment. Nixon, just like Hoover, keeps saying prosperity is just around the corner. Nixon says we really do not have inflation or unemployment; we just think we do. He's got figures to show you that prices are coming down, that there are more jobs.

Why couldn't the Enterprise, if it was going to put out a "progress edition," have said yes, we have had progress in the last 50 years; we have got all these plants, all these high wages, all these jobs and we are proud of them, but that's old-time progress, what we need now is the new-time progress. We've got to have plants that the people can live with. It will be progress when plant fumes don't take the paint off the houses; it will be progress when plants quit fouling the rivers, the bays, the streams and the Gulf.

Progress in 1971 is not the same as it was in 1921. Fifty years ago, there was scarcely a paved road in Texas, much less a million trailer trucks with poison spewing behind them. There was no radio, no TV and the movies were new. The great majority of Texans lived on farms. Now we have become industrialized and our greatest concern is to keep from building death traps for our people and our society. Let us be wary of progress 1971 style. Let's give it a good look before we buy it. I think the American people are doing that.

But the question comes up fast: what is real progress in 1971? It's just a little of what it's going to be more and more of in 1980, 1990 and the 2000s. Progress is awakening the American conscience to quit polluting, to quit fouling our streams. Never forget one thing, the worst polluter, the worst vandal is Man in his greed and selfishness.

Real progress in 1971 is to quit polluting Village Creek, quit polluting the Neches River and the bays. It is saving the Big Thicket, and the only good word the Enterprise has said for saving the Thicket is that maybe it ought to be saved, but who in the hell is going to visit it? I saved that editorial and put it in my will to have my heirs send it to the Enterprise for publication in the year 2000 when Rayburn Lake and Dam B will be mud holes with eight feet of cans and bottles and old refrigerators and cars on the bottom, and when people will be elbow to elbow fighting for their place in line just to walk through the Thicket, if by then it is not a pulpwood desert of slash pines. The Enterprise could make real progress if it showed that 95 per cent of the money spent on welfare in America goes to the disabled sick and hopelessly unemployed, and that only a small per cent goes to mothers of illegitimate children. That's another streak of racism that the haters have seized upon. It just doesn't exist to the ex-

358

tent Governor Maddox, Senator Ellender, Senator Bentsen and
Senator Stennis would like for you to believe.

Real progress in 1971 also espouses honesty in public office
and we have yet to see one word of criticism in the Enterprise
against Preston Smith's pandering to the Big Rich for personal
profit, against Ben Barnes' disgraceful conduct, yet the Enterprise will write pious editorials against pornography. You never
hear the Enterprise condemn Bill Heatley, Dr. Rex Baum or
"Greedy Gus" Mutscher for their stock scandals and the Enterprise, the great exponent of free enterprise, was painfully silent
when Nixon was coercing the Republicans to give away $250 mil-
lion to Lockheed. If Joy Roberts went broke, do you think Nixon
would give him a big loan?

TREE FARMS AND CLEARCUTTING   *September 2*

Now comes one William Smith, described as a "forestry specialist with the Texas Agricultural Extension Service," dis-
seminating tricky language and confusing rhetoric about the Big
Thicket. How he got into the act is easy to guess since A&M's
"forestry specialists" have long aided and abetted destruction of
the Big Thicket. So it is time to expose Mr. Smith as a phoney
who talks with a forked tongue. What he says is far from the
truth, that "scientific forest surveys of the East Texas piney
woods" show it is virtually the same today as it was in 1935. Mr.
Smith wants you to believe that the Big Thicket is the same as it
was in 1935.

All this came out in a story dated College Station and published in a number of Texas newspapers, including the Beaumont Journal and Dallas Morning News, both of which put mis-
leading headlines on the story. The Journal's headline, "Big
Thicket Never Changes," was of course not only false, but it does
great damage to the credibility of the Big Thicket Association
which has photographs to prove how much of the Big Thicket
has been bulldozed and shredded, preparatory to planting pine
trees in rows.

If the reader does not think as he goes along, he's almost sure to get the impression that the acreage of the Big Thicket is the same as it was 35 years ago. What Smith actually is saying is that the forest acreage is about the same in the four counties of Polk, Tyler, Hardin and Liberty, but he indulges in the kind of deceptive semantics that is characteristic of E. R. Wagoner of the Texas Forestry Association at Lufkin.

Big Thicket conservationists do not claim that the pine acreage has changed radically, what they claim, backed by photographic proof, is that the owners are destroying the Thicket, and it could still be classified as forest acreage after the Thicket is destroyed. Smith, either in ignorance or with malice and forethought, says that the forest acreage and the Big Thicket are the same. Thousands of acres of the Big Thicket have been bulldozed in recent years, the ground cleared for planting quick-growing slash pines in rows. Technically it is still forest land since it will be planted into a pulpwood forest, but it is no longer the Big Thicket. Thus Smith seeks to perpetrate a hoax by confusing the Big Thicket with a pulpwood desert. Smith was quoted as saying that he finds it difficult to understand the claims of conservationists who say that the Big Thicket is being destroyed at the rate of 50 acres a day and that the area will be a biological desert in five years. The reason Mr. Smith does not understand is because he doesn't know the difference between the Big Thicket and a tree farm, or maybe he does but he brazenly makes such a statement as, "The Big Thicket exists today only because private landowners have done a good job of stewardship of the area for more than 100 years." That statement is based on either ignorance or malice. By the 1930s, the Piney Woods, and I refer to the 10 counties in Southeast Texas, were almost denuded of timber, except for the depths of the Big Thicket where the timber companies could not operate on account of moisture. The original virgin, long leaf pine forest has been cut down. By the time FDR had become president, land in the Piney Woods was not worth paying the taxes on and a lot of timber companies could not pay the taxes.

In the '30s, the federal government stepped in and bought thousands of denuded, eroded acres and designated them national forests, Sam Houston National Forest, Crockett National Forest, Angelina National Forest. The federal government then began to replant the forests, with the land company owners looking on and that gave them an idea; they also began to replant, so don't try to tell me that the stewardship which Smith lauds has been going on for 100 years. It has been going on since the Depression when the land companies took their cue from the federal government and began replanting. No one is going to say that the land companies have not been good stewards of the land since they began replanting. They have done a marvelous job. They have kept the forest area largely intact, except for some regrettable housing developments, but in the last few years with the invention and manufacture of new machinery that could penetrate the water and mud guarding the interior of the Thicket, they have changed their use of the land. There is a new game plan, and that is why conservationists are up in arms.

Here's how they are doing it. Up until the 1960s, the land companies used what is called selective cutting of timber. The foresters would go through and mark the trees to be cut, leaving the hardwood and younger pines. Nearly all of the old hardwood was cut in the first half of this century. This selective cutting was praised by local people because it left the birds, the bees, the bobcats, the squirrels, the deer, all the wildlife and even the orchids. But then in the last few years the land companies became dedicated to the belief that only in clearcutting the Thicket and planting it in rows of pulpwood could they make a profit.

Smith's pitch is for the land companies, and we love the land companies just as much as he does. We agree with him that it is the lifeblood of East Texas' economy, "and with proper management it can continue without harm to the public interest." If the land companies had not set out to clearcut the Thicket, we would still be saying that the landowners are great custodians of the Thicket, but they are not any more, and that is why our cry continues to be Save The Thicket!

IS BIG BUSINESS FREE ENTERPRISE?   *September 23*

The average citizen will start believing Nixon's price freeze is working when the price of groceries goes down. They are still going up. You can't blame the retailers, their prices reflect the wholesale prices, but this freeze will continue to be a farce until the price of groceries goes down and stays down.

We know now that there never has been such a thing as free enterprise, it has been government subsidized free enterprise, but up until recent years the federal government has managed to hide its nurture of free enterprise under the guise of names like tax credits, investment credit, oil depletion allowance, agricultural supports and a web of laws that allow big companies to elude payment of income taxes. If there were such a thing as free enterprise and if it were not a myth, H. L. Hunt, the Dallas billionaire, would pay more than $5,000 in income taxes a year. Free enterprise as it has come to be understood does not mean small business, small retail stores, it means big business only.

Free enterprise is a long string of benefits that the government has on the statute books for Big Business. The attitude of big business was never better expressed than by the head of General Motors during the Eisenhower administration. I forget his name, but he was in Ike's cabinet. He said, "What's good for General Motors is good for the country," and he believed it, and that, my friend, is the philosophy behind the Nixon price and raise freeze. It was not meant to lower high prices, but to benefit Big Business.

It's the same trickle down theory that got a foothold in the government during the William McKinley administration, which was dedicated to big business. The McKinley theorists held that if big business prospered, the good times would seep down to you and me, but they never did. There was no Hoover Depression in Texas in the 1930s. There was always a Depression until World War II. In the first two decades of this century most of the time there was 3 to 4 cent cotton, 50 cent a bushel wheat, and you could not sell fresh vegetables or fruits or produce. If you had a good crop of anything the price went down so low that nobody would buy it. I could tell no difference in the '30s and the three decades that began with 1900. There were always bad times, and between 1900 and 1930, the Republicans were in power 26 of the 34 years, and all the Republican presidents were just like Richard Nixon, helping the Big Rich and letting the rest of the population scratch to survive, but be sure and make it profitable at the top. Naturally I don't trust Republicans. I have never trusted a Republican in the White House and I don't trust Tricky Dick. To my way of thinking, he's pulling a fast one on us gullible people, not only on the freeze but in everything else.

I still have the feeling that all of Tricky Dick's grandiose schemes, and he has had a new one every week since he took office, are going to come to some bad end. I'm just waiting for it, because I know it will happen. The first big mess is going to be Vietnam, and the next one is going to be his economics. Tricky Dick has only one thing in mind and that is to get re-elected.

The American people did not realize that the government is the guarantor for free enterprise until Nixon and Connally came right out and told Congress it had to lend Lockheed $250 million. That shook the average man: for the first time he realized that the Republican party and its administration and free enterprise are synonymous terms. I would like to point out here that the term free enterprise was invented by Republicans for the sole benefit of big business. This was the first time that a national administration, though, came out and openly admitted that it could not let a big business go broke.

THE TREE KILLERS ARE WORKING   *September 30*

The tree killers are slowly but surely stripping Southeast Texas of hardwood; the bulldozing is just another phase; it's the tree killers that are sickening to watch. There are about seven of them, mostly youths in a crew. They leave Kountze at 7 every morning and are driven north to the woods where they work.

They call their weapons "guns." They are giant hypodermic-like needles. The killer walks up to a tree, usually an oak, and jabs the spear like a needle into the bark. At once a load of poison is released by valve action. Then the man walks around the tree, jabbing it into the bark, and the tree has received a lethal dose and begins to die at once.

All hardwood is killed except magnolia, dogwood and holly. All oaks and beech are shot with the gun. This operation is going on in Tyler County now, but it has been carried on in Hardin County. Presumably, when all the hardwood is dead, slash pine will be planted where the hardwood stood. There is not much dogwood, magnolia and holly now. The tree killers, aided by the bulldozers, are preparing the way for the pulpwood desert of the future in Southeast Texas. The trees are being killed, hundreds, thousands every day, shot to death with the killer guns.

Why does the News print these stories about bulldozing the Thicket and killing oaks with poison guns? The News believes the people should realize that the nature of the woods is being drastically changed from a mixture of hardwood and pine to only pine. You have got enough sense to know the results will change everything.

PORTRAIT OF MISS NEEL   *November 11*

I have written hundreds of thousands of words in my 46 years as a newspaperman, but I have never written a published line about a woman who was probably the greatest person I ever met. Even now, after 50 years, I know that she had a greater influence on me than any other human being. The woman was Miss Bernice Ruth Neel, an English teacher, but more than that she was an evangelistic Christian, of a type I have never known or met since.

So why is it, I am asking myself, I now sit down to write about Miss Neel? Was it that for 50 years I have been afraid to tackle the subject? Was it that all these years I have held Miss Neel above any exercise in journalism?

What brings it on now is that recently there was held in the old administration building at Decatur, Texas, a reunion of the class of that junior college of 1921. I did not attend, but I see now that I should have moved heaven and earth to go because since then I have learned that Miss Neel and 13 classmates were there.

In case you don't know about Decatur College, it began its existence in the late 1890s and before it closed down and moved to Dallas about 15 years ago it was the oldest junior college in the world. It is located on one of the high hills in Decatur.

My father took me to enroll in that college in the fall of 1919. It was along in November, a couple of months after school had started. We had just picked a huge cotton crop on our farm in Cottle County on the southern edge of the Panhandle. I was 17 years old and deep down I thought I knew it all, but I was scared to death. We got on the Quanah, Acme & Pacific train at Paducah and rode it to Quanah, stopping at the Pease River crossing to let the engineer shoot ducks. The train had one passenger car, heated by a coal stove, and it was zero weather.

After a long wait at Quanah we boarded a Fort Worth & Denver passenger train. The ground was a foot deep in snow when we left Paducah, but as the train puffed south downgrade the snow began to get lighter. Vernon, Chillicothe, Electra, Wichita Falls, Henrietta, Bowie and finally Decatur. When we arrived most of the snow had melted. My father took me to the college and enrolled me and went back to Paducah, and I was alone the first time in my life. I was 17 years old.

Why did my father send me to Decatur College? He was a Methodist and it was strictly Baptist, and I mean strict. It was because of the president of the college: Dr. J. Lawrence Ward, who was kin by marriage to our family. My father would make fun of Dr. Ward and call him "prissy" but he had total admiration for him. Years later Dr. Ward preached his funeral and 20 years after that he preached my mother's funeral. Dr. Ward wore Woodrow Wilson glasses with lenses that shone like diamonds, probably illuminated by his sharp blue eyes. He always wore a suit, a high stiff collar and tie. He was always immaculate. He presided over chapel every morning, and he preached where ever called on Sundays, some times at a one room rural Baptist church called New South.

I was uncomfortable when I arrived at the college, mainly on account of my new shoes. I had 13 size feet squeezed into 10 size shoes. I had lived on a farm all my life and never had known more than 50 people, and here I was suddenly thrown into association with at least 200 strangers, all of whom I decided right off were potential enemies and I developed an instant antipathy and contempt. They were all dressed better than I. They all seemed less crude and more sophisticated, though I didn't know that word then. I enrolled in Spanish, English, math, history and a twice-a-week Bible course which was compulsory. The Spanish teacher, Mr. Read, was young, and I learned Spanish easily. History was taught by E. M. Gettys who had tuberculosis but kept it under control, and always seemed to be infinitely bored.

A man named W. M. Hughes was the geometry and trigonometry teacher. If you get it you got it, and if he knew you didn't have enough sense to grasp solid and trig he passed you anyway. He was the best domino player in town. There was a hotel downtown where there was a domino table and Mr. Hughes could be found there when he wasn't teaching.

The student body was disappointed in me because I was not an athlete. My cousin, John Fullingim, was the basketball and football star in the college before I came. His nickname was "Ox" and he was as strong as an ox. Mr. Hughes often looked at me and his look seemed to say, "Look at that Fullingim. It's hard to believe he is a cousin of Ox," but the football season was over by the time I arrived. I was too scared to go out for basketball because all the basketball I had ever played had been on an outdoor court, and I was sure I'd be laughed at if I came on the court, skinny legs, big feet and all.

Nevertheless I was enjoying college life and living in a dormitory. At first Miss Neel did not impress me, though she was all my sister had talked about the two years she attended before I went. Lena would come home to Paducah and talk about Miss Neel by the hour, and she would proudly show her books. Right off, I felt that Miss Neel was showing a special interest in me, but in truth she was showing no more interest in me than in anyone else. All of her students felt she was showing a special interest in them. Nevertheless I was certain I was one of her favorites, and I wanted to impress upon her how smart I was, which was a difficult thing to do considering.

For instance, she made an assignment, and I clipped a very sophisticated and amusing column out of the Dallas News, and worse, hired a man in the courthouse to type it, and then I turned it in as an original theme. The man, who I still consider to be a louse, told Miss Neel where I got the column, and she wrote a little note on the paper, quoting the typist. She did not say a word but there was the saddest look on her face and I felt my face, scalp, neck and even my hands burning as I turned red all over. From then on Miss Neel could have walked on me.

Her specialty was Tennyson, and nobody ever taught a course in poetry as did Miss Neel. Nowadays, Tennyson is as Victorian and as irrelevant and passe as Longfellow, but remember that 1921 was before Sinclair Lewis, before John Updike, before Hemingway, before Dylan Thomas, even before Picasso. 1921 was still Victorian. I read Harold Bell Wright as avidly as I read Faulkner today. The way Miss Neel taught Tennyson it was a course in Christianity. It was learning to know God. It was learning to doubt and resolve your doubts. Yet she never evangelized in class. She taught Tennyson. It was weeks before I knew that Miss Neel was an ardent Christian, and it was months before I realized that in teaching Tennyson, she was teaching an experience in Christianity. I don't think she ever had us memorize too much in Tennyson, but I memorized it anyway. I can still quote passages:

> *Strong Son of God, Immortal Love,*
> *Whom We that have not seen Thy face,*
> *By Faith and faith alone embrace,*
> *Believing what we cannot prove.*

For a whole nine months, we had Tennyson, and when it was over I had learned to appreciate good writing, learned what to look for in my reading and had learned that the strongest emotion man can have is his attempt to be on speaking terms with his Creator.

The second and last year I was there, 1921, I attended a revival at the First Baptist Church in Decatur, and I listened to the sermons every night. We were not forced to attend the revival, as we were required to attend church every Sunday, but I went anyway, just to have some place to go. I would sit near the back, fully conscious and rather proud that I was a Methodist, and was having no truck with those emotional Baptists. Then one night a heavy hand laid itself on my heart. It felt terrible. All at once I hated myself, more than usual. I hated myself anyway most of the time, for what 19-year-old doesn't? Just at that moment, Miss Neel who was sitting a lot of seats ahead of me turned around and looked at me, and all at once I knew what I wanted to do. I wanted to take the preacher by the hand and maybe the awful feeling would go away. I walked up to the altar and was met by the preacher.

In a little while, a wind began blowing in my chest and I felt very happy. So that was the way I was converted. They call it a lot of things, saved, converted, but I always call it the night the wind blew in my heart.

Now that I briefly touched upon the selfless career, startling influence and endearing personality of this remarkable woman, Miss Neel, I should at least give you an idea of her personal appearance 50 years ago, when she was the guiding star in the life of so many young people. She had eyes and skin that I always thought would wrinkle beautifully when she got old. She was a large woman, chunky and heavy, but she missed being fat. Years later, I was watching a lioness and I thought of Miss Neel, but Miss Neel was ineffably kind, generous. I remember a purple dress she wore, also a purple coat. I often wondered about a decorative pin she wore at her throat.

I never saw Miss Neel but once after I left the college and then I had graduated from the University of Oklahoma, but it was a constrained, irrelevant conversation as well as I remember. She had just returned from Brazil where she had been a missionary. She went to Brazil first, I think in about 1923, and she went back, off and on, until she retired. Until last week I did not know whether she was living or dead.

Maybe at the age of 17 or 19 somebody like Miss Neel is going to happen in everybody's life. The person, not especially meaning to, turns you the way you go after that. Mine went the writing way. If I had never known Miss Neel would I have ever known the wind in my heart which I recognized as God? I tremble when I think I may not. For what is known to Methodists and Baptists as heartfelt religion is known to modern day Pentecosts as getting the Holy Ghost. I can't believe there is sure knowledge unless it is heartfelt.

I still have a moldy pack of letters, probably 10 or 15, written to me from Brazil by Miss Neel in the 1920s. I have never reread the letters in all these 45 years, but I know they are there in that trunk and I know what they say. I remember every day what they say. It may be that I shall never reread them, for fear of the failures I have suffered for not heeding all Bernice Neel wrote.

But often I look at the picture, in sepia, I have of her in the trunk. If there ever was a walking saint to me it was Bernice Neel. There is a statue to Miss Neal 100 feet tall in my heart.

Now I know why I have never written about Bernice Neel: I could never find the right words, I could never say the right thing, I could never do justice to her, I could never present her in the flesh and in the spirit as she was, and that is strangely frustrating. One should be able to articulate about a force that has stirred one's life for 50 years.

She seemed like a saint. From the beginning Miss Neel seemed untouchable by human passions and sexual love, and I could never picture her as being in love with a man, or loved by one, or as married or wanting to get married. She always seemed above and beyond the human emotions that rend most of us apart.

GUNFIRE IN THE WOODS   *November 18*

I heard the woods are full of the sound of gunfire, and a man came through here Sunday with three bucks tied to the outside of his car, but few kills were reported locally, though many hunters are taking a week off beginning with the opening of deer season. Hunting was better in Tyler County. Hunters say the deer are running like crazy, too fast and too far away to hit.

DEBATE CHALLENGE
FROM HUBERT MEWHINNEY   *December 9*

Dear Arch:
With your kind permission, I should like to subscribe to your paper, for the next few months anyway. It seems that this dude from North Carolina is going to come down to Texas some time after the turn of the year and hold another hearing about that Big Thicket National Park. I should like to read what you have to say on the subject. I doubt not that it will be both plenteous and eloquent, no matter how deficient in botanical knowledge.

Since I do not know what your subscription rate is, I enclose a check for five dollars, drawn at random. Put me down, please, sir, for whatever number of issues five dollars will buy. I can always renew.

Since Kountze is more or less the center of these moonstruck fallacies about the Thicket, it occurs to me to ask if you would be interested in a debate on the subject, say, in three or four weekly installments of about three hundred words apiece. Or three hundred would be about enough for me. As the editor, you might want three or four thousand. I realize that it is presumptuous to ask for space in your paper. But usually I get money when I write something for one of the papers. I am offering this free of charge.

Come on, Arch, let's have a debate.

If for any reason you should take the notion, you are welcome to print this as a letter to the editor.

> *Respectfully,*
> *H. Mewhinney*
> *Cleveland, Texas*

THE PRINTER ACCEPTS THE CHALLENGE

Before you read another word of this column read the letter on this page. The letter is from Hubert Mewhinney who now lives in the boondocks of San Jacinto County. Mewhinney is after my hide. He wants to nail it upon the wall of his smokehouse along with hides of snakes, skunks and other varmints. He wants to debate me on the Big Thicket. The only reason Mewhinney issued the challenge to me is because he knows he can whip me.

If you don't know Mewhinney, I'm going to tell you a little about him. He's an authority on everything from reading Latin and Greek in the original to identifying plants in the Thicket by their scientific names. For years, before he retired several years ago, he was the No. 1 columnist on The Houston Post. He is called the newspaperman's newspaperman. All newspapermen envy Hubert Mewhinney. He's never lost a newspaper fight which is more than the Printer can say.

When Mewhinney retired he moved to Cleveland, Texas. The last time I saw Mewhinney he didn't look like he lived any place but back in the woods in San Jacinto County. He came to the Kountze News with his girl friend of about 30 (he's 70 if he's a day, but looks like he has the vitality of a man 35) and Dr. Mc-Leod of Sam Houston State College. All this girl did while he was here was bring him, and eventually me and McLeod, cold beers from the pickup truck outside. Mewhinney was wearing bib overalls of the kind brakemen and engineers wear.

What Mewhinney was doing here was telling me how stupid I am about the Thicket. I learned more in that hour he was here than I ever learned any place, but it was awful how he humiliated me. That is the man who now proposes to debate me. I'm scared to death of him, but I'm going to do it. He's almost certain to show me up as a nincompoop before all my readers. You can tell by his letter how sarcastic he can be. Actually, I love Mewhinney, although he is insulting. For instance, in the accompanying letter he tells you how ignorant I am about the Thicket.

This column gladly accepts the challenge to debate Mewhinney, but is fearful of losing. First thing, Mewhinney, we've got to decide what proposition we'll debate. You did not say, so first thing we have to do is agree on the agenda. Now Mewhinney, I'm going to outline my present beliefs about the Thicket. I would consider these subjects for debate. When it comes down to it I suppose this debate really doesn't need an agenda or propositions. Nevertheless, I'm going to start off in this preliminary announcement by summarizing what I have printed over and over in the Kountze News.

The Big Thicket area of Southeast Texas is being clearcut. For months now, one timber company has had a crew of men roving the woods poisoning all hardwood except holly, magnolia and dogwood. The size of this crew will be increased and another crew added soon. I believe that the timber companies should cease clearcutting and destroying hardwood.

I am not in favor of a national park as such, in the sense of Yellowstone. I want to save 60,000 acres of the Thicket, the entire Pine Island Bayou watershed, which includes the Black Creek area, Little Pine Island Bayou and the so-called Saratoga triangle. A fence 20 feet high should be built around this area. No concessions, roads or improvements of any kind should be allowed. There should be trails and primitive camping.

I know, Mewhinney, that you are going to say that there is no Big Thicket as such in Hardin County, that you can find the same soil, plants, animals and foliage in other counties of Southeast Texas. I say the traditional bear Thicket between here and Saratoga and Sour Lake is different. Where we are going to fall out the most, Mewhinney, would be your refusal to admit that the traditional Thicket has a spiritual quality. For instance, last week I was in a beech tree area that almost duplicated the depths of the Thicket in looks, but the only difference was in feeling. I always know when I'm in the real Thicket because I get the Holy Ghost and talk in tongues. I start singing, "I'm Bound For the Promised Land."

Right now, Mewhinney, the timber companies are "pushing" thousands of acres of hardwood in Southeast Texas. All the timber companies have fleets of bulldozers, and every morning in Mary's Cafe I drink coffee with the tree poisoners and the dozer operators and I say, how many oaks did you flatten today, how many nests did you destroy?

I am not going to argue that the timber companies are SOBs. I think that the timber companies, all corporations, are doing what they have to do, produce more pulpwood, but we must stop them from killing the hardwood. If you think I'm going to cuss the timber companies you have another think coming.

Okay, Mewhinney, I'm waiting for your first installment. You see in brief what I believe. Now you have the floor and let's make this long and drawn out. It will be the Lincoln-Douglas debate on the Thicket.

I wish I had Mewhinney's picture to run in the paper, but in case he's so ornery he won't send it to me, I'll tell you he looks like a villain out of Gunsmoke or Bonanza, sort of Burl Ivish. He's one of the meanest looking men I ever saw. He has grey hair and it's kinda long and he shaves when he feels like it. He was a terror on the Houston Post. He scares me to death just to look at him.

MEWHINNEY'S FIRST REPLY   *December 23*

Dear Archer,

I have always thought of you as a good-hearted fellow and an honest man (which while we are on the subject of conservation, might as well be listed as a scarce and endangered species).

It is benevolent of you to let me have a little space in your paper so that I can try to disabuse you of some of your more grievous lamentable delusions about the Big Thicket, if any such place really exists in any recognizable, identifiable or definable form.

But, if you will, please, sir, let me say at the beginning of this seminar that you are the most inconsistent lover of nature that I have run into lately. On the very same front page of your paper, December 9, 1971, where you offered to let me have some space to discuss your love for nature, you printed a picture of a cute little 10-year-old boy with the corpse of a Texas red wolf that he had shot.

Now, Arch, the Texas red wolf or Florida wolf (or Canis Niger, Bartram, as he is sometimes called) is a scarce and endangered species, too. Learned mammalogists have been holding conferences in an effort to figure out some way to save the Texas red wolf from the fate that overtook the buffalo, the passenger pigeon, the ivory-billed woodpecker, and the Carolina parakeet. I learn from the daily papers that some of the earnest lovers of nature in Houston have even formed a club known as Friends of the Red Wolf, to try to keep the Harris County commissioners from paying bounties for the scalps of this misunderstood and persecuted animal. And what do you do, Arch, you bleeding-heart lover of outdoor nature and ivory-billed woodpeckers? Why, you bum, you print a picture of this charming, skillful, but misguided and half-pint rifleman and the Texas red wolf that he has so expertly shot down. And it is obvious from the cutlines that you approve of his performance.

Why, pooh on you, Arch. That cute little boy has played the deuce. Admire his skill with a rifle, yes. And I speak here as a man who has fired a hundred thousand shots with various rifles and has even worn out the barrels of a few of them. If that cute little young one can take a wolf with the first and only shot from anything as light as a size .22, why, then, that cute little young one is a rifleman. I just don't think much of his judgement.

And I don't think much of yours either, Arch.

H. Mewhinney

THE PRINTER TURNS THE TABLE

Touché, Mewhinney!

Mewhinney has drawn first blood. Read his opening attack on this page. He says the Printer is a phoney for yelling conservation and then publishing the picture of a red wolf on the front page.

But was that picture of the wolf published two weeks ago that of a red wolf? The father of the boy who killed it said it was a grey wolf. Mewhinney seems quite certain. He even quoted the scientific name for it. He says it was a red wolf. We'll have to see about that. I have consulted some of the local experts and they are divided. Most of them said, simply, it looked like a timber wolf. The wolf's hair was about the color of a German police dog, a kind of grey yellow. Gerald Flowers said it had a kind of gold tinge to it. He said that's what the red wolf looks like.

Anyway, if the wolf in that picture is a red wolf the species is not endangered in Hardin County. There are droves of them. Everybody this fall has been seeing wolves. Around Batson their howling keeps residents awake. Is it possible, Mewhinney, that these are not the red wolves of which you write? If they are, would you say they are endangered with so many of them around? Another thing, Mewhinney, you go up and down my back with a rake, for publishing the picture. You were right. That's where you got me in the very first letter. I should not have published the picture at all for the obvious reason that it will encourage other hunters to shoot wolves, have their picture taken and published in the paper. I think really that there was nothing wrong in publishing the picture, only that I should have said, look folks, the boy killed the wolf; he hadn't oughta done it, but he did. This wolf is an endangered species (if it's a red wolf), and he should not be shot by hunters.

Like the time I published the picture of the golden eagle that was found dead. We made a picture of it and splashed it all over the front page with a story excoriating the killer, telling him the penalty, and describing in detail the heinous results of killing an eagle, either bald or golden.

Mewhinney, only a few weeks ago I wrote a letter to the Tyler County Booster at Woodville protesting the slew of dead snake pictures they run. One issue they had three. I said, don't kill the snakes; nature needs them. Not that I expected to have anyone refrain from killing snakes, knowing that man is a subhuman species when he faces a snake, a wolf or a bobcat. His first impulse is to kill.

But Mewhinney, if we are to save the red wolf from developers, lake builders, bulldozers and tree poisoners, we've got to have a place where they will be safe, and I say that place should be about 60,000 acres in the Saratoga triangle. Put up a high fence around it and keep all vehicles and concessions out. Now, Mewhinney, how are you going to answer that one? You are going to have to agree, that's what. The only place wildlife can be safe, the only place birds can be safe, the only place Thicket animals can be safe is a huge acreage set aside to perpetuate Thicket ecology.

MEWHINNEY'S FRONTAL ASSAULT   December 30

Dear Arch,
It does not take much of a botanist to recognize the native trees of East Texas.
It is no harder to tell a buckeye from a basswood than it is to tell a radish from a head of lettuce or to tell a peanut from a bale of hay.
I, therefore, claim no particular credit for knowing how to tell a buckeye from a basswood. I just wish that some of these dudes from the Sierra Club and the Big Thicket Association would learn how to do that, too. Then they might quit expressing all that amazement because beech trees, bald cypresses, mesquites, palmettoes and prickly pears can all be found growing wild within the Big Thicket of East Texas.
You are certainly right in saying they can all be found in the Big Thicket. They can also be found in every other part of East Texas. What have you boys in Hardin County got that the rest of East Texas hasn't got, too? So far as I can tell, what you have mostly got is a wilder imagination and a looser grasp on physical reality.
To show how far outside the Big Thicket those plants can be found, a listing of their ranges may be copied from any of numerous manuals.
Beech: From a few miles west of Conroe clear on up into Nova Scotia. Westward to Wisconsin.

Bald cypress: Texas to Massachusetts. The biggest bald cypress in Texas is nearly four hundred miles west of the Big Thicket, at the edge of the Frio River in Real County.

Mesquite: Texas, Oklahoma, Kansas, Arkansas, Louisiana, westward to California, southward into South America.

Palmetto: Texas to North Carolina.

Prickly pear: There are numerous species of prickly pears, all belonging to the genus Opuntia. They spread in every direction outside the Big Thicket westward into California, eastward into Cuba, northward into Alberta, and southward into Chile. Just to make it unanimous, they also grow in Wisconsin. Maybe they will be discovered in China next.

Indeed, there already seems to be a sort of cultural and botanical exchange going on between the Big Thicket and the People's Republic of China. It is frequently and proudly claimed that the biggest Chinese tallow tree in the world is growing right there in the Big Thicket.

Just the same, I still believe that those cunning and inscrutable Chinamen have an even bigger tallow tree hidden out somewhere in the vast and mysterious expanses of China. They are waiting to spring it on you boys at the precise moment when the discovery will prove the most embarrassing.

H. Mewhinney
Cleveland, Texas

YEAR 1972

WHY IS THE BIG THICKET UNIQUE?　　　　　　　　*January 6*

Hubert Mewhinney apparently meant his printed offering last week to be his opening blast against saving the Big Thicket for a national park, since the song he has been singing for several years now, always accompanied by music of the timber companies, is that the Thicket is not unique, that is, it is no different from the rest of East Texas. His long suit is to try to prove that the Thicket in Hardin County is not different from any other county in East Texas.

Last week, he cited a list of trees that are found not only in the Thicket but all the way from Montgomery County to Wisconsin. These include beech, bald cypress, mesquite and palmetto. If their presence in both East Texas and Wisconsin proves anything, it is difficult to see. Mewhinney is trumpeting the same tune that McLeod of Sam Houston State University began humming several years ago. He published a small booklet devoted to the thesis that the Thicket is as much in Walker County as in Hardin. The timber companies loudly applauded and installed him in their hall of fame.

Now let's get down to what Mewhinney is trying to say. That is, that the Thicket doesn't exist now and never existed, and what can be found in it can be found almost any place. The big thing Mewhinney overlooks is that all the plants and trees can be found in one place, the Thicket. Now I know that Mewhinney does not set himself up as an expert on the soils, plant life and trees of the Thicket, and I refuse to recognize him as an expert. Likewise I am not going to set myself up as an expert, but I am going to quote only recognized experts, namely H. B. Parks, V. L. Cory and Don O. Baird who compiled, edited and wrote the famous *Biological Survey of the East Texas Big Thicket Area* in about 1933, and published the first edition in 1936 and the second in 1938. For nearly 40 years it has been the first and last word on the Thicket. Now if Mewhinney does not have a copy of this booklet I will lend him one. Understand Hubert, this book was written by professional scientists, not amateurs. The Big Thicket has had this booklet reprinted and it is on sale at the museum in Saratoga.

Now let me quote from the survey, just enough to demolish Mewhinney's theory that there is nothing unique about the Thicket: "The Big Thicket of Texas is a temperate zone, mesophytic jungle. There are numerous small areas of similar vegetation scattered throughout the flatwoods of the Southern United States which are known as hammock land vegetation. The Big Thicket differs from others in being much more extensive, covering approximately a million acres, and in being little disturbed as yet by devastating lumbering operations and clearing for farms (remember this was written 40 years ago). The timber that has been harvested has been mainly pine, and that remaining is the original growth of magnolia, white oak, gums and other shade tolerant varieties."

The sandy soil of the Thicket and the great amount of rainfall that it attracts make its inner depths resemble a rain forest at all times. The survey says, "The average altitude of the Big Thicket is 100 feet. Water can be had anywhere at a depth of not more than 20 feet. Because of its nearness to the Gulf, its heavy forest cover, and the enormous amount of water stored within its soils, this section has a most even climate. Many frosts never invade its vastness. Droughts are almost unknown. The only severity of the climate is the Gulf storm. Several of these in times before history have cut great lines through this area. Because of the wonderful adaptability to plant growth, such scars are soon healed and records of these storms appear as peculiarly shaped ridges all running one direction. However, when the moss and leaves are removed, the ridge is found to be an immense log, a veteran of the forest, that preceded the present one and was laid low by some ancient Gulf storm."

Until the 1960s when the timber companies began bulldozing and poisoning the hardwood, the depths of the Thicket remained about as it was 40 years ago when Parks, Cory and Baird were surveying it scientifically, and even now the timber companies are just beginning to completely destroy the hardwood. The only way they can destroy the Thicket completely is by

doing what they are doing. Bulldoze it as level as Bolivar penin-
sula, fill up Black Creek, Cypress Creek and Pine Island Bayou,
make it level and plant it in a pulpwood desert with no wildlife
habitat in which deer and other game may breed.

Mewhinney can keep on saying that all the trees found in the
Thicket can be found elsewhere, but what he can't say is that
within 100 yards of a bald cypress tree in Wisconsin can be found
crayfish 24 inches long, and some of the rarest birds in the
United States flocking together. Mewhinney, you can find a Florida screech owl in almost any state, but you won't find him in
company with the Bachman sparrow, the Carolina wren, brown-
headed nuthatch, the tufted titmouse, the Carolina pine siskin,
the eastern vesper sparrow, the slate-colored junco, the red-eyed
towhee shewink, the American sparrow hawk, all at the same
time, the same place.

These birds will be inhabiting the overstory, for the places I
have been in the Thicket where I got the Holy Ghost and talked
in tongues were like huge caves, with branches overhead, shade
on the ground, a few shafts of sunlight coming through. One
time Jim Webster took me to a place like that, the trees full of
birds, very little underbrush, and the ground dotted with slime
molds. Mewhinney you are not going to find slime molds in January in Wisconsin.

All mixed in with the slime molds, the palmettoes, the beech,
the magnolia, the cotton mouth moccasin are the algae and the
diatoms, found in almost every damp location. Then there is the
fungi, including toadstool mushrooms. The Big Thicket is by
nature suited to the growth of this group. The survey says that
there are more unknown and undescribed species of fungi in
the Big Thicket, some of great beauty and good size, than in any
other place.

What makes the Thicket in a class by itself, Mewhinney, is the
appearance of all these things in one place. There is no other
place like it in the nation. We heard that testimony over and over
at the Big Thicket hearing in Beaumont last year. Now if you and
McLeod want to put yourselves up as authorities greater than
the scientist who testified, you can, but you are going to look
ridiculous.

But back to your argument that what's in the Thicket can be

found any place else in East Texas, or Wisconsin, maybe. In isolated parts, yes, but not as in the Thicket where it has all come together. One of the endangered plants is the pitcher plant. I know of one pitcher plant bog that covers a dozen or more acres. The orchids of the Thicket are not a myth. I make the flat statement that nowhere in the United States can you find all these things together as in the Big Thicket, and that makes it the only one of its kind, unique.

Forty years ago, Parks, Cory and Dr. Baird, who is now in his eighties and living at Huntsville as a retired biology professor, wrote these ominous words: "If the hardwood is removed, the nature of the forest will be radically changed and its value lessened for game, recreation, and for productive forest management."

In the face of that statement, why do the timber companies persist in their bulldozing and poisoning of hardwood? Long ago men knew that the hardwood is needed to produce good pine.

Gone will be the heavy mast of oaks, magnolia, beech, maple, gum, tupelo, holly, dogwood, linden, hawthorn, hickory, pecan, persimmon, chinquapin, grape, Virginia creeper, pawpaw, smilax and supple jack. The dense undergrowth of evergreens which gives the Thicket its character is also of great importance as it furnishes the same cover at all seasons as well as a winter browse during the critical winter months.

MEWHINNEY SAYS EDWARDS PLATEAU WORTHIER
January 13

Dear Arch,

There are 198 counties in Texas with smaller population than the population of Hardin County.

It is therefore immediately obvious that all 198 of those counties are wilder, more primeval, and better suited for a National Park than Hardin County. The fewer the people, the wilder and more primitive the environment has to be.

I have never thought of Kountze or even of Silsbee as being a teem-

ing and overcrowded metropolis. But may I suggest to you, Arch, that there are more people living right inside the city limits of Kountze than on the whole seven hundred thousand acres of Real County. Hardin County, taken as a whole, is fourteen times as populated as Real County.

And Real County, up there on the rough and rugged Edwards Plateau, is far the prettier of the two. The road into the Prade Ranch, where you drive for several miles with the wheels of your pickup truck in the sparkling waters of the Frio River and with the limestone walls of the Frio Canyon closing you in, is sometimes called the most unusual road in North America. If you are looking for rare trees, why, Lacey's oak is scarcer than any oak you are going to find in East Texas. If you are looking for rare shrubs with flowers on them, the hairy sycamore-leaf snowbell is scarcer than the snowbells and silverbells of East Texas. But if through some strange perversity you still insist that East Texas is worthier than the Edwards Plateau of having a National Park in it, let me suggest that there are 29 counties in the Piney Woods that are less populous and therefore more primitive than Hardin County. Also, as I believe I mentioned once before, the biggest bald cypress in Texas may turn up right there in Real County on the edge of the Frio River.

I just don't see what makes Hardin County so unusual or so primitive. It says here in the Texas Almanac *that more than three hundred million barrels of oil have been taken out of Hardin County. I can well believe that. The ghastly scars that the wells, the slush pits and the pipelines left on the landscape are still extremely noticeable in Hardin County.*

Respectfully,
H. Mewhinney

A 24-INCH CRAWFISH?   *January 20*

Dear Arch,

I never have spent much of my time studying crawfish, toadstools, pond scum or algae, although I do have a few of each on these pitiable four acres in San Jacinto County. Why, Arch, that stuff is exactly what is the matter with Hardin County already. As I said, Hardin County is low, flat, swampy, mosquito-bit and full of crawfish.

I quote from your eloquent column of January 6: "What he can't say is that within a hundred yards of a bald cypress tree in Wisconsin can be found crayfish 24 inches long . . ." I really do not know whether there are any bald cypress trees in Wisconsin or not. The only large and authoritative book about trees that I have here gives the range as "Texas, Oklahoma, Arkansas, and Louisiana; eastward to Florida, northward to Massachusetts, and west to Missouri." Not a word about Wisconsin.

I will freely admit that I do not believe there are any crawfish in Wisconsin 24 inches long. Indeed, I incline to doubt that there are any crawfish in Hardin County that are two feet long. The crawfish of Hardin County are numerous, ubiquitous, ferocious and obnoxious. But two feet long? Come off it, Arch. Go get your yardstick and measure that crawfish again.

Nevertheless, all the documentary evidence I have to support this doubt comes from an article in the Encyclopedia Britannica *signed by Horton Holcombe Hobbs, Jr., head curator of zoology, Smithsonian Institution. He says that the biggest crawfish in the world is a species from Tasmania, called Astacopis gouldi. But this species is only 16 inches long. Somehow or other, this fellow Hobbs had missed out on the giant crawfish of Hardin County. I can see some future National Park ranger lecturing to a bunch of awestruck tourists in Hardin County.*

"Ladies and gentlemen," he says, "behold with suitable amazement this towering toadstool, reaching toward the skies six feet farther than Jack's beanstalk. At the foot of it behold the Monster Crawfish of Hardin County, chained to the trunk of the toadstool with a log chain, to keep him from busting loose and grabbing one of you tourists."

H. Mewhinney
Cleveland, Texas

ARCHER TRAPS MEWHINNEY

Oh, you get a line and I'll get a pole, honey;
You get a line and I'll get a pole, babe;
You get a line and I'll get a pole;
We'll go down to the crawdad hole;
We'll get some fish or damn my soul, honey, baby mine.

Aha, Mewhinney, my proud beauty, now I have you in my power. You have fallen into a trap I set for you cunningly and deliberately. Knowing your penchant for bombast, for elaborating on trivia and inconsequentae, for embroidering insignificant detail, I stated that crayfish 24 inches long were residents of the Big Thicket. Witness your reaction above. It is magnificent, but it is froth.

You will remember that at the beginning of this debate I warned you that I would quote only authorities and that I would, when run to cover, quote the Bible on the Thicket, the *Biological Survey*, published in 1938 by Corey, Parks and Dr. Don Baird and others from Sam Houston State College and Texas A&M. I am sure that you will not dispute these authorities, so I quote with great delight this excerpt from the survey, page 22, on crayfish, 24-inch crawfish, that is:

"This group (crustacia) which is best known by the common name of crawfish is the least known of all the groups of animals. This division contains a large number of organisms beginning with the tiny Cyclops, an almost transparent minute monster which is not uncommon in creek or cistern water and is best known by his resistance to the crawfish, and to the fact that it possesses only one eye spot—up to the huge land lobster, a crawfish which lives in the tunnels along edge of the water courses and possesses the longest legs of any group of animals. Adults sometimes reach a total of 24 inches long. It is most probably that there are within the sand flats almost every variety of fresh water crustacia, thus offering an attractive opportunity for investigation."

Now, Mewhinney let that teach you a lesson: To quit indulging your passion for harping on trivia and stick to the subject: Resolved that there is a Big Thicket and it should be saved!

THE CRAWFISH-SHRIMP DEBATE　　　　　　　　　*February 3*

$5 - REWARD - $5
DEAD OR ALIVE
FOR A TWO-FOOT CRAWFISH FROM KOUNTZE
(NO SHRIMP, LOBSTERS OR CRABS ACCEPTED.)

I hate to tell you this, Arch, but that two-foot crawfish you have been bragging about lately is not even a crawfish in the first place. It is a strange-looking species of fresh water shrimp, technically known as Macrobrachium jamaicense. It is 10 inches long. Neither is it a specialty of Kountze, of Hardin County or of the Big Thicket. "This and closely related species," says the En-cyclopedia Britannica, "are found in America from Florida to Brazil and from lower California to Peru."

If you want to know what those shrimp look like, for apparently you have never seen one, go find the article entitled "Shrimp" in the Encyclopedia Britannica, Volume 20. *There is a photograph of this strange shrimp accompanying the article.*

Like several other kinds of shrimp, this one swims around with all ten of his legs curved backward under his belly. But the two legs that have the claws on them are much longer than the other eight. Indeed, they are as long as the body of the shrimp, which is 10 inches long. Therefore, to make the shrimp look large, fierce and monstrous, the photographer cut one of his claw legs off, straightened out the kinks in it, and laid it beside the 10-inch body of the shrimp.

Ten plus ten equal twenty. Or at least they used to equal twenty before you boys came along and started bragging about the mythical wonders of the Big Thicket. Now you could do the same thing, Arch. Since you are an unusually big man, you could cut one of your arms off, straighten out the kinks in it, lay it down beside your body, and have yourself measured and photographed as the 12-foot editor from the Big Thicket.

Why don't you?

Respectfully,
H. Mewhinney

THE THICKET FEEDS MY SOUL

Well, how is the so-called great debate by H. Mewhinney and the Printer turning out? As far as I'm concerned, I've said about all I have to say, and I will say the rest in this column. And what I say in this column will be my most significant statement, that is, to me it will be. I gather that Mewhinney has about run out of soap because he took up the pollution problem last week and commented favorably on the News' antipollution page, and that was so embarrassing I had to shift his column to the inside, but if Mewhinney is not through I'm achin' to hear any additional arguments he has opposing efforts to save the Thicket.

One morning last week, Frank James came in here about 8 a.m. and told me that he had just seen an ivory-bill woodpecker flying among the gigantic pecan trees at the Ola Ellis residence nursing center. Well, we went over there in Frank's pickup but we couldn't see a sign of any woodpecker, but hope stirs eternal in my breast that some day I will see an ivory-bill, but I don't have much hope.

There are people who have sworn that they have seen ivory-bills in the Thicket; those people live in and outside of Hardin County. The prospect that they might be hiding in the depths of the Thicket makes it more imperative that the Thicket be saved. In my mind, the ivory-bill is a symbol of the Thicket: both are endangered species. I have to take the word of Mrs. Hancock of Austin, who testified in a federal hearing at Austin, that she saw a pair of ivory-bills. I have to take the word of Neal Wright and Geraldine Watson that there are ivory-bills in the Thicket. The certainty that this magnificent bird has been seen here is a clear mandate to save the hardwood and the Thicket. Way back in my mind, the Thicket and the ivory-bill are tied together, one and the same. The greatest ambition I have now, a consuming ever-present passion is to see the ivory-bill. If I had six months to waste I would spend it in the Thicket peering, watching, hoping, waiting for the ivory-bill. The jungles of the Amazon, the mountains of the Incas in Peru, mean nothing to me compared to the prospect of sighting that magnificent bird. I had rather spend six months in the depths of the Thicket than traverse jungles of the Amazon where no white man has been. I have not overestimated its beauty. I have seen that with my own eyes.

In my final statement on the Thicket to Mewhinney, I want to talk about something that is more in the realm of feeling than in seeing. I know when I'm in the depths of the Thicket by the way I feel. It's not the trees, the overstory, the algae, the birds, the lichens that tell me I'm in the Thicket. Here a while back I was in a baygall that had all the elements of the Thicket, plus beech trees, but I did not have the feeling.

In the depths of the Thicket in the Pine Island Bayou and Black Creek watershed I get the Holy Ghost and talk in tongues. I am not fooling myself. I know what it is to get the Holy Ghost. I had never talked in tongues before my Thicket experience, but I have attended Pentecostal and Assembly of God churches and Nazarene churches all my adult life at various times. I think that if you can't get a religious reaction when you see such things as the Grand Canyon, Padre Island, the Thicket, much as the same as you get in a Pentecostal revival, then your religion needs to be broadened. This feeling that rocks me in the Thicket is religious, but different from the religious reaction I have when I see other natural wonders. I am not going to debase my feeling by attempting to describe it, but I know what I know, and if I am deluding myself then I thank God for the delusion.

The saving of the Thicket is a spiritual exercise for me. I cite all the arguments against killing, pushing, poisoning the hardwood, practices that are sadly going on now; I point to the destruction of the game, the wildlife, but way deep down in my mind I know that what is being destroyed is what is feeding my soul. I have to go out there every so often to get the feeling, to feed my soul, and here I am a native of the great plains talking like this. I am sure that all who love the woods feel exactly as I do though they may have not analyzed it. They have never lived on the high plains away from trees. I have heard people say: who wants to go into the Thicket and fight mosquitoes and wade in the mud and water? The Thicket is not all mud and water and mosquitoes, for in its depths there is a green overstory with a few slivers of sunlight sifting through to the earth covered with moss, ferns, lichens and algae.

The ivory-bill and the Thicket combine to effect a religious symbol of beauty that man needs and will need more as people find less and less elbow room. The grandchildren of the young will be glad to flee to the depths of the Thicket in their days after 2000 A.D.

GIANT PINE   *February 10*

I saw the biggest lobolly pine I ever saw on the Flournoy land on Batson Prairie. The tree measured 12 feet, 7 inches around, the tape being placed four and a half feet from the ground. The tree looked to be 175 feet tall and the crown spread was immense. The reason the tree was never cut was because when the tract was cut several years ago by a Liberty sawmill company, the tree was already too large for the sawmill, so it's likely the tree will just keep on growing.

IT'S MAYHAW SEASON   *April 20*

There are people who live in this country, who have lived here all their lives, whose parents and grandparents lived here, but who know less about the woods than the tourists and bird watchers the nestors claim to despise. You ask these old-timers what kind of bird is making that sound and they say, "Hell, I don't know." I know a businessman in Kountze who claims to be an authority on the woods merely because he has lived here all of his life and he hasn't ever been in the Thicket, and he couldn't identify a half dozen bird calls.

I'll take it back about many of the old-timers never getting into the woods. Some of them go in just far enough to dump their old refrigerators, their beer cans, their old ketchup bottles and other garbage and trash. One thing you can be sure about the bird watchers and the tree lovers who come in droves to see the Thicket, they are not going to leave one cigarette, one gum wrapper, one napkin or anything else that will pollute the woods. I've been watching them, and they are not polluters.

If clear cutting, bulldozing and tree poisoning continue in Hardin County at the rate of the last few years, mayhaw ponds will be a thing of the past. I know that the old-timers and so-called nestors will make fun of that statement, but they also said at the turn of the century, there will always be bears in this country, there will always be deer, but the bears were all gone by 1920 and there wasn't a deer in the country by 1935. The deer have been brought back, but it won't be so easy to bring back the mayhaw trees. I know a mayhaw pond of about one acre of gnarled twisted trees that must be 100 years old. They are beautiful in bloom in late January or February, and they have an uncanny sense of knowing when to bloom to avoid frost. I make a lot of mayhaw jelly, and I give nearly all of it away to local people and to tourists. I am proud of the mayhaw ponds and the mayhaw jelly. You give a stranger a little jar of mayhaw jelly and he begins to get a picture of Hardin County, deeply wooded, forested, teeming with birds and wildlife.

Their time of the year is one of the best. All during April when they are ripening, I have that lifted up feeling. It's sort of a pride that I live in Mayhaw country.

Mrs. Roxie Pelt of the famous Pelt Prairie was just in the shop, but I wasn't here. She left a big pasteboard box full of super mayhaws, so big, so red and so clean that I started eating them.

MY 19-FOOT, TALKING PLANT   *August 3*

There is a 19-foot high plant in my house that can talk, that is, it talks to me. I have had this plant 15 years. It looks like a tall stalk of cane except that its leaves are yellow-striped. I never did know the name of it. I bought it in the plant department of Newberry's right after I built my house. There are some plants like it in the post office, but those are dwarf size and spindly. My plant is robust, glittering, full bodied, exuberant, confident and enjoys life to the fullest.

The plant first talked to me when it reached a height of 16 feet which is only a few feet from the roof. If you have ever been in my house you know that it has no ceiling, but huge beams of Oregon fir. The house consists of the kitchen, the living room and the upstairs balcony, all under the beams. The bedrooms and bath rooms are under the balcony. The original plant grew rather slowly and it was 10 years before it reached a height of 15 feet.

One day I had company and they commented on the height of the plant. One of the visitors said, "What are you going to do when the plant reaches the roof?" I said, "I've never thought about that, but I guess I'll either cut a hole in the roof so that it can go through or chop the top of it off." When I said that I noticed that the plant shivered and rattled its myriad leaves, but I thought some errant breeze was responsible.

After the company left, the plant spoke. I was not surprised. I suppose I had been expecting it, because after all a living thing that has been growing in your living room for 15 years should be expected to speak up some day. I said, "Well, a new country heard from." The plant said, "If you cut my top off I will die, and if you cut a hole in your ceiling, I will die because I can't continue to live if exposed to outside weather."

"What is your solution?" I said. "I tell you what," the plant said. "I will start growing suckers, and quit growing taller. But for gosh sakes keep that dog of your sister's next door out of here. I get nervous all the time he's around."

Weeks went by and no suckers started at the bottom of the plants and I thought about changing the plant to a bigger pot. I had already changed pots twice, but the plant said "Don't disturb me in any way. I'm in the process of sprouting a sucker."

In a week or so here came Campbell and Lynn Loughmiller who had often discussed the plant with me and whether I should cut the top off or a hole in the roof. First thing Campbell said when he walked into the room was, "Well! I have decided what you ought to do with the plant. You ought to cut it down level with the earth in the pot and a new sucker will come on."

I said, "A new sucker is now being grown and will come out any day," and Campbell said, "Don't see any signs of a sucker." I said, "The plant told me that the other day, and the plant knows what it's talking about." Both Lynn and Campbell looked at me funny, and Campbell said, "Archer, are you flipping your lid?" I told them that the plant talked to me all the time, and that the plant didn't particularly like the Loughmillers who live near Tyler and come down here, pulling a trailer which they stay in on trips.

I also told them that the plant is a Democrat and once thanked me profusely for hanging the lighted picture of John F. Kennedy that Jackie Fowler, who runs the beer tavern up at Village Mills, gave me. This picture is a shiny metal filigreed frame and the photograph is in color. "You couldn't have pleased me more hanging that picture on the wall six inches from me," the plant said. The plant also is for saving the Big Thicket and it literally shook with anger the other day when Kirby's Jim Webster came into the room where I handed him his stipend of mayhaw jelly. "You must learn to like people, even though you disagree with them," I told the plant.

The plant was incensed by Loughmiller's advice to cut it down to earth level. Then one day the sucker shot out and in a week it was five inches high and in six months it was two feet high, and when the Loughmillers came back from a six-month tour of South America, with 5,000 color slides of scenery, the first thing they said was, "Look at the plant! It's got a sucker." "Not only that," I said, "but it's got four suckers coming out of the top branches so it won't get any higher. That's what it told me." "Now, Archer," said Campbell, "I think you ought to cut off the original stalk at the base and let the sucker grow." I said, "I'll ask the plant about that when you leave. The plant will not talk in front of company." When the Loughmiller's left, I asked the plant, and it said, "The sucker will die if you cut me off." Now the sucker is 10 feet high and growing every day. It's beautiful with its dark green leaves with yellow and white stripes. It's even prettier than the original which now has six ball-like, bush suckers near the top. It is still a foot from the roof.

Every once in a while the plant will say, "Go upstairs and play the organ, play 'Will There Be Any Stars In My Crown,' or 'Red River Valley.' It soothes me after I hear all that blood thirsty talk on the TV." But don't get the idea that this plant is just a blabber-mouth. It will go for days and weeks without saying a word, and I will forget that it can talk, then all of a sudden it will say, "What happened to those lallagagging Loughmillers? How's the Holy Ghost Thicket coming on?"

LET'S STOP THE BULLDOZING OF TREES *August 24*

For years, the forest industry has preached Smokey Bear's sermon and the News has printed all the Smokey Bear cartoons free of charge, deploring forest fires. Save the forest, don't burn them, Smokey has winningly urged in ten thousand little pictures supplied by the forest industry. The News is about the only paper in Southeast Texas that has printed every one of them for free.

Now comes 1972 and what does the forest industry do. It destroys the forest by bulldozing, a more lethal form of murder than fire. Its bulldozers go into the woods and kill every living thing. Go about six miles east of Kountze and look at the bulldozed tracts, go any place which has been bulldozed. It doesn't take a smart man to see that there is enough pulpwood in those windrows of dead trees to last all the paper mills in Texas a year. So I ask the timber industry, what is the difference in destroying a forest by fire and in destroying it by bulldozers? I will tell you the difference. It is far more destructive. The only difference is that you burn after you have killed all the hardwood, not before.

Now the timber industry wants to take over the national forests, bulldoze them and plant them in pulpwood pines. I say, over my dead body, and you ought to say the same thing. They are not going to do it, but the people of Southeast Texas ought to lay down in front of those bulldozers. I'm going to keep on publishing the little Smokey Bear messages against setting forest fires, because I don't believe in setting fire to the woods, but I want you to bear in mind every time you see a Smokey Bear cartoon that what the timber industry really means is to let them burn the woods after they have pushed the trees down into windrows.

If I were 25 years old right now, I think I'd go out and lay down under those bulldozers, and in saying that I think that's no alibi. I am seriously thinking of doing it even at the age of 70. The trouble is I would need plenty of help, and it's certain others with me would wind up in jail, but that would be exactly what I want for that would center the attention of the nation on the destruction of the Thicket and might save it.

So who will go with old Arch Fullingim to the Holy Ghost Thicket and lay down in front of the bulldozers? That's a call for volunteers. That's a call to Mrs. Edna Jagoe of Port Arthur, a prominent club woman, to round up some volunteers. That's a call to the Sierra clubs of Beaumont and of Houston to round

391

up some volunteers. There ought to be some way to stop those bulldozers, to shame them into silence. Sierra Club demonstrators stopped the cutting of the redwoods in California. We could stop the bulldozing in Hardin County and lay the ground work for stopping the proposed clearcutting of the national forests. We ought to be waving Smokey Bear placards and climbing trees in front of bulldozers.

NIXON AND MCGOVERN CAMPAIGN   *September 28*

Are the American people going to see through Tricky Dicky Nixon in time to deny him another four years in the White House?

Nixon has become almost a hermit in this election. He spends his time between his White House in California, Florida and at Camp David which was FDR's Shangri La. Nixon has abandoned all pretense of holding news conferences. The media calls his attitude a "low profile," but it's really a lowdown, stinking ornery profile. He's getting by with trickery in the Watergate affair in which the Democratic headquarters were bugged. It's now coming out day by day how he allowed big campaign contributors who buy and sell wheat to Russia after buying it up at a low price from farmers. What happened was that the farmers didn't know that Nixon was going to sell millions of bushels to Russia and China, so they sold their wheat, but he let the big millionaire wheat buying companies know it, and they waited until all the wheat was bought from the farmers at a low price and then they sold it to Russia and China at a big profit. Naturally, these companies were big campaign contributors. Nixon is good at that kind of trickery, but he has no comment.

Nixon has corrupted the Justice Department by refusing to let it honestly investigate the bugging and burglarizing of the Democratic headquarters. You can be sure the Justice Department will keep all this dirty business under cover until after the election. Do you want a man for president who has allowed his agricultural department to rob farmers of millions of dollars, and never raised his voice against it, and who also allowed his hatchet men to violate the law by burglarizing the Democratic headquarters? You may want him, but I don't.

It is no longer a question of McGovern vs Nixon, but it's a question of Nixon. This country can't stand four more years of Nixon, that is the poor people can't and that's you and me. I can understand why the rich are for Nixon, but I can't understand why a working man would be or why any salaried or working member of the middle class would be. Open your eyes and see who is supporting Nixon. It's Sammy Davis, Jr., who is a million-aire. Did you see Sammy Davis hugging Nixon at Miami? Bethlehem Steel is supporting Nixon, and Bethlehem Steel which had a net profit of $462,000,000 in 1970, paid no income tax. Tell me one thing that Nixon has done for the working man in the last four years? The price of food has doubled, and meat is priced so high that it breaks you to buy it. Everything you buy is twice the price you paid in 1968. I would vote against Tricky Dick for one reason only, if I don't have any other reasons, which I have, and that is the price of meat.

Nixon's Phase I and Phase II were tricks to enrich industry and pour it on the sore backs of the middle class consumers, not to mention the poor and the very poor. Everything went up but wages. What's Phase III going to be? I say it ought to be to get rid of Nixon. George McGovern says he will do away with Phases I and II. Well, that will be a good deal. Maybe the price of food and other necessities will go down to where they were when he went into office. I say we can't stand inflationary food prices.

Forget all about McGovern. Just think about Nixon. Mc-vern is going to do everything Nixon says he's not going to do, and if you know what's good for you, you will realize that. Nixon has lied to you about the war. He said in 1968 that, "If by November this war is not over, the American people will be justified in electing new leadership." Let's hold him to that. The war is still going on. He's brought all the combat troops home he says, but for them he has substituted our air force, and planes are getting shot down every day and pilots are being captured by the North Viets. We have spent 400 billion dollars on Vietnam and lost 55,000 men killed and 300,000 men wounded, and it's costing us millions of dollars every day. Yet, we are still bombing and killing. North Vietnam is not our enemy; it is the enemy of

South Vietnam, so why should we bomb them to bloody extinction. McGovern is right on the war, he is right on social security, he is right on cutting down the cost of defense.

Have you ever thought seriously to what state Nixon has guided us in the last four years? The workers in the munitions plants say now, don't stop the war, we've always got to have a war so we can keep our jobs. We've got to keep on making weapons and we've always got to have a way to use them. Let us keep on making weapons and let the leadership of this country devise ways to keep us in a war. I say, close down the war plants and stop the war, no matter how many lose their jobs. What do you say? If you say, keep on making guns and keep on inventing wars, then it's time you, no matter your age or sex, put on a uniform and breathed in a few bullets.

This country has come to a sorry stance when its President will tell the workers in a weapons plant, I'm not going to let you lose your jobs. We'll always have a war for you to supply.

Quoting Sargent Shriver again, he says that Tricky Dick is going to announce the end of the war, bombing and everything in the latter part of October, but that it will be just another trick, and I believe him. He will do anything to get elected, so I believe he will soon say that the war is over in Vietnam. That will be his final trick to get elected.

A DEMOCRATIC HERITAGE *October 5*

Living on that farm in the 1920s when we were on the extreme poverty level, but didn't know it, made me a Democrat and has kept me one. Poverty is still with us in this country, especially among the blacks who are 60 per cent unemployed in the cities, but we have no poverty anywhere today as we had on the farms of Cottle County in the 1920s. The diet was a starving sameness in the months when there was no garden. Before my poor mother left there she contracted pellagra because of the insufficient diet.

The poor people of this nation were poverty stricken from the time Abraham Lincoln was assassinated until Roosevelt was elected president. The Republicans ran this nation for nearly 75 years for the benefit of the rich, and Nixon is still doing it. I know that young people sometimes wonder what they would do without radio and television. They take those things for granted, but can you envision a USA without farms subsidies, without Social Security, medicare or federal money for education? All these things were done by the Democratic party. In tthe Republican years of the last century, and they all were Republican, and the first part of this century, Republicans governed the land for the benefit of the rich. Most of the voters of today know nothing about life in the 1920s or during the Depression. They know nothing of the poverty that Republican rule brought on the South and the rural areas of America. The people are forgetting again. The middle class has grown prosperous. There are no farms as there were in the 20's when the farmers made their poor living without outside jobs.

The thing I learned in the 1920s living on that poverty-stricken farm in Cottle County did not come to me until decades later. Now I know what counts is people, how we treat them, how they live. The Democratic party is not concerned about profits for the rich; its great concern is the welfare of the people.

I tremble for this nation if we turn our backs upon the people, if we again dedicate this nation to the perpetuation of the rich. The most symbolic part of the presidential campaign occurred today at Floresville, Texas, where Shriver was at a tamale supper with thousands of ordinary citizens, while six miles away Nixon and Connally were hosting the billionaires.

THE THICKET GOES FOR NIXON   *November 16*

Hardin County voted 44,000 to 27,000 for Nixon. That meant the Wallaceites, labor, blue collar and the affluent middle class voted for Nixon. They will regret it, just as they regretted voting for Hoover and Ike, and here let's get something straight for all time to come. Nixon hates labor. He hates labor because as a radical, right wing conservative he must always insure profits for corporations. Labor is going to get it in the neck in the next four years, and it will deserve every poleax blow it gets from Nixon, for it was the labor vote that put him in. This has been building up for four years. In 1968 a lot of the labor vote quit the Democratic party and joined the futile cause of Wallace, and although I espouse some of the Wallace goals, I know that he can never be elected president of the United States. It's an exercise in futility to vote for Wallace. He can never take over the Democratic party, either. The other night he sounded as if he thinks he might be able to, but it's an absurd hope.

Still the South has not got Wallace out of its system, and it will go for him bigger than ever if Wallace comes back in 1976, and he will if he is physically able, and I hope he is, for that would wreck the Republican party in the South. It was the attempted assassination of Wallace that gave Nixon his great majority. It never would have happened if Wallace had been a candidate, but Wallace could not have won, even against McGovern.

The South still has Wallace in its system. It went Republican only because it despised George McGovern, not because it liked Tricky Dicky. Agnew expects to succeed Nixon and he is popular in the South but Agnew can't compete with Wallace in the old Confederacy. Just as in 1928 when it was a good thing for labor, the blue collars, the bigots and the TV Archie Bunkers to all go over for Hoover, it is probably a good thing for that great segment of the voting public to vote for Nixon. Every so often they have to be shown that the Democratic party is the party of the working man, the great middle class, the blue collars. Before 1976, they will be shown again, for there is no way for the Republicans to run the country without unemployment, high prices and hard times. There is no way for the Republicans to run the country without making monumental foreign policy mistakes. They will repeat history in the next four years. The Republicans will do this because of the nature of the Republican party which is dedicated to the belief that only the rich must enjoy the fruits of labor.

YEAR 1973

THAT VILLAGE CREEK FRAGRANCE   *January 25*

One day last week I was driving across the Village Creek bottom on Highway 418, half listening to the radio, when all of a sudden I smelled the water in the creek and it shattered me. Just a whiff, and I sniffed and sniffed to get more, and when I didn't get it I pulled over to the side across the bridge and went down to the water and sniffed and smelled, and then stuck my hand and arm up to the elbow in the cold water of Village Creek, and got my coat sleeve wet and all the way to Silsbee I smelled the water of Village Creek, that sort of swampy, spring gushing smell, and I called up Alf who lives on Village Creek and said go down to the creek and smell and sniff. Spring is about six weeks away.

MARIJUANA & THE PENITENTIARY   *February 1*

It may not be right to smoke marijuana, but it certainly isn't right to clog up the penitentiary with boys and girls. I just don't believe that smoking pot should be crime enough to send an 18-year-old to the pen, or to even indict him. Until last week, abortion was a bad word in the minds of many people, but the Supreme Court set the nation right on that. Previously those who advocated abortion were bleeding heart left wing so and sos. Now the Supreme Court has ruled that abortion is a matter between a woman and her doctor.

I have to remind you that was the exact viewpoint of Frances Farenthold, while "Duckin'" Dolph Briscoe ranted and raved that abortion was something thought up by radical liberals. It is interesting to note that the Supreme Court vote was 7-2. Briscoe has not yet commented on the court's holding the Texas abortion law unconstitutional. He said he was passing the buck

397

to John Hill, the new attorney general. I hope that Hill has enough sense to agree with that 7-2 decision. Briscoe has been sounding off about his opposition to lowering marijuana punishment. He wants to keep on filling up the pen with young people who were perhaps experimenting and got caught.

The handwriting is on the wall that the Supreme Court will eventually rule on marijuana, holding that it should not be a first-time prison offense. Again, Mr. Briscoe will have to hang his head and refer the matter to Mr. Hill.

The Dallas Morning News seems to inspire all the kooks to blow their brains in letters. The News' editorial writers and letter writers exploit all the prejudices known to Americans. They manage to keep Dallas the hate capital of the world. For instance a letter writer in today's issue of The Dallas Morning News urges that all possessors of marijuana be shot. I don't think anyone knows exactly what to do about marijuana, but I am sure that most persons think that prison is not the answer. I heard over the radio the other day that Texas prisons are loaded with young people who got caught smoking pot or had a joint in their possession. If that is true, it is wrong. To send a boy or a girl to the pen for possession of a small amount is not only a gross waste of youth, but a waste of taxpayers' money. There are now more young people in prison for smoking pot than there are for driving while drunk. In fact, nobody goes to the pen on a DWI charge, and obviously DWI is more dangerous to the public than smoking pot. Nobody is tried these days on DWI offense, but turn a jury, especially a Dallas jury, loose on a boy who got caught smoking pot and they go crazy. Governor Dolph Briscoe says he's not for making possession a misdemeanor and the legislature seems to feel the same way, but smoking a joint as first offense should be probated by law.

NIXON TAKES WATERGATE BLAME   *May 10*

It was fitting that John Connally should announce his future allegiance to the Republican party on the heels of Nixon's confession that he is to blame for Watergate. JC ceased being a

Democrat when he came out for Nixon in 1972. That's why his statement didn't impress anybody but the Republicans. JC has always been an ambitious headline grabber. He vows that he wants no office out of the Republican party, but if he doesn't why go to the trouble of calling a press conference to say so? As usual, JC was a devious character; he'll fit right in with Tricky Dicky's secret operations.

JC says that he's quitting the Democratic party because it is too liberal. He's talking about the party of Franklin Delano Roosevelt who gave us Social Security. He's talking about the party of Lyndon Baines Johnson who gave us true civil rights and medicare. Obviously, JC is actually opposed to Social Security and medicare and civil rights. JC didn't actually pinpoint where he thinks the Democratic party is too liberal, but if he did he'd have to be opposed to all the legislation that has gone on the books in the last 40 years since FDR took office. You can put it down as gospel truth that the Republicans on their own have passed no legislation that benefited the people. Connally used the word "liberal" as if it were a dirty word. Some Democrats who voted for Nixon last time had better believe it is a good word. I want you to look back 40 years before the time of FDR. The Democrats who are liberals in Washington gave us everything we have with the Republicans screaming bloody murder.

The awful thing about Watergate was not the bugging of the Democratic headquarters itself, but the way Nixon and his aides tried to cover it up. It's inconceivable that Nixon didn't know all about it, that it all happened in the White House and he was in the dark. He praised Ehrlichman and Haldeman to high heaven then lamented that they lied to him. He says he's responsible, but not to blame, which is Tricky Dicky double-talk. His TV speech left me cynical. I didn't believe a word he said about his innocence. It's Nixon's compulsive nature to resort to shady tricks. Nixon was acting true to form.

From now on, Nixon can't very well brag about peace with honor or law and order. Law and order has become law and odor and smells all over Washington. There is no honor in Vietnam. Nixon has been trying to squelch the press and TV, but he had to go in the White House press room and tell the reporters they are doing a good job and to keep it up. This was something the whole world knew before Nixon said it; but it was nice to see him agreeing.

NIXON, IMPEACHMENT & CONNALLY   May 24

The typical hard-core right wing Republicans try to make one feel sorry for Tricky Dicky Nixon by reminding you that he cried, actually wept when he was giving his recent TV speech in which he blamed everybody but himself for Watergate. As for me, I didn't see any tears, though I think he tried manfully to squeeze out a few. The Republicans like to bring up the spectacle of Senator Edmund Muskie crying in the snow in New Hampshire, which is said to have started Muskie down the skids in the Democratic primaries. If we had known then what we know now, we would have cried along with Muskie. At that time, Muskie was ahead of Nixon in the national polls and Tricky Dicky soon after began the spying, bugging and slander that ruined Muskie as a presidential candidate. The Nixon villifiers followed him to Florida and authored handbills charging Muskie with sexual perversions. They also put out similar tracts on Humphrey. It has also been revealed that what Muskie was crying about in New Hampshire was the tissue of lies and propaganda that Nixon's crew saturated New Hampshire with.

John Connally is fitting right in with the cover-up and lying going on in the Republican party. When he announced that he was turning Republican he was almost convincing in this declaration that he had not conferred with Nixon on any matter, that he did not expect any appointment and would think carefully before he accepted it. Two days later he was appointed an adviser to Nixon. Does anyone actually believe that Connally was telling the truth when he said he had not been offered an appointment? Does anyone actually believe that Connally had no intention of joining the Nixon crew again? Connally is in Washington because he thinks he's on the ground floor for the Republican nomination for president. While the Watergate investigators are digging up all the shady deeds of the Republicans I hope they get to Texas and unearth all the shady money

Connally turned over to the Committee to Re-elect the President (CREEP: which utterly describes that organization). JC did not actually collect the money but he talked a lot of money bags into giving it.

The media is full of talk about impeachment proceedings against Nixon. The House would have to vote for it and the senate would try him. I hope it never gets that far; I'd like to see Nixon have to bull his term out. The last person I want to see president is Spiro Agnew whose derogatory attacks on the press have lasted four years.

When the press was digging up the dirt on the Nixon administration, it soured responsible people on Agnew. Yet suppose the Senate hearings and the trials prove that Nixon not only knew about Watergate and the cover-up but planned it, will Congress then be forced to impeach him? Two weeks ago half of the American people, according to the Gallop poll, believed Nixon lied when he said he knew nothing about Watergate, either the burglary or the cover-up, but today that percentage has increased considerably. The hard-core Republicans in Texas are still making light of Watergate. They say there is nothing to it What they are doing is putting their stamp of approval on all kinds of crimes, burglary, slander, bribery, perjury and conspiracy. The worst thing about Watergate was not the burglary, but CREEP'S attempt to destroy the Democratic party and all its candidates by means of slander, tainted money, bugging and bribery. The next worst thing about Watergate was the attempt to cover it up. Citizens who go around making light of Watergate had better reassess the situation. Watergate has become the worst political crime in the history of the United States, even worse than the Teapot Dome of the 1920s.

If Nixon survives Watergate how can he pose as the supreme leader of the forces for law and order? The demonstrations by the long hairs were miniscule compared with Watergate. The youth only wanted the United States out of Southeast Asia. All the blacks wanted were jobs and true equality. It's shameful that the Dallas Morning News is still treating Watergate as if it were a laughable caper. That newspaper and its letter writers daily defend Nixon and his confederates and at the same time malign Edward Kennedy. Shame on the Dallas News editorial writers for its apparent endorsement of the high crimes and misdemeanors of which the Nixon White House has been guilty.

John Connally was through in the Democratic party in Texas and he knew it. He could never become the Democratic candidate for president. He is now 56 years old and this is the last go-around for him, if he wants to be president, and he most certainly does. Connally should feel right at home in the Watergate party. JC as governor pushed only legislation that benefited the rich, so that is where he belongs now.

"REALLY NOW MR. FULLINGIM"   *May 24*

Dear Editor:

I thoroughly enjoyed your article on the Kountze baseball team which appeared in your paper Thursday, May 17. It is one of the best stories I have ever read or written.

I started reading the story and thought the lead looked pretty familiar. Then I was shocked when I read the second paragraph and found the exact quote I used in my story. That, in my belief, is incredible.

Really now Mr. Fullingim, rewriting a story is one thing, but using it exactly with the same quotes is something else.

I would like to give you some good, sound advice, which obviously you desperately need. If you ever do this to a copyrighted story, which, admittedly, is doubtful for a small town newspaper, you could find yourself in serious trouble . . . ever heard of PLAGIARISM?

The next time you use one of my stories, I expect compensation.

Yours very truly,
Ron Cook
Beaumont Enterprise

EDITOR'S NOTE: I am shocked that you raised hell because the News copied your story in the Enterprise. We have been doing that for years. If it weren't for the Enterprise and the Journal, plus The Silsbee Bee and other assorted publications, we'd never get out a paper. That's why we make so many factual errors. My only gripe is that you don't have more stories about Kountze sports. What happened to that last game we played? Not a line about it in the paper. Now I've got to call Ted

Tate and write it myself. You are laying down on the job. I had no idea that you wanted credit for the story. If there was a by-line on it, I am sure Dee would have printed it. I'll try to be more careful from now on and give the Enterprise credit. If you won't accept my apologies, go ahead and sue. You'll have to get in line.

WHO CORRUPTED THE WATERGATE MEN?   *June 21*

The thing about the Senate Watergate hearings that is tragic is the parade, one after the other, of personable young men, who told in sober, conscientious tones how they were corrupted, how they lied, committed perjury, burned records and assisted in the cover-up. These young men, Magruder, Sloan and Porter, were not ordinary young men. They looked like Eagle Scouts, the all-American boys, they looked like heroes, not villains, and they talked frankly and I believe truthfully about how they corrupted and abused the election process. After a time, you begin to wonder, as does Senator Baker, who corrupted them, how could they have done such a thing? Of the first dozen witnesses, all were young men, only James McCord and Maurice Stans were men of years. Gradually you begin to think that these highly educated young men had been personally picked by Richard Nixon.

So who corrupted them? Did they corrupt each other? That's not likely, for the young are never corrupted by the young. How did these young men become debauched to the extent that they would perjure themselves and engage in a criminal conspiracy? All of them had the same answer. They were doing it for Richard Nixon, the implication was that what they did would have his approval and commendation. O, how they worshipped Nixon! Actually, I don't think any of these men should have to go to jail, but the people who inspired them to commit the crimes should not only go to jail, but should rot in jail.

All of these young men vowed that the President didn't know of their criminal activities; Magruder said that they failed Nixon, but nobody ever asked Magruder or any of the others, did you think that the President would have commended you. Would have been proud of you? How would they have answered? I believe they would have answered, we did it for the President.

LEGISLATORS, THE PEOPLE
& A NEW CONSTITUTION

September 13

The best you can say for the average member of the Texas Legislature is that he is a clown. He acts like a clown on the floor of his legislative body. Yet again he has given us an amendment to vote on to raise his salary. This time it ought to pass, but tell me one thing, how can you vote for a pay raise for legislators when you know how they voted in the last session, how they clowned up, how they consorted with lobbyists, how they bent the knee to corporate interests? The people of Texas are not as dumb as those legislators think. That's why four times in a row the people of Texas have refused to vote an amendment that would give them a pay raise. The people are not as dumb as the legislators think. When they start voting for a corporate income tax, a statewide telephone regulation bill, when they quit confirming zoombie, rubber-stamp members of environmental boards, when they start passing meaningful lobby bills, and a bill to truly finance education without pouring it on the sore backs of Texas consumers, then the people may vote them a raise.

The legislature down at Austin thinks it's fooling the people of Texas. They think we don't know they are principally clowns and womanizers who drink their fill of the lobbyists' liquor and work harder at seducing secretaries than they do in passing really good legislation. I can think of few legislators at Austin who have not been thoroughly corrupted from the first day they arrived in Austin.

I'll admit that the legislators need a raise, but they simply don't deserve it. Their record is too dismal. Look at the bills they passed and those they should have passed and one concludes they are overpaid. I am incensed when I consider that the legislature will rewrite the Constitution, and at the whim of every lobbyist of the oil, insurance and banking companies. Oh, the lobbyists will make it worth their time to sit in the constitution convention and do their bidding; the legislators will have all the liquor they can guzzle and all the broads they can nuzzle, and they'll write a constitution that even Vidor doesn't deserve. And when it's over Speaker Price Daniel will tell us how wonderful it is, and you know what we the people will do after watching the clowns sweat, get drunk and make love? We'll vote it down, and that will be a good thing.

⚬⚭⚬

NIXON, CONNALLY
& IMPEACHMENT HEARINGS   *September 27*

John Connally is now going around the country trying to endear himself to Republicans, trying to convince them that he would make a good presidential candidate, but I have been a Connally watcher a long time. I have studied that man and he won't do. You can blame him for most of the ills Texas has right now, especially the almost unbelievable mess the state school system is in. This was started by Connally and is continuing with Briscoe following the same worn out policy.

To make up your mind as to what kind of a Republican president Connally would make you have to look back and see what kind of governor he made. To do so, see if you can remember a single thing that he did for you or for Texas that could have made him an outstanding governor. Oh, he gave us the sales tax, but he warded off a corporation income tax, he shielded the oil, banking and utility companies. He gave the lobbyists a permanent home in Austin. If you asked him right now what he thought of the legislative scandals growing out of Sharpstown he would say they didn't amount to much, just as he says Watergate doesn't amount to much. Connally was a governor for the Texas Big Rich, just as he would be president for the nation's Big Rich, and he would shake them down for political favors, even more than Nixon has.

The Eastern media seem to feel that Big John, as they call him, has a certain frankness and charisma that are to be admired and commended. What they don't know now is that JC's charisma is phoney, his frankness is fake, his sincerity is all show. The most anybody could say for JC when he was running for president of

405

the University of Texas student council in Austin some 30 years ago was that he was good looking and that's still the most one can say for him. Otherwise, he was a phoney and still is.

JC wants to be president. He has always known that he could not be nominated as a Democrat because he could not get by the Kennedys, the Wallaces or the labor unions. Already they had him spotted as a phoney Democrat. JC is not a Republican. He just wants to be president.

Everytime you hear Ted Kennedy on TV or in the press he is working for, promoting, abetting the interest of education, health, peace and the things to which the Democratic party is dedicated, and what do you hear from JC? A defense of Nixon, of Watergate, of Kissinger. Let me remind you, dear reader, that JC only offers approval of hiding the tapes, for the Russian grain deal, for the energy crisis, that he is following the Nixon line to the bitter end, because after all, Agnew might be forced to resign and he might be appointed vice president. If that should take place, he would have to be confirmed by the senate and then we would know where Senator Bentsen is.

Meanwhile, the Watergate hearings are back with us, and I am happy again. I have my color TV in perfect condition again, thanks to Warrick's and when I'm not watching it at the shop I'll be at the house drinking it all in to the last horrendous syllable. During the time Watergate has been off the air I've come to some conclusions. I don't trust Senator Baker as I do Senator Weicker, and I have been watching Uncle Sam Ervin's voting in the Senate. I take the Congressional Record thanks to Jack Brooks, and Uncle Sam is a radical, right wing conservative who voted for Nixon more than he voted against him, or has in the past up to the time of Watergate. My favorite on the Watergate panel is the senator from Hawaii, and he is my choice for vice president in 1974; I hasten to add at this point in time.

The last time Watergate was on TV, the Kountze News was scarcely worth reading and it may not be this time if I get tied up watching it, but would you expect me to tell you what's going on in the commissioners court if Segretti was telling how he ruined Muskie in New Hampshire by lying about both Muskie and his wife. So bear with me. We've had a pretty good paper since Watergate went off the tube, and we'll try to write and listen to the tube at the same time.

⤳

MINORITIES & OUR SINS   *October 11*

I used to be a Civil War buff, but I always referred to it as the War Between the States. I would read every book that came out on the Civil War. Besides that, through the years I had collected a sizeable library on the War. It was The War to me. I could and still can name every general of the Southern army. I could trace every movement of Stonewall Jackson, Jeb Stuart, Robert E. Lee, Albert Sydney Johnson, Joseph Johnston. I could describe the battles of Shiloh, Gettysburg, Atlanta, Mansfield, Pea Ridge and Vicksburg in detail. I knew that precisely at 3:30 p.m. on a hot July afternoon, General Lee ordered Pickett's charge at Gettysburg, and at the same time ordered A. P. Hill to follow him, but alas A. P. Hill never came up the hill at Cemetery Ridge and the South lost the war.

Now nothing about the Civil War thrills me. I try to avoid reading about it. The sight of H. A. Hooks wearing his Confederate general's uniform turns my stomach. I don't even thrill to the sound of Dixie any more. It used to cause goose bumps every time I heard it. Now when I hear it I feel sad; not that I hate Dixie; I just feel sad. So what caused all this great change in me? Why even in the late 1950s, I was busy helping plan a big celebration for the 100th anniversary of the war. We even talked about a Confederate monument for the courthouse square, and there was some money raised.

The 1960s brought the change in me as well as a lot of other people. For the first time I began to see that the Civil War was fought to free the slaves, and that the slaves were looked upon as animals by their owners. My people owned no slaves. They left the South in the 1850s as poor as Job's turkey. They had no plantation, no slaves, they were poor, just as poor as the Negroes. But they believed in the Southern cause. They believed the South was right and that they were fighting for their rights. In 1960, John Fitzgerald Kennedy was elected president of the United States and I revere that day, because Kennedy caused me

407

to see the light. From him I learned that a black man should have the same rights, the same opportunities as a white man. It finally came to me that the South was wrong in that war, that what we were really fighting for was to keep black people in slavery, and I knew that was wrong. After Kennedy was killed, Lyndon Johnson made JFK's dream come true. The civil rights law that Johnson passed was Kennedy's dream. I thank the Lord that even though I was nearly 60 years old then, I finally was able to get on the right side.

It's the same way about the Indians. They were here first and we took the land away from them. Through 300 years we lied to them. Stole from them, and massacred them, and even today an Indian battle that the Indians lost is usually referred to as a battle, whereas if the white man lost the battle to the Indians it is referred to as a massacre, for instance the battle of the Little Big Horn is still referred to by some as a massacre. The way we treated the Indians was a sin and the way we kept the black man in slavery was a sin, and if there is one thing in the Bible that is true it is, "Be sure your sin will find you out," meaning that you will pay for your sin over and over, and I am not sure how we as a nation will pay for our sins against the Negro and the Indian but I am sure that we will eventually pay. Most likely in an unexpected way that will be cruel and costly.

We have always mistreated minorities in this country, and now we are still doing it, Mexicans, Indians, Negroes, even Chinese and Japanese during World War II. I learned to respect minorities from JFK, and I note with hope that his youngest brother Ted Kennedy is a champion of the aged, youth, the sick, the disabled, as well as minorities. Actually, I believe that Ted Kennedy is greater than his dead brothers, John and Robert. His is the humane voice in Washington; his is the voice that pleads for decency and fairness. His is the voice that is highlighting the cruelty of Richard Nixon's various vetoes.

But back to the original subject, I thank God that the light dawned on me about the Civil War, that I saw the light in my lifetime. I can understand how my grandfathers and uncles and other assorted kin were conscientious in fighting for the Confederacy, but I think that the Collins', the Overstreets' and many other Hardin County citizens who hid out in the Big Thicket to keep from fighting, were smarter. They probably saw that the South was fighting to perpetuate the Big Rich on the plantations in the South and they wanted no part of it. Hindsight comes easier than foresight, as the Watergate hearings prove, but some never even get hindsight.

THE NIXON LEGACY & 1976   *October 18*

Come gather round you know-it-all patriots who voted for Nixon and Agnew, and let's talk about the price of flour and bread. That's something you rednecks who cussed George McGovern's alleged "counter culture" can dig. Barely two months ago you could go to the grocery store and buy a five-pound sack of flour for 49 cents and nearly all through 1972 you could buy the same sack for 39 cents on special. Last week, I had to pay $1.11 for a five-pound sack of flour at a local store. So what happened.

Don't go away now. I'm going to start at the beginning and leave out nothin'. The price of flour seemed secure and untouched by inflation until Mr. Nixon decided to sell the 1972 wheat crop to Russia. The way he sold it was to enrich the grain speculators, who contributed thousands of dollars to his campaign. That immediately shot up the price of wheat. One month wheat was selling for $1.65 a bushel and the next month it was up to $3 a bushel. The first people to be defrauded were the farmers.

Last week I saw a picture of a Russian ship unloading wheat in an Italian port. That's like the timber companies screaming to high heaven that we've got a timber shortage and must have clear cutting in the national forests and at the same time the west coast ports are crowded with Japanese vessels loading timber for Japan. Wheat is aptly called the staff of life, and when Nixon made the crooked wheat deal he wrecked the U.S. economy.

All during the campaign Democrats were warning the electorate against Tricky Dick's shenanigans, but the voters were listening only to Nixon who was warning against McGovern's counter culture. What did that mean? I meant, according to Nixon, that McGovern had embraced and endorsed woman's lib, hippies, yippies, long hair, homosexuality, Negroes, Mexicans and a welfare state. Now we know that compared with Nixon, McGovern was a calm, sincere, honest Democrat who was lied on by the Republicans and the worst part of it was that some Democrats believed it. Now they are paying for it.

Nixon's chief apostle of law and order was vice president Spiro Agnew, and look what happened to him. When Old Spiro stood in that courtroom in Baltimore and told the Federal judge that he had accepted kickbacks that he didn't report in his income tax, that wiped out all of Agnew's mouthings of five years for law and order. It put him in a class with Nixon who has not yet resigned, who has not yet admitted that he knew about Watergate and covered it up.

I was never an admirer of Agnew, and I think he got exactly what was coming to him. I always thought that a man who could demean the press as Agnew did was a crook, and I am not like Walter Cronkite who got on TV and said he was not happy over what happened to Agnew. I was glad that he got caught up in his corruption. He was a mean, spiteful man. He lived a lie; he posed as a heroic figure, but all the time he knew that he was guilty of government crimes. I wonder now what his buddy Frank Sinatra will say, and how his two other buddies, Bob Hope and John Wayne, can explain Spiro's crimes. So it didn't madden me about Agnew. I always thought that he was not fit to be vice president of the United States, and so I say good riddance. The country would be better served if Nixon himself would resign and let Speaker of the House Carl Albert take over, but Nixon is tricky. He knows all the tricks, and he may be sly and cunning enough to stay in the White House until 1976.

Now a final word to the Democrats who voted for Nixon. I am thinking ahead to 1976. Experience is a dear school but a fool learns in no other. In 1976, will you disregard all the horrors of the administration and start yelling Chappaquiddick if Senator Kennedy is the nominee for president? Will you yell Chappaquiddick like you yelled counter culture at poor old George McGovern? If you do, Nixon and Agnew and their grain deal, their Watergate, their bribes and their selling of the government to the highest bidders will not have taught you anything. If you yell Chappaquiddick in 1976 you deserve everything you will get from Nixon and Agnew. I am aware that Hardin County voted for Nixon in 1972. He got 60 per cent of the vote. That was disgraceful, and reflects on the IQ and acumen of the people. Vow now to never again be misled by crooked politicians who tried to buy the Democratic process in America.

There is a brain-damaged writer named Robert Baskin who has a column in The Dallas Morning News and his latest is to foresee a possible Kennedy-Bentsen ticket in 1976 and that scares Baskin witless. This vision came to Bentsen after Ted Kennedy made a speech in the Senate praising Bentsen. Baskin is a bootlicker of Connally and Shivers and he backs all Republicans. Baskin paints a dreary picture of LBJ while he was vice president. But I imagine that LBJ thought it was worth it to endure being vice president for a short time. The very fact that Baskin fears a Kennedy-Bentsen accord sells me on the idea, but for one thing. Baskin has never been right in his prognostications.

NIXON SHOULD RESIGN   *November 8*

Richard Nixon should resign as President of the United States, and if he doesn't resign he should be impeached as soon as possible. The way Nixon acted at his recent press conference indicates to me that George Meany was right. Nixon is emotionally unstable and he's getting worse. He came on in that press conference with a big smile that was so hollow and shallow that it gave one the shakes just seeing it. The worst thing he did was jump on the news media. Now I watch all three of the networks from time to time, and I can't see any difference. I read the headlines in all the papers and I don't see any difference there. I'll admit that the Dallas News still reads on its editorial page as if Watergate never happened. But the point I am trying to make is that Nixon was not crucified by the media, but by the American people. He was not crucified by the Democrats, but by both Democrats and Republicans.

Nixon says he will never resign but what is he going to say

411

when the prosecutors expose his closest friend, Bebe Rebozo. The media is not making up all the new horrors that are surfacing every day. But let's go back to his press conference. Who but a mentally unstable man would say that he has no respect for the media or that they spoke outrageous lies, and then not pinpoint the lies. Nixon finally wiped the smile off his face at that conference and then spoke like a man who was angry and confused. If things keep getting worse in Washington public opinion will finally force Congress to impeach Nixon, and then if Nixon sees that he does not have the votes to win, he will resign.

Would a sane man have carried on the way Nixon did at the press conference? I know that if I had said what he did I would be worried about my sanity, but of course Nixon sees himself as cool in a crisis. He sees himself as acting normal. You can never convince a crazy man that he's not sane.

THE PEOPLE HAVE IMPEACHED NIXON   *November 22*

The chickens have come home to roost for Tricky Dick. The nation is remembering how every time he was elected to Congress, to the Senate, to Vice President, he called the Democrats traitors and communists. So now where do we find Mr. Nixon? He's the president who sold out to ITT, the oil companies, the grain dealers, the milk industry, and the man whose bosom friend took $100,000 from Howard Hughes. Caught, Nixon ran and hid and let the law deal with the criminals in his employ, who he inspired. He corrupted a whole slew of young men, Dean, Magruder, Haldeman, even Ziegler, the former Disneyland usher, but when they got caught committing crimes to elect their adored boss, he turned his back on them. He gave them a Judas kiss and showed no remorse for their going to prison.

Nixon is guilty of high crimes and misdemeanors, including selling the government to the highest bidders, corrupting the CIA and the FBI, and turning men like Kleindienst into liars and he ought to be impeached, if he doesn't resign. Eventually the American people who have awakened to his evil and perfidy will hound out of office all those who are now defending him.

Has Nixon changed any? Has he repented any? No. Look at his present tactics to avoid punishment. He is seeing congressmen in batches of 50, promising them goodies. And he still thinks Haldeman and Ehrlichman are noble public servants. Nixon can never change. He has been bad for the USA, and the proof of that can be seen daily in the letter column in the Beaumont Enterprise and the Dallas Morning News, which actually defend the crimes of Nixon, blindly turning away from facts, penning their paranoic, twisted minds, and Nixon is equated with religion, and patriotism. Most of these letters are turned out by the John Birch Society. I have seen the same letters written by different persons appear in both newspapers.

Nixon himself is paranoid or else he would have quit in shame and disgrace, but he will find out if he stays that it would have been better if he had resigned. The American people can live over Richard Nixon. They have now formed opinions that will never change and our system is greater than any president, as long as we have a Congress and a Supreme Court. Congress may not impeach Nixon, but the people have.

RELY ON PEOPLE, NOT THINGS   *November 29*

Ralph Nader's new crusade to do away with spray cans because they are not only killing the environment but us, leaves me passive and nonchalant. I never did like spray cans anyway. When I press the button down to spray something, it sprays my face. Likewise the energy crisis does not scare me at all. I can do without the electricity and the gas if I have to.

Most of my life I lived without electricity and gas. Out on the farm in Cottle County we had coal oil lamps, and our mode of transportation was via wagon or horseback. I never entertained the idea of making a long weekend trip. People stayed put the first 25 years of this century, and they'd be better off if they stayed put now. You can call me an old fogey or in my dotage, but I have lived through both times, and I think people were happier when they didn't have to go to Rayburn Lake every weekend, or to Toledo Bend, or Parkdale Mall, or use spray cans.

When I was a teenager there was no such thing as a radio, let alone TV. What did we do to pass the time? We worked in the fields all day and at night we stayed home except on Saturday when we went to a singing or a party. We relied on people, our association with them, to give us a good feeling. Nowadays, people don't rely on people because they don't really love people. They rely on things, gadgets, gimmicks, not people.

So I rather welcome the shortages. I predict we are going to learn a lot about ourselves, our country and our economy in the next decade. It may be that I'll eventually have to start rustling wood for my beautiful fireplace. I'd welcome that, too.

I HAVE LITTLE ENTHUSIASM NOW   *December 6*

It's getting harder and harder to put out this paper each week. For the first time in my 50-year career of working on newspapers I have to admit that I have little enthusiasm. It's been coming on me gradually for several years ever since the doctor gave me some high blood pressure pills and the side effects caused double vision in my right eye. Since then I have not been able to read at a distance beyond six inches. But I have been able to live with that. I still read voraciously.

If I told the truth, I suppose I would have to admit that I keep holding on to show Blair, Birdwell, Lamar McDonald and Christian that they can't run me out of town. Another reason is that I would like to be publishing the paper in 1976 when I hope a Democrat is elected president, preferably Ted Kennedy. Also I get a great satisfaction out of throwing up to the rednecks, who just couldn't stand George McGovern's so-called, counter culture, what a big mess they got into when they voted for Nixon.

MARIJUANA AND DWI

The 31 marijuana cases on the docket for trial in district court here are not only a disgrace to the sheriff's department but to the court. Not that the pot violators were arrested. No complaint there, but that when you know the district court record on DWI cases, the pot cases loom pretty small. No pot smoker has ever been arrested for driving while drunk on pot. I've never read of a fatal wreck caused by a pot smoker, though I am sure it has happened. The point I'm trying to make is that the laws and the court go to pieces over a boy smoking a joint, but do nothing that works to send a DWI person to the pen and get him off the highway. I don't feel endangered by the pot smokers but I durn sure feel that my life is not worth a nickel with the DWIs cluttering the highways. I urge the law to concentrate on the No. 1 menace.

AMNESTY FOR NIXON? *December 20*

You can order bumper stickers that say "Support The President," 1,000 for $150. Bumper strips reading, "Get Off His Back," also are available at the same price, according to pro-Nixon propaganda we have received. There are some people who might attach such a sticker on the bumper of their car, but I don't know who they are. Some radical, right wing, conservative, John Birch-type kooks.

Like everything else in the Nixon administration the "Support The President," stickers start off assuming the American people don't support the President when he is right. It's like the sign that says, "America, Love It Or Leave It," which assumed that if you were not for the Vietnam War, for Watergate and for Nixon you did not love America.

I don't support the President when he tries to blame all his misdeeds on the Democrats, like when he said he took his vice-presidential papers as an income tax deduction for $200,000, because LBJ told him to, like when he blamed two Democrats for selling out to the milk czars for $2 million, like when he spent $1 million on his homes in Florida and California. If you will think back, Nixon always says like Flip Wilson, "The Democrats made me do it." Some of these days, he's going to forget and say, like Flip, "The devil made me do it," when he is caught up in his high crimes and misdemeanors.

The only senator who has really said a good word for Nixon lately is Senator Ted Kennedy who praised an official act of Nixon. Anyway, if every Democrat in Congress were on his feet every hour of the day, cussing Nixon, they would never equal the volume of abuse that Nixon heaped on FDR, Truman or the Kennedys. Remember Tricky Dicky's battle cry against Adlai Stevenson in 1952 was "20 years of treason," so now the shoe is on the other foot.

The reason Truman always hated Nixon was because Nixon convinced a lot of Americans that General George Marshall was a traitor when the communists took over Red China. If you ask me that was a good thing. At least the Chinese are eating and eating well now; they have no prostitutes, no dope rings, all without freedom, I'll admit, but old Chang is not there to keep the Chinese coolies in opium-dazed slavery. What the Republicans have forgotten, but what the Democrats still remember, is how Nixon was on the backs of the Democrats for 20 years, with his lies, contempt, dirty tricks. So don't tell me to get off Nixon's sore back. I'll get off his back when he does what old Spiro did.

If I were to put any kind of Nixon sticker on my bumper it would be "No Amnesty for Nixon," emphasizing that Spiro got amnesty and those who turned state's evidence in the Watergate trials are getting amnesty, but there is no amnesty because of Nixon and Spiro for the thousands of American boys who refused to fight a war that was not for our country, but for the Vietnamese who used that war to turn thousands of our soldiers into drug addicts, a war that was fought to enrich the ammunition makers and promote Pentagon generals who drive to work in limousines. Spiro got off lightly. Mitchell is not in jail yet, neither is Stans, Haldeman or Ehrlichman and Nixon is still against the boys who had to flee the country to keep from fighting that evil war. So I say no amnesty for Nixon.

YEAR 1974

RELIGIOUS BEAUTY   *February 7*

I saw Hattie Williams, Kountze's great tamale maker and preacher, and I asked her what she was praying for these days and she said, "The human race." She has her Bible with her always as she sits on the front porch of her house and waits for customers. Her religion, and the way she practices it, has made her beautiful.

WILL THE REAL LLOYD BENTSEN STAND UP?   *February 14*

Will the real U.S. Senator Lloyd Bentsen stand up? Since he announced for the senate and ignominiously defeated Senator Ralph Yarborough there have been so many Bentsens on the scene that it's difficult to put your finger on one and say this is the real Lloyd Bentsen. But let's start at the beginning and not leave out nothin'. Bentsen ran a demagogic, contemptible race against Yarborough. He ran as a redneck demagogue. He accused Yarborough of being an atheist, a hippy demonstrator, a man who was opposed to reading the Bible. He dredged up Yarborough's vote against the two southerners who Nixon appointed to the Supreme Court. Bentsen knew these two men were not only incompetent, but racist and corrupt. Yet, Bentsen told the voters that Yarborough was voting against the South. I could go on for two pages about how Bentsen distorted Yarborough's noble record, how he spread lies and how he spent hundreds of thousands of dollars in spreading the misinformation.

That was Lloyd Bentsen and it still rankles. You must remember that Bentsen had the backing of big oil in Texas, including John Connally, the big rich and the clique who has run Texas for 40 years by controlling the Texas daily press. But once Bent-

417

sen was elected, he started running for president of the United States. At first it made me laugh, but I am not laughing anymore, for Bentsen has voted exactly as a candidate for president should vote. He has voted against convictions he had in Texas for decades, while he was becoming super rich.

Bentsen is a hard nosed man, with hard fists and a merciless, sometimes cruel attitude. I have watched the senate career of Lloyd Bentsen carefully from the day he went to the senate. I have read all his official stories sent to newspapers. At first it seemed inconceivable to me that Bentsen could ever make himself presentable to national Democratic leaders, but in the past few years he has earned the admiration of Senator Mike Mansfield and Senator Ted Kennedy, though here a while back Bentsen went to great pains to disavow any more than a senate friendship with Ted Kennedy.

At first the nation laughed but they are not laughing any more, for Bentsen is living up to his role of voting and speaking as a liberal candidate for the Democratic presidential nomination should. The thing that nags and worries me is: will Bentsen be the first Democratic nominee in history who poses as a liberal and is really at heart a John Connally, an Allan Shivers, an old-time Price Daniel? Bentsen knows as well as you and I that the Democratic party is never going to nominate for president any man who is not a liberal, for that is what the national Democratic party is.

It's too early to put a final assessment on Bentsen. Every time he acts like a national Democrat he comes home to Texas and almost convinces you that he's not only been to see John Connally, but has been consorting with Shivers. As for me, I am almost proud of his voting record to date. I wish for certain that it came naturally and not because he's running for president.

However I am confident that the Democrats will not fail to nominate a progressive, a moderate, a liberator what ever you want to call it; the party has never failed to nominate a liberal and I don't believe Bentsen can fool people like Humphrey, Mondale and Tunney. In time, the real Lloyd Bentsen will stand up in all his glory or all his humiliation and shame.

MAYBE I SHOULD RETIRE   *February 21*

I am 72 years old and rich, so why shouldn't I retire? There are a few highly precious things I want to do before I walk that lonesome valley, and if I don't retire soon I know I'll never do them. If I was poor and penniless I'll admit that I would keep on working, but like I said I'm rich and the reason I'm rich is because Lamar, Birdwell, McDonald and George Christian tried to run me out of town. I recall in horror when I think how it used to be when Lamar was publishing his ad in the News. I'd have to literally beg him to pay off. He never would pay until the end of the month and then I'd have to go up there with my hat in my hand. Before he'd pay me he'd always threaten me and tell me how good he was to me to be paying a measly $56 a week for the ad. He'd always tell me who he wanted me to support for city council, mayor or school trustee. Half the time I supported the candidates he didn't like and that was the reason he finally quit and decided to run me out of town.

I am not doing as good a job as I want to in putting out the News. The reason is that I have lost interest in going to meetings. I should be covering the city council and the school board word for word, though Superintendent Hughes doesn't want any publicity unless he writes it himself, and the city council is glad I'm not present. Whenever the press does not cover the city council it always gets in the same mess it is in now. And when the press does not cover the school board meetings the superintendent and the board get to thinking that they, not the people, own the schools.

The News needs an editor who will attend every meeting of the city council and the school board, and I'm not going to do it, I'm just too tired to sit up half the night with the board or the council.

MY LAST ISSUE   *February 28*

This is the last issue of the News that I'll publish. Dee and I have sold the paper. However, this column will continue to ap-

A career nears its end.

pear indefinitely, possibly a year. A lot of people take this paper just because of this column, not because they exactly agree with what I say, but they want to read what I have to say whether they agree with it or not. I shall write mainly on state and national topics.

I wanted to keep on publishing the News until 1976, when I am sure Ted Kennedy will be candidate for president, but Buddy Moore, the new owner, says that if Ted is the Democratic candidate in 1976, and I'm still living and writing, I can boost his candidacy in the News. One thing most of you must remember, is that my opinions do not necessarily reflect those of Buddy. You will see from the start that the paper is his and will reflect his style, conviction and ideas of putting out a paper.

The newsprint situation triggered our decision to sell the paper, but there were other compelling reasons. One is that I am 72 years old and rich and should retire. I have not been doing the kind of job that needs to be done. I have not been covering sports and meetings. I have been making few pictures. I have not been publishing enough local news.

Also, I want to continue my 35-year search for the ivory-bill woodpecker. I will have time now to go into the depths of my beloved Holy Ghost Thicket. I can help with the Big Thicket museum at Saratoga. I will have about three months of chores to do, and then I'm going to settle down in my beautiful house on Williford Road and write the book that I have been writing in my head for the last five years.

All I'm going to tell you about the book is that it will have less than 200 pages, compared to the 400 page novel I wrote in 1949 and never got printed. I think I can get this one printed, but this is the last reference I will make to it and don't ask me about it, because if you do I may talk and a person can talk a book to death before writing it. I have talked many books to death. I'm damn sure not going to talk this one to death.

ONE YEAR OF WATERGATE *March 14*

One of the most absurd aspects of Nixon's recent appearances on TV is his contention that he is not responsible for the misdeeds of his closest aids and associates and therefore is no crook. "I am not a crook," Nixon said, but about 27 of his White House staff have been indicted for perjury, lying, burglary, obstruction of justice, taking bribes and various other crimes. The entire Nation should have looked at Watergate differently from the start. They should have laid down premises that if the White House Staff committed crimes, then Nixon did. The President is solely responsible for Watergate and related crimes, and it does not do any good to say that Nixon didn't know.

My guess is that if the House impeaches Nixon, he will be forced to resign as Agnew did and that would be best. Then the grand jury would be free to indict him for specific crimes and let him be tried by a jury of his peers. Nixon said that a year of Watergate was enough, a statement which in itself denotes cover-up, permissive crimes and contempt for law. It appears to mean that Mr. Nixon thinks he has already suffered enough, but he's likely to find out that Watergate will be around two or three years from now.

As for those people who keep saying "I'm sick of Watergate," they should be ashamed. Those I know who say that are great law and order people when it comes to brown or black minorities or poor white trash but not when it comes to their own kind. A year of Watergate turned Mr. Nixon's party upside down, and Republicans like George Bush keep saying that Nixon did it, the Republican party didn't. If that be true then why do the Republican leaders keep defending Nixon. And there's Gerald Ford the new vice president, who absolves the Republican party and places the blame on the White House staff. The Republican party elected Nixon. The Republican party still upholds him, defends him, makes excuses for him. Nixon is the head of the Republican party and responsible for its actions. Because the Republican party has always been the party of great wealth, it seeks to use that wealth to perpetuate itself.

A year of Watergate enough? Yes, if you want to bury your head in the sand. Yes, if you think law and order is a joke. Yes, if you want to abolish the Constitution and the judicial system.

CONRAD IN COTTLE COUNTY   *March 28*

One dry summer on the farm in Cottle County in the middle 1920s, I filled out a blank cut from a magazine and ordered the complete works of Joseph Conrad, who wrote sea stories. I was enraptured by the sea which I had never seen, but I had always read every story I could find about the sea. I knew that some day I would be near the sea and get my fill of it. In due time the books came, some 40 volumes, packed in a long wooden box. I was so proud of the shipment that I kept the books in the same box for 10 years.

That summer I read nearly all of the Conrad books. I was utterly fascinated, in a kind of spell. The seas and the Malay Islands that Conrad wrote about were strange in comparison to the hot dry lands of the Panhandle and that summer I did not love my surroundings. In fact I spent some Saturdays and Sundays sitting high in a cottonwood tree in colorful Salt Creek Canyon reading Joseph Conrad. This canyon was just below our house and was a purple, red, yellow, orange, blue gash in the earth about a half mile wide. I loved that canyon with all my soul.

Conrad was first brought to my attention in my first year at the University of Oklahoma. Nobody told me about him, but I was impressed by what H. L. Mencken had to say about him, also by references to him in Century, Harper's and Atlantic Monthly magazines. Conrad's books had a major influence on my life in the 1920s. Above all I wanted to go to sea. I did not care for a job, to acquire property that would hold me down in one place. I wanted to go to sea.

I was paying out the books by the month. I kept them always in the box under my bed so my father would not see them. He didn't believe in reading novels, not because they were or were not immoral, but, he said, "They're all a pack of lies." He was nearly 60 at the time and had a big belly and I knew he could not see the box under the bed if I pushed it back far enough.

All that summer I traveled with Conrad all over the world in his ships, meeting Lord Jim, the nigger of the *Narcissus*, the superbly delineated characters of *Youth* and *The Heart of Darkness*, and the sharply chiseled characters in *Victory*. Sometimes my Mammy and I would go for a walk and I would tell her what was in the book I was currently reading. No matter what I did, my Mammy always approved, just as most mothers do. I still read Joseph Conrad stories but never with the utter concentration and excitement that I knew that hot, dry summer they came to me. So it was entirely natural for me to finally work my way to the sea. That happened in 1926 in Havana, Cuba, when I signed on a Danish freighter for Japan, carrying a hold full of sugar. But once on the sea, it was little like Conrad's. Still I would find myself standing on deck admiring the white caps and imagine that a seven-masted, fully rigged schooner would show up over the horizon. I learned then what beauty there was in the sea itself, and understood that Conrad had to invent and invent and invent in order to make the sea and its environs and inhabitants mean what he wanted them to mean.

CALL FOR NIXON'S RESIGNATION   *May 16*

Now the Republicans, not the Democrats, want Richard Nixon to resign as president of the United States. I have been saying for a year that Nixon should not resign, but that the Constitutional process for removing a president should function, that is, should Nixon leave office, it should be through impeachment. It is now tumbling in everyday that the leaders of the Republican party don't want Nixon impeached, they want him to resign. Leading Republicans in the House and Senate and the nation's leading Republican newspapers, including the Chicago Tribune and Los Angeles Times, are yelling for Nixon to quit. But their reason is self-serving and selfish. They don't want the true and complete story of Watergate to come out on the floor of the senate when it would be seen on TV by all America. They want to save the Republicans in the House and Senate. They can visualize a cozy, harmonious period of relaxation if Vice President Ford takes the place of Nixon. They now see that the only way Watergate is going to get off the back of Richard Nixon is to get rid of Nixon.

You don't hear of any Democratic papers calling for Nixon's

resignation. Only the Republicans are raising the hue and cry, so let's make it clear that Republicans, not Democrats, are now hounding Nixon to resign. When Spiro Agnew was forced out of office by the Republicans in the face of a horde of criminal charges against him, the facts never did come out. Nixon could go the same way, but it can not be said that the Democrats did it.

Not everybody has turned against Nixon. There are die-hards all over the country, and they would continue to support Nixon under any circumstances. They makes excuses for him. Most sickening are those people who try to excuse Nixon by comparing Watergate with Kennedy's Bay of Pigs, Johnson's Bobby Baker affair and Truman's salty language, and especially Senator Kennedy's Chappaquiddick. The difference between Ted Kennedy and Nixon is that Kennedy pled guilty to the charge against him and took his punishment. Nixon is still in the woodwork delving in secrecy. Kennedy's crime was against a person who was the victim of an accident, whereas, Nixon's crimes are against the Constitution and law of the nation. John Kennedy took all the blame for the Bay of Pigs, although it was all set up and ready to go when Kennedy replaced Ike. Harry Truman has never tried to hide anything. Now Nixon has a Jesuit Catholic priest who excuses his profanity and obscenity by calling his cussing "emotional therapy."

FORD RUNS HOT & COLD   *May 30*

I'm getting nauseated with Vice President Gerald Ford's excuses, his running hot and cold. It hasn't been five years since Ford was screaming for the impeachment of Justice William Douglas, and yelling for all the information the Supreme Court had. Now he's changed his tune; but the law hasn't changed. Ford, like all Republicans, is concerned about his own security, not about the fate of this country. Nixon says he's going to hang on as long as he has one senator for him, meaning that in order to save his hide he would take the country down with him, but the time may come this year, if the House impeaches Nixon, that the Republicans will rise in wrath and demand he resign. Ford would be just as bad as Nixon, and if he took Nixon's place he might get the idea that he would make a better president. We know now that the Republican party does not represent the people of this country and never has.

If you want to become convinced that Ford is going to be just as bad as Nixon, last week he took a swing at the Kennedy-Mills health bill which Nixon is opposing. The major difference between Nixon's health bill and the Kennedy-Mills bill is that the latter would be financed and administered by Social Security. Nixon would turn health insurance over to those insurance companies who deal in fine print in those ads you shake out of your Sunday paper every week. If Nixon's bill passes, there will be great riches for the insurance companies, but no help for the poor. Nixon's health insurance plan is for the benefit of the rich, not the poor, whereas the Kennedy-Mills bill will be as certain as Social Security.

Ford has changed his tune so many different times about Nixon that one finds it difficult to have any confidence in him.

NIXON'S RESIGNATION IN CHARACTER   *August 15*

Unlike all the sad young men who took orders from Richard Nixon and who admitted they did wrong before they went to prison, Nixon expressed no regret in his resignation speech. He did not even say that he was resigning because he was going to be impeached and kicked out of office by the Senate if he did not resign. He said only that he was resigning because he had lost his base of support in the Senate, meaning the radical, right wing Republicans and the few equally radical, redneck southerners like Strom Thurmond who were sticking by him.

Nixon confessed nothing; he said only that he had made some mistakes. Mistakes hell! Those mistakes were crimes which already sent 20 co-conspirators to prison. So we are going to have to deal with Richard Nixon some more. President Jerry Ford said thank God the nightmare is over. That's what he thinks. We don't know yet what Jaworski is going to do, whether he will try

Nixon for the crimes or let him go, but a Washington grand jury is ready to indict him. Nixon said he's not going to sit down and enjoy the California sunshine. He says he's going to continue to work for peace. Should we turn Nixon loose in the world again?

It's going to be pretty painful for the people of this country when Haldeman, Ehrlichman and Mitchell go on trial, are found guilty, and are sent to prison and their ringleader, Richard Nixon, is still roaming the boondocks working for peace. If Nixon is not prosecuted by Jaworski then all the others should go free, including those in prison and those who have served their time in prison. All should be pardoned, but Richard Nixon should face the bar of justice. We have heard over and over that no man is above the law, and Richard Nixon isn't either.

Nixon's resignation speech did not help him any. He admitted nothing. I was infuriated. Some commentators said it was beautiful, touching, but to me it was the old Nixon, admitting nothing, not even admitting that he was resigning to keep from being impeached. My true belief is that Nixon resigned in order to get his $60,000 a year pension, $198,000 a year for an office staff, and free office space. For the key word of the Nixon credo has always been money, money!

As Nixon boarded Air Force One for California I was reminded of the time Truman left Washington riding in a car to the train station and traveling to Missouri carrying his own suitcases.

DOUBLE–TALK & NIXON PARDON   *September 5*

My honeymoon with President Gerald Ford ended with his first press conference. Then he laid several important issues on the line. When Nixon was impeached by the House some newsman asked him if he would pardon Nixon. Ford said, "I don't think the American people would stand for it." Now he says that he thinks Nixon has been punished enough and that one of his options is to grant a pardon to Nixon whether he goes on trial or not. That's double talk, saying one thing at one time and something else another. Here's another example of his double talk. While he was vice president he kept saying that he would not run for president in 1976. Now he says he will. Both Agnew and Nixon said they wouldn't resign, but both of them did. Is Ford following in their footsteps? If there's any fairness or justice in our system, and I believe there is, Nixon should be prosecuted, and Ford should not grant him a pardon. If Nixon goes free, then all the Watergate criminals should go free. It's like Congressman Charles Wilson said to me recently, "Are you going to let Nixon go free because he lied?" Still Wilson thinks that Nixon has been punished enough and should not be prosecuted. The deserters and draft evaders who are out of the country have also been punished enough.

Nixon has not been punished except by the Republican party which forced him to resign. Nixon has neither confessed nor admitted any crime. He's drawing a huge pension which he doesn't deserve; and which should be taken away from him.

YEAR 1975

As the time gets near for me to quit writing this column, it gets harder and harder to write. I think the big reason is that I'm anxious to go to the hospital and have a hemmorhoid operation. Now don't laugh, it's a most painful ailment. I'll go either to the veteran's hospital in Houston or San Antonio.

But my problem today is what am I going to write? For years I had no trouble writing this column. I'd have three or four things in mind to write and I'd sit down at the front table in the shop and knock this column out in no time. Now I debate about whether to cuss Ford or Kissinger.

I'm getting to where I don't trust Kissinger as much as I did. Last week he went to California to make a speech and stopped off to see Nixon, with whom he still has an enjoyable rapport. That makes me think that Kissinger was right in with Nixon and knew all about it during Watergate. For all I know he is still taking advice from Nixon.

Now a few unkind words about President Ford. It worries me that I can't hate him as I hated Nixon, Holy Ike and other assorted Republicans. Ford is a good old boy, and I doubt if he knows the difference between political right and wrong. He almost proved that he didn't when he pardoned Nixon, and now he has dreamed up a big scheme to tax Arab oil, in which the gasoline users get to pay the bill. He has harsh words for a gasoline ration plan that the Democrats and labor favor. Ford keeps saying he wants no part of a ration plan. Just look at World War II's ration plan. He keeps calling it a failure. What that ration plan did in 1942–46 was win the war. There was a black market and violations, but it was only a small per cent of the total product. People at least knew how much gas they were going to get and how much it was going to cost them.

A month ago, Ford had his "WIN" stickers printed and they

lasted two weeks. In my books, Ford is too dumb to be President and it is a good thing that Congress is taking over.

THE LAST COLUMN   *February 27*

I am almost convinced now that Senator Bentsen is another John Connally. It was Big John who persuaded Bentsen to run his scandalous campaign against Ralph Yarborough, so what Texans need to get in their heads is to think of Connally every time they think of Bentsen. House Speaker Billy Clayton of Lubbock, along with Briscoe and Lieutenant Governor Hobby, are the No. 1 supporters of Bentsen. Look at it this way: All the Democratic presidents of this century, Wilson, Truman, Kennedy and Johnson were liberals, not conservative like Bentsen, who is the epitome of corrupt Texas money, and wants to be president. If there is anything to Bentsen that puts him in the class with Kennedy, FDR, Wilson or Truman it is not visible. Bentsen is not the kind of Democrat who is elected president of the United States. Every Democratic president we have had since Jefferson has been a liberal, a president for all the people. We don't need a president who would be a caretaker of the Texas oil industry and a person who takes advice from John Connally.

Archer Fullingim:
A Country Editor's View of Life

was set in Baskerville type by G & S Typesetters, Austin
was printed by The Whitley Company, Austin, on
paper from Lone Star Paper Company, Austin
bound by Universal Book Binders, San Antonio
and designed by
Barbara Mathews Whitehead
1975